CATALINA ISLAND
HANDBOOK

A GUIDE TO CALIFORNIA'S CHANNEL ISLANDS

FOURTH EDITION

CATALINA ISLAND
HANDBOOK

A GUIDE TO CALIFORNIA'S CHANNEL ISLANDS

FOURTH EDITION

CHICKI MALLAN

**PHOTOS BY
OZ MALLAN**

MOON
PUBLICATIONS INC.

CATALINA ISLAND HANDBOOK
A GUIDE TO CALIFORNIA'S CHANNEL ISLANDS

PUBLISHED BY
Moon Publications, Inc.
722 Wall Street
Chico, California 95928 USA
tel. (916) 345-5473

PRINTED BY
Colorcraft, Ltd., Hong Kong

© Text Copyright Chicki Mallan 1992. All rights reserved.
© Maps Copyright Moon Publications 1992. All rights reserved.
© Photos Copyright Oz Mallan. All rights reserved
  Some photos and illustrations are used by permission
  and are the property of the original copyright owners.

LIBRARY OF CONGRESS CATALOGING IN PUBLICATION DATA
Mallan, Chicki.
  Catalina Island Handbook : A Guide to California's Channel Islands
  / by Chicki Mallan.
    p.   cm.
  Rev. ed. of: Guide to Catalina and California's Channel Islands.
3rd ed. 1990.
  Includes bibliographical references and index.
  ISBN 0-918373-42-5 : $10.95
  1. Santa Catalina Island (Calif.)—Guidebooks. 2. Channel Islands
(Calif.)—Guidebooks. I. Mallan, Chicki, 1933–   Guide to Catalina
and California's Channel Islands. II. Title.
F868.L8M26   1992   92–8065
917.94'91—dc20   CIP

Please send all comments,
corrections, additions,
amendments, and critiques to:

**CHICKI MALLAN
C/O MOON PUBLICATIONS
722 WALL STREET
CHICO, CA 95928 USA**

PRINTING HISTORY
First edition
  1984
Second edition
  March 1989
Third edition
  August 1990
Fourth edition
  May 1992

Printed in Hong Kong

Cover photograph by Oz Mallan

To the "Cousins."
May they keep the special memories of Catalina forever bright:
the smell of the sea, hamburgers and sympathy,
french fries and love—the back-door.

ACKNOWLEDGEMENTS

Special thanks to Patti Lange, daughter and sure-footed Catalina researcher. Also thanks to other Catalina Islanders who took the time to help us out—Wayne Griffin, Chamber of Commerce; Misty Gaye, Island Naturalist; John Phelps and Odie Hernandez, Harbor Dept.; Lyn Lehr and Audrey Bombard, Two Harbors; Patricia Moor, Curator of the Catalina Museum; Shirley Davy and Gail Hodges, BBDO; Rudy Piltch, Ron Doutt, and Donna Harrison at the SCI Co.: and all the Islanders who are always so helpful with our project.

Thanks to the entire Moon staff for the TLC and quality help they continue to bestow on this often-flustered author: Beth Rhudy, Taran March, Mark Arends, Annie Hikido, Dave Hurst, Mark Voss, Nancy Kennedy, Asha Johnson, Anne-Marie Nicoara, and thanks to Mark Morris for swift editing. Bob Race and Brian Bardwell make the best maps in the travel-book business. Let us not forget the front office people who take a book and make the magic of promoting and selling look easy: Donna Galassi, Cindy Fahey, Lucinda Stram, Julie Mason, Rick Johnson, and Mars Datura.

Husband Oz Mallan's photos and Kathy Escovedo-Sanders's drawings depicting scenes of Catalina add a special dimension of beauty to the book. In my office, thanks to Karol Saritas for being so flexible, for reading my mind, and for learning WordStar 6.0 so quickly! Special thanks to Oz who continues to help put it all together, and to the **Big Eight,** my kids, who keep adding to my rooting section with more and more grands, who cheer me on and make it all worthwhile.

IS THIS BOOK OUT OF DATE?

Between the time this book went to press and the time it got onto the shelves, motels have closed, restaurants have changed hands, and prices have probably gone up. Because of this, all prices herein should be regarded as approximations and are not guaranteed by the publisher of author. Because keeping this book accurate and timely means fourth and later editions, we would appreciate hearing about and errors or omissions you may encounter in *Catalina Island Handbook*. Also, if you have any noteworthy experiences (good or bad) with establishments listed in this book, please pass it along to us. If an attraction is out of place on a map, tell us; if the best restaurant in town is not included, we'd like to know. All contributions will be deeply appreciated and properly acknowledged. Address your letters to:

Chicki Mallan
C/o Moon Publications, Inc.
722 Wall St.
Chico, CA 95928

CONTENTS

MAP SYMBOLS

WATER   INTERSTATE HIGHWAY   FREEWAY
O   CITY   MAIN HIGHWAY
o   TOWN   U. S. HIGHWAY   SECONDARY ROAD
■   SIGHT OR POINT OF INTEREST   UNPAVED ROAD
▲   MOUNTAIN   STATE HIGHWAY   BRIDGE

All maps in this book are oriented with north at the top of the map unless otherwise noted.

ABBREVIATIONS

C.—century   OW—one way   RT—round trip
F—farenheit   pp—per person   tel.—telephone number

MAPS

CHARTS

KATHY ESCOVIDO-SANDERS

INTRODUCTION

An island is a special place. There's a dreamlike quality about a bit of land surrounded by the beautiful sea. Birds, fish, and seals frolic in splashing ocean spray for the benefit of anyone watching—or not watching. Tall peaks give the sun and moon a dramatic stage on which to perform their magic each day—and the show is always different. For those who have not yet discovered their "special island," may we recommend Santa Catalina?

In Avalon, simple things take on new meaning: walking along the beachfront's serpentine wall, watching the harbor lights when the bay is filled with boats, listening to the special music of a clinking halyard on a mast. Here you'll smell fresh air on a breezy morning, and sit for hours under the palm trees on Casino Point watching the changing colors of the sea. And even if you're not a fisherman, when the cannon booms across the harbor the infectious excitement will rush you along with other beach-goers to see a marlin winched up to the pier's scales.

That's just part of what Catalina is about, but if that much sounds good, cross the channel and have a look. Take a hike into the interior, see untamed bison peacefully grazing on a hillside with the Pacific Ocean as a backdrop, study plants that have been extinct on the Mainland for thousands of years, see California as it looked before we discovered cement—or cars, or high-rise buildings. Crossing the channel for the first time, there's a whole set of experiences that you'll remember for a lifetime: watching the porpoises following along, diving in and out of the ship's wake, the surprise of finding your "sea legs" while carrying coffee and a sandwich to the upper deck, meeting fellow travelers also curious about islands. But probably the most indelible memory of all is first seeing the white speck on the horizon that slowly becomes Avalon's hallmark, the great white Moorish-style Casino building on the bay. Avalon, on the crescent-shaped cove, is a Mediterranean-like village climbing hillsides dotted with vivid-colored bougainvilleas. Tall eucalyptus trees line zigzag roads that circle into the cleavage of the Island. The Casino presides over it all.

Many people already have that special feeling about Catalina because there's something of interest for every visitor. Boaters, hikers, campers, horsemen, cyclists, divers, anglers, sun worshipers, and jet-setters will find all they're looking for, as will historians, naturalists, archaeologists, and botanists. Vacationers can choose nonstop activities around Avalon town—or in your own boat discover the magic of a small cove and complete solitude, just you and nature's wonders. Parents can relax as their children are happily occupied on Avalon's beaches, splashing in the water, or with organized play. It doesn't have to be summer; winters are mild, spring is glorious, but there are some who swear the most beautiful time of year is the fall. Come on over; once is all it takes, and Catalina will become your "special island."

SOUTHERN CALIFORNIA COASTLINE AND THE CHANNEL ISLANDS

SANTA BARBARA

SANTA BARBARA CHANNEL

SAN MIGUEL I.
SANTA ROSA I.
SANTA CRUZ I.

VENTURA

GULL I.
ANACAPA IS.

LOS ANGELES

LONG BEACH

SANTA BARBARA I.

SAN NICOLAS I.

SAN PEDRO CHANNEL

SANTA CATALINA I.

OUTER SANTA BARBARA CHANNEL

PACIFIC OCEAN

SAN CLEMENTE I.

SAN DIEGO

UNITED STATES
MEXICO

0   20 mi
0   20 km

© MOON PUBLICATIONS, INC.

KATHY ESCOVIDO-SANDERS

THE LAND

Santa Catalina Island is one of the eight California Channel Islands stretching along the Southern California coast. Catalina itself has a 120-million-year geological history. Early paleontologists assumed that it was once attached to the Mainland, but recent studies and more modern scientific methods are raising some doubts about this theory. Catalina, only 19 miles from the Mainland at its closest point, sits on the Pacific tectonic plate, while most of California and the rest of the U.S. are on the North American plate. Plate movements and volcanic eruptions are responsible for the formation of Catalina Island, though this is not true of all the Channel Islands. The two most common types of Island rock are the result of this formation process: igneous (volcanic) and metamorphic (usually sedimentary rock that has changed under pressure, heat, or chemical action).

The Indians of the Mainland used a descriptive phrase when they spoke of Catalina Island: *wexaj momte asunga wow*—"mountain ranges that rise from the sea." Most of the Island consists of mountains interspersed with meadows and valleys. Black Jack (2,006 feet) and Mt. Orizaba (2,097 feet) are the two highest peaks. Some of the coastal cliffs fall abruptly to the sea, leaving not even a path's space along the ocean, while in other areas the hills slope gently to sandy beaches below. The 21-mile-long Island has an east-west orientation. On the western (or windward) side, the Pacific crashes against the tall, rugged coast. Off the eastern (or lee) coast that faces the Mainland, the sea is calm and placid. Catalina's widest section is at Long Point directly across from China Point on the windward side (approximately 7½ miles). The Island's east and west sides have a natural cleavage at Two Harbors—a half-mile-wide isthmus six miles from the west end—which is the narrowest point. A deep undersea ledge girdles the Island's landmass, fostering a rich habitat for marinelife. Catalina's steep canyon walls create a climate that helps sustain types of vegetation that are unique to the Island.

Catalina's inland roads wind around the rugged mountain tops overlooking the sea.

Water

Although surrounded by water, Catalina's drinkable kind has always been a problem. In the early days, the Indians and the first settlers relied on the few natural springs scattered over the

Island, plus the few streams which still run to the sea after a good wet year. Today, the utility company maintains a dam, reservoir, and pipeline to accommodate the Island's freshwater needs.

CLIMATE

Many people mistakenly believe that Catalina is a tropical island. Though the sun shines an average of 267 days a year, its climate is in fact similar to the Southern California coast. Thanks to cooling marine breezes, Catalina is generally moister and cooler in the summer months than the Mainland; in winter, with help from the warm Japanese current, it's generally a few degrees milder.

In summer, the average temperature ranges from 70-76° F. In the winter, the temperature ranges from 49-63° F. The average rainfall is 14 inches per year, but the extremes can be great. Some years (as on the California Mainland), as much as 30 inches of rain fall, while the drought years of 1977-78 brought virtually none. The average sea temperature in the winter is 56-59° F, in the summer 67-70° F. The winter months almost always bring a northeastern (Santa Ana) storm or two. These Santa Ana conditions can turn the calm Pacific into a raging sea. Its high winds are infrequent but dangerous; sometimes reaching 50 knots, they occur Nov. to

An occasional storm hits Catalina Island, pounding her placid shores with a turbulent surf.

March. Fog can be expected in all seasons, but in winter it covers a wider area and lasts longer. In May and June, Catalina hosts the fog until about noon. Many visitors consider Catalina's biggest attraction the lack of smog. This is due to westerly winds and the Island's distance from the Mainland.

FLORA

Though the plantlife is similar to the Mainland's, Catalina's resident species are slightly different. Some plants that thrive on the Island today existed on the Mainland 20,000 years ago, but as the Mainland became drier, many of those plants died out. Of approximately 600 species on Catalina, 396 are native.

Some of the wildflowers found on Catalina are:

> bright eyes
> brodiaea (blue dick)
> bush lupine
> bush sunflower
> shore heliotrope
> California bindweed
> California island poppy
> sumac (lemonade berry)
> California lilac
> tree tobacco
> tree poppy
> everlasting flower
> violet nightshade
> fiesta flower
> wild apple
> giant sea dahlia
> wild four o'clock
> ground pink
> wild sweet pea
> Indian paintbrush
> woodland star
> yellow pansy

Trees

Early accounts by miners and settlers mention an abundance of pine trees. Yet, the pines introduced in recent years haven't thrived on Catalina because of the frequent dry seasons. Thanks to Philip Wrigley's conservancy program, introduced in 1972, hikers to the interior can see 10 adult mahogany trees in an obscure canyon.

Some of the trees seen on Catalina are:

> California holly (toyon)
> elderberry
> Catalina ironwood
> greasewood
> Catalina manzanita
> island oak
> Catalina wild cherry
> mountain mahogany
> cottonwood
> scrub oak

PLANT LORE

Indians and pioneers, as well as modern-day herbologists, have told of the culinary and medicinal uses of a number of Catalina's plant species. Some of these may be more lore than fact; others have proven still useful today. One is the **prickly pear**, a common edible fruit which grows on cacti, found not only in Catalina but in many other parts of the world. A deep purplish-red, this fruit is sweet and juicy when ripe, and according to some, makes a great fruit pudding. A good way to get rid of the thorns and skin without injury is to leave the fruit attached to the plant and carefully peel. Otherwise, a fork makes a good handle while peeling the nasties off.

The **Catalina cherry tree** grows well on the Island; a large grove on the west end carries the appropriate name of Cherry Cove. The reddish-black cherry has little flesh around its seed, but is quite refreshing. It's said to have been one of the favorite fruits of the Indians. **Sumac**, or lemonade berry, is said to provide a refreshing drink called "lemonade" by the Mexicans. **Wild sage**, which grows profusely on the Mainland,

SHOOTING STARS

Shooting Stars are February's
    flowers,
Carpeting the Deer Trail bowers,
Dainty, delicate, fragrant showers,
February's Stars.

Five petaled, bent back on the stem,
Stamens forward, nature's gem,
Hidden in a fern-filled glen,
Rose-orchid Stars.

Golden rings, the heart of you,
Bill of purple, another's hue,
Beauty's crown, climber's view,
Long-stemmed treasures.

MARIPOSA LILY

Three-petaled, dainty
Flush of the dawn,
Velvet red heart of you,
Slender stem long,

Bearing another bud,
Unfolds to light,
Mariposa Lily,
Lovely and bright.

Growing in wild oats,
Planted by God,
Speaking of Love divine,
Ne'er of the sod.

verses by
Ann Cloud Reynolds

DIANA LASICH HARPER

ANN CLOUD REYNOLDS

From the 1920s into the '50s, Ann was a familiar sight in Avalon with her walking staff, floppy straw hat, rucksack, and beach towel around her shoulders heading into Catalina's hills. She reveled in nature's offerings, from Cottonwood Canyon to Silver Peak and all in between. As others know the floor plan of their home, Ann knew Catalina's interior, every rock, mountain, valley, and wild flower. She wrote three small books, all including poetry and a feeling that she was part of the land and the Indians from the past. Ann (now deceased), always referred to "Hiker" in her books. Hiker was Ann. Hiker found Indian caves with ancient markings, spent nights under the stars long before most, fed the ravens, spoke to the goats, took pictures of wildflowers, and sang from the hilltops:

> Echoing across the years,
> Comes the call,
> Brings the tears,
> Of joy, to know the Indians all,
> Listen ever for the call—*Yo te hoy!*

is gathered by herbologists for home remedies—it's great added to turkey stuffing and other cooks' specialties. Wild cucumber and radish, beach strawberry, toyon berry, blackberry, and wild currant were most likely eaten by the original inhabitants of the Island and are a treat when found by today's residents.

Remedies

Two plants used as remedies for rattlesnake bites are the **wild carrot** and **rattlesnake weed**. A poultice of the fresh leaves was applied to the wound. If, in the course of an illness, copious perspiring was required, a drink was made and administered from the leaves of the large **elderberry** tree *(Sambucus mexicanus)*. *Yerba mansa (Anemopsis california)* was chewed raw for mucous membrane sickness, and it was also

made into powder for knife wounds. **Snake cactus** was used to fight high fever. The aborigines were thought to have made a liniment remedy for rheumatism from an extract of the **white willow**.

Narcotics

Historians believe that the Gabrielino Indians took part in Chingichnich religious ceremonies involving **jimson weed**. This ceremony was a cult of initiation for adolescents entering manhood. The jimson weed *(Datura metaloides)* is a highly effective narcotic. After a three-day fast, young men were given a drink made of jimson leaves. Afterward, they would dance until they passed out. Their dreams during this time were thought to be prophetic and held great significance for the rest of their lives. This group is referred to as the "Toloache Cult." Old-timers have described the **yerba santa** as having the power to induce a "gentle sleep," but it's rarely found on the Island today.

Miscellaneous

Long and coarsely fibrous, the tuberous root of the **soap plant** works well as a scrub brush. The *Chenopodium californicum*, a parsnip-like root, also provides a detergent in lieu of soap. **Poison oak** grows on the Island, and if you are sensitive, contact with it can cause discomfort any season of the year. Leaves, bare branches, or even smoke from a burning bush can bring on an itchy rash.

Restoration

Today, the Catalina Conservancy maintains a native plant nursery at Middle Ranch. Here seedlings of plants are coaxed along and then planted throughout the interior. This restoration is an ongoing project that some dreamers believe will eventually present the Island as it was 150 years ago.

KATHY ESCOVIDO-SANDERS

FAUNA

LAND CREATURES

Goats

The hills of Catalina Island are lined with a network of narrow paths. These are mostly goat trails. Since goat bones have not been found in the Indian kitchen middens, it's assumed that goats arrived after the Spanish era. Some historians claim Spanish explorers brought goats to ensure a supply of meat for their travels. Though naturalists now disagree with that theory, another has yet to be suggested. Allowed to run free for years, the goats eventually grew in number to thousands. Goats nibble every living thing, including the endemic plants on the Island; the destruction of grasses, shrubs, and trees was overwhelming. For that reason, the Conservancy has rid the Island of most of the feral goats.

Backpackers and hikers still see a few running along the trails. Their coats vary from white to brown to black or a mixture of all three; the most common is the shaggy black and brown goat. Some billies have large horn-spreads measuring three feet and more. These ornery animals command the sheerest cliffs, and frequently climb down to the water's edge to lick salt from the ocean-sprayed rocks.

Wild Pigs

The feral pig was introduced to Catalina in the mid-1920s to hold down the rattlesnake population. These pigs are mean when cornered and have multiplied to a couple thousand. They occasionally come into Avalon and damage the golf course by digging up the greens, but for the most part they stay in the backcountry, running loose on the roughly 47,884 acres at their disposal. To keep the herds down, boar and goat hunts are organized through the Camp and Cove Agency at Two Harbors.

Bison

In 1924, when William Farnum, a Western moviemaker, was filming Zane Grey's *The Vanishing American,* 14 bison were brought to the Island for the film. Rounding up the bison afterward proved to be too difficult, so in the end they were left to roam. By 1934, the herd had increased to 19, then 30 additional bison were brought from Colorado to supplement the herd. Today's population is held to 200-400—ideal for the ecosystem. When the herd gets too large, bison are culled; the animals are sent to the Mainland to be butchered and frozen, then shipped back as expensive hamburger—buffalo chili and buffalo burgers are sold at the Airport-In-The-Sky as well as other cafes on the Island.

When an old bull is challenged by a younger one, a fierce battle generally follows. The young bull is usually sent scurrying, but in some cases the old bull is run out of the herd. Considered a rogue, he thereafter roams the hills alone. Fencing at every road entry into Avalon from the interior and a large metal bump-gate for cars ordinarily keep the animals in the hills and out of town, but there are exceptions. When a bull finds entry into Avalon it always causes unusual excitement. Early one morning in 1978 the town awoke to see a rogue wandering down the beach in Avalon. Before anyone could do anything, he had trotted up Sumner St. and darted onto the Pitch and Putt golf course adjoining Avalon's elementary school. The whole affair soon turned into a noisy roundup with cheering children and a siren-blaring police car chasing the running bull back and forth the length of the golf course, trying to guide him through the gate, missing at least eight times. Finally, he fled toward the peaceful environment of the interior.

Deer

Although anthropologist Alfred L. Kroeber briefly mentions Catalina's deer in his 1925 *Handbook of Indians of California,* many historians date the introduction of deer to the Island to 1930, when 18 mule deer were brought for refuge by the California Fish and Game Commission. They too have adapted to the environment, multiplying to the point where deer hunts must be organized periodically to keep the population down. In years of little rain the deer come into town to feast on rosebuds, pansy blossoms, and other garden delicacies. During one severe drought, they did considerable damage. To avert total devastation, many of the animals were trapped in huge cages, shipped to the Mainland, and set free in a wild area where ample forage was available.

Catalina Island Foxes

The small island fox seen on Catalina as well as many of the other Channel islands is a diminutive form of the Mainland gray fox. Its color is variegated gray, black, rust, and white. It is seldom seen by the casual observer. However, it has been said that on a summer evening if you study the shoreline when the flying-fish boat

Buffalos spend time roaming the hills; here a small herd is gathered around a welcome waterhole.

aims its powerful light toward shore, you might see a pair of glowing eyes. Fish often get confused or mistakenly follow the light beam and land on the rocky beach, stranded. They don't remain long, as the small fox with his sharp vision is also watching and waiting for just this opportunity for a fresh seafood snack.

According to Misty Gay, Catalina's naturalist, the fox is a subspecies endimic to Santa Catalina Island. Six of the eight Channel islands have Channel Island foxes; on each the fox has evolved into a separate and unique subspecies. It is Catalina's largest native mammalian predator.

Rodents

The ground squirrel is also endemic to the island. This small gray-brown squirrel, which lives in subterranean tunnels, has an unmistakable clacketing chatter. Also native to Catalina and close relatives to the ground squirrel are the western harvest mouse and deer mouse.

Other Animals

Islanders have their share of house pets—the usual dogs, cats, canaries, and parrots. Thoroughbred Arabian horses are raised at Rancho Escondido, a 537-acre private ranch owned by the Wrigley family. At Middle Ranch, now part of the Catalina Conservancy, is the pony center where kids from Avalon learn to ride, some of whom travel to the Mainland to participate in horse shows and do quite well.

WATER CREATURES

Sea Lions

Herds of this "circus seal," intelligent and easily trained, range the California waters and are protected by law from hunters; some specimens in the wild live as long as 18 years; in captivity they can live longer. Ranging in color from tan or gray to almost black, the California sea lion cow may be more than six feet long and weigh over 300 pounds, while the bulls can grow to nine feet and 1,000 pounds. A large male usually

has a prominent crest on its forehead.

Though sea lions don't pup on Catalina, they do on some of the other Channel islands. The sea lions return to the place of their birth to mate each year in late spring or early summer. These enormous bulls battle for favorite locations for their breeding harems, even while the cows are still birthing. Pups are usually born in June, though some are born as early as May and as late as July. Today only the harbor seals pup on Catalina, producing a single pup in the spring. The pups then have the summer—a gentle season of mild weather—and an abundant supply of fish to encourage their rapid growth.

Naturalists studying the Catalina area report the sea lion population is on the increase once again. If you have any interest in the habits of these intelligent, inquisitive pinnipeds ("fin-foot-

Sea lions enjoy summer fun and frolic near Catalina's Seal Rocks.

ed" ones), the ideal way to observe their habits is from a boat and with a pair of binoculars. The experience of watching them lolling on the rocks in the summer sun or gently nudging their pups into the water for a swimming lesson is well worth the time. You may pick the day that one of the rare pinnipeds, such as the elephant seal, visits the Island.

AIR CREATURES

Like most communities near the Pacific, Catalina hosts an abundance of waterfowl, including the cormorant, many varieties of seagull, the tern, grebe, and pelican. You'll also find many species of common Mainland birds such as the sparrow, finch, warbler, hummingbird, and mockingbird. At one time there were hundreds of quail; now, hunting them is limited to years when there's a good hatch (which is very rare). The black raven and the bald eagle were held sacred by the Catalina Indian. Ravens are still plentiful on the Island, but by the mid-1900s the magnificent eagles had all but vanished. For many years, they built their nests on sheer cliffs that overlooked the sea, but nests are rarely seen now.

The Catalina Conservancy and the Institute for Wildlife Studies have undertaken the painstaking task of reintroducing the bald eagle to the Island. In 1980, a nesting platform was built and 14 eaglets were fed and observed until they were able to fend for themselves. Since then other eaglets have been released, making a total of 37. A 1991 count placed the eagle population at 17. As Island naturalist Misty Gay explains, some of the eagles fly away from the Island and others die of natural causes, although one is known to have been shot.

Despite setbacks, the program is considered successful; in 1987, a nest was built and eggs were laid. None of the eggs hatched, but that first nest was definitely a good sign that the eagles were adapting to their new home on Catalina. Nesting eagles care for their young for up to five months. By then they're nearly the size of an adult. The nest (of necessity) is large, and it's not unusual to see an eagle carrying a stick (as big around as a human arm) through the air for the building process. One of the largest nests on record weighed a ton and was six feet across.

When hiking in the interior, you may glimpse them soaring on updrafts along the cliff sides or over the sea or reservoirs watching with a keen eye for an errant fish, an important part of their diet. Thanks to the Conservancy these birds are the beginning of a new community of bald eagles on Catalina Island.

Another bird originally native to Catalina is the peregrine falcon. The Conservancy has released these into the interior as well.

KATHY ESCOVIDO-SANDERS

HISTORY

THE FIRST ISLANDERS

Prehistory
Catalina Island has a mysterious and complex history. For the last 30,000 years, no fewer than five aboriginal cultures have occupied California's Channel Islands. But the history of man is clouded; there are few definite answers to long-asked questions. For a brief period, there was wild speculation that Catalina's first inhabitants may have been a cultured race of white giants, survivors from a sunken continent. Old ships' logs and other written accounts refer to the "white-skinned" Indian communities on Catalina Island, but no evidence exists that whites inhabited the islands.

It's now thought that during the Pleistocene Ice Age (50,000 B.C.), when the level of the sea fell, men and animals crossed the Bering land bridge from Asia to the American continent. For nearly 50,000 years, humans made an epic trek southward spreading throughout North, Central, and South America until approximately 1000 B.C., when they reached Tierra del Fuego and could go no farther.

With the possible exceptions of Alaska and remote sections of Canada, the use of stone tools continued on Santa Catalina longer than anywhere else in North America. Perhaps this was because of the unlimited quantities of soapstone and obsidian available for making tools, cooking utensils, and ceremonial objects, as well as the isolation of the Island from outside cultural influences and other sources of materials.

Gabrielino Indians
Much of our knowledge about early man in the Channel Islands is speculative. Although deep layers of excavated cultural material from middens (ancient refuse heaps) clearly establish that a sizable number of people have lived on Catalina Island since 2000 B.C., early anthropologists and archaeologists believed that the more modern Indians of the Channel Islands (referred to variously as "Chumash, Gabrielino," and "Shoshonean") can be traced as far back as 500 B.C.

Alfred L. Kroeber, an anthropologist distinguished for his studies of early California Indians, wrote that the "remains" found on the majority of the Channel Islands show all the characteristics of Chumash civilization in its most perfect state. However, the Indians on Catalina called themselves "Pimugnans" (they called the Island "Pimu" or "Pimugna") and enjoyed a lively interaction with the Chumash. Their ancestors were from the early Shoshonean linguistic group that migrated from the Great Plains.

At the peak of their civilization, 2,500 Indians lived on the Island at three major sites: Little Harbor, Avalon, and Two Harbors. Hundreds of other sites have been found; some were permanent and others were temporary bases for hunting and gathering expeditions. Since the sea supplied the major part of the Indian diet, the permanent sites were located near a freshwater supply that was reasonably close to the shoreline. It appears that the Two Harbors area had the largest community, while the site at Little Harbor was the oldest.

The Pimugnans were later called Gabrielinos. This and other names for natives were taken from the missions that eventually became the homes of the last survivors of the Southern California tribes: the Obispeno, Purismeno, and Diegueno, from San Luis Obispo, La Purisma Concepcion, and San Diego. As time passed, these coastal and Island Indians intermingled and developed a shared culture due to an ongoing trade between the people of the Channel Islands and the Mainland. They have since all come to be called "Canalinos."

In an old sea log Friar Torquemada, interpreter for Friar Ascension, the adventurous missionary who accompanied the Vizcaino expedition in 1602, described the Indians as a warm, friendly people and physically hardy. The Indian houses on Catalina were described by Miguel Costanso, an engineer with the 1769 Portola expedition, as circular, thatched domes 60 feet in diameter, spacious enough to hold three to four families. The men and children usually went naked; the women wore otter-skin aprons. At night otter-skin robes were also used as blankets.

The Gabrielinos or Pimugnans of Catalina were energetic traders with a flourishing stoneware trade: archaeologists have found Catalina steatite artifacts in Indian sites as far

away as Nevada and New Mexico. Many artifacts were removed from the Island in the early 1900s and moved to the now defunct Heye Foundation's Museum of American Indians in New York.

Religious Beliefs
Many of the Islanders' customs differed from those of the Gabrielinos on the Mainland. According to Bernice Eastman Johnston, noted author associated with the Southwest Museum of Los Angeles, the Mainland Gabrielinos found something sinister in the isolation granted their tribesmen by the rough waters of the channel. Even though brisk trading went on between them, and the Mainland Indians had learned many of the elements of the vigorous Chingichnich cult from the religious genius of the men of Santa Catalina, it was whispered that the Islanders were fierce wizards.

Legends tell of a mysterious temple complex where the Indians from all the Channel Islands gathered once a year to worship Chingichnich, their sun-god. Their highly formalized and ritualized religion involved temples called *yuva'r,* sacred open-air enclosures with elaborate poles and banners decorated in feathers. An image of Chingichnich was placed in the *yuva'r* and only old men possessing great "power" could enter. Lengthy and involved ceremonies were performed for every important event in life: birth, puberty, marriage, and death. Offerings of food and goods were presented not only to Chingichnich but also to the owl, raven, crow, and eagle.

THE SPANISH ERA

Early Explorers

The first known white explorer to visit the Indians of Catalina was Juan Rodriguez Cabrillo, a Portuguese navigator sailing under the Spanish flag. He claimed the Island in 1542 and called it San Salvador. Sixty years later, Sebastian Vizcaino claimed it for King Philip III and renamed the Island. Because his arrival on November 24, 1602 coincided with the Catholic feast of St. Catherine of Alexandria, Vizcaino and his men named the island Santa Catalina in her honor. The Indians gave the crew an enthusiastic, hospitable welcome, and the ship remained in various Catalina harbors for several days. Much has been learned from their logs about the Catalina Indians. We know that they caught fish on barbless hooks and kept dogs as pets—dogs that "do not bark, but howl like coyotes."

After Vizcaino's visit, however, the Channel Islands were ignored for more thán 150 years. In 1769 an expedition headed by Gaspar de Portola and Friar Junipero Serra claimed all of California for Spain. Catalina was considered as a possible mission location, but the shortage of missionaries and the Island's distance from the Mainland made this impractical. So time and outsiders continued to pass Catalina by.

The Sea Otter Trade

At the end of the 1700s the Catalina Indians still enjoyed a peaceful, primitive life-style, though this was not to last much longer. As Spain established presidios, missions, and pueblos along the California coast, ships discovered the safe harbors of Catalina—and the sea otter. This small, intelligent mammal furnished the most valuable fur found on the entire coast from California to Alaska.

Violent competition began among ships and crews to monopolize the feeding grounds of these animals, which had gamboled freely for centuries in the waters of the Channel Islands. Their velvet-like skins, sold regularly to Chinese merchants in Canton, also brought exorbitant

prices from Russian nobility. However, foreign vessels were forbidden by the Spanish colonial government to trade along the California coast. If caught the ship either had its cargo confiscated or had to pay a 100% duty.

The brig *Lelia Byrd* was the first American ship on record to anchor in Catalina waters. Captain William Shaler, his hold loaded with otter skins, put into the Spanish harbor of San Diego desperate for food, water, and repairs. The authorities became suspicious; when they threatened to search the ship, Shaler was forced to make a run for the open sea. He limped into the Bay of the Seven Moons (Avalon Bay) in May 1804. His ship, leaking badly, was careened and with the aid of the friendly Catalina Indians he caulked his vessel with lime and tallow. Six weeks later, Shaler sailed on to the Hawaiian Islands and sold his precious cargo of skins to King Kamehameha. It was the sea otter that indirectly caused the extinction of the Catalina Indian.

Final Chapter

The end began in 1806 when a business alliance was formed between the Russian-American Fur Company based in Sitka, Alaska, and two American traders, Joseph O'Cain and Jonathan Winship. With a captive crew of Aleuts and Kodiak Indians, the Russian trappers sailed south along the coast from their colony in Alaska to hunt the sea otter at any risk. The peaceful Catalina Islanders were no match for them.

The frenzied hunting lasted for several years, during which not only were the otters almost exterminated, but the Pimugnans were looted, the women raped, and many men slaughtered. By 1832 the population had been decimated, and the few remaining Indians sought refuge with the Mainland missionaries at San Gabriel and San Fernando. Most died within several years, unable to cope with the transition from the Stone Age to the lifestyle and diseases of a more modern civilization.

The Chinese

As early as 1847, a small group of Chinese immigrants entered the United States to make their home in California. Lured from poor towns in China by the stories of high-paying jobs in the gold mines, by 1852 20,000 Chinese were in the state. In those first years California politicians and entrepreneurs welcomed the Chinese as hard-working, dependable laborers willing to work for pennies an hour. They held the lowliest jobs in cigar factories, laundries, kitchens, private homes, railroads, ranches, and gold mines. Resentment against the Chinese developed when, despite their low wages, with enormous frugality and perseverance they often ended up wealthier than their American coworkers.

The Chinese were subjected to a variety of indignities and violent acts ridiculing their dress, almond-shaped eyes, food habits (Chinese ate bamboo shoots, seaweed, salt ginger, and dried duck liver). This jingoism fueled anti-immigration legislation.

The cry "California for the Americans" brought about various laws over the years. One enacted during the 1850s stated that an immigration head-tax of $50 was to be paid by every foreigner entering the state. Until then, many sea captains arranged with landowners and businessmen to pick up in China and deliver cheap laborers—all penniless. Under the new law, the captain would have to pay the fee unless he managed to sneak past customs. Corrupt sailing masters arriving from the Orient would avoid customs in the larger northern ports and continue south to Monterey. If they were unsuccessful in finding buyers for their human cargo, they continued on to Catalina, where the Chinese were hidden in Ironbound Bay, Lobster

Bay, or Smuggler's Cove to wait for smaller ships to transport them to San Pedro on the Mainland and new work.

Even after the laws were repealed there were still periodic political "clean-ups"; Chinese operating restaurants and laundries in San Francisco were rounded up and loaded on ships supposedly destined for China. However, most were simply hidden on Catalina and other Channel islands until things settled down once more; then the captives were returned to their waiting employers.

Catalina also was used by smugglers as a warehouse for contraband; itinerant sheepherders tended animals on the Island; and fur traders made their secret headquarters there. In those early years, Catalina was the scene of both legal and illegal trading activities, neither of which benefited the development of the Island.

Gold

George Yount, a pioneer and otter hunter in the 1830s, told stories on the Mainland of gold-bearing rock he'd seen on Catalina Island. In 1863, miners from everywhere flocked across the channel in anything that floated, and the purple hills of Catalina became the scene of a turbulent gold-mining boom. For "$2 including grub," optimistic miners traveled on boats already loaded with lumber, tools, and provisions to supply the operating mines.

Such sloops as the *Ned Beale,* the *Anna Maria,* and the schooner *Commerce* all plied the waters between San Pedro and Catalina's Two Harbors. Phineas Banning, who was destined to play an important part in the history of Catalina Island, advertised that his steamer *Cricket* and his schooner *San Diego* were available to those who wished to charter them for trips to the "very rich mines" on Catalina.

According to old records at the *L.A. County Recorder*, most of the mining activity was located in the vicinity of Cherry Valley, Two Harbors, and Silver Canyon. Although operating expenses of mining the gold were too high to make it profitable, dreams of grandeur kept these miners groping. Names of claims were as rich as the hopes of the owners: Gem of the Ocean, Pacific Gold, Silver and Galena Co., Diamond Mining, and General Wright Mining Company. Curiously, the last is the name of the Union general responsible for ordering miners on the Island to abandon their claims and leave their dreams behind.

AN AMERICAN CALIFORNIA

During this period of development in the early 1800s, many countries cast a wandering eye to the coast of California. Russia, England, France, and America recognized its potential. The coast was perfect for harboring and stocking ships for the long journey to the Orient. The moderate climate provided a long growing season on fertile farmlands. Mexico welcomed foreigners to California, but only those who wished to become naturalized citizens. The Mexicans encouraged trade, placed a price tag on it, but then found it difficult to collect the tariffs. As a result, many American clipper ships battled the gales around Cape Horn and made a lively profit bringing manufactured goods to the isolated rancheros along the California coast. The picture changed when California became a state of America in 1850.

A Silver Saddle
Thomas Robbins, an American from Massachusetts, made his first trip to California in 1823. As mate on the *Rover* he got his first glimpse of the Catalina hills rising from the Pa-

cific. After several subsequent trips to California he settled in Santa Barbara, ran a general store, and continued sailing in channel waters as captain of the schooner *Santa Barbara*. In 1834, he married Encarnacion, the daughter of a rich Santa Barbara landowner, Carlos Carrillo. Because he was known as a good friend to Mexican as well as American officials, Robbins's general store became a gathering place for seafarers who stopped at Santa Barbara.

In the service of Mexican Governor Alvarado, Robbins later commanded the government schooner *California* and came to know all the Channel islands. In 1839, he asked the governor for possession of Catalina Island. Alvarado did not issue the grant to Robbins or any of the other petitioners for the Island. But in 1846, before the Mexican War when American "takeover" rumors were rife, provisional Governor Pio Pico signed away Catalina Island to Robbins as a last gesture of his authority. The favorite story of the event suggests that on the 4th of July, with the Americans about to take full control, Governor Pio Pico passed through Santa Barbara on his way to meet with General Castro. The long-sought Catalina grant was swapped with Robbins in exchange for a silver saddle and a fresh horse. After Robbins, many title changes affected the fortunes of Catalina Island.

Guadalupe Treaty
In 1848, with the signing of the Guadalupe Hidalgo Treaty which ended the Mexican War, Catalina was annexed to California, along with Santa Barbara, San Clemente, and the Anacapas.

Civil War
Occupation of the Island by Union Army troops during the Civil War finally put an end to the mining activities. For years, historians maintained that this action was taken because the Union believed that the miners were actually Confederate sympathizers who planned to seize Catalina to use as a base for illicit pirate activities by Southern privateers. However, research shows that the Union Army's Commander of

the Department of the Pacific, Brigadier General George Wright, ordered a company of infantry to take possession of Catalina; he had been having trouble with certain Indian tribes that refused to stay on their reservations north of San Francisco, and he wanted to move them to the Island. A letter written during that period by General Wright described the condition of the Island:

From a special report which I have just received from the commanding officer on the island, I am well satisfied that it is better adapted for an Indian reservation than I at first supposed. It appears that we found on the island some 80 to 100 people, some few of them mining and the others engaged in stock raising. There are twelve or fifteen small valleys embracing an area of 1,000 or 1,200 acres of good fertile land. The island has on it a large number of wild goats estimated at 15,000, besides quail and small game. It has an abundant supply of fresh running water which can easily be conducted to any part of the island.

Army officials in Washington rejected this proposal and the plan was scrapped. From this letter it would appear that the water situation was well under control. However, the letter that follows describes the problem:

In continuation of my report of January 19, 1864, I can now say from personal observation that the so-called big spring has not sufficient water to attempt to lead it to this post, there being not more than half an inch of water at most. This being the case we will refer to the only living stream of any size on the island distant from the isthmus in an air line about six miles, but from the broken and rolling nature of the country will take, in my judgment, ten miles of pipe to reach the post.

SANTA CATALINA ISLAND CO.

OWNERSHIP OF SANTA CATALINA ISLAND

KING OF SPAIN
Through Spanish occupation of California begun in 1769

|

MEXICO
Through successful revolt against Spain, accomplished in 1822

|

THOMAS M. ROBBINS
By grant on July 4, 1846, from Governor Pio Pico

|

JOSE MARIA COVARRUBIAS
By deed of August 31, 1850, his title being confirmed by
U.S. Land Commission and U.S. Patent

|

ALBERT PACKARD
By deed of October 13, 1853

¾   ¼

JAMES RAY   EUGENE L. SULLIVAN
Deed May 14, 1864   Deed June 9, 1858

WALTER HAWXHURST   CHAS. M. HITCHCOCK
Sheriff's deed August 6, 1867   Deed Feb 4, 1864

JAMES LICK
By deeds May 23, 1864; May 23, 1865; June 27, 1866; September 16, 1867

|

TRUSTEES OF JAMES LICK TRUST
By deed June 2, 1874

J.B. BANNING   Lots in Avalon sold to various
Deed Sept. 30, 1891   individuals

TRUSTEES OF JAMES LICK TRUST
By Sheriff's Sale

|

WILLIAM BANNING
By deed September 20, 1892

|

SANTA CATALINA ISLAND COMPANY
Incorporated October 16, 1894; by deed of May 7, 1896

|

The Santa Catalina Island Company now owns approximately 13%
of Santa Catalina Island.

|

Santa Catalina Island Conservancy owns approximately 86% of total land area,
by deed of February 18, 1975.

|

University of Southern California — Marine Science Center — Big Fisherman's Cove
By deeds of March 8, 1965 and January 26, 1972

Lots in Avalon sold to various individuals approximately 1%

Water continued to be a problem for years. The war itself never reached Catalina, but while there, the soldiers constructed a barracks. The barracks still stands, and has since been transformed into a privately owned yacht club. Although Wright's letters implied that Catalina belonged to the government, in fact it was legally deeded at that time to a man named James Lick.

TITLE HISTORY

After Thomas Robbins, Catalina had several owners. Fellow Santa Barbaran Jose Maria Covarrubias bought the Island from Robbins for $10,000. Next, Albert Packard, a lawyer also from Santa Barbara, gained ownership in 1853 for the all-time bargain price of $1000. James Lick, eccentric founder of the Lick Observatory, was the next owner. He arrived in San Francisco in 1847 with $40,000 in gold. While other newcomers mined, he began to buy choice pieces of real estate in the city. In 1861, he built the magnificent Lick House, then rented it out and lodged alone in one of its cheapest rooms. At a time when his yearly income was $200,000, he traveled around San Francisco in a dilapidated old buggy pulled by an aged horse. While the public laughed, he continued augmenting his fortune.

In Los Angeles, Lick acquired Los Feliz Rancho, now the location of Griffith Park, and from 1863-67 he purchased Catalina Island in quarter shares from four separate owners for $23,000 each. (See chart p. 18.) Much to his credit, he enjoyed using his money for others—and he funded an old ladies' home, an orphan shelter, a library association, a society for the prevention of cruelty to animals, free public baths, and a memorial to his mother. James Lick died in 1876 and was buried beneath the dome of his powerful telescope on Mt. Hamilton near San Jose, which later developed into the Lick Observatory.

The SCI Company

Lick's trustees sold Catalina in 1887 to the ambitious George R. Shatto for $200,000. Shatto was the first to create and subdivide the town of Avalon. However, he was unable to keep up the mortgage payments and the Lick trustees took the Island back, reselling it in 1892 to William Banning for $128,740. In 1896, he deeded the Island to the newly formed Santa Catalina Island Company (SCI Co.). The company was family owned, the stock held by three Banning brothers—William, Hancock, and J.B.—and their two sisters—Katherine and Anna. The Banning brothers turned themselves enthusiastically to developing Catalina Island into a pleasure resort. However, after some major changes to Avalon (see "Casino Point"), the plan was

KATHY ESCOVIDO-SANDERS

thwarted by the 1915 fire that damaged a good part of the town. Progress came to a halt for lack of capital.

The Wrigley Era

In 1919, chewing gum magnate William Wrigley Jr. bought the major interest in SCI Company for $3,000,000, announcing that "the development of Santa Catalina Island will be one of the greatest pleasures of my life." A man of his word, he created a fabulous resort within a few short years.

Until his death in 1932, Wrigley indulged his love affair with Catalina. He invested huge amounts of money in building projects such as an enormous ballroom housed in the Casino, the first completely round structure built in Southern California. He created a bird park and invited the public to visit (free of charge) the literally thousands of extraordinary birds that paraded around the "largest bird cage in the world" (built from the ribs of the old Sugarloaf Casino). He developed a baseball field and brought his Chicago Cubs over every year for spring training. He put in costly new utility systems. Catalina soon became the favored vacation spot for the stars and celebrities of Hollywood's Golden Era, as well as an attainable vacationland for regular people . . . as it is today.

In 1932, his son Philip K. Wrigley assumed control of the company and continued to improve the Island. Though under a different name, Catalina today still rests in the hands of the Wrigleys. Currently, Philip's son, William Wrigley, is seated as the SCI Company's director, and nephew Paxson Offield, who lives on the Island, is president of the company.

WW II

This growth cycle was interrupted by WW II, when Catalina became a training area for Merchant Marine, Army, Coast Guard, and Navy personnel, including the mysterious OSS (Office of Strategic Service). From 1941-45, tourists were not permitted on the Island. The St. Catherine Hotel was taken over by the Merchant Marine for a cooking school. It never regained its original beauty or its popularity, and in 1965 the

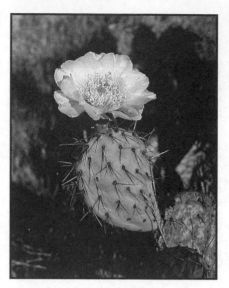

tuna cactus flower

classic old hotel was demolished. Several years passed before Catalina was "rediscovered" once again.

SANTA CATALINA ISLAND CONSERVANCY

The Beginning

Since William Wrigley Jr. bought Catalina Island in 1919, few changes had affected the interior of the Island. Mr. Wrigley purchased controlling interest in the Santa Catalina Island Company (SCI Co.) primarily because he thought the island some day would be the last remaining vestige of early California and that it was too precious a commodity to be subjected to massive development. The Santa Catalina Island Company turned its interest to establishing Avalon, the Island's only city, as a major resort and vacation destination. These efforts were accomplished.

Catalina's interior, however, remained unspoiled, with very little vehicular traffic but still a favorite for hikers and boaters who reveled in the beauty of the area. In 1972, William Wrigley Jr.'s son, Philip K., created a nonprofit foundation, the Santa Catalina Island Conservancy, to ensure the continued preservation of the majority of the Island. "The property can never revert to private ownership, so the wildlands, open space and nature areas will be there for the enjoyment of generations to come."

Los Angeles County Involvement
In 1974, an easement agreement gave Los Angeles County the right to share the use of 41,000 acres of Catalina's interior and coastline for parks, conservation, and recreation purposes for 50 years. In 1975, the Santa Catalina Island Conservancy acquired title to 42,129 acres and other assets from SCI Co. and now owns about 86% of Catalina Island, which includes the acreage and coastline covered by the agreement with Los Angeles County. This partnership of Conservancy and county was created to bring the Catalina Island experience to as many people as the area is able to accommodate without damage to the Island's fragile ecology. However, only the Conservancy bears the considerable financial responsibility for the preserve, including maintaining roads, the airport, and paying taxes. To help meet these substantial financial responsibilities, the Conservancy solicits memberships.

Preservation
The Conservancy has worked to halt deterioration of Catalina's natural resources, enabling threatened plant and animal species to reestablish. In the 1800s and early 1900s, domestic sheep were allowed to graze and proliferate freely. Along with the goats and wild pigs, these herbivores depleted many native grasses and other plants, which encouraged the growth of cactus in their place. The restoration program has begun to replenish many of these plants, and the animal populations are kept at numbers the interior lands are able to support. The sheep were removed entirely in 1923.

Airport-In-The-Sky
Until 1946, the only planes that landed at Catalina Island were small amphibians. Shortly before WW II, the tops of two mountains were leveled off and the canyon in between filled in to build an airport runway. However, when the war started, logs, boulders, and barbed wire were strung all across the runway to prevent its being used in the event of enemy attack. Building resumed immediately after the war and the runway was refinished and a modern terminal erected. The airport, called the Airport-In-The-Sky, overlooks rolling hills to the ocean in the background and is owned and operated by the Santa Catalina Island Conservancy.

Airport-In-The-Sky

CATALINA CONSERVANCY

BLACK INDICATES AREAS PROTECTED
BY S.C.I. CONSERVANCY

United Airlines flew DC-3s for several years from Los Angeles to Catalina. There are several regularly scheduled flights to the Airport-In-The-Sky today; service from San Diego, Orange County, and Los Angeles is available a couple times a week. The 3,200-foot asphalt runway will still handle planes up to and including DC-3s. Many small private planes visit Catalina every year and the number of Islanders who fly and park their planes here continues to grow. There is a daily $5 tie-down and parking fee.

The airport, 10 road miles from Avalon, is served by a shuttle which runs frequently to Avalon and to Two Harbors (both $8 one way, $11 roundtrip). The Runway Cafe is open from

8:30 a.m.-4 p.m. daily and you may eat on the lovely red-tiled Spanish patio or inside the pilots' lounge. The Runway Cafe specializes in (among other things) buffalo burgers and buffalo chili along with a regular menu; tel. (310) 510-2196. For airport shuttle-bus information and general airport information, call 510-0143. Private planes are welcome from 8 a.m.-7 p.m. mid-May to mid-Oct., 8 a.m.-5 p.m. the rest of the year.

Natural History Museum
Open to the public, the Conservancy-owned and -operated airport is fast becoming the inland hub of Conservancy activities. A small natural history museum here displays much of the Indian history of Catalina, along with plant, animal, and geology exhibits. Lectures and seminars are given by Catalina resident naturalist, Misty Gay. The Conservancy publishes a great pictorial and review of the island, "Santa Catalina, an Island Adventure," which is available at the Sugarloaf Bookstore in Avalon. College-student interns assist in interpreting the Island for visitors and staff at the Catalina Conservancy Natural History Center. Guided nature hikes are also offered.

Education
One of the newer extensions developed by the Conservancy is the education program, which fosters direct participation. Conservancy representatives travel to the Mainland to provide in-

---

CATALINA CONSERVANCY MEMBERSHIP FEES

Initiation fees:

Student	$10
Participating Member	$25
Supporting Member	$50
Donor	$100
Sustaining Member	$500

Annual pledge for support groups:

Catalina Caballeros	$100
Catalina Marineros	$100

formative slide presentations and lectures. These give up-to-date information about the *real* treasures of Catalina Island. For more information, call (310) 510-1421.

Intern Program
University science students participate in a program that brings them to the Island for a summer of study and college credit. These interns bunk at Middle Ranch and are given a crash course in the native plants and animals of Catalina. They assist naturalist Misty Gay in projects in the interior. For more information, call (310) 510-1421.

Membership
There are two Conservancy support groups, organized around special interests. The Catalina Marineros is a group for people interested in boating and sailing along the Catalina coastline. Catalina Caballeros involve members who enjoy horseback riding through the interior of the Island and they join together annually for rides. A Conservancy membership is a satisfying way to ensure that the Island will remain the great untainted open space it is now.

There are many ways to get involved; classes of membership are based on contribution amounts (tax deductible). All members receive the Catalina Conservancy newsletter and other special mailings. For more information, contact Douglas Propst, President, Santa Catalina Island Conservancy, P.O. Box 2739, Avalon, CA 90704, tel. (310) 510-1421.

GETTING THERE

DEPARTURE TERMINALS FROM SOUTHERN CALIFORNIA

There are a variety of ways to get to Catalina Island from Southern California. Several boat lines depart from five handy locations (Newport Beach, Long Beach, Redondo Beach, San Pedro, and San Diego). You have a choice of two boating destinations on Catalina, Avalon or Two Harbors. If you're in a hurry, there's helicopter and plane service to Pebbly Beach or the Airport-In-The-Sky. Reservations are a must on all transportation to (and from) the Island. Even with reservations you should arrive at all debarkation points at least an hour early to buy your ticket and check in. If you already have a ticket, it must be stamped before you get in line to board. Being early also allows time to park your car. Parking facilities are ample at each location; the fees vary. On the Mainland transfers between air and boat terminals can be made via Super Shuttle tel. (213) 777-8000 or Super Express tel. (213) 670-7080. You may bring as much luggage as you like, but keep in mind that on all boats passengers handle their own. For a more detailed description of boat rides to Catalina, see "Kidstuff."

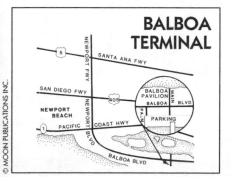

TRANSPORT COMPANIES SERVING CATALINA ISLAND

Catalina Express
The newest and fastest ships run between Catalina and the Catalina Express Port in Long Beach, Catalina Air Sea Terminal in San Pedro, and (seasonally) Redondo Beach Marina. Comfortable, with airline-style seats, drinks and snacks are available.

© MOON PUBLICATIONS INC.

From Long Beach roundtrip fares: adults $32, seniors $28.50, children $23.50, under two $1.50. Group rates for 20 or more. Ask about the Captain's Lounge which seats eight, $40 one way for the room in addition to the regular fare, by reservation only; includes a complimentary bottle of champagne. The Express offers an early-morning trip originating in Avalon and Two Harbors during the summer season. There is a $3 one-way charge for bicycles and surfboards. For roundtrip reservations and current schedule, call (310) 519-1212 in Redondo/Long Beach, or 510-1212 in Catalina.

Catalina Passenger Service
From mid-March through Nov. (limited service Dec. through mid-March), *The Catalina Flyer* departs Newport Harbor each morning at 9 a.m., departing Avalon 4:30 p.m. Fares: adult $28 RT, child 12 and under $15 RT. Credit cards accepted. If you're bringing a bicycle, mention this when making reservations; there's a $3 fee.

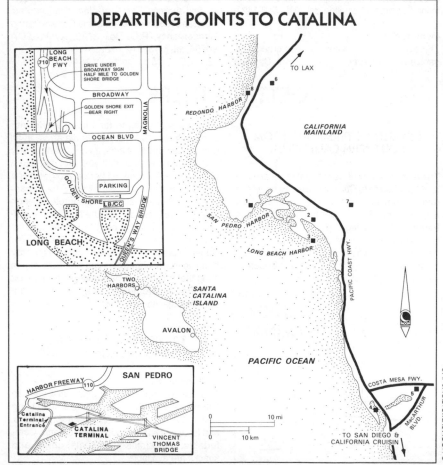

DEPARTING POINTS TO CATALINA

LONG BEACH FWY
710
DRIVE UNDER BROADWAY SIGN HALF MILE TO GOLDEN SHORE BRIDGE
BROADWAY
GOLDEN SHORE EXIT —BEAR RIGHT
MAGNOLIA
OCEAN BLVD
GOLDEN SHORE
PARKING
LB/CC
LONG BEACH
QUEEN'S WAY BRIDGE

TO LAX
REDONDO HARBOR
CALIFORNIA MAINLAND
SAN PEDRO HARBOR
LONG BEACH HARBOR
PACIFIC COAST HWY.

TWO HARBORS
SANTA CATALINA ISLAND
AVALON
PACIFIC OCEAN

HARBOR FREEWAY 110
SAN PEDRO
Catalina Terminal Entrance
CATALINA TERMINAL
VINCENT THOMAS BRIDGE

0   10 mi
0   10 km

COSTA MESA FWY.
MacARTHUR BLVD.
TO SAN DIEGO & CALIFORNIA CRUISIN'

Catalina dinghies (Oz Mallan)

(clockwise from top left) **1.** scuba diver comes up for *real* air; **2.** Catalina boaters;
3. communing with the fishes (all photos: Oz Mallan)

The Catalina Flyer is a fast catamaran with sundeck, full-service cocktail lounges, and a private stateroom for groups of up to 125 people. The trip between Newport and Catalina takes 75 minutes. For reservations call (714) 673-5245, 400 Main St., Balboa, CA 92661. On board are a small snack bar, comfortable inside seats, open deck, and video games.

Catalina Cruises

Catalina Cruises leaves from the Catalina Terminal daily. The cruise between Long Beach and Avalon on Catalina Cruises takes approximately two hours, part of which is a tour through massive Long Beach Harbor, past the permanently docked *Queen Mary* and the geodome hangar housing Howard Hughes's giant plane, the *Spruce Goose*.

Fares: adult $28 RT, child under 12 $18, child under two $1.50, senior citizens $24. Group rates on request. Bikes and surfboards are permitted for $3 (space available), but only at specific sailing times. Wheels must be removed and attached to frame. Ask about other sports equipment including scuba gear.

Each three-deck ship carries 700 passengers, with tables and chairs on the inside and wooden benches on the open decks. Two snack bars sell light snacks and drinks, including beer and wine. During the summer season, there are a minimum of four scheduled roundtrips a day, with weekend variations; ask about departures that go to Two Harbors. After Nov., call for the winter schedule. For reservations and schedules, from the Long Beach area call (310) 253-9800 or (800) 888-5939. Credit cards accepted. You'll find a small cafeteria, upstairs restaurant, and gift shop at the Catalina Terminal in Long Beach.

Helicopter

Island Express Helicopter Service, tel. (800)

DEPARTING POINTS TO CATALINA

1. **Catalina Air Sea Terminal** (San Pedro to Avalon and Two Harbors) Take Harbor Fwy. South (110) to the Terminal Island-Long Beach exit to Harbor Blvd. Follow signs to Catalina Terminal entrance across Harbor Blvd. From Long Beach take Ocean Blvd. west to the Harbor Blvd. exit from the Vincent Thomas Bridge.

2. **Catalina Terminal** (Long Beach to Avalon and Two Harbors) Go south on the Long Beach Fwy. (710), turn off at Downtown Long Beach exit to Golden Shore exit and follow signs to terminal.

3. **Helicopter Service** (Long Beach to Avalon) Go south on the Long Beach Fwy. (710) to Harbor Scenic Dr. exit, last exit before Queen Mary. Turn left at bottom of exit ramp and go 100 feet past stop sign. Heliport is small building on right, on ocean side.

4. **Newport Boat Terminal** (Newport to Avalon) From Pacific Coast Highway (Hwy. 1) turn south on Newport Blvd. to Balboa Blvd. Travel two miles on Balboa Blvd. to Balboa Pavilion on left.

5. **John Wayne Airport** (Orange County to Avalon) From 405 Freeway, exit Century Blvd. West, follow signs for departure to terminal six. Check-in counter near Republic and Delta.

6. **Long Beach Municipal Airport—Charter Service** (Long Beach to Avalon) San Diego Freeway (405) to Lakewood Blvd. North turnoff. Turn left at second traffic light (Douglas Dr.) off Lakewood Blvd. to airport terminal.

7. **Redondo Beach Marina** (Redondo to Avalon) From the San Diego Fwy. (405), exit on Crenshaw Blvd. and travel south to 190th St. Take 190th St. west until Harbor Dr. Go south on Harbor Dr. to Redondo Beach Marina. From LAX travel south on Pacific Coast Hwy. (1). Take a right on Beryl St., then a left on Harbor Dr. to Redondo Beach Marina.

San Diego Terminal. (Not on Map) Departs from B St. Cruise Ship Terminal just south of the Star of India on Harbor Drive in downtown. For more information, contact California Crusin' at (619) 235--8600.

2-AVALON, (310) 491-5550 or 510-2525, offers daily flights between Long Beach (at the bow of the *Queen Mary*), the Sea/Air Terminal in San Pedro, and Avalon. One-way ticket, $55, roundtrip ticket $95. Commuter books are $236.50 including tax for five one-way tickets, or 10 one-way tickets for $473 including tax. You're allowed one bag; extra luggage allowed only if space is available. Courtesy van service in Avalon. Commuter books are good for one year. Free parking in Long Beach.

Helitrans
From the Catalina Air Sea Terminal in San Pedro, Helitrans, a commuter jet-helicopter service, offers daily flights to Avalon. Flying time is a swift 18 minutes. Fare: adult $55 OW, $96 RT; two to three pieces of luggage allowed free. In Southern California call toll-free from the Los Angeles area (800) 262-1472 or (310) 548-1314 for prices, winter schedule, and reservations. Ask about air tours of Catalina Island.

Island Express Helicopter Service
Daily flights between Avalon and Catalina Air Sea Terminal in San Pedro and the Catalina Express Port at the *Queen Mary*. For reservations and more fare information call (800) 2-AVALON, (310) 491-5550, or in Avalon 510-2525.

SeaJet
From San Diego (or Oceanside) to Avalon, SeaJet's 110-foot sleek, computer-stabilized catamarans offer a full-day package which includes roundtrip transportation, continental breakfast with champagne, indoor/outdoor seating, six hours in Avalon, with choice of two tours. Adult package, $69; ask about family, senior, junior, and military discount rates. Phone (619) 696-0088, (800) 622-CJET.

Island Hopper/Catalina Airlines
Makes daily flights year-round between San Diego and Catalina. Departure from Montgomery Field in San Diego at 10 a.m. and 3 p.m., from Catalina's Airport-In-The-Sky at 11:15 a.m. and 2 p.m. Fares are $65 OW, $110 RT, children under two are free. For information call (800) 339-0FLY or (619) 279-4595; 3760 Green Curtis Dr., San Diego, CA 92123.

Pacific Coast Airlines
For a slightly different itinerary, Pacific Coast Airlines flies Thurs.-Mon. from John Wayne Airport in Orange County making a stopover to pick up passengers at LAX. The morning flight departs Orange County at 7 a.m., departs LAX at 9:45 a.m., arriving in Catalina's Airport-In-The-Sky at 10:15 a.m. The afternoon flight leaves Orange County at 2:45 p.m., departs LAX at 3:30 p.m. and arrives in Catalina at 4 p.m. Fares range from $49-70 OW. For information call (800) 426-5400 or (714) 261-1600; 4600 Campus Dr. 103, Newport Beach, CA 92660.

KATHY ESCOVEDO-SANDERS

HEALTH AND HELP

Hospital And Paramedics

Avalon Municipal Hospital, 100 Falls Canyon Rd., which has a close affiliation with Long Beach Memorial Medical Center on the Mainland, has a highly efficient emergency room, a fully equipped lab, and X-ray facility. One full-time doctor is a permanent resident of Avalon, and during the summer months interns come to the Island to help out. At least 20 doctors are on call when in town. In case of a serious emergency, call 911 or 510-0700 for an ambulance. In extreme situations the Medivac helicoptor can transport emergency cases to several hospitals on the Mainland in about 25 minutes.

Working hand in hand with the local medical staff, Avalon's highly trained paramedics have saved hundreds of lives with their quick response to emergency situations. *Bay Watch,* the Los Angeles County lifeguard vessel docked at the Avalon Mole, is manned by paramedics who handle boating and other water-related emergencies.

Other Facilities

The Marine Science Center at Two Harbors has one of the few hyperbaric chambers on the Southern California coast, designed to treat divers with the bends (nitrogen poisoning). For simple complaints you can be treated at the Avalon Clinic, 100 Falls Canyon Rd. (next door to the hospital), tel. 510-0096. In the event of a sudden toothache that can't wait until you go home, call resident dentist Dr. B.A. Calise, 204 Metropole, tel. 510-0322, in Avalon.

HEALTH CARE

Water

Avalon has good clean water straight from the sky and the sea. Yes, Catalina has a desalination plant which presently provides 25% of the Island's water. The plant, located at Pebbly Beach, is state of the art, and soon may increase the amount of sea water converted and then mixed with the Island's existing water-delivery system.

However, if you're hiking through the interior, bring water with you. Water at the county campgrounds is potable, but don't drink the water in streams or lakes. This is good advice wherever you hike since more and more cases of giardiasis are turning up across the States. If you must drink the water—purify it. Don't get lazy in this department; you can become very sick drinking contaminated water and you can't tell by looking at it—unless you travel with a microscope! The easiest way is to use purification tablets; Hidroclonozone and Halazone are two, but many brands are available at drugstores. Another common method is to carry a small plastic bottle of liquid bleach (use 8-10 drops per quart). Whichever you use, let the water stand for 20 minutes to improve the flavor. If you're not prepared with any of the above, boiling the water for 20-30 minutes will purify it; that method uses a heck of a lot of fuel when you're carrying it on your back. Several compact purifiers are on the market which solve the water problem.

When camping on the beach where fresh water is scarce, use sea water to wash dishes and even yourself. Liquid Ivory or Joy detergents both suds well in salt water. It only takes a small squirt to do a good job. (A rub of soap on the bottom of pots and pans before use over an open fire makes for easy cleaning of the pots after cooking.)

Sunburn

Sunburn can spoil a vacation quicker than anything else. Approach the sun cautiously. Expose yourself for short periods the first few days; wear a hat and sunglasses. Use a good sunscreen, and apply it to all exposed areas of the body (don't forget your feet, hands, nose, backs of your knees, and top of your forehead—especially if you have a receding hairline). Remember that after every time you go into the water, sunscreen lotion must be reapplied. Even after a few days of desensitizing your skin, when spending a day snorkeling wear a T-shirt in the water to protect your exposed back, and thoroughly douse the back of your neck with sunscreen lotion.

If you still get a painful sunburn, stay out of the sun. Cover up with clothes if it's impossible to find protective deep shade (like in the depths of a dark, thick forest). Even in the shade (such as under a beach umbrella), the reflection of the sun off the sand or water will burn your skin. Reburning the skin can result in painful blisters that easily become infected. Soothing suntan lotions, aloe gel, coconut oil, vinegar, cool tea, and preparations like Solarcaine will help relieve the pain. Drink plenty of liquids (especially water) and take tepid showers. The best cure is just spending a couple of days out of the sun.

Water Safety

The usual precautions apply: don't swim alone in isolated places, and don't take small children to rough surf areas, especially if there isn't a lifeguard. Familiarize yourself with the beach before splashing into the surf. In Avalon the surf is usually gentle during the summer months, but at Pebbly Beach and on the Island's back side the surf is much stronger and there are no lifeguards. While swimming, if you feel yourself being pulled out to sea, don't panic and don't wear yourself out trying to swim to shore. Instead, swim parallel to the beach in

---

EMERGENCY TELEPHONE NUMBERS

Police, paramedics,
  and fire dept. . . . . . . 911 or 510-0203
Hospital. . . . . 911 or 510-0700
Harbormaster. 510-0535
Sheriff's Dept . . . . 911 or 510-0174

Emergency Toll-free Mainland Numbers

Pollution and Oil Spills . (800) 424-8802
Runaway Hotline. . . . . . (800) 448-4663

Emergency Mainland Numbers—Toll

Coast Guard Search and
  Rescue . . . . (213) 590-2225
FBI . . . . (213) 477-6565
Poison Control Center. . (213) 484-5151

either direction, and usually after swimming three or four yards you'll be out of the undertow—then swim to shore. Pebbly Beach, especially, is noted for undertows.

Self Help
The smart traveler carries a first-aid kit of some kind. If backpacking, at least carry the following:

- ✓ alcohol
- ✓ adhesive tape
- ✓ aspirin
- ✓ baking soda
- ✓ bandages
- ✓ cornstarch
- ✓ gauze
- ✓ hydrogen peroxide
- ✓ iodine
- ✓ insect repellent
- ✓ Lomotil
- ✓ needle
- ✓ pain pills
- ✓ antibiotic ointment
- ✓ pain killer
- ✓ sunscreen
- ✓ tweezers
- ✓ water purification tablets

Even if not out in the wilderness you should carry at least a few bandages, aspirin, and an antibiotic ointment, powder, or both. Keep wounds as clean and dry as possible. If you're planning to backpack in the interior another great addition to your kit is David Werner's book, *Where There Is No Doctor*. It can be ordered for $8.39 from the Hesperian Foundation, Box 1692, Palo Alto, CA 94302. Werner drew on his experience living in Mexico's isolated backcountry to create this practical, informative book. Make sure your tetanus vaccination is current before you leave home, especially if you're backpacking in isolated regions.

SIMPLE FIRST-AID GUIDE

Acute Allergic Reaction
This, the most serious complication of insect bites or stings, can be fatal. Common symptoms are hives, rash, pallor, nausea, tightness in chest or throat, trouble in speaking or breathing. Be alert for symptoms. If they appear, get prompt medical help. Start CPR if needed and continue until medical help is available.

Animal Bites
Bites, especially on face and neck, need immediate medical attention. If possible, catch and hold the animal for observation, taking care not to be bitten. Wash the wound with soap and water (hold under running water for two to three minutes unless bleeding is heavy). Do not use iodine or other antiseptic. Bandage. This also applies to bites by human beings. In case of human bites the danger of infection is high.

Bee or Wasp Stings
If available apply cold compresses quickly. Try to remove stinger by gentle scraping with clean fingernail and continue cold applications till pain is gone. Be alert for symptoms of acute allergic reaction or infection requiring medical aid.

Bleeding
For severe bleeding apply direct pressure to the wound with bandage or the heel of the hand. Do not remove blood-soaked clothes, just add others on top and continue pressure till bleeding stops. Elevate bleeding part above heart level. If bleeding continues, apply pressure bandage to arterial points. Do not put on tourniquet unless advised by a physician. Do not use iodine or other disinfectant. Get medical aid.

Blister
It is better not to open a blister if you can rest

the foot. If you can't, wash foot with soap and water; make a small hole at the base of the blister with a needle sterilized in alcohol or in a match flame; drain and cover with a bandage or moleskin. If a blister breaks on its own, wash with soap and water, bandage, and be alert for signs of infection (redness, festering) that call for further attention.

Burns

Minor burns (redness, swelling, pain): apply cold water, or immerse burned part in cold water immediately. Use burn medication if necessary. With deeper burns blisters develop. Immerse in cold water (not ice water) or apply cold compresses for one to two hours. Blot dry and protect with sterile bandage. Do not use antiseptic, ointment, or home remedies. Consult a doctor. With very deep burns skin layers are destroyed; skin may be charred. Cover with sterile cloth; be alert for breathing difficulties and treat for shock if necessary. Do not remove clothing stuck to burn. Do not apply ice. Do not use burn remedies. Get medical help quickly.

Cuts

Wash small cuts with clean water and soap. Hold wound under running water. Bandage. Use hydrogen peroxide or other antiseptic. For large wounds see "Bleeding" above. If a finger or toe has been cut off, treat severed end to control bleeding. Put severed part in clean cloth for the doctor (it may be possible to reattach it by surgery). Treat for shock if necessary. Get medical help at once.

Diving Accident

There may be injury to the cervical spine (such as a broken neck). Call for medical help. (See "Drowning" and "Fractures" below.)

Drowning

Clear airway and start CPR even before trying to get water out of lungs. Continue CPR till medical help arrives. In case of vomiting, turn victim's head to one side to prevent the inhaling of vomitus.

Food Poisoning

Symptoms appear a varying number of hours after eating and are generally like those of the flu—headache, diarrhea, vomiting, abdominal cramps, fever, a general sick feeling. See a doctor. A rare form, botulism, has a high fatality rate. Symptoms are double vision, inability to swallow, difficulty in speaking, respiratory paralysis. Get to emergency facility at once.

Fractures

Until medical help arrives, do not move the victim unless absolutely necessary. Suspected victims of back, neck, or hip injuries should not be moved. Suspected breaks of arms or legs should be splinted to avoid further damage before victim is moved, if moving is necessary.

Heat Exhaustion

Symptoms are cool moist skin, profuse sweating, headache, fatigue, and drowsiness, with essentially normal body temperature. Remove victim to cool surroundings, raise feet and legs, loosen clothing, and apply cool cloths. Give sips of salt water—one teaspoon of salt to a glass of water—for rehydration. If victim vomits, stop fluids, and take the victim to emergency facility as soon as possible.

Heat Stroke

Rush victim to hospital. Heat stroke can be fatal. Victim may be unconscious or severely confused. Skin feels hot, is red and dry, with no perspiration. Body temperature is high. Pulse is rapid. Remove victim to cool area, sponge with cool water or rubbing alcohol; use fans or air conditioning and wrap in wet sheets, but do not overchill. Massage arms and legs to increase circulation. Do not give large amount of liquids. Do not give liquids if victim is unconscious.

Jellyfish Stings

Symptom is acute pain and may include feeling of paralysis. Immerse in ice water for five to ten minutes or apply aromatic spirits of ammonia to remove venom from skin. Be alert for symptoms of acute allergic reaction and/or shock. If this happens, get victim to hospital as soon as possible.

Motion Sickness

Get a prescription from your doctor if boat travel is anticipated and this condition is a problem. Many over-the-counter remedies are sold in the U.S.: Bonine and Dramamine are two. Medication administered in adhesive patches behind the ear is also available by prescription. If you prefer not to take chemicals or get drowsy, try the Sea Band, a cloth band that you place around the pressure point of the wrists. It works through acupressure, without drugs. For more information write: Sea Band, 1645 Palm Beach Lake Blvd., Suite 220, W. Palm Beach, FL 33401, tel. (305) 684-4508.

Muscle Cramps

Usually a result of unaccustomed exertion. "Working" the muscle or kneading with hand relieves cramp. If in water head for shore (don't panic—you can swim even with a muscle cramp), or knead muscle with hand. Call for help if needed.

Mushroom Poisoning

Even a small ingestion may be serious. Induce vomiting immediately if there is any question of mushroom poisoning. Symptoms —vomiting, diarrhea, difficulty breathing— may begin in one to two hours or up to 24 hours. Convulsions and delirium may develop. Go to a doctor or emergency facility at once.

Nosebleed

Press bleeding nostril closed, pinch nostrils together, or pack with sterile cotton or gauze. Apply cold water to nose and face. Victim should sit up, leaning forward, or lie down with head and shoulders raised. If bleeding does not stop in ten minutes get medical help.

Obstructed Airway

Find out if victim can talk by asking, "Can you talk?" If he can talk, encourage him to try to cough obstruction out. If he can't speak, a trained person must apply the Heimlich Maneuver. If you are alone and choking, try to forcefully cough object out. Or press your fist into your upper abdomen with a quick upward thrust, or lean forward and quickly press your upper abdomen over any firm object with rounded edge (back of chair, edge of sink, porch railing). Keep trying till the object comes out.

Poison Oak

After contact, wash affected area with alkali-base laundry soap, lathering well. Cortisone creams are helpful when itching and blisters develop.

Puncture Wounds

They often do not bleed, so try to squeeze out some blood. Wash thoroughly with soap and water and apply a sterile bandage. Check with doctor about tetanus. If pain, heat, throbbing, or redness develop, get medical attention at once.

Rabies

Bites from bats, raccoons, rats, or other wild animals are the most common source of rabies today. If bitten try to capture the animal (avoid getting bitten again), so that it can be observed; do not kill the animal unless necessary and try not to injure the head so the brain can be examined. Even if the animal can't be found, you must see a doctor, who may decide to use antirabies immunization. In any case, flush the bite with water and apply a dry dressing; keep victim quiet and see a doctor as soon as possible.

Scrapes

Sponge with soap and water; dry. Apply antibiotic ointment or powder and cover with a non-stick dressing (or tape on a piece of cellophane). When healing starts, stop ointment and use antiseptic powder to help scab form. Ask doctor about tetanus.

continues

Shock

Can be a side effect in any kind of injury. Get immediate medical help. Symptoms may be pallor, clammy feeling to the skin, shallow breathing, fast pulse, weakness, or thirst. Loosen clothing, cover victim with blanket but do not apply other heat, and lay him on his back with feet raised. If necessary, start CPR. Do not give water or other fluids.

Snakebite

If snake is not poisonous, toothmarks usually appear in an even row. Wash the bite with soap and water and apply sterile bandage. See a doctor. If snake is poisonous, puncture marks (one to six) can usually be seen. Kill the snake for identification if possible, taking care not to be bitten. Keep the victim quiet, immobilize the bitten arm or leg, keeping it on a lower level than the heart. If possible, phone ahead to be sure antivenin is available and get medical treatment as soon as possible. Do not give alcohol in any form. If treatment must be delayed and snakebite kit is available, use as directed.

Spider Bites

The black widow bite may produce only a light reaction at the place of the bite, but severe pain, a general sick feeling, sweating, abdominal cramps, and breathing and speaking difficulty may develop. The more dangerous brown recluse spider's venom produces severe reaction at the bite, generally in two to eight hours, plus chills, fever, joint pain, nausea, and vomiting. Apply a cold compress to the bite in either case. Get medical aid quickly.

Sprain

Treat as a fracture till injured part has been x-rayed. Raise the sprained ankle or other joint and apply cold compresses or immerse in cold water. If swelling is pronounced, try not to use the injured part. Get prompt medical help.

Sunburn

For skin that is moderately red and slightly swollen, apply wet dressings of gauze dipped in a solution of one tablespoon baking soda and one tablespoon cornstarch to two quarts of cool water. Or take a cool bath with a cup of baking soda mixed in the water. Sunburn remedies are helpful in relieving pain. See a doctor if burn is severe.

Sunstroke

This is a severe emergency. Skin is hot and dry; body temperature is high. The victim may be delirious or unconscious. Get medical help immediately. (See "Heat Stroke," above)

Ticks

Cover ticks with mineral oil or kerosene to exclude air from ticks and they will usually drop off or can be lifted off with tweezers in 30 minutes. To avoid infection, take care to remove the whole tick. Wash area with soap and water.

To Save A Knocked Out Tooth

Rinse tooth in cool water. Do not scrub tooth. If possible, replace tooth in socket and hold it in place. If this cannot be done, put the tooth under the tongue, or wrap it in a wet cloth, or drop it in a glass of milk. See a dentist immediately.

KATHY ESCOVEDO-SANDERS

PRACTICALITIES

INFORMATION

Chamber Of Commerce
This office is located at the foot of the Pleasure Pier. You can obtain helpful information here on just about any Island-related subject; they're especially helpful for making hotel reservations by providing a list of daily hotel vacancies. Ask for a free directory of businesses in Avalon. Open daily from 8 a.m.-5 p.m., tel. 510-1520.

News Media
A local paper, the *Catalina Islander,* is published once a week. You can purchase it at Sugarloaf Book Store, 403 Crescent Ave., Leo's Drug Store, or at the *Islander* office at 615 Crescent Avenue. This small newspaper is mailed to thousands of Mainlanders who enjoy keeping up with Catalina activities. Seasonal schedule changes for transportation are reported, as well as business information. A classified ad section often lists summer and winter housing rentals.

Another local paper, the *Avalon Bay News,* is available every Thursday. It includes current Island news as well as feature stories focusing on Island history. Subscription rate is $30 annually; 117 Whittley Ave., tel. 510-1500, and available at local stores, including Fred and Sally's Market and Avalon Liquor. Mainland newspapers are sold at Sugarloaf Bookstore, tel. 510-0077, and at several racks around town and on the mole.

Bookstores
The **Sugarloaf Bookstore**, 403 Crescent Ave., carries a tremendous collection of magazines, guidebooks, paperbacks, cold drinks, candy, beer, wine, and ice cream. **R. Franklin Pyke Bookseller**, 228 Metropole Ave., tel. 510-2588, carries books from cheap (secondhand paperbacks) to expensive (local history, and fine collector items), chart guides and maps, both old and new, as well as early local photos and postcards. Catalina pottery is bought and sold, and local artwork is on display. Open Tues.-Sun. 10-5 and by appointment; credit cards accepted.

SERVICES

Mail
The post office (tel. 510-0084) in the **Atwater Hotel Building** can be reached either from Metropole St. (across from Von's) or from Sumner Ave. (next to the Atwater Hotel). If you plan to stay on the Island for more than a day or two and would like to receive mail, have it addressed to you care of General Delivery, Avalon, CA 90704. There's no mail delivery in Avalon; it all comes to post office boxes or the general delivery window. Mail deposited by 3 p.m. will leave Avalon the same day. Mail drops are on the corner of Crescent and Metropole and in the post office. **Federal Express** mail is brought to the Island via Catalina Flying Boats from Long Beach.

Avalon's streets are swept daily.

Telephone
For all parts of Catalina the telephone area code is 310. Public telephone booths are located in the post office arcade, the plaza, and on the green pier. Calls to Orange County and Los Angeles County are usually less than $1 for three minutes. Western Union: tel. (800) 325-6000, in Avalon 510-0600.

Restrooms
Men's and women's public restrooms in Avalon are located at the foot of the Pleasure Pier, Boat Terminal Mole, Bird Park, Casino walkway, Island Plaza, and at Pebbly Beach. At the Buffalo Nickel look for the sign that says "Buffalo Heads." A drinking fountain is located on each end of Middle Beach.

Public Showers
At the foot of the green Pleasure Pier, coin-operated showers are open to the public. Bring your own towel, soap, and a quarter for each three minutes of shower you desire. Outside on the beach, saltwater showers are available to rinse the sand off. More public showers are located on the Casino walkway.

Lockers
If you're just visiting for the day and need someplace to leave your gear while swimming or eating, storage lockers are available at the Island Plaza and on the mole.

Groceries
Von's Market, 123 Metropole Ave., tel. 510-0280, and **Fred and Sally's Market**, 117 Catalina Ave., tel. 510-1199, both deliver for a small fee; check time schedule at the store.

Laundromat
Catalina Coin Wash, 113 Metropole Ave., tel. 510-9027, charges $2.50 for a wash and dry. Cottonwood Coin Laundry, 220 Metropole Ave., 510-1244, charges $2.50-3 for a wash and dry.

Dry Cleaners
Avalon Bay News doubles as a dry-cleaning depot. Clothes are sent to the Mainland to be

Avalon's only gas station is located at Pebbly Beach.

cleaned. Turnaround time can be lengthy but it's a great convenience otherwise; 117 Whittley Ave., 510-1500.

Drug Store

Prescriptions are filled at **Leo's Drug Store**, 401 Crescent Ave., tel. 510-0189. Well stocked with camera supplies, film, gifts, and other sundries.

Hardware

Chet's Hardware is Avalon's general store and carries a little bit of everything from household goods to fishing supplies. Open year-round in the Atwater Arcade opposite the post office, tel. 510-0990.

Banks

There are two banks on the Island, both in Avalon: **Southern California Bank**, offering Touch and Go ATM service; 303 Crescent Ave., tel. 510-2265; and **Bank of San Pedro**, 307 Crescent Ave., tel. 510-1170. Open weekdays 9 a.m.-3 p.m., Saturday 9 a.m.-noon.

Credit Cards

Business is run much as it is on the Mainland; most businesses accept credit cards. Many do not accept personal checks, but most shops and businesses will accept well-known traveler's checks with proper identification.

Diving Supplies

Divers can find just about everything they need at several shops in Avalon. **Catalina Divers Supply** is located on the green Pleasure Pier, tel. 510-0330; **Island Marine**, is at 125 Metropole Ave., in Cricket Alley, tel. 510-0238. **Catalina Scuba** is located in the lobby of the Bay View Hotel, 124 Whittley Ave., 510-2594, a favored hotel which caters to divers visiting the Island.

Fishing Supplies And License

Avalon Boat Stand, on the Pleasure Pier, for years has been the familiar spot for fishing supplies and small talk; tel. 510-0455. Two more with well-stocked shelves are Island Marine, at 125 Metropole Ave., tel. 510-0238, and **Chet's Hardware** store, in the Atwater Arcade opposite the post office, tel. 510-0990.

Government

Many visitors are surprised that Catalina is in America, a tax-paying, sixth-class city of Los Angeles County, state of California. The Los Angeles County Health, Fire, and Building Inspection departments provide services for Avalon and Catalina Island. The city receives its police protection under a contract from the Los Angeles County Sheriff's Department. Avalon has jurisdiction for three miles out to sea including moorings, sanitation, and police protection. It functions under a city council with an appointed city manager and the mayor is directly elected by the voters.

The Law

Although the police department is run by the Los Angeles County Sheriff's Department, there is a resident judge, and a jail and courthouse administered through Avalon. **Note:** Drinking of any alcoholic beverage on the beach or city streets is prohibited by city ordinance. This is vigorously enforced. Avalon has a local attorney if you should need one; call G.J. Sanders, tel. 510-2903.

SHOPPING

For a small town, Avalon has an immense number of unique shops selling a wide variety of stylish sportswear, hand-painted T-shirts, shells, toys, smart children's duds, original Catalina art, and, and, and, and . . . ! Most shops accept credit cards. Because Avalon clothing shops carry top-of-the-line famous-name sportswear, at summer's end many merchants put on a very popular sale. Such crowds turn out (all the way from the Mainland) that bargain-hunters are admitted inside the shops only a few at a time.

Art Shops

Upton's House of Wood was originated by the late Avalon artist Bud Upton and his son Roger. Bud was a prodigious artist who painted scenes from all over the Island. He captured eras in time and small vignettes of the Catalina panorama from many years past until he died in 1989 at the age of 88. The quaint wooden house in the House of Wood window was just one of his clever creations and his sense of humor is evident in his "infamous" gold buffalo chip. As well as original paintings, carvings, and knickknacks, the shopper will find unique Catalina-made souvenirs; 517 Crescent Ave., tel. 510-0125, open daily during the summer.

Don't miss a stop at the **Off White Gallery**, a showroom for several of Catalina's most talented artists. You'll see watercolors by Frank Loudin, oil paintings by Denise Burns, locally designed and handcrafted gold jewelry by Dave Stein, and bronze sculpture by J. Quillan. Located on the corner of Crescent Ave. and Whittley at Hotel Villa Portofino, tel. 510-1183; open year-round.

While strolling through the Metropole Marketplace, make a stop at **Perico Gallery** for something different again—pen and inks, watercolors, and prints of Catalina created by local artists. You'll also find a superb collection of Catalina bird tiles. Open year-round, tel. 510-1342. Check out the **Old Catalina Pottery Exhibit and Retail Shop,** a great source for buying and selling Catalina pottery. Located in the El Encanto Marketplace, with two display rooms: one with exhibits worth thousands of dollars of collector's items, the other a store with a variety of goods for sale; 101 Marilla, tel. 510-2376 and 510-1515.

Browse through Tonya's Art Gallery with original paintings and sculptures in the El Encanto; tel. 510-0151. Another place where it's easy to spend time window-shopping is the **Antique Store,** the only place of its kind on the Island, with antiques and collectibles located at 120 Sumner Ave., tel. 510-0559.

Shell Shops

While many shops on the Island stock shells, collectors might want to take a look at **Mermaid's Garden** at the Metropole Marketplace. Along with shells you'll find shell jewelry and other gifts from the Island, tel. 510-0295. **The Little Shell Shop**, 105 Pebbly Beach Rd., is open daily 10:30 a.m.-noon and 2-4 p.m.; tel. 510-2127.

Gold And Silver Shops

The **Catalina Gold Company** has wonderful chains and unique pieces created by talented artisans. The shop also deals in pearls and diamonds. It is rumored that the gold prices here are *much* cheaper than on the Mainland. Located at the Metropole Marketplace, tel. 510-0457; open year-round. **Patricia's** is a gallery of handcrafted gold and silver jewelry. Many of the silver pieces come from Taxco, Mexico, and included among the fine gifts are handblown glass and arty tiles. Located just inside the arch at the El Encanto, tel. 510-1448.

Gift Shops

At 523 Crescent Ave. allow time to browse in a marvelous shop filled with surprises in every corner. **Grand Traditions** is a gourmet, bed, bath, and wine shop. And it doesn't stop there, with clever educational children's toys, unusual decorator baskets, exotic dried flowers, and too much more to try to list. Open year-round; 523 Crescent Ave., on the corner of Claressa, tel. 510-1278. The **Hen House Gifts**, in the Island Tour Plaza, has a large selection of fun things from unusual children's jewelry, Nativity scenes, chimes, and music boxes to T-shirts, bears, and dolls. Open daily from Easter through October, weekends in the winter; tel. 510-1912.

Catalina Design Center offers handmade jewelry, woodwork, ceramics, windsocks, and more. Located at 125 Sumner Ave., tel. 510-2600; open year-round. The **Now And Then Shop** has gathered a collection of antiques, children's clothing, toys, jewelry, and other collectibles. Take a look at the **Catalina Trading Co.,** 125 Metropole Ave. (in Cricket Alley), tel. 510-0782. They create beautiful personal gift baskets, and stock unique gift items and gourmet foods. **Especially Yours,** 205 Crescent Ave. (Metropole Marketplace), tel. 510-2535, specializes in handcrafted Victorian items.

Catalina Designs, 125 Sumner, tel. 510-2600, carries Pacific Coast jewelry and crafts. Look for **Le Bouquet de Catalina** in the Post Office arcade building, tel. 510-1278. You'll find flowers, balloons, dried floral arrangements, and lovely glass designs. At **Sherri's Stationery and Gifts,** 205 Crescent Ave., tel. 510-2984, shoppers will find a selection similar to most Mainland Hallmark shops. **Catalina Confetti,** tel. 510-2511, offers a little bit of everything including candy and fudge.

Good Junk

Renato's Bits 'N Pieces has items from new and used Italian jewelry, to Catalina pottery, to furniture; 116 Claressa Ave., tel. 510-2947.

Clothing Stores

Men and women find an excellent choice of active sportswear and shoes, including most of the big names, at the **Catalina Island Dept. Store.** Great selection of trendy sweatshirts and sweaters for those cool evenings on the water. It's located at 421 Crescent Ave., tel. 510-0151, opposite the green Pleasure Pier; open year-round. One of Avalon's upscale men's shops is **Buoys and Gulls**, offering two floors of quality resort, yachting, and beach attire. Located at 407 Crescent Ave., tel. 510-0416. **Catalina Gear** carries men's and women's active wear and accessories, including such brands as Patagonia. Open year-round; located at 226 Crescent Ave., tel. 510-2488.

Carlotta's Mexican Shop has been offering charming clothing, jewelry, and accessories from Mexico, Guatemala, and Indonesia for many years in the same location at the El Encanto. Look for designer T-shirts by Kat and Vicki Fleming jewelry. Open daily from April through Oct., and weekends in the winter season; tel. 510-1953.

Ladley's Menswear offers fine casual styles, featuring surfwear to imported clothing; 205 Crescent Avenue. At **Peggy's Gifts and Souvenirs** look for a great selection of hats, bags, and shirts. Located next to Leo's Drug Store, 104 Sumner Ave., tel. 510-0690. Wander on up to 233 Sumner Ave. for a spree at the **Whale's Tale.** At this fashionable boutique, shoppers will find feminine fancies, finery, and gifts, including jumpsuits, swimwear, and exclusive dresses. Open year-round, located across from the Golf Gardens, tel. 510-1097.

At **Trix,** you'll find trendy sportswear, accessories, and women's clothing; 107 Sumner Ave., tel. 510-2622. **Weezie's** offers swimsuits, sportswear, and casual women's clothing; 415 Crescent Ave., tel. 510-1612. Look for **Resort Wear,** in the Metropole Marketplace. **Island Madness,** 319 Beacon Ave., tel. 510-2377, carries clothes and gear for beach-goers and surf lovers.

Children's Shops
Looking for that special gift for the little ones? In Avalon there are so many choices your problem will be making a decision. At the **Toy Attic** you'll find a variety of toys, games, books, and beach and water toys. As for dolls choose from quality Madame Alexander or Raikes and Gund Bears. It's located at 119 Claressa, tel. 510-1TOY. The well-dressed child shops at **Melody's**. The selection contains children's clothing from infants and up. Located at 106 Sumner Ave., tel 510-0706; open year-round.

The **Sand Box Children's Boutique** carries a grand selection of bright trendy clothing and more. Even the kids hate to leave. From infant sizes and up. Located at 519 Crescent Ave., tel. 510-2130. **Catalina Kids,** 205 Crescent Ave., tel. 510-1559, dresses the kids in T-shirts, chic beach outfits, and smart accessories, for infants and up.

Shoes
Catalina Department Store and **Buoys and Gulls** have good selections of sporty footwear.

WHAT TO TAKE

Clothes
Go simple. Dress to suit your life-style. There isn't a place on the Island that requires a tie. Sundresses and shorts are acceptable everywhere, as are Levi's and T-shirts. Take at least one swimsuit, and a sweater or a light jacket for the boat ride; it can get cool on the water once the sun goes down. Sandals are good for pavement and hot sand, and a good pair of walking shoes will carry you comfortably over the hiking trails around Avalon or the interior. There are laundromats in Avalon, so you needn't take your entire wardrobe.

Winter Visits
If you're visiting Avalon in the winter the weather is much the same as it is along the coast of Southern California: around 56-63°F, often rainy (average yearly rainfall is 14 inches, nearly all of it occurring between mid-Oct. and mid-April). If you plan to be outdoors a lot, bring warm clothes and a raincoat.

Children
If you have kids, bring them! This is a great place for the young at heart at any age. For summer fun take several swimsuits for each; kids live on the beach and spend most of their time in the safe waters of Avalon (all small children need supervision). Bring their favorite beach toys and flotation vests or arm rings for safety. Don't forget beach towels. See "Kidstuff" for more details.

Food
Most visitors choose to buy their food on the Island, where there is a variety of choices, ranging from restaurants to convenience stores (see "Avalon—Food"). Some, however, prefer to carry a cooler or picnic basket over on the boat; there are picnic areas in a variety of scenic places on the Island. Just remember, you'll be doing a lot of walking so you'll only want to carry what you need.

Cooking facilities are limited but there are free barbecue pits on the mole, close to where the boat disembarks. There's a $1 pp fee and a $100 refundable deposit to use the picnic grounds located past the golf course, about a one-mile walk from the mole. A fire permit is needed for barbecues; for details check with the visitor's information center on Crescent Ave. opposite the green Pleasure Pier.

Photo Equipment
Catalina is a photographer's paradise. There's a picture to take wherever you look: the bay, the Casino, the purple hills, a buffalo, or sun worshipers on the beach. Bring an ample supply of film—it's cheaper at your favorite discount store on the Mainland. However, if you run short, camera supplies (including rentals) are available at many Island locations, including **Leo's Drug Store** on the corner of Sumner and Crescent and **Island Photo & Video,** at 121 Metropole, tel. 510-2614; processing here is a little pricey. (See "Cameras and Picture Taking" for more information.)

Pets

If you plan to bring your pet with you to Catalina, it travels free on the boat but must be leashed and muzzled; check with your carrier ahead of time. On the plane pets require a regular-priced ticket. For your convenience and in an effort to keep Avalon as clean as possible, the Avalon Humane Society has provided a fenced-in area for your pet to relieve himself alongside the roadway on the Casino side of the bay. Check the Avalon map.

Avalon also has some regulations pertaining to your pets in town. For a helpful pamphlet containing excerpts of the municipal code concerning animals, ask at the chamber of commerce office at the foot of the Pleasure Pier, or write to the Avalon Humane Society, Box 1584, Avalon, CA 90704. **Note:** Pets are not allowed on Crescent Ave. or any beach at any time! Pets must be on leashes when on Avalon city streets.

Swimming And Diving Equipment

If you enjoy snorkeling, bring your fins and mask. There are many clear deep coves close by that are alive with colorful fish darting through kelp forests. If you're a diver, you may bring your air tanks with you on the boat; air is available in Avalon on the Pleasure Pier. If you don't want to carry it all, tanks and equipment can be rented on the Pleasure Pier at **Catalina Divers Supply,** tel. 510-0330 in Avalon and at **Catalina Scuba,** located at the Bay View Hotel, tel. 510-2594.

Insurance And ID

Carry proper identification and a medical insurance card with you. If you need to use a medical facility, your card will expedite matters, just as it does on the Mainland.

CAMERAS AND PICTURE TAKING

Land and sea combine to provide unforgettable panoramas, well worth taking home with you on film to savor again at your leisure. Instamatic or disc cameras are easy to carry and uncomplicated, while 35mm cameras offer higher-quality pictures, have become easier than ever

Divers can rent equipment or bring it over on the boat.

to use, and are available in any price range. They can come equipped with built-in light meter, automatic exposure, self-focus, and self-advance—with little more to do than aim and click.

Whether in the interior with the magnificent bison, along an isolated coast, or in Avalon, picture taking is a natural. Don't miss this chance; bring your camera!

X-ray Protection

If you bring your film from home by air where you must go through an X-ray security device; remember to take precautions. Each time film is passed through the machine, a little damage is done, especially in high ASA film. It's cumulative, and perhaps one time won't make much difference, but most photographers won't take the chance.

With today's tight security at airports, some guards insist on passing your film and camera through the X-ray machine. But whenever possible, request hand inspection. Another alternative is to place it in protective lead bags and pack it in your checked luggage. Lead-lined bags are available at camera shops in two sizes. The larger size holds up to 22 rolls of 35mm film; the smaller size holds eight. If you use fast film, ASA 400 or higher, buy the double lead-lined bag designed to protect more sensitive film. It's also efficient to have an extra lead-lined bag for carrying your film-loaded camera if you want to drop it into a piece of carry-on luggage. (And for nonphotographers, the bag protects medications from X-ray damage.)

If you decide to request hand examination make it simple for the security guard. Have the film out of boxes and place plastic cartridge containers together in one clear Ziploc plastic bag that you can hand him for quick examination both coming and going. Whenever possible, load the camera after going through security.

Film Processing

For processing film the traveler has several options. Most people take their film home and have it processed at a familiar lab. However, for the traveler shooting lots of film and staying for more than three weeks, another option is to buy prepaid Kodak mailers before you leave home and simply drop the film in the Avalon post office. Be sure to put postage on the inside envelope that will be sent to your home address.

In Avalon good photo processing is done at several locations, including **Leo's Drug Store**, 401 Crescent Ave., tel. 510-0189. For instant processing go to **Island Photo**, where you can get same-day service and one-hour printing; 125 Metropole Ave., tel. 510-0479. Remember, outside of Island Photo instant service, film is sent to the Mainland, and therefore takes longer to get back. If on the Island for a short visit, be sure to ask the date it will be back.

Camera Protection

Take a few precautions with your camera while traveling. At the beach remember that a combination of wind and sand can really gum up the works and scratch the lens. On 35mm cameras use a clear skylight filter instead of a lens cap so

the camera can hang around your neck or over your shoulder always at the ready for that spectacular shot that comes when least expected. And if something is going to get scratched, better an $18 filter than a $300 lens. It also helps to carry as little equipment as possible.

If you plan to be in small boats that put you close to the water, keep the cameras temporarily in Ziploc bags when not in use. Don't *store* cameras in plastic bags for any length of time, because the moisture that builds up in the bag is the same as being in the rain. It's always wise to keep cameras out of sight when camping. Put your name and address on the camera. Chances are if it gets left behind or stolen it won't matter whether your name is there or not, and don't expect to see it again; however, miracles do happen. You can put a rider on most homeowner's insurance policies for a nominal sum that will cover the cost if a camera is lost or stolen.

CATALINA CALENDAR OF EVENTS

Jan.	Avalon Benefit 50-mile run
March	Catalina 10K Race
	Catalina Marathon Race
	Annual Avalon Underwater Clean-up
April	Easter Sunrise Service and Pageant
May	Memorial Dance
June	Catalina Island Chamber Music Festival
	Del Rey Yacht Club Race in Avalon
	Exchange Club Fishing Tournament
July	Dixieland Jazz Jamboree
	Metropolitan Yacht Club Annual Opening
	Fourth of July Town Fireworks
	Fourth of July Casino Dance
Aug.	Coors U.S. Championship Outrigger Race
Sept.	Catalina Art Festival Billfish Tournament
Oct.	Gold Cup Marlin Tournament
Nov.	Rotary Club 10K Run
Dec.	New Year's Eve Dance

KATHY ESCOVEDO-SANDERS

AVALON
INTRODUCTION

HISTORY

In 1987, Avalon turned 100 years old. The town has obviously changed in many ways: in 1887 Avalon was a beautiful tent city, where residential lots were auctioned off for as little as $150; today you're lucky to buy one for $50,000 (and at that price you won't see the ocean). In the early days, water was at a premium, sold on street corners by the gallon after being hauled to the Island in barges from the Mainland.

Today, the Edison Company and modern technology have made water a little easier to come by with reservoirs and pumping stations (but water will always be a problem since its source is unpredictable Mother Nature). The town has cable TV, offering the latest movies, concerts, and soaps, as well as the even more dramatic weekly meetings of the Avalon City

Council. New hotels and homes continue to spring up in the one-square-mile town. Vacationers now have the choice of newly built jet-set-style resorts or historical "quaint" and "charming" old inns—there's even a campground in Avalon.

Most agree that the changes have greatly improved Avalon. But great care has been taken not to destroy the natural beauty of the bay, even though it's loaded most weekends with small boats. The harbor is kept clean, a project in which most boaters are happy to participate. The mountains surrounding the town are as beautiful as ever. There are not now nor will there ever be buildings marring the natural rhythm of the rolling hills.

Timms Harbor And Shatto City
When the first Spanish ships sailed to Catalina Island, the harbor now called Avalon was known by the Pimugna Indians as the Bay of the Seven

Moons. Since then, the name has been altered to reflect the changing owners, residents, and destiny of the Island. Under the ownership of James Lick (1867-87), the Bay of the Seven Moons was serviced by Captain A.W. Timms, who renamed it for himself: Timms Harbor. He also controlled the harbor at San Pedro, which he called Timms Point. Thus, his three sailing vessels operated from Timms to Timms. When George Shatto purchased the Island in 1887, the new owner renamed it for himself: Shatto City.

George Shatto had a dream of transforming the simple tent city into a dazzling, modern tourist center. Drawing up a city plan, he laid out properties and streets and auctioned them off—from $150 for a 20-foot lot to $2000 for a larger bay-view site. On these small lots people pitched tents or built lean-tos that could be taken down at the end of their vacations. Small lots were also leased to summer campers for $25 yearly. What's now known as Avalon is the only land on Catalina Island ever sold to private parties. Shatto built the Hotel Metropole, a gathering spot for the social elite, as well as for the sportsfishermen drawn to the harbor for the rich schools of gamefish that surrounded it.

The Tuna Club was spawned in 1898 by eight of these fishermen who gathered on the Metropole's large porch for long nights of endless fish stories. Along with Charles Fredric Holder, noted fisherman and writer, these sportsmen set down the rules. To belong you had to be one of the few who had taken "a tuna weighing 100 pounds or over or a swordfish or marlin swordfish weighing 200 pounds or over on regulation heavy tackle; or a tuna weighing 60 pounds or over or a marlin swordfish or broadbill weighing 100 pounds or over on regulation light tackle." This active club's first building, constructed at the turn of the century, was destroyed in the 1915 fire. The present structure was built in 1916 at the same location on the edge of the bay. The original club goals still apply, and the Tuna Club carries on as a place where gentlemen anglers mingle, as well as honor and protect the sports-fishing waters of Catalina (oh yes, there are women members also).

Avalon

George Shatto's 20-year-old sister-in-law, Etta Whitney, christened the harbor "Avalon" from a phrase out of Tennyson's *Idylls of the King:*

> To the island-valley of Avalon:
> Where falls not hail or rain or any snow;
> Nor ever wind blows loudly; but it lies
> Deep-meadow'd happy fair with orchard
>   lawns
> And bowery hollows crown'd with
>   summer sea . . .

Etta's choice took hold. Soon Avalon was well on its way to becoming the tourist attraction of Shatto's dream, with the completed Hotel Metropole, and Banning's two steamers shuttling people across the channel. But this was not enough for Shatto to meet his financial obligations. After only four years of investment, Shatto's schemes failed and he was forced to sell.

The Banning Family's Avalon

In 1892, the new owner, William Banning, became the first of his family to realize Catalina's true potential. By 1896 the rest of the family followed, forming the Santa Catalina Island Company (SCI Company) to further develop Avalon as a tourist center. The town grew: beaches were dotted with more and more tents, and hundreds of vacationers swam in Avalon's clear waters, fished for their dinner, and listened to the music of the Metropole orchestra that floated over the bay.

There was even the new thrill of glass-bottom boats, invented and perfected by Charley Feige in 1896. The adventurous could ride on a stagecoach over the rough back roads of the interior. William Banning was the finest amateur six-in-hand stagecoach driver in the United States. (His father, Phineas Banning, was the builder of quality stagecoaches in Wilmington, California, and a pioneer who ran a stage line along the Southern California coast.) The Bannings also constructed a steep incline railway, providing a stunning view of the town and bay from atop Buena Vista Park, as well as a dance pavilion and a public golf course. All of these attractions, along with the glass-bottom boats, were includ-

A swimming scene from the late 1890s. Sugarloaf Rock on the point was later removed and replaced by the Casino in 1929.

SANTA CATALINA ISLAND CO.

ed in the price of the boat ticket to Avalon, or offered for very little extra.

A Growing Town

As more people visited Catalina, the permanent population increased, though the winter population leveled out at 300-400. Other entrepreneurs could see the money to be made, and competition developed over transportation to Avalon. This was the beginning of a nine-year waterfront war, during which barbed-wire fences were raised, torn down, and raised again to keep passengers brought by non-SCI Company transport away from Avalon. Bloody beachfront battles were a common occurrence each summer. The Avalon Freeholders Improvement Association was formed in 1909 to bring peace to the Island community. Though they were unsuccessful, the Municipal Pier (now called the Pleasure Pier) was built under its sponsorship. Turbulent years of civic government followed. Lawsuits were filed and the battle for waterfront rights continued. In 1913, after a hard-fought election—backed by proof that it had 500 residents—Avalon was incorporated as a sixth-class city, the 30th city in Los Angeles County.

The Banning Company, however, was still responsible for providing water for the town. Many townspeople felt that the Bannings were not exerting their best efforts to establish a good water system. Much of the water was hauled in on steamers from the Mainland and locally on small boats from Torqua Springs, an expensive proposition. The Bannings' dream was coming to life, but profits were slim and the strings of control were inexorably slipping from their hands.

The Fire Of 1915

A devastating fire on November 29, 1915, leveled one-third of Avalon, horrifically demonstrating the need for a viable water system. For years an aura of suspicion surrounded the mysterious start of the conflagration. Was this someone's way to get rid of the Bannings and perhaps put an end to the ongoing problems of the new city of Avalon? No one knows. After this catastrophe the Bannings implemented an electric plant and saltwater mains for fire protection and sanitation. Drinking water was still hauled in. To replace the fire-gutted Metropole, the SCI Company completed the St. Catherine Hotel in Descanso Bay by the summer season of 1918. But the financial blow caused by the fire was more than the company could absorb. So after 27 years of Banning management, William Wrigley Jr. purchased the Santa Catalina Island Company in 1919. Wrigley proceeded to build and broaden Catalina above and beyond the wildest dreams of either George Shatto or the Banning family.

"WHERE IS VINEGAR HILL?" A TOURIST ASKED

The oldtime locals know of the area called Vinegar Hill. Up Marilla Street at Vieudelou sits the oldest house in Avalon. It was in this general area back in the 1920s that some locals indulged in the manufacture of moonshine. The "revenooers" would come from overtown (islander talk for the Mainland), break up the stills with axes and clubs, and dump the whole mess down Marilla Street. The smell after a few days of fermenting on the street caused the area to become known as (right!) Vinegar Hill.

Wrigley's Island

From 1919 until the beginning of WW II, Avalon's facilities and popularity did nothing but grow. It was the "in" place for Southern Californians to visit. Wrigley was a wise and daring businessman, not afraid to spend money advertising the Island. The Wrigley $10 package deal included roundtrip transportation from Los Angeles, a night at the luxurious St. Catherine Hotel, four meals, and an excursion in a glass-bottom boat. He built the Island Villas to replace the tent city that had grown larger every summer during the Bannings' ownership. The villas were small canvas-topped bungalows lined up in close rows where families could stay inexpensively.

Wrigley sponsored the Wrigley Ocean Marathon in January 1927, awarding $25,000 to the winner of a swimming race from Two Harbors to the San Pedro shore (22 miles). A 17-year-old Canadian, George Young, had bicycled from Toronto, Canada, to take part, and out of 103 contestants only he completed the swim. His official time of 15 hours, 46 minutes, was made in 56-62° waters. Over and above the $25,000, Wrigley had offered a special prize of $15,000 to any woman who finished. Hours after Young had landed, two determined women were forcibly removed from the water and awarded $2500 each for their efforts. Since then, many swimmers have both succeeded and failed. On September 21, 1952, Florence Chadwick swam the channel in 13 hours, 42 minutes. In 1958, Greta Anderson swam to and from the Mainland in a 26-hour period.

P.K. Wrigley

After the death of William Wrigley Jr. in 1932, his son Philip K. Wrigley ("P.K.") assumed the leadership of the family-owned SCI Company, carrying on the Wrigley tradition of making Avalon an exciting place to visit and an ideal place to live. Everyday utilities taken for granted on the Mainland improved on the Island. William Wrigley Jr. built Thompson Reservoir; pipes were connected; cables were laid. Today, the Southern California Edison Company provides electricity and water.

COMMUNICATIONS

Early Methods

Signal fires between the Island and the Mainland Indians were the first means of communication across the channel. Later, it became common to send messages on infrequently passing boats. By the 1850s, letters arrived by boat once or twice a month. During the gold rush, the miners kept homing pigeons; records show that as late as 1899, carrier pigeons were sent to Los Angeles in as little as 45 minutes! In contrast, a letter sent in 1864 from Two Harbors took 10 days to reach Wilmington, a stagecoach stop on the Southern California coast. Today, Avalon's post office still cannot match the record of feathered "air mail."

Telephones

In 1902, the world's first commercial wireless radio station was opened in Avalon. In 1903, the Banning Company built a telephone line from Avalon to Two Harbors via Middle Ranch and Little Harbor. Pacific Telephone and Telegraph installed the first commercial telephone system in 1919 at Pebbly Beach, with a sister station at San Pedro. In 1923, Pacific T&T laid two 23-mile-long, 300-ton submarine cables to the Mainland. The Avalon telephone system, one of the longest-lived "number please" systems in operation in the country, wasn't replaced by direct dialing until 1979.

Retired Avalon operators still tell stories about the personal-style communication that lasted for so long. If, for instance, an Islander was spending the evening at a friend's but was expecting an important phone call, he'd just lift the receiver and ask the operator to transfer it; today you pay for that same service, called "call forwarding." The operators knew which numbers were those of the elderly and infirm. Would-be catastrophes were averted by an operator quickly sending a police car to check out an irregularity of a light on her switchboard. One little old lady, a regular patient at the hospital, in spite of repeated instructions on how to use the buzzer to get a nurse, insisted on using her phone to tell the operator to "get that nurse in here right now!" With small-town care and concern the telephone operator would in turn call the hospital main office to pass on the request. Today, Catalina has direct dialing like everywhere else in the United States.

Broadcasting

Catalina's first radio broadcasting station, little more than a crystal set, was built in 1921 by Lawrence Gordon Mott at his residence on Clarissa Avenue. During the winter of 1922-23, he maintained contact with the McMillan Expedition at the North Pole—for three weeks, he was the only contact the expedition had with the outside world. In the late '20s and '30s, radio shows were common on the Island. Strolling announcer Gary Breckner was a familiar sight in Avalon, especially when the SS *Catalina* was about to dock. Radio shows consisted of random street interviews with vacationers or regular broadcasts of big-band music from the Casino. One of the world's first civilian microwave radio systems was installed in 1946, and in 1952 a 10,000-watt radio station, KBIG, was built in the interior of the Island.

Newspapers

The first newspaper printed in Avalon was the *Catalina Wireless,* a small daily published by the *Los Angeles Times* in 1903, which used the wireless telegraph to communicate news between Avalon and the Mainland. This, however, proved unprofitable and lasted only a short time. Another short-lived paper was a summer tabloid published in the early 1900s by Ernest Windle

CATALINA ISLANDER

Avalon's "number please" operators shortly before the system was abandoned for a telephone service installed in 1979, at the time one of the most sophisticated in all of North America.

and George Channing. In 1912, a new *Catalina Wireless* appeared, surviving as a weekly until the big fire of 1915. In 1913, Ernest Windle founded the *Catalina Islander,* which is now produced weekly using the most modern computerized technology. The newest weekly paper, begun in 1990, is the *Avalon Bay News.*

EDUCATION

From two students in 1888, the Avalon school system has grown to 370-400 children in grades kindergarten through 12, with 20 teachers. Over the years the "schoolhouse" has been located in a variety of buildings, including the Congregational Church, the Whittley St. School House, the old Sugarloaf Casino, and the present Casino. The 1902 election approved funds to buy property for a schoolhouse. Fourteen votes were cast, all in favor. In 1923, Avalon Schools became affiliated with the Long Beach School System. William Wrigley Jr. donated a six-acre lot in Falls Canyon, the current site of the elementary and high schools. A handful of students are bused from the Two Harbors coastal area of the interior, a 45-minute trip each way. A new, red, one-room schoolhouse at Two Harbors run by the Long Beach School System now makes it possible for kindergarteners through fourth-graders (about 14 students) to be instructed close to home.

MUSIC AND STORIES

Many people who have been impressed by Catalina's natural beauty have communicated this awareness in songs and stories. Al Jolson's "Avalon" continues to perpetuate the town's popularity, and in the '50s the Four Preps' popular "26 Miles Across the Sea" was heard repeatedly on pop radio stations. Catalina has inspired fictitious Indian legends as well as contemporary stories. Even Leroi, the well-fed and much-loved town cat usually found napping in the sun on the Pleasure Pier, had his story written and published by Avalon author Elizabeth Grieson.

Reunions

Graduates have always considered themselves a special group of people, fortunate to have grown up in the homey, small-town atmosphere of Catalina Island. Class reunions are held regularly. The largest was held in 1982, open to all students who had ever attended Avalon schools. It was a tremendous turnout; 1,500 people of all ages came from around the world for a weekend of street parties, barbecues, picnics, and informal get-togethers. It culminated in a grand dinner dance at the Casino Ballroom. The proceeds were donated to the Avalon School to buy modern computer equipment. Businesses like Eric's Hamburger Stand, an institution and student hangout on Pleasure Pier, dropped prices to the "old days" level. Treasured mementos such as old photos, school sweaters, yearbooks, athletic awards, and trophies were displayed in shop windows.

ISLAND LIVING

Life has its trade-offs, and the pleasant things about living on Catalina Island may not all be measurable in the usual terms. Perhaps the nicest thing about Avalon is its small-town warmth combined with the bonus of the Island's natural beauty. Everyone knows everyone else. Some of the families on the Island trace their roots back to the early settlers, and the Catalina Island Museum presents special certificates to longtime Island residents. Islanders value their history, and old-timers' memories are guarded carefully on taped interviews. In Avalon, social activities abound. Mom isn't a taxi since the kids can walk everywhere. Crime is rare. When tragedy hits, the whole town rallies. And the most amazing thing is that all this is less than an hour from L.A.

Of the one million people who travel to Santa Catalina Island every year, there are always a few who decide that this is the way of life they would like to pursue permanently. So the year-round population (about 2,500) of Avalon grows—but not rapidly. Housing is a major problem in Avalon. Because the town is small, there's a restricted number of dwellings, and the cost of housing is very high.

The hardier pioneer-types adapt to Island living, and it's a joy; but those people who aren't flexible should dismiss the thought. What's considered an adventure for one person could turn into a nightmare for another. Everything that is eaten, drunk, worn, built, or driven must be brought from the Mainland by barge. And though freight service is excellent 90% of the year, the barge is occasionally halted by a raging wind or an irate sea. Rarely do two days in a row go by, however, that the barge or boat can't make it. When this does happen, grocery store shelves start to empty and the fresh milk and bread supply gets very low. There's no outgoing or incoming mail, no Mainland newspapers, and of course if you happen to be on the Mainland, you're stuck there until the storm subsides. Sometimes the sea crashes over the beaches and rushes across the road and sidewalk on Crescent Avenue. In 1982, the ocean really flexed its muscles, tearing out part of the seawall around the Casino and almost destroying the road and boardwalk to Pebbly Beach.

Water: Troubles

Other times it's the rain that affects the Islanders —or the lack of it. Avalon depends *almost* entirely on rainfall for fresh water—75% is captured in dams and reservoirs before it runs into the sea. Another 25% comes from the ocean, converted by a high-tech desalination plant implemented in 1991. Thompson Reservoir holds 326 million gallons. Two pumping stations and eight miles of pipeline are required to convey the water 800 feet up over "The Summit" and back down to Avalon town, where it is mixed with the desalinated water before delivery to consumers. During the drought years of 1977-78 and again in 1991-92, Islanders were forced to learn a new way of life. Each family was allowed to use only a given amount of water each month; after two warnings their water was turned down to a dribble by the Edison Company. This didn't happen to many; for most the water shortage was dealt with effectively.

Houses step up the sides of steep hills, reminiscent of sunny Mediterranean villages.

Five-minute Navy showers became the norm and faucets were never left to run for any chore. Households learned the easiest ways to recycle their washing machine water—pumping or hand-dipping it into the garden. If toilets weren't already hooked up to a saltwater line, they were converted. All fire hoses use salt water, and during the drought the streets were hosed down with salt water. If one had a swimming pool and wanted to keep it filled, water was brought from the Mainland in huge tanks on a barge at the pool-owner's expense. These measures proved effective, and many Islanders have continued this frugality with water as a way of life.

On the other hand, some years the skies open and water comes in a nonstop deluge. The streams get high, all the reservoirs fill to capacity, and overflow plays havoc with the interior roads. Children who live in any one of the many coves around the Island have to travel to and from school in Avalon by boat when interior roads get washed out. Though houses in Avalon are built up the sides of the hills, surprisingly none has ever slid down, as in some Mainland areas.

Shopping

Avalon has a great selection of small shops that carry almost everything needed for day-to-day living. You can buy TVs, refrigerators, and other appliances, but for large furniture and specialty items most go to the Mainland. Goods cost more on the Island since everything must come over on the barge and freight costs are steep. Most Islanders feel, though, that the slight increase in price balances their diminished auto expenses. A few people *(very few)* go to the Mainland for groceries and haul them back to Catalina on the boat. (There are even those who refuse to pay freight charges. One man carried most of an automobile to the Island on the boat every week, piece by piece, hidden in boxes and suitcases. Eventually he did have to ship the motor and a few large parts, but he put his car together, content to have saved a lot of money.)

KATHY ESCOVIDO-SANDERS

KATHY ESCOVIDO-SANDERS

CASINO POINT

HISTORY

From prehistory, a large, loaf-shaped rock has jutted out into the sea, around which the Bay of the Seven Moons curved in a gentle crescent. Though the profile and name have changed, from this spot, once known as Sugarloaf Point, you can clearly see the hills of the Mainland on a crystalline day.

A Second Sugarloaf

In the 1890s, the Banning brothers tried blasting a tunnel between Avalon Bay and Descanso Bay (at that time known as Banning Cove). The cove was to be the site of the Bannings' home and the tunnel through Sugarloaf Point would provide easy access. The Banning house was built in the cove in 1895; the tunnel collapsed in 1906. However, what appeared to be a setback provided a firm foundation for a new road which followed the coastline from Casino Point to Descanso Bay. The collapse of the tunnel, the first of several changes to the skyline at the Point, left

two distinct rock formations instead of one: Big Sugarloaf and Little Sugarloaf.

Big Sugarloaf Bites The Dust

In the devastating fire of 1915, many of Avalon's premier buildings were destroyed. One of the victims was the large, gracious Hotel Metropole on Crescent Avenue, then considered one of the finest hotels in Southern California. By 1917, the Metropole had yet to be rebuilt, and the Bannings decided that Big Sugarloaf should be leveled, with the new hotel constructed in its place. They blasted the rock completely away with black powder—a tricky demolition job in those times. After removing the last of the rock in 1918, the long-awaited hotel, called the St. Catherine, was finally built—not on Sugarloaf Point but in Banning Cove (renamed Descanso Bay). At that time, Little Sugarloaf was still a landmark for sailors because it could be seen from great distances. It was also the location of a treacherously steep stairway built in 1896 where enterprising Island boys offered a steady arm (for 25 cents) to the less hardy who wished to climb to the peak. It was also the favored place to shoot off fireworks on the Fourth of July.

More Construction
The next alteration to the Point took place in 1920, with the addition of the "Sugarloaf Casino" (not to be confused with the present-day Casino). The Sugarloaf was an octagonal, steel-framed stucco building surrounded by a large wood-planked deck. The dance floor, large enough for 250 couples, was also used as a roller-skating rink. One of its two wings once housed a Chinese Tea Room, as well as an elementary school, until the Falls Canyon School was completed in 1925.

Ocean Access
In 1921, a freight wharf was added on the Avalon side of the Point. Shortly after, a ramp and float were installed to receive passengers fly-ing into Avalon from Wilmington on Curtiss Flying Boats and bimotored Sikorskys. This continued until 1931 when the Hamilton Beach Amphibian Airport was completed.

The Casino
The destiny of Sugarloaf Point was decided in 1928, when William Wrigley Jr. chose it as the location for a mammoth new casino. The smaller Sugarloaf Casino was dismantled and its octagonal steel frame was placed well up into Avalon Canyon to become the world's largest birdcage, subsequently expanding into the Catalina Bird Park. In March 1929, the last of Little Sugarloaf was blasted away, and the spectacular new Casino began to take shape. Over the years there have been other changes. Landfill provided a parking lot. During WW II a battery of antiaircraft guns was mounted there and a large wooden armory was constructed. Mer-

When determining the design of the Casino, William Wrigley Jr. imposed several restrictions before construction began: that Sugarloaf Rock on the point and Mrs. Wrigley's flower garden at the base of the cliff be preserved. The spit of land, being triangular in shape, dictated a cir-cular building as the most logical. Wrigley envisioned a Moorish-style structure with a theater on the bottom level and a large ballroom above. Today the Casino stands alone. Sugarloaf Rock was ultimately removed during the construction.

chant seaman trainees practiced maneuvers on a wooden ship's bow that had been constructed on the wharf. It was quite common to see the gleeps (as the trainees were called by the Islanders) marching in their white or navy-blue uniforms along the Casino Road. The wartime buildings have since been removed.

Diving

In 1951, the new attraction on the Point was a diving bell. Viewers descended in a metal tank surrounded with small windows that looked out upon darting fish and undulating giant brown kelp in the clear waters of Catalina. The bell was removed 10 years later, though divers continue to enjoy exploring in this underwater park. Only now they dive with the aid of wetsuits and compressed-air tanks.

Storms

In 1964, the seawall was reinforced and a short breakwater was built with rocks from the Pebbly Beach quarry. This protects Avalon during the northeastern storms each winter. The Catalina Channel can turn vicious on occasion. In February 1982, Casino Point bore the fury of one of the worst storms ever recorded on the Island. All through the night the ocean crashed repeatedly over the seawall and breakwater, tearing away giant chunks of cement and hurling them onto the area as though they were toy blocks. Fortunately, outside of some water seepage in the lower-level rooms, the Casino—staid lady of Avalon—suffered no harm.

THE CASINO BUILDING

The present Casino is basically the same as the day it was completed in 1929. The years have proved it a sturdy monument to the builders of the past. Large enough to hold Catalina's entire year-round population, it is the city's civil-defense shelter. Stored in its many corners and caverns are enough water and emergency supplies to last two weeks. The Casino has become a landmark. Its image *is* Catalina. It gleams white against the sea in the brilliant sun-

John Gabriel Beckman, who did the original art for the Casino Building in 1929, returned in 1987 to add more tile-work above the theater box office.

shine and at night lights create dramatic shadows on its walls.

Building the Casino was a tremendous engineering feat. Designed by Los Angeles architects Walter Webber and Sumner A. Spaulding, the Mediterranean design with Moorish Alhambra influences won a special award from the American Institute of Architects in 1930. A cantilevered structure, two 178-foot girders weighing 50 tons each span the building at right angles. Steel and concrete columns and beams support most of the weight of the roof and all floor weight except that of the ballroom. The exterior buttresses carry a vertical load. With its 40-foot-deep foundation, 100,000 sacks of cement and 25,000 yards of concrete, it's a monolith that has already stood for over 50 years, and it will continue its constant vigil over Avalon Bay for many years to come.

Avalon Theater

The main floor of the Casino holds the Avalon Theater, the Catalina Island Museum, and the art gallery. The movie theater was designed in the late '20s, around the time "talking pictures" were introduced. Though Wrigley, along with most, didn't have much faith in the success of the talkies, he insisted on perfect acoustics for the theater's sound system. His system was so well designed that in 1931, when the Radio City Music Hall was being built in New York City, engineers involved in that project visited the Island to study the acoustics of the Avalon Theater.

A large Page organ was installed in the theater to provide musical accompaniment to the

AVALON

BAY OF AVALON

silent movies that, as fate had it, soon faded into the past. Still, the Page was used for several years to add drama and excitement to early talkies shown in the Casino. Organ music itself

was popular entertainment in the '20s and '30s, and free concerts were given every day in the summer.

Today, the Page organ has great historical value. During the spring of 1979, six men from the Los Angeles Chapter of the American Theatre Organ Society performed the tedious, time-consuming task of replacing leather and felt parts that had been gnawed away by mice who lived in the vast mechanism of the organ during its many years of nonuse. They repaired electrical connections and gave the organ a general overhaul for the 50th anniversary of the Casino when, once again, the organ came to full vibrant life. This full-scale pipe organ has 16 ranks of pipes, with 73-85 pipes per rank. The pipes are made of lead, tin, zinc, and wood—manufactured in Germany. The largest pipe measures 16 feet and the shortest is one-quarter inch long.

Today's Theater
The grand-scale art-deco murals in the auditorium have survived the past 55 years intact. They were painted in 1929 by John Gabriel Beckman, a well-known young artist who also painted Grauman's Chinese Theater in Hollywood. He went on to become an art director for Columbia Studios. In 1986, Beckman was commissioned to complete the tile mural along the box office wall. It had been designed in 1929, but never finished. Over 50 years later the tile was set. Considered to be one of the finest examples of art deco today, in 1929 the work was called "futuristic." Motifs include hooded friars, exotic birds and flowers, leaping goats, a waterfall, and elegant monkeys. These theater walls have an intrinsic history and value, which is probably why they have never been replaced or painted over.

Although the theater was primarily designed to show movies, many live stage productions have also been performed. During WW II, the theater was used as a classroom for merchant seamen as well as for USO shows, alive with Hollywood's finest stars: Bob Hope, Alice Faye, Kate Smith, Danny Kaye, and Spike Jones, to name a few. Boxing was a weekly event for the

The museum is a step into Catalina's past. Among Indian artifacts and changing exhibits, various vignettes of the past hundred years include such memorabilia as this from the SS Catalina and SS Avalon, which made thousands of crossings between the Mainland and the Island.

servicemen, along with band concerts and radio shows. Today, community groups use the theater regularly for local entertainment, as do convention groups from all over. The theater shows a first-run single feature twice nightly during the summer, at 7 p.m. and at about 9:30 p.m.; adult $7, child $3.

The Catalina Museum

This growing museum is well worth visiting. Its three primary areas of interest are archaeology, history, and natural history. Its displays of Indian artifacts from various parts of the Island chronicle the history of Catalina from the days of earliest Indian habitation. See photographs from the 1880s and listen to taped interviews of Catalina old-timers—priceless history if you have time to tune in. Quartered in the Casino's bottom level, the museum's entrance is on the south side of the building. Admission is free.

The Museum Society is a private, nonprofit corporation. It conducts research, offers free lectures on Island-related topics, stages slide shows with taped commentary, and organizes tours of the historical Holly Hill House. Membership is invited; donations and other financial support (tax-deductible) are welcomed. For more information write to Catalina Island Museum, Box 366, Avalon, CA 90704. The museum is open daily 10:30-4 p.m., year-round; a $1 admission (children under 12 free) is paid at the door.

Art Gallery And Festival

Next to the museum, also on the lower level, is the entrance to the Catalina Art Gallery, admission free. The exhibits, which change frequently, represent both Island and visiting artists. The active Catalina Art Association initiated the Art Festival more than 20 years ago. Held in late September, this event has since become one of the most prestigious art festivals in Southern California and beyond. The Casino ballroom is the scene of the Invitational Exhibit on the first night of the three-day show. Award-winning artists are invited to take part in this judging. The streets of Avalon become an outdoor gallery hosting an array of international artists and art enthusiasts. Avalon is proud to have many local artists represented in winning categories. Cash prizes are awarded for the best art entered. For more information, write to the Catalina Art Association, Box 235, Avalon, CA 90704.

Ballroom

The top floor of this Moorish-flavored structure is the world-famous Casino ballroom, scene of massive crowds during the golden era of the big bands. In those days the big white steamer SS *Catalina* carried thousands of passengers to the Island to hear such greats as Glen Miller, Benny Goodman, and Kay Kyser. Designed to give the largest unobstructed dancing area possible, the engineering allowed for 20,000 square feet of dance floor. Built to accommodate 1,500 couples, it very often did. The dance floor is surrounded by a 14-foot open balcony that provides a romantic setting from which to view the lights of town at night. In 1929, when the Casino was opened, only sodas and ice-cream sundaes were offered at the bar, in the tradition of Wrigley's attitude that Avalon would provide wholesome entertainment for the entire family. Even after Prohibition was repealed, it was not until immediately after WW II that the Casino ballroom began serving liquor.

In 1987, the Casino ballroom was refurbished: new paint, new carpet, new drapes, a new stage, and new kitchen. It is also run by the Santa Catalina Island Company, which encourages the public (both on the Mainland and in Avalon) to rent the ballroom for the evening or afternoon for weddings, receptions, banquets, dances, or other private events. For more information on having an event at the Casino, call (310) 510-2444. Catering is available.

Building Maintenance

Maintenance of the Casino is a major expense of the Santa Catalina Island Company. About 570,000 gallons of water a month are used during peak season and the monthly electricity usage has reached as much as 66,000 kilowatts. A resident maintenance man lives in an apartment at the top of the east wing. This apartment has been occupied by only three families since 1929. Bill Bowman was the early maintenance man from 1929 to 1947.

Next, Dale Eisenhut was hired as the electrical engineer. He and his wife, Donna (now the librarian at the Avalon County Library), moved in with their three young daughters. The giant building—as unique a home to grow up in as one could imagine—became the romping backdrop for the unfolding lives and energies of growing kids. These little girls tricycled around a balcony, which by night metamorphosed into a splendid promenade filled with romance-minded young couples. There was an occasional at-

Catalina Casino

tempt at "tightrope" walking across a 10-story-high balustrade, and with the passing years the roar of motorcycles was frequently heard as they climbed the broad indoor ramps to the front door of the Eisenhut apartment.

Today, Frank Buck holds the position. One important duty is the special cleaning and waxing of the 59-year-old dance floor. Not only has the floor been constantly maintained, but it has actually been enhanced by continuous use. The late Dale Eisenhut commented that the floor was the cleanest and brightest he'd ever seen after a crowd of 4,835 people had danced on it all evening.

(top) Cherry Cove (Oz Mallan); (bottom) Arch Rock, Anacapa Island (Channel Islands National Park) (top) Catalina cruise ship; (bottom) harbor view of west end cove (photos: Oz Mallan)

ACCOMMODATIONS

The variety of accommodations on Catalina can be as luxurious or as Spartan as your wallet and taste dictate. You can stay on top of a hill with its invigorating walk and views, or you can remain on the flats—close to all downtown activities and just a short walk from the beach. Note: With the exception of Banning House Lodge Bed and Breakfast Inn, and winter camping cabins at Two Harbors, the only lodgings on the Island are within Avalon city limits.

Many hotels and motels offer package deals. During summer months most require a two-day weekend minimum stay, and on holiday weekends a three-day minimum. Condominiums and houses, which offer cooking facilities, are also available. Make reservations as early as possible for summer stays and don't hesitate to visit Avalon in the winter. Winter rates, which begin the middle of October, are cheaper, the weather is usually beautiful, and you'll find fewer tourists, giving Islanders more time to show you what their Island is really like. A local city ordinance states that children (under 18) cannot occupy an overnight accommodation unless accompanied by a parent or guardian.

Services And Reservations

Many hotels serve complimentary coffee or breakfast, some provide courtesy transportation to or from the mole or heliport, and some have jacuzzis, patios, and barbecues. During the summer, reservations will ensure a room; in the winter you could chance it and probably get a room that suits you. A simple one-call system is handled through the **Avalon Chamber of Commerce**, tel. 510-1520; they have a good list of current reservations available and will in turn transfer your call to the hotel of your choice. Rates are quite fluid in today's economy and Catalina is definitely affected by the seasons—call and double check for the most current prices. Rates on the hotel chart do not include a seven percent city bed tax and are based on double occupancy.

HOTELS

Picturesque Hotels

El Terado Terrace stretches across a small canyon, each unit with complete cooking facilities. There's a stunning view from **Zane Grey Hotel**, the historical former home of the late Western novelist and big-game fisherman. **Glenmore Plaza Hotel**, built in 1881, is charming; for a special occasion stay in the unique suite in the cupola (round bed included). The **Catalina Island Inn** was built in 1906, and the turn-of-the-century flavor has been tastefully preserved. Another with yesteryear charm, the **Hotel Catalina** has its own small movie theater (seats 30).

Modern

Some of the more modern accommodations are **Hotel Vincente's**, where all rooms have king-size beds, refrigerators, color televisions, heat, and fans. Suites have ocean views. **Seaport Village** is attractive, from small rooms to suites and with all the conveniences, including a jacuzzi; some have lovely views of the harbor.

When you call, ask about their package deals, including transportation from the Mainland. **Hotel Villa Portofino** has a beachfront location, queen- and king-size beds, some suites with ocean view; downtown and close to all activities. Excellent restaurant and bar on premises.

CATALINA ACCOMMODATIONS

1. Zane Grey Hotel
2. Snidow Hotel
3. Seaport Village Inn
4. Marilla Inn
5. El Rancho Hotel
6. El Terado Terrace
7. Catalina Beach House
8. Hotel Vincente's
9. Hotel Catalina
10. Cloud 7
11. Hotel Villa Portofino
12. Bayview House
13. Buena Vista Hotel
14. Catalina Island Inn
15. Catalina Cottagesl
16. Casa Mariquita
17. Gull House
18. La Paloma
19. Catalina Lodge
20. Atwater Hotel
21. Glenmore Plaza Hotel
22. Hotel MacRae
23. Hotel Vista del Mar
24. Pavilion Lodge
25. Catherine Hotel
26. Garden House Inn
27. Seacrest Inn
28. Old Turner Inn
29. Blue Dolphin House
30. Catalina Canyon Hotel
31. Inn On Mt. Ada
32. Edgewater Hotel
33. Hotel Metropole

CATALINA ACCOMMODATIONS

MAP #	NAME	PHONE	RATES	TRANSPORT	OCEAN VIEW	RESTAURANT	CONTINENTAL BREAKFAST
20	Atwater Hotel	(213) 510-1788	$35–120	no	no	yes	no
	Banning House	(213) 510-0303	$100–175	yes	yes	no	no
12	Bayview Hotel	(213) 510-0600	$40–60	no	yes	no	yes
29	Blue Dolphin House	(213) 510-1811	$135	no	no	no	no
13	Buena Vista Hotel	(213) 510-0340	$80–130	no	yes	no	no
16	Casa Mariquita	(213) 510-1192	$80–275	yes	yes	no	no
7	Catalina Beach House	(213) 510-1078	$50–80	yes	yes	no	yes
30	Catalina Canyon Hotel	(213) 510-0325	$70–110	yes	yes	yes	no
15	Catalina Cottages	(213) 510-1010	$20–77	no	no	no	no
14	Catalina Island Inn	(213) 510-1623	$75–185	yes	yes	no	yes
19	Catalina Lodge	(213) 510-1070	$79	yes	no	no	yes
25	Catherine Hotel	(213) 510-0170	$75–100	no	yes	yes	no
10	Cloud 7	(213) 510-0454	$40–100	yes	yes	no	yes
	Cove of Catalina Resort	(213) 510-1220	$225-up	yes	yes	no	no
32	Edgewater Hotel	(213) 510-0347	$160–265	no	yes	no	yes
5	El Rancho Hotel	(213) 510-0603	$40–75	no	yes	no	no
6	El Terado Terrace	(213) 510-0831	$65–210	no	yes	no	yes
26	Garden House Inn	(213) 510-0356	$125–250	no	yes	yes	yes
21	Glenmore Plaza Hotel	(213) 510-0017	$89–175	yes	yes	yes	no
17	Gull House	(213) 510-2547	$125–135	yes	no	no	yes
9	Hotel Catalina	(213) 510-0027	$85–110	no	yes	no	yes
22	Hotel MacRae	(213) 510-0246	$42	no	yes	yes	yes
33	Hotel Metropole	(213) 510-1884	$75–225	yes	yes	yes	yes
11	Hotel Villa Portofino	(213) 510-0555	$82–225	yes	yes	yes	yes
8	Hotel Vincente's	(213) 510-1115	$85–275	no	yes	no	yes
23	Hotel Vista Del Mar	(213) 510-1452	$85–275	yes	yes	yes	yes
31	Inn on Mt. Ada	(213) 510-2030	$190–580	yes	yes	yes	yes
18	La Paloma	(213) 510-0737	$90–145	yes	yes	no	no
4	Marilla Inn	(213) 510-1651	$50–80	yes	yes	no	no
28	Old Turner Inn	(213) 510-2236	$110–175	no	no	no	yes
	Pacific Isle	(213) 510-1148	$75–185	no	yes	no	no
24	Pavilion Lodge	(800) 4AVALON	$49–149	no	no	no	no
27	Seacrest Inn	(213) 510-0196	$135–185	yes	no	no	yes
3	Seaport Village Inn	(213) 510-0344	$69–189	yes	yes	no	yes
2	Snidow Hotel	(213) 510-0746	$150	yes	yes	no	yes
1	Zane Grey Hotel	(213) 510-0966	$80–130	yes	yes	no	yes

Located above town in a lovely canyon, the Catalina Canyon Hotel offers visitors a secluded resort with a continental restaurant on the grounds.

Luxury

Avalon luxury hotels are not that much more expensive than the average hotel and well worth the splurge. The **Hotel Vista Del Mar** is one of Avalon's newest hotels located in the center of town on Crescent Ave. overlooking Avalon Bay and the beach. Upscale rooms include cable color TV, a wet bar, refrigerator, air-conditioning, telephones, fireplaces, and some are equipped with jacuzzis. Continental breakfast is served in the cool green atrium.

The pink **Hotel St. Lauren** was designed to resemble the old circular building that was built on the same spot at the turn of the century. The lovely new structure has amenities the old homestead probably never dreamed of, such as jacuzzi tubs, rooms for the handicapped, an elevator, smoking and nonsmoking rooms, color TV, phones, video rentals, honeymoon suites, and conference rooms. Guests are invited to a continental breakfast with an ocean view—all of this a half block from the beach. Ask about year-round packages. No pets.

Catalina Canyon Resort Hotel is built into a beautiful canyon a couple of miles from downtown. The hotel offers modern Mainland touches such as telephones, pool, conference rooms, and a terrific restaurant on the premises; a complete resort hotel. Courtesy transportation takes guests back and forth to town, or it's a relaxing walk beyond the Catalina Island Golf Club.

The new **Hotel Metropole**, a unique hotel with 45 rooms offering various amenities depending on whether you choose standard, superior, or suites. Your choices include jacuzzi, ocean view, balcony, fireplace; an elevator serves the upper floors. Some rooms look over a charming courtyard with fountains and plants. Transportation is provided to and from the mole or heliport. Packages available. Rates begin at $75 to $275 depending on room and season; price includes continental breakfast. For more information call (800) 541-8528 or 510-1884.

The **Cove of Catalina Resort** is a group of beautiful luxury villas located at Hamilton Cove with a security gate for total privacy. Twenty-three one- and two-bedroom furnished condos have all the conveniences of home, equipped kitchens, dishwashers, laundry facilities, and most with ocean views. Guests have free use of all facilities including clubhouse, exercise room, saunas, and a spa and pool that overlook the ocean. A putting green (complete with bubbling stream) and two tennis courts adjoin the villas. A 100-foot pier reaches into the harbor where there are presently 36 moorings for private boats. As a villa guest, boaters have priority reservations through the Avalon Harbor Dept. to moor their boats. Price of villa includes the use of a golf cart that can be taken into Avalon town. Rates are $225 and up for a one-bedroom condo (two persons), and $300 and up for two bedroom (four persons). For information phone 510-1220, reservations 510-2759.

DOWNTOWN

Built in 1960, the **Pavilion Lodge** in 1991 was the recipient of a $1.8 million renovation and remodeling transformation. The hotel now has new air-conditioning/heating, new bathrooms, new room furnishings and bright colors for all units. A lovely garden courtyard is lined with chaises lounges, and morning coffee is complimentary. The Pavilion's 72 rooms are conveniently located just "14 steps" from South Beach and the blue Pacific, as well as all downtown activities and restaurants. Courtesy baggage delivery is provided to and from the transportation terminal at the Cabrillo Mole. Rates are variable according to season from a low of $49 to a high of $149. For hotel information and reservations, call from California (800) 4-AVALON, (310) 510-2500, or write Box 737, Avalon, CA 90704.

BED AND BREAKFAST

When planning a vacation everyone has a fantasy of finding dreamlike accommodations. Some fantasies star high-rise hotels, with lush amenities, room service, nightclub, color TV, sauna, spa, and pool, breathtaking views, and an assortment of gourmet dining rooms. But wait! Of all things, more and more people fantasize about a stay in a homey atmosphere that offers cushy quilts, a touch of simplicity, clean air away from the bustle of the city, a view of glittering stars at night, a chance to meet warm and friendly fellow guests, and waking to the aroma of coffee and cinnamon rolls in the morning. Put all of this together and you come up with something called a bed and breakfast.

For years the low-key bed and breakfast has been a popular way of traveling in Europe, but it's only been in the past 10 years or so that it's really caught on in the States. B&B aficionados are the first to tell you that all B&Bs are not the stuff that fantasies are made of. "Continental breakfast," a catch phrase, can mean a number of things. It can be a stale, packaged sweet roll and a cup of weak coffee. Or it can be a wonderful farm-style offering that is enough to hold you all day. The building itself can be a converted old farmhouse, a stately old home, or it can be an old hotel that doesn't live up to the standards of a chain. It would be safe to say that if it's your first time out and you're not staying at a recommended establishment (many good B&B books published), it's going to be a surprise one way or the other.

entrance to the Inn on Mt. Ada

On Catalina Island there are four lovely establishments:

The Inn On Mount Ada

This lovely white "mansion" on a hill overlooking Avalon Bay was formerly the home of the William Wrigley Jr. family. At night the lovely building is lit and gives the impression of floating over the bay. The home was built in 1919 after the Wrigleys bought Catalina Island. Totally refurbished and renovated to accommodate visitors of the 1980s and 1990s, Marlene McAdam and Susie Griffin have created a luxurious, pleasant B&B. Each bedroom is comfy and attractive, and some have fireplaces. The house is beautifully decorated with antiques that fit the era, and the views are spectacular—Ada Wrigley loved it because she could watch the sun rise *and* set. The public rooms are many and spacious, including a formal living room and dining room, expansive terrace, a cozy sun room always stocked for help-yourself snacks, including homemade cookies, fresh fruit, hot and cold drinks. Wine and hors d'oeuvres are served at cocktail hour. A hearty "Catalina" breakfast, light lunch, and dinner are included in the price as is the use of a golf cart.

All six rooms have beautiful views and different prices; winter rates begin at $190 to summer's high of $580. No smoking; children over 14 are welcome. Want to have a wedding party? The entire Inn rents for $2850 per night, midweek and winter months, $3500 per night, weekends and summer. These are base prices, call for wedding details. For reservations call 510-2030 or write to P.O. Box 2560, Avalon, CA 90704.

The "Old" Turner Inn

A quiet country setting located in the heart of Avalon near the beach. Completely renovated in 1987, the inn is convenient to all the activities of town. The Old Turner Inn has five guest rooms (four with wood-burning fireplaces), handmade linens, and lovely antique furniture. Guests enjoy a superb continental-plus breakfast buffet and wine and snacks are served in the afternoon. Bikes are available for touring the island. Rates are $110 to $175. Located at 232 Catalina Ave., tel. 510-2236, the mailing address is P.O. Box 97, Avalon, CA 90704.

Garden House Inn

Built in the early 1900s, the three-story building has nine rooms (including a two-room suite on the ground floor) with lovely early '30s decor, queen-size beds, private terraces, some rooms with a harbor view, one block from the beach. The inn offers phones and TV, cold buffet breakfast, afternoon snacks, evening sherry, and cookies. Rates run $125 to $250, winter discounts are given. Children over 16 are welcome, no pets, and no smoking. The inn is located on the corner of Third and Clarissa; mailing address is P.O. Box 1881, Avalon, CA 90704, tel. 510-0356.

Gull House

Gull house offers two suites with separate entrances, living room, and in the rear-yard patio a small pool, spa, and barbecue. Owners Hattie and Bob Michalis give special attention to anniversary and honeymoon couples. The roomy suites are comfortable and offer much privacy. Continental breakfast is served each morning under an umbrella on a cheery patio. Rates are $125-135; closed approximately November through April. Gull House is located at 344 Whittley Avenue. For more information and reservations call 510-2547 or write to P.O. Box 1381, Avalon, CA 90704.

Romance

Seacrest Inn offers an elderly, cozy getaway with complimentary continental breakfast, in-room fireplaces, whirlpool spa for two, plus non-smoking rooms. Ask about travel packages including boat or air transportation. Located close to the beach at 201 Clarissa, Box 128, Avalon, CA 90704, tel. (310) 510-0196.

Budget

Bayview Hotel is a divers' favorite with on premise dive shop, gear rinse, dry rack, storage space, patio, and spa. Ask about family rates. At **Casa Mariquita**, if they know you are on your honeymoon, you'll find a bottle of champagne in your room. The **La Paloma** is a shady group of bungalows off the main drag with 1940s charm. These older hotels are few in number so make summer reservations as early as possible; many rooms have shared bathroom facilities.

Rock Bottom
If money is a serious consideration, try the **Hermosa Hotel** (they advertise cheap sleep!). Others to try are the **Catalina Beach House**, and **El Rancho Hotel**.

CAMPING

The cheapest way to stay in Avalon is to bring your tent and camp at the **Hermit Gulch Campground**, which can accommodate 200 people, handicapped accessible, $6 per person per night. It's a one-mile walk from the Mole past the golf course on Avalon Canyon Rd.; or take a tram from the plaza, $2. Call the campground for tram schedule at 510-8368. Campers find toilets, indoor hot showers, fire rings, picnic tables, barbecues, and a group campfire area. Reservations are necessary, open year-round. Information from the Los Angeles County Office in the **Avalon Plaza**, tel. 510-0688.

OTHER RENTALS

Many visitors save on vacation costs by renting a house or condo and sharing it with another family or group. The condos are all fairly new and in many cases offer a swimming pool. Because of current water rationing due to the severe drought, many pools are closed on the Island. Most of the rental cottages are older, but some are larger than many of the condos. If you're interested in this option, buy a copy of the *Catalina Islander*, Box 428, Avalon, CA 90704, tel. 510-0500, fax (213) 510-2882, the *Avalon Bay News*, 117 Whittley Ave., tel. 510-1500, check the classified ads, or deal through one of several property managers: Beach Realty, tel. 510-0039; CPS Property Services, tel. 510-2242; Davis-Baker Realty Co., tel. 510-2276; Santa Catalina Island Co., tel. 510-2000; Hunt & Associates Realtors, tel. 510-2721.

KATHY ESCOVEDO-SANDERS

FOOD

In Avalon, eating can be a gratifying dining experience or merely the exercising of a necessary daily habit. The town offers walk-away hot-dog stands, a clam bake delivered to your boat, carry-out tacos, fresh shrimp cocktails in paper cups, and chocolate-covered frozen fruit, as well as culinary delights at a variety of first-class restaurants. As of this printing the big chain burger take-outs haven't yet invaded the Island, but Kentucky Fried Chicken is about to make a breakthrough! There's little difference in price between comparable restaurants in Catalina and Southern California. If in some instances you notice the price is slightly higher on Catalina, remember that you're on an island; everything you eat starts out on the Mainland and must be barged across the ocean.

CHOICE PLACES

There are several good Mexican restaurants with atmosphere to match. **Mi Casita** serves excellent Mexican food as does the charming Mexican marketplace **El Encanto** patio. For a family-style cafe and a quick spicy lunch try **Saldana's Taco Shop**. For authentic tasty Mexican food in a bar-like atmosphere try **El Marcelino Mexican Restaurant** at 128 Catalina Ave., tel. 510-2768; the only place in town open for food after the bars close. Try their mound of nachos with homemade beans or the carne asada tacos.

A few coffee shops like **Joe's Place**, the **Pancake Cottage,** and **Sally's Waffle Shop** open for the early fishermen. The **Busy Bee** offers a great view of the bay, boats, and Casino along with full cocktail service and homemade french fries, and they grind their own beef for delicious half-pound burgers. Another outdoor cafe at the **Metropole Marketplace** offers good food and crowd-watching tables where the pigeons strut close by hoping for a small crumb.

The newly opened **Boardwalk Cafe** at the St. Catherine Hotel has you eating fresh seafood, salads, and daily tasty specials on an outdoor patio with live music on the weekends. **Armstrong's** specializes in seafood, as does

Pirrone's, which also offers a complete continental menu, cocktails, lunch, and a buffet brunch where customers fix their own omelettes.

Italian-food lovers have several choices: The exquisite **Ristorante Villa Portofino** serves dinner year-round, lunch, and Sunday brunch in the summer, with full cocktail service and entertainment. Excellent northern Italian cuisine is featured and the warm romantic atmosphere invites lingering over a Frangelica or cappuccino. **Antonio's Pizzeria and Catalina Cabaret** serves tasty pizza and creative sandwiches with lively entertainment suitable for the whole family. **The Prego,** with soft, candle-lit interior, and luscious Italian dishes (try the eggplant parmesan and baseball-sized meatballs) is reminiscent of a small Italian trattoria in Florence.

For those who like spicy old favorites try **The Blue Parrot**—great tropical setting and American food with a Caribbean flair. Cajun prawns with linguini and seafood stew are good starters for fish lovers. Also, it's the only place in town that serves sushi: 205 Crescent Ave., tel. 510-2465. The newly opened **Pacifica** calls itself traditional French cuisine with an Oriental flavor. The menu (dinner only) boasts such delicacies as abalone à la francaise, abalone in a lemon-butter sauce, and Sanglier, roasted rack of boar; 101 Marilla Ave. (in the El Encanto), tel. 510-7224.

The meat-and-potato gang have many choices to dine on juicy steaks and tender prime rib dinners, many with salad bar. For a lively evening and good food, choose between **El Galleon, Channel House, Harbor Grill,** or **Solomon's Landing** on the upper level of the El Encanto; all on Crescent Avenue. Chinese food is great at **Mr. Ning's Chinese Garden** next to the Atwater Hotel, 127 Sumner Ave., tel. 510-1161.

FAST FOODS

At **Original Antonio's Pizzeria,** expect genuine pizza, gourmet sandwiches, beer and wine—even some of Mamma Mia's "day-old" spaghetti plus jukebox music of the 1950s. Food to go; for delivery call 510-0060. Open daily year-round, 114 Sumner.

Avalon Seafood: Open-air take-out restaurant on the Green Pleasure Pier, specializing in fresh fish and chips—cooked to perfection. Fish market, bait, gamefish cleaned, and official weigh station; tel. 510-0197.

Bayside Bakery And Deli serves a delicious variety of deli sandwiches, salads, European pastries, and other baked goods, including a breakfast pita and nonfat frozen yogurt. Food to go. Open year-round, tel. 510-2632.

Coney Island West: On a sunny sidewalk patio, enjoy fabulous hamburgers, hot dogs, or fish and chips, and a cold glass of beer or wine. Metropole Marketplace, 205 Crescent, tel. 510-0763.

Lori's Good Stuff: Open 11-4 behind Joe's Place at the foot of the Pleasure Pier. Lori knows the real meaning of scrumptious fresh fruit shakes, plus thick meaty sandwiches along with healthy salads and special iced teas; tel. 510-2489.

Pelican Cove Sandwiches And Delicatessen: For a unique Avalon lunchtime experience join the friendly people at **Pelican Cove,** 103 Cabrillo Way (on the way to the mole across from the basketball court), tel. 510-2881.

For tasty, generous submarine sandwiches, salads, super iced Italian coffee, and the Island's "best" cheesecake, go to **Tug's Deli** in the Metropole Marketplace, 205 Crescent Ave., tel. 510-0927

Shipwreck Joey's: On the Casino dock, have breakfast, lunch, and munchies until 6 p.m. while watching the boats in the harbor. Check winter schedule. **Trader Jim's** is the nearest thing to a health-food store in Avalon. Along with a good selection of bulk grains, nuts, spices, and natural foods to go, customers will enjoy the tried and true espresso bar as well as occasional live music in the shady courtyard of the Metropole Marketplace, tel. 510-1450.

For a special occasion with a dash of originality, call the **Catalina Clambake.** A party in a can will be delivered to your door—or your deck—complete with flowers, wine, and candles for the romantic. Choices include fish, lobster, shrimp, salmon, swordfish, ribs, chicken, and the trimmings. A little pricey, but what ser-

continued on p. 68

EATERIES OF AVALON

NAME	ADDRESS	PHONE	MEALS	COMMENTS
Antonio's Pizzeria	114 Sumner Ave.	510-0060	L, D	lively atmosphere with Italian food, pizza delivered
Antonio's Pizzeria and Catalina Cabaret	230 Crescent Ave.	510-0008	B, L, and D	Dixieland jazz, live entertainment, Boppo the clown
Armstrong's Fish Market and Seafood Restaurant	306 Crescent Ave.	510-0113	L, D	pleasant dining by the sea
Avalon Seafood	Pleasure Pier	510-0197	L, D	fish market/fast food, shrimp cocktails to go or watch Rosie cook your abalone steak
Blue Parrot	205 Crescent Ave.	510-2465	L, D	upstairs, nice view—American w/Caribbean flair, good spicy stuff; sushi bar
Buffalo Nickel	Pebbly Beach Rd. at airport	510-1323	L, D	rooftop patio, continental dinner, courtesy transport
Bouy 25	Metropole Marketplace	510-1618	L, D	Sunday brunch, Bob Salsbury Jazz Band Mon. and Tues.
Busy Bee	304 Crescent Ave.	510-1983	B, L, and D	patio by the sea, great burgers, cocktails
Cafe Metropole	107 Metropole	510-0302	L	outdoor patio, great sandwiches, vegetarian selection
Cafe Prego	603 Crescent Ave.	510-1218	L, D	Italian food, intimate
Canyon Restaurant and Lounge	883 Los Lomos Rd.	510-0327	B, L, and D	continental dinners, tropical drinks
Casino Restaurant	Casino Point	510-2000	D	catered special-occasion dinners
Avalon Bake Shoppe	122 Catalina Ave.	510-0361	B	coffee and the freshest donuts
Catalina Island Gourmet	P.O. Box 2050	510-2598	L, D	buffalo salami and jerky
Channel Hopper	4 Cabrillo Mole (where the boat leaves)	510-1971	L	take-out sandwiches, call ahead to have sandwiches ready at boat time
Channel House	205 Crescent Ave.	510-1617	B, L, and D	great Belgian waffles, patio
Descanso Beach Club	follow palm trees beyond the Casino	510-0484	L, D	private club open to the public, on the beach, good sandwiches, weekly barbecue
Doug's Harbor Reef Restaurant	Two Harbors	510-0303	L, D	tropical atmosphere, outdoor patio, good steaks
El Encanto Patio Restaurant	101 Marilla Ave.	510-0883	L, D	enjoyable Mexican patio
El Galleon	411 Crescent Ave.	510-1188	L, D	good steaks, lively atmosphere, good music in summer, sidewalk cafe
El Marcelino Mexican Restaurant	128 Catalina Ave.	510-2768	L	bar atmosphere, good Mexican food

EATERIES OF AVALON

NAME	ADDRESS	PHONE	MEALS	COMMENTS
Eric's	Pleasure Pier	510-0894	L	homemade chili
Harbor Grill	313 Crescent Ave.	510-0171	B, L, and D	good salad bar, cocktails
Joe's Place	510 Crescent Ave.	510-0491	B, L, and D	for the early riser
Kentucky Fried Chicken	107 Metropole	510-2147	L, D	same old, same old
Lady Catherines	708 Crescent Ave.	510-0170	D	happy hour, champagne brunch
Lori's Good Stuff	510 Crescent Ave.	510-2489	L	fresh fruity shakes, vegetable sandwiches
Lloyd's of Avalon	315 Crescent Ave.	510-0541	L	take-out hamburgers and fries, homemade candy
Luau Larry's	509 Crescent Ave.	510-1919	L, D	oceanfront, lively
Mi Casita	111 Clarissa	510-1772	L, D	Mexican food
Mr. Ning's Chinese Garden	127 Sumner Ave.	510-1161	L, D	good Chinese cuisine in the Atwater Hotel building
Pacifica	101 Marilla Ave. (in El Canto Marketplace)	510-7224	D	expensive American, Pacific, or French cuisine with Oriental flair; roasted rack of boar, buffalo steaks in sauce
Pancake Cottage	118 Catalina Ave.	510-0726	B, L	breakfast house
Pete's Snack Bar	132 Sumner Ave.	510-0523	B, L	patio, great omeletes
Picnic Fry	104 Clarissa Ave.	510-0587	L	budget (take-out only) frozen chocolate bananas, Mexican food
Pirrone's Restaurant	417 Crescent Ave.	510-0333	B, L, and D	features seafood, prime rib, chicken steak
Ristorante Villa Portofino	209 Crescent Ave.	510-0508	L, D	first-class continental food for special occasions
Runway Cafe	at the airport	510-2196	B, L	good buffalo burgers, omelettes, soft tacos
Saldana's Taco Shop	113 Catalina Ave.	510-1176	L, D	Mexican food
Sally's Waffle Shop	505 Crescent Ave.	510-0355	B, L	great waffles
The Sand Trap Patio Restaurant	on the road to stables	510-1349	B, L	terrific sandwiches
Solomon's Landing	El Encanto Upstairs	510-1474	L, D	oyster bar, large upstairs patio with ocean view, salad bar
Sunset Buffet Cruise	on board MV *Phoenix*	510-2000	D	reservations, seasonal dinner cruise
Tug's Deli	in the Metropole Marketplace	510-0927	B, L, and D	Deli-style sandwiches (big!), salads, Italian-style killer cheesecake, gourmet bagels
Twilight Dining Tour	Two Harbors	510-2000	D	reservations required, boat trip included, seasonal, flying fish trip on return

vice! Call before 2 p.m. for same-day delivery, tel. 510-0598.

JUST A LITTLE BEYOND AVALON TOWN

Buffalo Nickel

The strolling visitor will enjoy breakfast (Sat. and Sun. only), lunch, and dinner at the Buffalo Nickel at the heliport in Pebbly Beach. The breakfast burrito is a local favorite. Buffalo dishes include buffalo chili, buffalo burgers, and buffalo steaks, all made with Catalina-grown buffalo. If a mile walk doesn't appeal to you, the Nickel offers complimentary transportation back and forth to Avalon; call 510-1323.

Outdoor Dining

Take a stroll to the **Sand Trap** (formerly the Pitch and Putt golf course) and have a tasty lunch alfresco. Customers have a choice of excellent sandwiches, omelettes, and special "soft" tacos, beer and wine. Open evenings for private parties only. Year-round hours, breakfast and lunch 7:30 a.m.-3 p.m.; prices range from $2 to $6.

Farther out of the city at Catalina's Airport-In-The-Sky, visitors will find the **Runway Cafe;** open 8 a.m.-4 p.m. year-round. Island vacationers who want a change of pace can enjoy a ride into Catalina's interior from Avalon on an airport van or tour bus. Or pilots can fly in on a private plane. One of the Runway specialties is buffalo burgers. Check out **Doug's Harbor Reef Restaurant and Saloon** in Two Harbors.

DESSERT

Are you just looking for something sweet? Try **Lloyd's** (an Island institution) on the corner of Crescent Ave. and Sumner, and watch *real* taffy being pulled on machines that have been operating since before WW II. There's a difference between real saltwater taffy and the imitation. The real stuff is rather hard to bite into at first, but with a little mastication softens up and has the nostalgic taste of old-fashioned candy. The imitation has wax added, making a soft, slick texture that is easy to bite down on. Try a bag—then *you'll* be the expert. Lloyd's also sells freshly made chocolate fudge, divinity, and pralines. All can be mailed to anywhere in the world.

Avalon Bake Shop makes fresh donuts every day, plus a full line of goodies from 5:30 a.m.-3 p.m.; 122 Catalina St., tel. 510-0361. In the Metropole Marketplace you'll find the **Catalina Cookie Co.,** with mouth-watering homestyle cookies, and **Olaf's,** serving ice cream in

Take a one-mile walk from the waterfront through Avalon Valley to the Avalon Picnic Grounds.

giant waffle cones. The **Sweet Shoppe,** next to Mi Casita, has a complete soda fountain along with a tantalizing display of pastries and candy.

PICNICS

There are barbecue pits the visitor can use free of charge along the mole. A pleasant one-mile walk past the horse stables on Avalon Canyon Rd. brings you to another picnic area ($1 pp) with tables and large barbecue pits. Toilet facilities are available. Ask at the visitor's information center, 605 Crescent, across the street from the Pleasure Pier, or call 510-2500 for information.

Bring your picnic basket or cooler over on the boat, or shop at one of the two grocery stores in Avalon: **Fred and Sally's Market,** 117 Catalina Ave., tel. 510-1199; and **Von's Market,** 123 Metropole, tel. 510-0280. Fred and Sally's sells tasty barbecued chicken and ribs; call early—they sell out fast. Both of these markets are not only well stocked with food, but also with crowds of people in the narrow aisles. **Sophie's Place,** 417 Crescent, tel. 510-0656, offers tasty deli sandwiches and trimmings—as well as the latest golf gossip.

BILL MEISTER

KID STUFF

Catalina is a family kind of place where parents bring their young children year after year, generation after generation. This is an island of adventure and learning for kids, who then grow up and often return with their own children. This chapter deals with what to bring and the many things you can show and do with the kids, as well as many activities they can do on their own. This information is pertinent to "kids-at-heart" of any age, who are certain to get a childlike thrill on a trip to Catalina.

What To Take

For summer travel, bring beach towels and a couple of changes of swimwear. Small children should have hats to protect their heads from the sun, along with sunscreen. Even when the sky is overcast the sun's rays will burn; the reflection from water and the white sand increases the risk. If you forget to bring these necessities from home, drugstores and gift shops carry lotions and sun hats. Take 10 or 20 small plastic sandwich bags and 20 small plastic garbage bags; these come in handy for stashing wet

bathing suits and dirty clothes, as well as toting and saving a variety of things during your vacation.

THE TRIP

Flying

Getting to your destination is a large part—if not the largest part—of a child's visit to Catalina. If your youngster hasn't yet had the opportunity to travel on a small plane or helicopter, you might choose to fly to Catalina. This adds to the thrill of the trip and is a quick way to get there— only about a 20-minute flight from San Pedro Harbor or Long Beach to the Island or a little longer from Los Angeles, San Diego, and Las Vegas. However, if the budget squeaks at airfare (see "Getting There"), boats are an enjoyable, economical way to go.

Boat Travel

Depending on which boat you choose to cross the channel to Catalina, the trip can take anywhere from 55 minutes to two hours. Do your children get carsick? If so, you may presume your child will get an upset stomach at sea. And if not, it's still wise to be prepared. Many over-the-counter remedies are available for motion sickness. Ask the druggist to give you one that doesn't cause drowsiness (unless you *want* your child to sleep the two hours crossing the channel). To be effective the medication should be taken at least an hour before departure. Seasick pills are sold onboard, but by the time you decide you need it (usually outside of the break-water) it's too late to do any good.

The best place to sit during a rough crossing is in the center of the lower deck. However, fresh breezes will often help allay queasiness; outside seating is available. On a clear summer day, sitting on the open deck, it's easy to get sunburned in two hours, so use protective lotions freely and sunblock for sensitive skin. Being sunburned can really take the zest out of a vacation. Windburn should also be avoided. A good coating of lotion prevents chapping. When you travel in the winter months remember that even though the sun may be shining in the harbor, warm jackets and hats are recommended; the winter wind off the ocean can get very chilly in mid-channel. On cross-channel boats, enclosed decks offer either tables and chairs or airline-type seats with trays; bring a deck of cards or other amusements in case it's the kind of day you want to spend inside.

SIGHTS

The Harbors

If you've got a few days to visit Long Beach or San Pedro before boarding a Catalina boat, along with the activities described in this part of the book you might want to check out the many guided tours with reduced fares for children along the harborfront of Long Beach and San Pedro. The first part of the trip from the Mainland takes you past harbors full of ships and many fascinating landmarks. Later, you'll cross channel waters teeming with sealife.

Departing from Long Beach Harbor, you'll pass the permanently docked **Queen Mary,** which is one of the largest of the old passenger ships that regularly crossed the Atlantic Ocean

It's fun for kids to travel across the channel on a boat. They might see flying fish, seals, porpoises, or even a gray whale.

KIDS' MAP OF AVALON

DESCANSO BEACH

CATALINA MUSEUM & AVALON THEATRE

CRAB HUNTING ROCKS

BOAT INFORMATION, SIGHTSEEING TOURS & TICKETS

MOLE

TO LOVERS COVE

ROSIE'S SEAFOOD (BAIT)

SHORE BOATS

PLEASURE PIER

JOE'S RENT-A-BOAT

VOLLEYBALL & BASKETBALL COURTS

RECREATION PARK

NORTH BEACH

ARCADE

MIDDLE BEACH

SOUTH BEACH

SWIM LESSONS & BEACH ACTIVITIES

CRESCENT AVE.

OLIVE ST.

LOWER TERRACE RD.

MARILLA AVE.

WHITTLEY AVE.

WHITTLEY AVE.

BEACON ST.

LIBRARY

MINIATURE GOLF

METROPOLE AVE.

SUMNER AVE.

CATALINA AVE.

CLARISSA AVE.

TREMONT ST.

VISITORS COUNTRY CLUB

TENNIS COURTS

GOLF COURSE

PITCH N' PUTT GOLF

AVALON CANYON RD.

0   0.1 mi
0   0.1 km

STABLES

© MOON PUBLICATIONS, INC.

between New York and Great Britain. She not only carried passengers paying for luxury service but also brought thousands of immigrants from Europe to this country. Their quarters were on the lower decks deep within the ship below the waterline. The deeper the deck, the lower the class, and the cheaper the fare.

Today, the *Queen Mary* is a fantastic tourist complex with a hotel on board in the original staterooms, a variety of trendy shops, and non-guests can pay admission for a tour of the large ship. Its many cafes are open to the public for breakfast, lunch, and dinner onboard. The colorful ceremony of the changing of the guard, with their bright red British uniforms and tall fur hats, takes place several times a day in front of the ship, just as it's done in London. These guards add a touch of old England to the seaside community of Long Beach. For hotel reservations call (310) 432-6964.

Spruce Goose

After passing the *Queen Mary*, you'll see the largest plane in the world in the *Spruce Goose* Geodome hangar in Long Beach Harbor. Airborne only once, the *Goose* was built of spruce wood by Howard Hughes. Along with the plane, there are many exhibits in the enormous hangar, and a film of the *Goose* on its one and only flight with Howard Hughes in the cockpit is shown all day. The lighting and design of the geodome give the impression that the huge plane is sitting in the outdoors with a night sky overhead. Climb the stairway to get a closer look into the cockpit. The plane really is immense and well worth a trip. Informational books, souvenirs, and snacks are sold in the geodome.

Admission to the complex includes both the *Spruce Goose* and the *Queen Mary:* $17.50 adult, $9.50 kids 3-12, free under three. Hours are 9 a.m. to 8 p.m. Good wheelchair access, lots of parking available at the south end of the Long Beach Freeway, $5 cars, $6 oversized vehicles. Transportation is available from the Catalina Landing to the *Queen Mary* and *Spruce Goose* complex; tel. (310) 435-3511.

Shipping

As you pass through either the Long Beach or San Pedro harbors, you'll see many large ships from all over the world. Some are giant tankers bringing oil to be refined from as far away as the Middle East and North Atlantic. Other ships are enormous "container craft" carrying goods and flying flags from the far-flung corners of the globe. Giant cranes handle these containers quickly and efficiently. Can you and your kids guess what country the ships hail from by identifying the flags and the language the names are written in?

The Breakwater

Looking much like a stone wall, this breakwater for many miles parallels the Long Beach and San Pedro coastline, shielding the working part of these harbors from heavy winter storms. Powerful winds can turn the Pacific Ocean into a churning, heaving body of water. The breakwater is a deeply planted barrier. Thousands of huge rocks were hauled on flat barges by tugboats (from Catalina's quarries) and piled on the bottom of the ocean, building a wall high and wide enough to make the harbors safe and calm. Because of the ongoing action of the waves upon the breakwater, it needs constant repair.

The boat to Catalina frequently passes rock-laden barges pulled by a tugboat from Catalina's two rock quarries, one very close to Avalon just beyond Pebbly Beach, and the other at Empire Landing toward the west end of the Island near Two Harbors. The rock quarries are built on mountains of stone. With dynamite and mechanical equipment, the mountains are broken up into smaller chunks of rock (some weighing as much as a couple of tons), which are then loaded onto barges with giant cranes, taken across the channel, and dumped at the spot where the breakwater is being built or repaired. Projects like this take years to complete.

On The Boat

While you motor through the breakwater, the boat travels within the speed limit of the har-

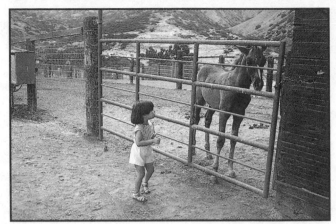

a little visitor getting acquainted with one of Catalina's young horses

bor. Fast-moving boats leave a wake behind, and a small boat caught in that wake could flip over. When you pass through the entrance to the breakwater, you'll see a large flashing light that warns ships traveling at night or in fog that they're near the harbor. Once the boat leaves the harbor and the seawall, it picks up speed. Sometimes it's difficult to get your "sea legs" if the deck is pitching. If it's a calm sea the deck won't move much, but don't be surprised if it's still hard to stand!

Sealife

Watch the water for fish. Different sealife swim the channel, depending on the time of year and the currents. In the winter months, you'll see mammoth gray whales traveling south to Mexican waters to bear their young in **Scammon's Bay** off Baja California. Every year they travel 6,000 miles from their summer feeding grounds in the Bering Sea to Mexico and then back. When a whale blows a tall stream of water straight up into the air and then dive to the bottom with a flap of its giant tail, it's called "sounding." Often several of the huge mammals travel together—this group is called a "pod."

In the summer, passengers often see porpoises playing in the wake of the boat. They leap out of the water, jump the waves, and dive back into the wake as they follow along. These popular mammals seem to enjoy showing off. Toward the end of the summer, look for flying fish skimming over the tops of the waves. A colorful, translucent, bubble-like tube or balloon floating in the water is a jellyfish. If you encounter one while swimming, don't touch it and don't stick around; it can give you a painful sting. As the boat gets closer to the Island, sea-gazers might see a seal that has strayed from the hauling ground located near the east end of the Island. Most of the pinnipeds that live on Catalina are California sea lions; intelligent and playful, they're the variety that's trained for circus acts. Sometimes the brown pelicans put on a show if they find a school of fish. Attacking the sea like divebombers, they fill their pouchlike bills with as many small shiny fish as possible. A flock of squawking seagulls meets the arriving passenger boats in the harbor every day, waiting for a free lunch thrown by the galley crew.

Docking In Avalon

Depending on the weather, the mountains of the Island will be visible rising out of the sea during most of the trip. From several miles away the white Casino is apparent. As the ship approaches the harbor, the speed is reduced and the captain carefully negotiates the large boat snugly against the dock. Deck hands throw the lines ashore as waiting departing passengers watch. The gangplanks are put into position and you've arrived at Catalina's **Cabrillo Mole.** Follow the Mainland ticket seller's instructions, and make return reservations as soon as you arrive; the ticket offices for all ships are conveniently located on the mole. Even if you've already purchased your tickets, return reservations must be made and tickets stamped at the Catalina office with your return date and time.

IN AVALON

Hotels

With kids, there are several things to keep in mind when choosing a hotel. Some have outside areas where you can wash the sand off before entering. Some also have lockers where you can store beach toys so you won't have to lug them to your room; others have outside clotheslines to hang up wet suits and towels. If all these things are important to you, ask about them when you make reservations. Be sure to find out if there's a hotel courtesy car waiting at the mole. With children and luggage it can be a big help, especially if your hotel is at the top of one of the many hills. If the service is not provided, the tram ($1 pp if running) will take you to the central Island plaza; several taxis also meet the boat. If none is in sight, use the public phone on the mole to call Avalon Taxi (510-0705/0025); $6-7 will usually get you and your luggage to the hotel.

Beaches

Avalon is small, a one-square-mile community, and children quickly learn the lay of the land. The biggest attractions for kids are the beach and the water. Avalon is on the lee (protected) side of the Island, so the surf is calm. Although it's a very safe area for children to swim and play in, a Los Angeles County lifeguard is on duty every day until dusk. Small children should be supervised at all times. The beaches in the center of town are sandy and drop off to deep water very quickly—sooner than most Mainland beaches. **South Beach** has a float anchored some 50 feet offshore during the summer months.

North Beach (a very small sandy area) has a retaining wall with steps down to the water's edge. It gets deep quickly when the tide is in and can be quite surgy. This beach is not recommended for small children or any child who cannot swim. A walk along the shoreline from the mole past Abalone Point will bring you to Lovers Cove. This rocky beach (without lifeguard) becomes very deep very quickly, so it's not a good play area for toddlers or young children who can't swim. However, because it's a fish preserve, it's a good place to introduce the older *swimming* child to snorkeling.

AVALON RECREATION DEPARTMENT

The following is the summer schedule (from June through Labor Day) of supervised activities for kids offered by the Avalon Recreation Department. Unless otherwise noted, the number to call for information and schedules is 510-1987.

Day Camp

Monday through Fri. from 9 a.m. to 2 p.m., children (4-12 years) can attend a day camp at the City Park. Each child must bring a bag lunch and a drink that will not spoil (no refrigeration). A fun-filled half day of various activities includes field trips, games, supervised beach games, and arts and crafts. Shoes necessary; $7 daily fee, $30 weekly fee. For reservations call 510-0928/1987.

Beach Games

During the summer months, a variety of supervised beach games are offered for kids of all ages. Three days a week there are sandcastle building contests with prizes. Beach activities, swimming races, balloon toss, and active games keep the kids happily occupied for a portion of the day, free. Call for scheduled events.

The City Park

At the end of Crescent Ave., this small park is a good place for your little ones to get acquainted with other children; it's the hub of the recreation program. Arts and crafts occur weekly. There's a small playground with swings here, and activities go on from 9 a.m. to 3 p.m., tel. 510-0928. Another playground is located next to the volleyball courts, on the left side when walking to town from the mole.

Fishing
A favorite pastime for little kids is fishing off the Pleasure Pier. Mornings, twice a week, the city organizes fishing derbies for the kids (four years and up), with a ribbon and prize to the fisherman who brings in the biggest and the most. To participate they need minimal fishing equipment: bait and a fishing pole (a dropline works fine). If you've forgotten to bring yours, they're for sale at Joe's Rent-A-Boat on the Pleasure Pier for about $3, including a hook. Rosie at the fish market sells frozen squid and anchovies by the small bag for bait; balls of cheese, peas, and wads of bread work, too. Note: An outside saltwater shower is located near the Pleasure Pier to use after this activity.

Los Angeles County Library
Once a week from July 1 'til Labor Day the library offers a special story time for children preschool and up. Librarian Donna Eisenhut welcomes children with an up-to-date selection of children's books. The library is at 215 Sumner Avenue. For information, call 510-1050.

Beach Bingo
All ages meet at South Beach Mondays and Wednesdays at 6 p.m. for beach bingo, 50 cents per card. Lots of great prizes.

Mini Golf Tournament
At the Golf Gardens on Thursdays. Kids have to be enrolled in day camp to participate.

Volleyball/Basketball
Bring a group or come to make friends at the volleyball/basketball court parallel to South Beach. Basketballs and volleyballs are available Mon. through Fri.; small fee and deposit required.

Lip-sync Contest
Come to the Wrigley Plaza Stage on Friday at 6:45 p.m. with your tape ready to play. Individual or group acts welcome—bring your best costumes, showmanship, props, whatever it takes. Yes, there are prizes! First-place winners will be invited back for the final competition for a grand prize around Labor Day weekend.

BEACH BUMMING

Rock Crabs And Tidepools

Little children seem to wake up at the crack of dawn, vacation or not, so it's wise to have a couple of surprises up your sleeve to keep them occupied. One

shore crab

morning, surprise them by taking them crab hunting. Six- to nine-year-olds seem to enjoy this the most; younger kids might not be sure-footed enough. You'll be clambering around some big rocks by the ocean, and all involved will probably get wet, so dress for the beach—swimsuits and tennis shoes. This activity is best done at low tide; on the night before, check the tide timetable on the end of the pier at the harbormaster's office.

Crabs love raw hamburger. If you're out before the grocery stores are open (Fred and Sally's Market opens at 7 a.m.), most restaurants will sell you a raw hamburger patty. Give each child a small plastic bag of meat and one with cracker crumbs for the tidepools if the tide is really low. One burger patty should do

limpet

for two children for about half an hour.

Walk along the boardwalk toward Casino Point past the Tuna Club. Below the rails are large rocks along the edge of the water. Look to see if you spot any of these small crabs out scavenging a meal. If you have a sharp eye, you'll see lots of them about one to three inches in size, even though they're almost the color of the rocks. Put the tiniest pinch of raw meat on *enjoying Avalon Bay while eating lunch*

the top of a rock (not in the water), and these awkward little creatures will rush sidelong to grab the meat in their great claws.

If you have very curious children who want to examine the crabs up close, have them pick them up carefully from behind; they will pinch if given a chance. Treat them kindly and return them gently back to the rocks. Mean- *sea star* der toward the Casino along the rocks. If it's really low tide, investigate the small tidepools; the sea is alive with little creatures, wispy grasses, kelp, and sea urchins. The water is clear enough to watch the fish scrambling for the cracker crumbs (crunched up very fine). This is a pleasant, relaxing way to show your children some of the wonders of sealife and work up an appetite for breakfast.

Bird And Fish Feeding

All small children love to feed animals, and Avalon has a large resident family of pigeons that strut around town, especially near the Busy Bee Cafe. The pigeons love cracker or bread crumbs and they'll practically do a jig for stale popcorn. The end of the Pleasure Pier is a good place to feed the fish. They'll gather in groups close to the surface for cracker crumbs; however, sometimes a clownish seagull will get there before

the fish do. The seagull is such a glutton that it'll try eating just about anything, even if it's not edible. Most animals, fish and gulls included, are just like us: they seem the hungriest early in the morning and at dusk.

Boating For Kids

If your kids are 11 or older, renting a rowboat is always an adventure. Rowing around the harbor gives them plenty of exercise and they can even fish if they like. The cost is $10 per hour at Joe's Rent-A-Boat on the Pleasure Pier, and they must know how to swim. Joe also rents paddleboards for $5 per hour.

Beachcombing

Another early-morning activity is beachcombing. Priceless treasures can be found on any of the beaches on Catalina before the crowds arrive. Most children enjoy searching for shells along the waterline. Be sure to bring a plastic bag to hold them. One of the favorites is a small purple shell called the purple olive shell. At one time they were used for money (called *wampum*) by the Catalina Indians, who also used them for making necklaces and ornaments. Other Indians on the Mainland who didn't live close to the ocean would trade precious goods to the Catalina Indians for these shells. Look for tiny mussel shells and baby clamshells. Perhaps you'll be lucky enough to find a rare, delicate chambered nautilus.

Another bit of booty found on the beach are tiny bits of colored glass, "ocean jewels" that have been smoothed and polished by the constant movement of the surf and friction with the sand and rocks. Collect these to sparkle in a pretty glass jar full of water set on a sunny windowsill. Sea-hewn driftwood can be found in intriguing shapes, and who knows what else you'll find. The best part of beachcombing is the surprise you have each day when you look to see what fascinating bits of flotsam and jetsam the sea has carried in on the last tide. Older (and richer) beachcombers use metal detectors on the sand to find loose change that inevitably gets lost each day.

Older Kids

Biking on the Island is great fun for the whole family. Pack a picnic and bike up to the Wrigley Memorial and Botanical Garden, out to Pebbly Beach, or along the road leading to the Casino. See "Getting Around in Avalon" for more details about bicycles.

DIVING

Diving Catalina is a unique experience with crystal-clear water and fascinating marinelife. Excellent diving locations within 30 feet of the shoreline eliminate tedious walks with heavy equipment over long beaches or rocky shores. Campsites for beach dives are conveniently located on both sides of the Island. Most of the coves along the lee (protected) side offer kelp forests as well as steep cliffs and caves which were thrust into the foundation of the Island millions of years ago now alive with sealife. There are wrecks to be explored which, along with the caves, are reachable by rental boats available on the Pleasure Pier.

Catalina's nearly transparent waters offer visibility ranging from 40 to 80 feet, depending on the time of year. Summer blooms of plankton lessen minimum visibility to 30 feet; in the winter visibility can be as much as 100 feet. Bring your underwater camera! Summer water temperature averages 67-70°, winter 56-59°. Call the Avalon Harbor Department to check on weather conditions, tel. 510-0535.

Dive Instruction

If your fantasy is learning to use scuba equipment and roaming the seven seas, you can combine a vacation on Catalina Island with an

*Catalina Divers Supply
on the Pleasure Pier
in Avalon Bay*

Catalina's Underwater Park

ON HARDY

intensive certification course. Catalina is an ideal place to learn to dive. On the lee side, the water is very clear; the steep drops make for short surface swims; there's only a little surf to contend with; and the marinelife is abundant.

The **Argo Diving Service** offers a certification program as well as a variety of underwater adventures. Certification instruction for beginners costs $200 for about 24 hours of diving. If you're already certified and would like an introduction to the territory, Argo also offers guided tours, private or semiprivate, for almost any adventure you dream up: observing, handling, and feeding fish; underwater photography; night diving; exploring kelp beds and wrecks; taking game such as abalone, scallops, and lobster. Fee for boat and crew is $60 hourly for one to six divers in Catalina waters. An open-boat trip including dives, instructor/guide, tank, refill, weight belt, lunch, drinks, pick-up and delivery to your hotel is $85 for a day-long trip. For a free packet loaded with good diving information, write to Argo Diving Services, Box 1201, Avalon, CA 90704, tel. 510-2208.

Catalina Aquatic Rentals offers introductory classes as well as certification courses either privately or in groups. Equipment rental, sales, and air are available at **The Float** in Hamilton Cove. To get there take the shore boat from the green Pleasure Pier. For reservations and information call 510-1811.

Dive Boats And Trucks

Diving is a popular pastime in Catalina, and several boats are available and equipped for divers. The **King Neptune** travels with two compressors for quick 3,000-pound air fills, plus a subsurface platform for easy access. The boat travels 18 knots, so few dive spots are more than an hour away. For more information call 510-0600. The *Argonaut* is a divers' charter boat, but will also charter for other activities. Costs $60/hour, including drinks and lunch. For further information, call Jon Hardy at 510-2208. **Catalina Divers Supply** parks its equipment truck on Casino Point on most weekends of the year—fill your air tanks for $3.50 and $4. Gear reservations require a deposit. Group rates and package deals available. **Snorkel Mobile** is at Lovers Cove during summer vacation 10 a.m. till 6 p.m. or by special arrangement. Their booth is at the Pleasure Pier, open daily from 8 a.m. 'til dark during the summer months; winter hours are shorter. Prerequisites for renting diving supplies are a valid diver's certification card and a driver's license. Full line of rental gear is available. Snorkeling tours and packages are offered during the season. For more information, call 510-0330 or write Box 126, Avalon, CA 90704.

CATALINA DIVERS' MAP

TWO HARBORS

ESCONDIDO RD.

TWO HARBORS RD.

AIRPORT RD.

OLD STAGE RD.

MIDDLE RANCH RD.

AVALON

MOON

0   3mi

0   3km

• = DIVE SITES

AVALON SHORELINE

WRECK OF VALIANT
80-120 FT. DEEP

SEAPLANE LANDING AREA

HAMILTON
BEACH

CATALINA UNDERWATER PARK

LOVERS COVE

GAME PRESERVE

SNORKEL
AREA

30 YDS.

SCUBA AREA

CASINO POINT

W-52   W-51

C.D.S.
DIVE STATION

AVALON BAY

CABRILLO MOLE

SNORKEL
AREA

BALBOA BAY
ISLAND BEACH CLUB
&
C.D.S. AQUATIC
SPORTS CENTER

CASINO

CATALINA
DIVERS SUPPLY

AVALON

AVALON

CATALINA UNDERWATER PARK

50 FT. DEEP

50 FT. DEEP

FISH HABITAT

WRECK
50 FT. DEEP

60 FT. DEEP

OLD STEEL PIER

KELP FOREST

WRECK 36 FT. DEEP

UNDERWATER CLIFFS
& PINNACLES

C.D.S. DIVE STATION
AIR & EQUIPMENT

SEA WALL

CASINO POINT BREAKWATER

CASINO

PARKING

© MOON PUBLICATIONS, INC.

CATALINA DIVERS' MAP KEY

1. Game Preserve. Open to snorkel divers and glass bottom sightseeing boats only. Look—but don't touch!

2. Permit from Harbor Master required to scuba dive within city limits except in Catalina Underwater Park.

3. Catalina Underwater Park, the first on West Coast. Excellent scuba or snorkel area. Explore, photo. No taking of game or salvage. Dive station provides air and rentals.

4. Fine snorkel areas flank Descanso Beach Club. Dive, dine and drink in the relaxed atmosphere of a private club.

5. to 6. Rocks and Kelp to 40 feet deep. Explore, photo.

7. Large kelp bed to 60 feet deep. Lobster, bass, yellowtail.

8. Moorings, sand bottom, rest area for halibut.

9. Fine snorkel and scuba. Abalone, all fish, explore, photo.

10. Very clear cove at point; sand, rock, and kelp, fine for photos.

11. Deep water, vertical cliffs to 130 feet deep. Caution: strong current and boat traffic.

12. Fine snorkel and scuba. Lobster.

13. Rocks, kelp, and sand to 100 feet deep. Lobster, yellowtail.

14. Fair anchorage and snorkel are. Halibut and abalone east.

15. Many small scenic coves, fine photo, exploring.

16. to 17. Steep drop-off at rock quarry. Green abalone, shallow, kelp.

18. Small coves, caves, clear water. Excellent photo, explore, lobster.

20. Kelp bed, abalone, bass, lobster; buoyed reef south, best.

21. Moorings, yacht services, and air, in season. Landing permit required.

22. Buoyed reef 20–80 feet deep; kelp, rocks. Explore, photo. Lobster, bass, yellowtail. Caution: occasional heavy current.

23. Moorings, white sand 20–40 feet deep. Fine visibility. Photo and beginners.

24. East and west, explore, photo, abalone, lobster. Caution: strong current on point.

25. Many scenic coves west, photo, explore, abalone.

26. Steep drop-off to 140 feet deep. Caution: strong current and swell.

27. Kelp beds to 60 feet deep. Explore, abalone, lobster, exposed to westerlies.

28. Fair exposed anchorage, kelp to 40 feet deep. Photo, explore, lobster.

29. Cliffs to 140 feet deep. Photo, lobster, scallops.

30. Deep water, photo, lobster, scallops. Caution: current and swell.

31. Shallow inside, moorings, wreck of *Ning Po* awash east. West shore outside, kelp and rocks to 40 feet deep. Explore, lobster, halibut.

32. Protected anchorage, reef awash west, photo, explore, abalone, lobster. Coast northwest, kelp and large rocks, fine exploring, abalone, lobster.

33. Coast south, kelp rocks to 80 feet deep. Explore, lobster, abalone, scallops.

34. Kelp beds to 80 feet deep. Lobster, abalone, scallops.

35. Kelp bed 100 yards off Point; explore, lobster, abalone, scallop.

36. Beach looks inviting but shorebreak treacherous. Good offshore kelp beds east; lobster, often poor visibility.

37. to 38. Kelp beds, huge rocks, and caves to 60 feet deep. Explore, abalone, lobster. Caution: current and boat traffic off Church Rock.

39. Seal colony, seasonal. Area southeast, abalone, lobster when calm.

40. Deep water, explore, photo, abalone. Caution: boat traffic.

41. Pebbly Beach area. Caution: seaplane traffic.

DIVE LOCATIONS

The First Underwater Park

Set aside in 1965 by the Avalon City Council, this is a unique underwater park on the lee side, directly off Casino Point. It's the only place within city limits where snorkeling or scuba diving is permitted. Several wrecks have been placed in the park near some of the finest kelp forests in the world, and artificial reef areas have been established to provide additional fish habitats. In this same area are deep underwater cliffs and pinnacles waiting to be explored by the adventurous. The park is often used as the underwater backdrop for Hollywood films. **Note**: Removal of game and specimens from the underwater park is prohibited, as well as salvaging artifacts placed there to serve as subject matter for photography. Spearfishing is also illegal.

The *Valiant*

A short distance from Avalon in Descanso Bay is the wreck of the *Valiant*, a deep-dive site (90-100 feet) on the outer edge of the Descanso Bay Moorings. The *Catalina Islander* newspaper covered the sinking in 1930:

The palatial yacht was 163 feet long and carried 3,000 gallons of fuel . . . it recently made a 7,500-mile cruise to the Pacific. . . . The explosion occurred while the owner, Mr. Charles S. Howard, and his guests were at dinner Saturday evening, December 13. The vessel carried a crew of 22 who were also on board at the time. . . . Anchored some 500 yards from the pier at the Hotel St. Catherine, the explosion reverberated through the town of Avalon. . . . Immediately following the blast, flames shot out from the huge hole in the starboard side near the engine room . . . the fire department responded immediately but the vessel was too far from the pier to be reached . . . the flames illuminated the sky for miles.

The *Valiant* burned for three days and then sank. Divers still occasionally find a small coin-like token that says "good for one drink MV Valiant," an inside joke among guests who sailed during Prohibition days. One of the most costly shipwrecks in Catalina waters, the valuable metals were salvaged long ago. But it's reported that over $75,000 in cash and gems went to the bottom, and no one has ever claimed to have found it! It's necessary to obtain a (free) permit from the Harbor Department to dive the *Valiant* or any other spot within city limits, with the exception of the underwater park off Casino Point.

Casino Point divers

Sue-Jac

A more recent shipwreck (1980) is the *Sue-Jac*. This modern 70-foot schooner went down during a severe northeaster while bystanders watched Los Angeles County's Bay Watch crew rescue all aboard—three crew members and one dog. The *Sue-Jac* sank gently and came to rest on a 90-foot-deep slope, bow down, almost in one piece. An experienced diver can swim through an entrance into the cabin and then out the skylight—an exciting dive destination.

Other Wrecks

Many believe that in 1598 a Spanish galleon struck a rock and sank with a reported $2 million in bullion and artifacts. In 1602, some of the goods from the wreckage were found on Catalina shores, and in 1850 what may have been part of its hull was found off Ship Rock in six-plus fathoms. In 1852, a Spanish frigate sank near the Island with a $1.2 million cargo. In 1920, the *North Star* sank; in 1924 the *Taurus,* a 551-ton U.S. schooner, went down; 1926 took the *William G. Irwin* to the bottom and in 1929 the *Charles F. Crocker,* an 860-ton U.S. barkentine, foundered. The list continues with the USS *Koka* sinking in 1937. Ten years later, in 1947, the *Rossino II* hit bottom off Catalina Head. Basic NOAA charts show some spots by wreck symbol with "PA" (position approximate).

SPECIAL DIVERS' ACCOMMODATIONS

A few hotels encourage diving clientele by providing facilities for storing and cleaning equipment. It's smart to mention your equipment when making reservations.

Bay View Hotel

An older hotel with men's and women's showers and toilets on each floor. Wash-down facilities for dive gear, outdoor shower, barbecue pits, jacuzzi, accommodates groups up to 150. Courtesy car on request. Summer rates $55 and up single or double, winter rates available; 124 Whittley, Box 1017, Avalon, CA 90704, tel. 510-0600.

Blue Dolphin House

Ideal for groups, families, or clubs. Four units, two-bedroom suites with fully equipped kitchens, ceiling fans, color cable TV, heating, linens, and towels provided, one block to the beach. Accommodates up to six people. Off-season rates offered. Rental for up to four people is $150 per night. Facilities for washing and drying diving gear, outdoor shower. Located at 603 Beacon; mailing address is Box 2605, Avalon, CA 90704, tel. 510-1811.

La Paloma Cottages

Located in the heart of Avalon (1½ blocks to the beach). Housekeeping cottages and apartments, some with view, peaceful and quiet, wisteria-covered walkways and gardens, kitchens and private baths, TV, radio, heat, barbecue, patios, luggage storage, courtesy car, coffee. Seasonal rates, $85 and up, closed January. Box 1505, Avalon, CA 90704, tel. 510-0737.

Seaport Village Inn

Views, beach one-half block away, color TV, spa, sundeck, complimentary coffee, one- and two-bedroom family suites with kitchen, studio suites, view rooms, transportation from boat. Group and package rates from $74 double. In Avalon tel. 510-0344, in San Diego tel. (619) 571-0663, in Southern California tel. (800) 2-CATALINA.

OTHER SPORTS

Horseback Riding

Catalina Stables and Kennel is located on Avalon Canyon Rd. just past the golf links on the left side of the street. You can ride the picturesque mountain and valley trails on a western saddle. A pony ring is used daily by an active group of Catalina riders. Rentals are available by the hour or day, with one-hour guided rides at $25 pp. For information, call 510-0478.

Golf

The nine-hole, 32-par Catalina Golf Course offers a challenge to all golfers, duffers and experts alike. The course, with its narrow fairways hugged by rugged hills, is considered tricky. Tall eucalyptus trees spill welcome shade across the grass, while thick groups of scattered fig trees provide a juicy fruit snack in late summer, yours for the taking. Out-of-bounds is tall dry grass and brambles. Be prepared for an up-and-down climb.

The course is kept in good condition—though occasionally a wild boar makes his way onto the green and digs in the tender grass, but the patient attendants make quick repairs. There's a small putting green but no driving range. In years past, this was the scene of the Bobby Jones Tournament, Bobby himself participating. Since 1968, the Catalina Golf Course has been the site of the prestigious Catalina Junior Golf Tournament. Held the weekend following Easter Sunday, talented juniors from all over California compete. Several young adults on the pro circuit today began their careers playing in this tournament—Amy Alcott and Craig Stadler to name two.

A pro shop sells the basics: clubs, balls, gloves, hats, and tees. Rentals include clubs and motorized carts. Pro David Lafata gives lessons in the off-season, either group or private. At the old pitch and putt course on the street just below the Country Club is the **Sand Trap**, a great outdoor sandwich shop that also serves breakfast. To reach the Country Club, walk to the end of Sumner Ave. and on up the small hill (well marked with a sign that says Catalina Visitors Country Club). This is where you pay your fees for both courses; call 510-0530 for more information. Greens fee: $10 for nine holes, $10 golf cart rental for nine holes.

Tennis

Laykold tennis courts are available (free) throughout the summer at the Avalon School Grounds in Falls Canyon. From mid-Sept. to mid-June, the courts are available before 11 a.m. and after 2:30 p.m. Bring your own equipment. The Las Casitas tennis courts are Laykold 60 by 120 courts, reserved through the recreation department, tel. 510-0928. Equipment not available.

At the Catalina Visitor's Country Club you'll find Pacific Pave tennis courts. Rackets and balls can be rented. The courts are lit for night use. (For directions to the Country Club see "Golf.") Fees: $10 hourly, racket rental $1. Reservations are a good idea, up to 24 hours ahead.

MORE WATER SPORTS

Wave Jammers

Explore the hidden coves of Catalina on a **Yamaha Wave Jammer.** Enough room for two people, instruction and rentals are available. Take the shoreboat at the green Pleasure Pier to **The Float** at Hamilton Cove. Reservations recommended, tel. 510-1811.

Water-skiing

Avalon's lee side has calm ocean water where the water-skiing is ideal. You must bring your own equipment and boat; as of this printing, no rentals are available. Avalon Harbor areas are well marked and the speed limit for all boats and dinghies within the harbor is five mph or "wakeless speed," whichever is less.

Paddleboards

Avalon's calm, clear, surf-free waters are perfect for exploring the bay on a board. Rent one on the Pleasure Pier at Joe's Rent-A-Boat; $5 per hour plus $2.50 deposit.

Para-sailing

Experience a thrill of a lifetime, and enjoy the most spectacular view of Catalina as you soar overhead. No need to get wet as you'll be taking off and landing directly in the boat. Simply stand there as the wind fills the para-sail and gently lifts you into the sky. **Para-Sailing Catalina With Island Cruzers** is next to Brown's Bikes across from the basketball courts; tel. 510-1777.

HUNTING

The Catalina hills are rich with wild goat, boar, deer, quail, and turkey. Each year the hunts are determined by the "hatch." Some years only bow hunting is allowed; other years guns are permitted. All hunting is directed by Doug Bombard of the Catalina Hunting Program. A package deal is offered that includes food, lodging, transportation while on Catalina Island, guide fees, and game cleaning for return shipment to the Mainland. It does not include tags or transportation to and from the Island. All hunters must have tags and a valid California hunting license in their possession on arrival at the Hunting Lodge. There's always a waiting list of hunters for the Island hunts; applications are

---

HUNTING FEES

Antlerless Season	$200 pp per day
Buck Season	$400 pp per day
Boar and Goat Season	$200 pp per day
Non-hunter (observer only) . . .	$85 pp per day
Boar Tag (limit one per day)	$50
Goat Tag: Trophy (limit one per day).	$40
Goat Tag: Non-Trophy (limit one per day) .	$25

---

taken and then names are drawn. Call 510-0303 for detailed information.

Getting There

All hunters are requested to use the same means of transportation—the *Catalina Express*. It departs from the San Pedro terminal at the foot of the Harbor Freeway and across Harbor Boulevard. This minimizes confusion in picking up and delivering hunters, allowing more time for hunting.

Clothes And Equipment

No rifles, shotguns, or bows are available at the Hunting Lodge. Pistols and handguns may not be used for hunting on Conservancy lands. Bring a set of field glasses, a good supply of ammunition or arrows, plus a warm jacket and good hiking boots.

FISHING

If there's an ocean and a boat, you'll usually find a fisherman. The water along the Southern California coast is noted for being rich with sealife of all varieties. Visiting sportsmen revel in the knowledge that they have a good to excellent chance of catching a trophy in Southern California fishing beds. The biggest question is deciding what variety they want to go for.

Catalina is renowned for its excellent fishing, notably for marlin. The roar of the Avalon cannon alerts the town that another marlin has been brought into the Pleasure Pier at **Rosie's Fish Market**. Amidst crowds of visitors and fishing buffs, an Avalon ceremony follows: the big fish is hung on the pier's scale, a bottle of champagne is presented to the angler, and a photo is taken to record the exciting moment. Sea bass, rock cod, sand dabs, button perch, and sheepshead are some of the more delicious fish also brought in. If you're a lucky diver, you can find lobster and abalone.

Tackle rentals from **Joe's Rent-A-Boat** (on the green Pleasure Pier): still-fishing rods, $5; trolling rods complete with lures and hooks, $8. Bait available. **Note**: Please respect the non-

Joe's Rent-A-Boat stand on the Pleasure Pier rents boats and fishing equipment.

fishing areas—Lovers Cove and the underwater park off Casino Point—and be aware of the fishing seasons. If in doubt, ask the harbormaster at the end of the Pleasure Pier. A valid California fishing license is required, available at Joe's and **Island Marine**, 125 Metropole Ave. (in Cricket Alley).

BOAT RENTALS

A variety of boats can be rented at **Joe's Rent-A-Boat** on the Pleasure Pier. They can be taken to any one of the many coves along the Catalina coast for fishing, picnicking, skin diving, or just sightseeing. If you don't bring your own fishing tackle you can rent or buy most of the equipment needed here at Joe's. Take a bright flashlight with you if you're planning to be out after sunset on a boat without running lights. Joe's is open Easter week through October. For reservations, call 510-0455. **Note**: Coast Guard regulations limit these small boats to six passengers. **Island Marine and Sports**, 125 Metropole Ave. (in Cricket Alley), tel. 510-0238, also rents and sells fishing gear, bait, and diving and boating supplies. If you need outboard or inboard parts, they carry Evinrude and Mercury.

Charter Boats

If you'd like to try for big fish and/or want to indulge in a little luxury, this is the way to go. Charters generally come with a skipper and, in some cases, a deck hand. Some provide you with lunch and drinks for the day. They all have a different set of rules and prices; most are negotiable.

Keeper Charters

Experience the ultimate fishing machine. Catch marlin, yellowtail, tuna, and other deep-sea fish aboard the *Keeper.* The boat is equipped with reels and custom rods. The cost is $100/hour, four-hour minimum. Includes lunch, beverages, all fishing tackle, and tax; the only thing you need to bring is a valid fishing license. Half day is $381.50, includes beverages and tax. Call for reservations at the **Catalina Island Inn,** tel. 510-1624.

Descanso Charters

An exciting day of fishing, island sightseeing, snorkeling, or just relaxing can be yours on Descanso Charters. The late-model Bertram 30-foot sportfisher will accommodate four passengers for fishing and six for sightseeing. Top-notch tackle provided. Family outings welcome. For information and reservations call 510-1573

(Avalon), (213) 457-4697 (Mainland), Box 1031, Avalon, CA 90704.

Tackle

What kind of fishing tackle to use! Choice of equipment grows every year. You can quiz 10 fishermen and get 10 answers to a simple question like "What's the best tackle to catch a yellowtail?" Are you one who uses the same tackle whether fishing surf, pier, or live bait? Is your favorite the conventional reel or the spinning type? Brass, plastic, or chrome plate? How about the line? Is it 20-pound line, 50, or maybe 12? And then there's the rod, which can be eight feet or six feet. What's a beginner to do?! One thing is to get a fellow fisherman to recommend a good tackle shop, find a salesperson who instills confidence, and start handling the options. As for price, you usually get what you pay for.

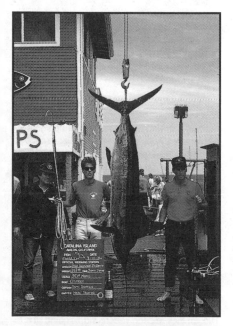

The cannon booms and beachers rush to the pier to see a marlin brought in to Avalon.

THE FISH

Tuna Family

The variety of fish in Southern California waters is enormous. The tuna family includes among others albacore, yellowfin, bigeye, and bluefin tuna. These are all good eating fish, and many fishermen make sensational canned (or jarred) tuna from these big babies; wahoo is also a taste treat for tuna lovers. In the late 1940s and '50s commercial fishermen made a killing for several years with huge schools of albacore running between Catalina and the Mainland. For whatever reason, albacore are seldom seen in those same quantities in the '90s.

Flatfish

Sole, sand dabs, and turbot are all flatfish. Sand dabs are particularly popular with local fishermen in Catalina, usually caught in water 300 feet deep or more. Sand dabs are small fish up to about a pound and great eating (once filleted); sole grow to about six pounds and turbot to about two pounds, all great table fare.

Sheepshead

This toothy fish can be a 30-pound catch. It dines regularly on shellfish in kelp and rock beds and is part of the wrasse family. The young female is generally an all-over pink color, and the male is more colorful with a white lower jar, black head, and red and black striped body; but this is one of the fish (as well as giant black sea bass and marlin, among others) that change sex during their development. As the small pink females grow, they begin to change color and sex. Trimmings of mussels, squid, abalone, and shrimp make good bait. Sheepshead can be found in 60 feet of water, or the surf, or even at several hundred feet when fishing for rock cod.

Sculpin

Look out for this fish. Although it's great eating, and bought in a fish market it is perfectly safe, when fishing—beware. The sculpin is the only venemous fish common to Southern California. Rather an ugly creature, it's rust and white colored with a high spiky dorsal. A bottom dweller, it seldom grows to more than three pounds and has a large mouth. The only safe way to handle this fellow is by grabbing the lower jaw with the thumb and forefinger. Though without teeth, the fish has spiny fins and rays that carry a toxic substance that, when introduced into a person, will produce severe pain, shock, and nausea; the only remedy seems to be time. They are good eating fish with fine white flesh, but catching them is better left to the experienced fishermen. The roe is poisonous.

Barracuda
At one time this was a very common fish locally; however, overfishing and pollution have thinned out the numbers. A 28-inch limit is helping the barracuda to make a comeback. This fish strikes both lures and bait, really goes for anchovy bait, and puts up a good fight. They show up around Southern California in late Jan., lingering into Feb. and March, and can be big: from seven to nine pounds, though the average size is four to six pounds.

Bonito
Bonito is an inshore fish that's found almost year-round. This is a good fighting fish and can weigh from 2 to over 12 pounds. Sometimes called the poor man's tuna, the fish is attracted to surface commotion—splashing—and tackle shops even sell lures called "bonito splashers." They strike at free-swimming anchovy bait as well as lures. This fish is good eating when smoked.

Halibut
This bottom fish eats anything that passes it by, dead or alive. It's a lethargic fish that hides on the bottom after flipping sand over its body, and with bulging eyes just hangs around waiting for its prey. Another victim of overfishing in local waters, they were large in the past, up to 50 pounds. Nowadays a 10-pounder is a good size. There's a size limit of 22 inches as well as a bag limit of five fish. According to Charlie Davis,

fishing guru of the Pacific coast, the halibut got its name in England, where in the early days all flat fish were called "butts." All butts were saved for priests, or "holy" men, thus *holybutts*, now halibut.

Kelp Or Calico Bass
Found around reefs, rock jetties, breakwaters, and kelp beds, this bass grows to over 10 pounds. It will take most live baits and a variety of lures, but especially likes anchovy, squid, and jack mackerel. It has a large mouth and a three- or four-pound bass can easily consume a bait that weighs half a pound. Favorite time to fish from a local breakwater is about an hour before and several hours after dark. Best fishing is when there's a full moon just a few hours after sundown. This is a great eating fish and cannot be sold; a protected species, its size limit is 12 inches.

Black Sea Bass
This is great trophy material! The black sea bass is the largest of the bass family along the California coast. Very slow growing, it can attain weights of 500 pounds, and since it's estimated that a 300-pounder is 20 years old, the 500-pounder is really a granddaddy. A bottom feeder, it takes most bait but favors bonito, mackerel, squid, barracuda, and whitefish—heavy tackle is in order. A night feeder that usually schools, good catches are made after sundown. When young (under 50 pounds), they're silvery with large purple spots that disappear as the fish dies. The older bass is brownish-black with a bronze blush. These are caught in rocky areas and kelp beds in depths of 60 to 200 feet. Look for these near Anacapa, Santa Barbara, and San Nicolas islands. Great eating!

White Sea Bass
Another favorite eating fish is the white sea bass. It grows to about 70 pounds, but a fish weighing 50 pounds is considered a prize catch. Though they're seen year-round, the best time to catch them is from Jan. through June. Live squid is a desired bait, and fishing after dark can be most effective, but sardines and Pacific green

horsin' around (Oz Mallan)

(clockwise from top) **1.** Elephant seal (Channel Island National Park); **2.** Channel Islands fox (Channel Island National Park); **3.** Island buffalo (Oz Mallan)

SOUTHERN CALIFORNIA FISH-LANDING LOCATIONS

Fishermen can bring their catches into the following Southern California cities and will find a weighing station, good facilities, and supplies:

Avalon, Catalina Island	Hermosa Beach
Gaviota	Redondo Beach
Goleta	Long Beach
Santa Barbara	Seal Beach
Ventura	Huntington Beach
Oxnard	Newport Beach
Port Hueneme	Balboa
Paradise Cove	Laguna Beach
Malibu	Dana Point
Santa Monica	San Clemente
Venice	Oceanside
Marina del Rey	Mission Bay
Manhattan Beach	San Diego

---

mackerel also do the job. **Note**: Don't put your bare hand into the very sharp gills of this fish.

Marlin

Most fishermen feel that once they've caught the big trophy, the marlin, they've made it to the big time. Marlin were first caught around Catalina Island at the beginning of the century. At that time they were almost exclusively caught with trolled flying fish. Though not considered a deluxe food fish in the States, it's been fished by the ton by the Japanese, who make a very popular wiener-like sausage in Japan. Overfishing has diminished the size of the fish. Marlin arrive in Southern California about July and stay as long as the water temperatures and food are to their liking, sometime as long as December. Marlins make for "fun" fishing. They spend most of their time close to the surface, and can be seen jumping if they're in the area. It's not unusual to see a marlin "sleeping" or "sunning" with its tail and the hump of the shoulders out of the water.

Non-fishing Supplies

There are many more varieties of fish that make great sportfishing and/or terrific eating in Southern California. Fishing is not only great for the fisherman, but it's a relaxing way to spend a day on the ocean for the nonfisherman companion. But do make sure you bring a few things to stay comfortable: sunscreen, sun hat, lots of water or other beverages, ice, an extra shirt (a hot sun can burn right through a white T-shirt), motion sickness medication if it's a problem, first-aid kit, waterproof poncho, binoculars, and don't forget the camera and lots of film. Most serious fishermen carry protective gloves. Birdwatchers—bring along a birding book.

KATHY ESCOVEDO-SANDERS

AFTER DARK

It's perfectly safe and highly recommended to meander Avalon's streets after dark. This is a magic time of dancing lights, shimmering sights, and the moon rising dramatically from behind Mt. Ada. Take a romantic walk along Pebbly Beach Road to Abalone Point (aptly named Lovers Cove) for a glimpse of Avalon after dark. Stroll along the serpentine wall of the waterfront; follow the front street, Crescent Ave., past the Tuna Club and the Yacht Club to the Casino. Be sure to take a boat ride over the black silky water for a glimpse of flying fish, or stargaze on a harbor cruise.

ENTERTAINMENT

Movies
The **Casino Theater**, tel. 510-0179, presents first-run movies which change weekly. Two showings—7 and 9:30 p.m.; adult $7, senior $4, child $3. Get there when the box office opens at 7 p.m. (or earlier if it's a popular film— there'll be a line); this will give you a few minutes to inspect the monumental art-deco murals painted 50 years ago by John Beckman. When the movie is over, stroll around the theater to the edge of the seawall for another impressive view of the bay and glimmering Avalon town.

During the summer, the Page organ is played by Bob Salisburg Friday and Saturday nights before the first showing.

Dances
About 10 times a year the big-band sound comes to the world-famous **Casino ballroom**. These events generally begin at 8:30 p.m. and last until 1 a.m. or on Saturday afternoons from 12-4 p.m. The 20,000-square-foot ballroom, which now accommodates 1,200 dancers, is veneered with seven hardwoods laid over cork for an ideal dancing surface. The open balcony encircling the ballroom presents a breathtaking view of stars, moon, and sea. Liquor is served at the bar, and food is sometimes available. For special dances, such as on New Year's Eve and other special dates, an excellent meal is catered in the ballroom. Prices vary according to the event. Drinks average $4. Call the Avalon Chamber of Commerce, tel. 510-1520 or 510-2000, or your local Ticketron office for scheduled bands and ticket information. The Casino ballroom is available for private parties for $2000, tel. 510-0244.

Live Theater
Avalon's amateur theater group is called ACT, **Avalon Community Theater**. This energetic

local company presents several productions during the year. Popular with visitors and home-town audiences, the plays are staged at Tremont Hall (at the end of Tremont St.) and admission is generally adult $6, child $2.50.

Nightclubs

Avalon's nightspots come alive after the sun goes down. The **Channel House Restaurant** at the Metropole Marketplace advertises "light jazz" evenings, seafood, steaks, fabulous bar, patio and decor; 205 Crescent Ave., tel. 510-1617. **Solomon's Landing** is located on the top floor of the **El Encanto Mexican Marketplace** at the end of Crescent Avenue. There's live music and dancing here during the summer months with D.J. Jon Fondy, and the view from the patio is fabulous. **The Galleon** restaurant and bar across from Middle Beach (also on Crescent Ave.) sports a small sidewalk cafe, a great crowd-watching spot, but it's inside where you'll find the action—good live music in the summer and your chance to get up and sing with the help of Karoke—a machine that gives your singing star quality. Don't forget the **Chi-Chi**, 107 Sumner, for a lively afternoon or evening of live music and dancing seven nights a week all summer.

Sportsmen don't despair! For that baseball game or early season football exhibition game you just can't miss, rush to **J.L.'s Locker Room**, 126 Sumner Ave., tel. 510-0258. This is Avalon's only sports bar, with five large-screen TVs dedicated to sports viewers. Drinks are approximately $3.50; open 10 a.m.-2 a.m., cash only. If you just want a quiet spot to share a late-evening espresso with a special person, drop by the **Ristorante Villa Portofino** at 101 Crescent Avenue. **Billy's Bar** at the Catherine Hotel offers casual dining, dancing, spirits, and upbeat summer entertainment, tel. 510-0170.

Arcades

Avalon's two game arcades are located on either end of Crescent Avenue. **Avalon Arcade** is at 601 Crescent, tel. 510-0291; **Mardi Gras Arcade** is at 225 Crescent, tel. 510-0967. Like most arcades everywhere, they have all the latest electronic games, are well lit, and generally crowded with young kids.

Miniature Golf

Golf Gardens is open every day from April through October and weekends during the winter months. This 18-hole park is on a one-acre garden set back one block from the beach. Enter from the Island Plaza. Adults $5, kids (under four feet) $3. Open from 9 a.m. 'til 11 p.m., tel. 510-1200.

Stroll through the El Encanto Marketplace where a variety of stores make evening shopping an event.

Browsing Avalon

Evening is a favorite time for a stroll through the shops. The **Metropole Marketplace** is a browsers' paradise with 30 shops, several clothing stores, gift shops with unique Catalina souvenirs, and an art/gift shop where you can find original drawings and paintings of Catalina. For an after-dinner treat the **Catalina Cookie Company**, home of the "killer brownie," sells homestyle cookies and luscious old-fashioned handmade chocolate turtles and fudge. Or for ice cream go to **Catalina Ice Cream** parlor. You might prefer to walk up a flight of stairs to the **The Blue Parrot** for a drink or dinner on their outdoor patio and enjoy the view over the harbor. After leaving the Metropole Marketplace, wander up Crescent to the **El Encanto Mexican Marketplace**, with its bubbling fountain, Latin atmosphere, shops, and restaurants.

Keith Sheets is just one of the narrator/guides that make the Flying Fish trip fun.

EVENING CRUISES

Shore Boat

An important service for the boating community is the shore boat. The several shore boats which dock at the Pleasure Pier run every hour, shuttling passengers to and from their boats. This is also a fun way to spend an hour sightseeing on the bay; you'll get a close-up view of the many vessels that visit Avalon Harbor—from the small fishing boats to the super-deluxe powerboats docked in the outer harbor to the sleek-lined sailboats. Fare: $2.50 pp for inner and outer harbor.

Harbor Cruise

The shore boat travels to White's Landing three times a day at 3, 6, and 9 p.m., May through Sept., for $10 RT. For those mooring their boats at White's Landing, it's an opportunity for a night out on the town. A harbor cruise around Avalon Bay is also offered for $3 adults, $1.50 children, $2.75 seniors for as long as you care to cruise.

Flying Fish

A boat trip on the *Blanche W* to see the flying fish leaves the Pleasure Pier every evening at dark. These trips start in May and continue into Sept., when the warm Pacific lures the four-winged fish to the waters surrounding Catalina. The boat is an open launch equipped with a 40-million-candlepower searchlight. Attracted by the light, these unusual fish glide as far as 50 feet along the water. They often fly over the boat and have even been known to land in a viewer's lap. The species found in Catalina waters grows 19-24 inches in length and can weigh 1½ to 2 pounds, Goliaths compared to the tiny flying fish common in the South Pacific. They have blue backs and silver bellies, with practically transparent fins that serve as wings. When the wings dry out, the fish plummets back into the water.

The *Blanche W* motors north along the Island's coast, the powerful light playing up and down the steep cliffs that edge the water. It's quite common to see wild goats scattered along the hillside, eyes glowing silver in the light. Be sure to bring a sweater or light jacket because the ocean air after dark can be chilly—even in summer. The trip lasts one hour; adult $6, child $4, senior $5. Tickets and reservations are available from the visitor's information center on Crescent Avenue. For more information and schedules, call 510-2000 in Avalon.

Underwater Gardens

The *Moonstone* is a glass-bottom boat equipped with a powerful light that shines down around its glass wells. A powerful diesel-driven craft, its four sheets of laminated quarter-inch glass allow an unusually clear view of the marine environment. The boat operates year-round, with night trips as long as the weather permits. On this evening trip you may see a hungry sea lion swimming gracefully through the water, chasing after the flying fish that are attracted to the brilliant underwater light. Here's a good opportunity to see certain species of marinelife that hide or

GETTING MARRIED ON CATALINA

Catalina has always been known as the "Isle of Romance" so it's not unusual that more and more couples choose to get married on the Island. Pick a hilltop or a cove, and more than likely a wedding can be planned around it. Newspapers all over the country are filled with curious weddings; couples have tied the knot in hot-air baloons, on boats at sea, skydiving, on horseback, and recently, Catalina's famous marine gardens were the location of a "watery wedding." Kathy Dodge and Michael Michelin, in complete scuba gear, wet suits, plus a floating white veil for the bride were wed underwater with witnesses and videos. Guess what they did for their honeymoon— they spent a week scuba diving.

Weddings By The Sea

Even for traditionalists—couples who just want a plain old wedding with a bouquet of flowers—Catalina has everything to offer. **Weddings By The Sea** suggests a variety of settings from which to choose: garden spots, courtyards, hotel patios, as well as beautiful vistas around the Island. If a couple wants something unique, these wedding specialists are full of ideas. They will assist with coordinating music, photography, video, catering, and flowers. Weddings By The Sea will help you with your vows or use those created yourself. For more information call Anne

Marshall, 510-0-I DO, Box 2173, Avalon, CA 90704. Another choice is **Island Romance.** They will make all the arrangements to ensure that special day on Catalina will be all that it can be. Contact Nancy Russel, wedding and group coordinator, Box 2096, Avalon CA 90704, tel. 510-2096.

Note: The Inn on Mt. Ada is available for $2500, including the rooms. For more information call 510-2030; Box 2560, Avalon, CA 90704. Don't forget the wedding license!

Added Touches

For wedding pictures there are several choices in Avalon: **Elegant Wedding Photography** offers professionally trained, reliable photographers with full studio facilities. Contact Edward Dunn tel. 510-2252. Beautiful fresh flowers (and balloons) are available from **The Other Store** in the Metropole Marketplace, they deliver; tel. 510-2143. **The Avalon Bake Shop** is a full-line bakery that will bake wedding cakes. To order, call 510-0361; Box 2301, 122 Catalina St., Avalon, CA 90704. You can buy a ring at the **Catalina Gold Co.** at the Metropole Marketplace. Any number of restaurants in town would be perfect for a reception—and there's always the Casino ballroom.

cruising on the Blanche W's *Flying Fish trip*

sleep during the day, such as the Catalina lobster. Tickets are sold on the Pleasure Pier and reservations should be made ahead of time. Fare: adult $4.75, child $2.50, senior $3.25.

DINING AND BOATING TRIPS

Sunset Buffet Cruise

At dusk, the **Phoenix,** a large paddle-wheel glass-bottom boat, is converted into a floating buffet supper boat. Cruising leisurely to the rhythm of a live band, it travels north to Long Point. Dancing on the gently rocking deck is a challenge. Leave your wallet at home; all drinks and a sumptuous buffet supper served during the cruise are included in the $32.50 pp fare (children $17.50, seniors $28.50).

It's an unforgettable way to watch the sun set behind the golden Catalina hills. Reservations are a must. Tickets are available in the Island Plaza ticket office and visitor's information center on Crescent Ave., or call 510-2000 in Avalon. Operates four nights a week, departing 6 p.m. mid-May to the end of September. On Sunday the same ship, the *Phoenix,* offers a

Brunch Cruise departing at 10 a.m. for a coastline voyage and a delicious brunch buffet. Adults $14.50, children 5-11 $9, seniors $13.

Twilight Dining

The 5½-hour trip begins at 4:30 p.m. with a 14-mile sightseeing cruise along Catalina's stunning coastline on a comfortable 90-passenger motor vessel to Two Harbors at the Isthmus. This is a special evening of romantic cruising

Cruising the coast is great fun on a Twilight Dining trip.

under the stars, good food, dancing, and a chance to see the fauna that make Catalina unique. On the outgoing passage you'll enjoy the birds, the mountains, the goats, the setting sun, the conviviality of fellow passengers, and of course the comic crew. Once docked, take a walk along Two Harbors' palm-lined beach before your complimentary cocktail and delightful buffet dinner at **Doug's Harbor Reef Restaurant**. Then it's time for music and dancing.

There's more. On your cruise back to Avalon, scan the seas for flying fish, aided by the *Blanche W* 's 40-million-candlepower searchlight. Be sure to bring a light jacket for the return trip. If you still get cold, tell one of the crew; they always carry a good supply of blankets since late evening on the ocean is usually chilly. Get full information and make your reservations for this trip at the Catalina Visitor's Information Center across from the green Pleasure Pier or call

510-2000. Twice a week, summer only, beginning June 15; $32.50 adults, children $17.50, seniors $28.50.

Barbecue It Yourself At The Beach

Every evening the **Descanso Beach Club** fires up its giant barbecue and invites the public to bring their own steaks, fish, or whatever to roast over the hot charcoal. The cost is $6.95 for salads, a baked potato with all the trimmings, bread and butter, and table service. A bar provides alcoholic and nonalcoholic drinks. With all the tropical splendor of a beach open to the sea and sky, you'll truly enjoy this repast under the stars. To get to the Descanso Beach Club, follow the palm trees past the Casino. For reservations call 510-2780 in Avalon. Summer only. Plans to build a new hotel in this cove are in the works, but until construction begins, the barbecues are a great way to go.

WRIGLEY MEMORIAL
AND BOTANICAL GARDEN

William Wrigley Jr. maintained his enthusiasm for Catalina Island from his first visit in 1919 until his death in 1932. He generously spent millions for the development of the Island and put his energies into many projects that are still an important part of the Island's culture today. After his death, the Santa Catalina Island Company built an imposing memorial for him at the head of Avalon Canyon. The Wrigley

Memorial and Botanical Garden, including the site of the memorial, covers almost 38 acres.

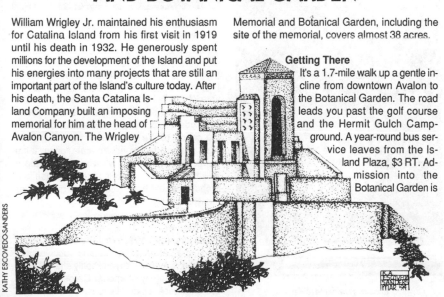

Getting There

It's a 1.7-mile walk up a gentle incline from downtown Avalon to the Botanical Garden. The road leads you past the golf course and the Hermit Gulch Campground. A year-round bus service leaves from the Island Plaza, $3 RT. Admission into the Botanical Garden is

KATHY ESCOVEDO-SANDERS

free for children under 12 and for anyone who belongs to the Wrigley Memorial Foundation. For all other visitors the charge is $1. If you're interested in joining the Wrigley Memorial Foundation, write P.O. Box 88, Avalon, CA 90704, tel. 510-2288.

The Monument
Wrigley's memorial was constructed mostly from native Catalina materials. A graceful lookout tower, it stands 232 feet wide, 180 feet deep, and 130 feet high from the bottom of its wide circular stairway to the top of its main 80-foot tower. Climb the stairs for a stunning view of the Botanical Garden that spreads across the canyon floor below. From the now-defunct Catalina tile production plant initiated by Wrigley, red roof tiles and colorful handmade glazed tiles were used for the interior. Blue flagstones from Little Harbor surface the ramp and both terraces

a walker's first view of the Wrigley Memorial from the road

of the tower. Pink and green marble was brought from Georgia only because it had the coloration to provide the desired finishing effects. At one time Wrigley's body was entombed here, but it has since been moved. In the '50s mischievous local kids would take portable music, climb into the center of the monument, and dance the night away on the luxurious marble floor over the tomb. However, from what is written about William Wrigley, he was a fun-loving man and probably would have had a good giggle over the whole thing.

The Garden
It was originally Mrs. Wrigley's idea to begin planting a garden of cactus and succulents in picturesque Avalon Canyon shortly after 1919. In 1969, the Wrigley Memorial Garden Foundation undertook a plan of expansion and revital-

another view of the tower

CATALINA'S ENDEMIC PLANTS

CATALINA MAHOGANY
(Cerocarpus traskiae)
Catalina mahogany is a large ever-green shrub or
small tree which grows to about 15 feet. The young
shoots are reddish brown. The grayish-green leaves are
thick and leathery; the lower surface covered with dense fur-like hair.
The small whitish floweres usually grow in clusters, and are produced
in great abundance. Following flowering, the seeds, or fruits, grow a
long, hairy twisted tail which gives the plant a most unusual appearance.

ST. CATHERINE'S LACE
(Eriogonum giganteum giganteum)
St. Catherine's lace is usually broader than it is tall
and is generally thought of as an ever-green
shrub. The flowere on this beautiful plant are
borne on long stems well above its silvery
gray-green leaves, and grow in clusters which
form a flat, lacy canopy. The plant is soft
grayish-white in May and June, then turns to
ivory, beige, and light brown, and finally in
autumn it turns a rich russet color.

CATALINA MANZANITA
(Arctostaphylos catalinae)
Catalina manzanita is a spreading evergreen
shrub or small tree which stands as much as
eight feet tall with smooth, dark red bark and
bright green hairy leaves. The leaves are oblong or
elliptical and have a leathery texture. The flowers
bloom from January to March in large spreading clusters at the tips of
the branches and individual flowers are urn-shaped, white, fragrant
and about one-half inch long. The fruit is about three-eighths inch
thick and is pinkish-yellow when forming and usually turns golden
brown to dark brown when mature.

CATALINA LIVE-FOREVER
(Dudleya hassei)
This low-growing succulent rosette-type perennial has
numerous slender, pencil-shaped leaves, which are
bluish to light green. The yellow-white, star-shaped
flowers are borne on fleshy pink stalks which are
five to 15 inches long. It blooms in May and June.

ENDEMIC PLANTS CONTINUED

CATALINA IRONWOOD
(Lyonothamnus floribundus floribundus)
Catalina ironwood is a handsome slender-crowned
evergreen tree which grows 50-70 feet tall with a single
trunk or with a number of stems arising from the
ground. The dark green leaves are three to six inches
long and are generally entire or whole with an occasional
tendency toward a fern-like dissection. It has reddish-brown
stringy bark. The small white flowers, borne in large flat-topped
clusters four to eight inches across, mature in June and July.

YERBA SANTA
(Eriodictyon traskiae traskiae)
This evergreen shrub (not pictured) has shredding bark and a pungent fragrance. It
has an open, sprawling growth habit. The leaves are grayish-white and woolly,
usually toothed and mostly crowded toward the ends of branches. The whitish-purple flowers
cluster on the branch tips, and bloom in May and June.

CATALINA BEDSTRAW
(Galium catalinense)
This plant (not pictured) is a perennial herb with four-angled slender woody stems and branches.
This dense, low-growing under-shrub with inconspicuous whitish flowers blooms from April
through July.

ization, and this garden has since grown into a comprehensive botanical showcase attracting visitors, researchers, students, and teachers. It's a living laboratory for the study of plants endemic to Catalina. It also provides a thriving natural habitat for further study of specimens of particular interest and value—learning how they may be used to ecological advantage. There are hundreds of plant species available for your inspection.

Botanical Studies
All eight known plants endemic to Catalina are included in the garden's collection. In addition, a number of special plants from Santa Rosa, San Clemente, and other Santa Barbara Channel islands, many of them extremely rare, have recently been planted. The garden includes an herbarium and an area for students to study the herbarium specimens. There is an excellent library used for research by the students. **Note:** An herbarium is a collection of dried plant specimens usually mounted and arranged for reference.

KATHY ESCOVEDO-SANDERS

GETTING AROUND IN AVALON

Avalon town is small, just one square mile. It boasts clean, fresh air, broad walkways along the ocean with spectacular coastal views, and narrow, scenic streets up Mediterranean-like hillsides. Visitors cannot bring autos to the Island, and Islanders can ship them over only with a special permit. But there's plenty of public and private transportation, car and bike rentals, and—always the best—your own two feet.

Walking
By far the most popular way to get around this small town is by foot. Many Islanders remember when autos were used only for business and deliveries. In those days the city fathers didn't think twice about barricading a street for a roller-skating party, since there wasn't enough traffic to hinder and no one ever complained. During WW II part of Crescent Avenue was routinely closed off for Saturday night street dances for the servicemen stationed on the Island. Most Avalon streets were built before cars were common transportation, so streets and sidewalks are narrow. Walking these delightful winding

streets or alongside the clear blue water surrounding this smog-free island community remains a favorite pastime of visitors and residents alike.

Foot Traffic
A section of Crescent Ave., the main street which fronts the bay, is reserved for foot traffic (even dogs on leashes are not allowed). One side of the street is lined with shops, restaurants, and small hotels, while the other parallels the beach and Pleasure Pier. Bikes are not allowed.

Shuttle Bus
The shuttle bus around town and to the Botanical Garden operates sporadically with no set schedule or even days of operation during the slow months. It's most likely to run on weekends in summer months for $2 pp.

Bike Rentals
Brown's Bikes, at 107 Pebbly Beach Rd., tel. 510-0986, charges $4 per hour, $12/full day for a single-speed bike, with five- and 18-speed

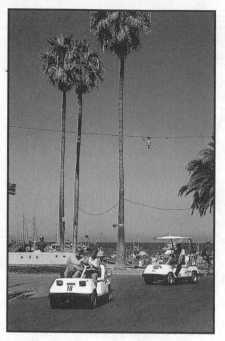

While there are more autos in Avalon than ever, most people get around in golf carts; they're for rent at several places in Avalon.

bikes and tandems available. Ask about special group rentals and baby seats. These bikes may not be taken out of the city limits.

Bring Your Own Bike
Each boat company handles bicycle portage in its own way. See "Getting There" in the "Intro-

duction." Bikes are allowed on the roads of the interior but a bike permit is needed for insurance purposes. The $50 permit is valid for one year and available from the Catalina Conservancy at 206 Metropole Ave., tel. 510-1421. Don't bother chancing it as Conservancy rangers and patrolling sheriff vehicles always check for permits. If you go, be in shape, bring water, and be ready for a wonderful biking experience. Trips to the Botanical Garden, Pebbly Beach, and the Casino make good rides for youngsters and adults.

Taxi
There is one taxi company operating within Avalon city limits: **Catalina Cab Company**. It runs year-round, with a stand on Crescent Ave. across from the Metropole Marketplace, and is easy to find. Several taxis meet each boat; $5-7 will get you up most of the Avalon hills.

Car Rentals
Catalina Auto and Bike Rentals, on the corner of Metropole and Crescent, tel. 510-0111, rents manual-shift "towncar" compacts for four people by the hour for $30 with a $30 deposit; for six people at $50/hour with a $50 deposit. A map of Avalon comes with all rentals. You can drive within the city limits only; this includes Botanical Garden and Pebbly Beach. **Island Rentals**, 125 Pebbly Beach Rd., tel. 510-1456, wants $30 an hour with a $30 deposit. **Cartopia Car Rental**, 615 Crescent Ave., rents electric golf-type carts for about $30 per hour with a $30 deposit.

WALKING TOURS OF AVALON

In Avalon strike out on foot. Avalon is a small town with narrow streets to explore and many architecturally unusual houses to view, some constructed on the original 20-foot-wide lots laid out by George Shatto, who developed Avalon in the late 1800s. Land is scarce in Avalon and property values have skyrocketed over the years, so landowners have used remodeling techniques to garner every possible inch of living space. About half the homes are built on the level streets just up from the Pleasure Pier, called the "flats" by the Islanders, while the other half climb the hills, giving Avalon a sunny Mediterranean-island appearance. On these walking tours you'll discover homes built before there were many roads in Avalon; a few still can only be reached by a flight of stairs up a hill to the front door.

Take your camera, your *Catalina Island Handbook,* and, if you're prone to sunburn, a hat and sunscreen. Be prepared for a few steep climbs.

Whittley Walk
From Crescent Ave. on the shoreline start up Whittley. Turn left at East Whittley, the first street you come to, and follow its steep curve up around to the right. As you walk up East Whittley you pass several small houses; the second from the corner on the right was built in 1903 for $500 and is still occupied by the Trout family, descendants of the 1911 owners. Originally the little house was built on one of the small lots leased from Banning's SCI Company. When Whittley St. was widened the house next door on the corner of Whittley and East Whittley was moved eight feet and pushed right up under the eaves of the Trout house. After Wrigley purchased the Island, the Trouts were able to buy the land beneath their house. Farther on your right you come to the Christian Science church and a Spanish-style house with a red-tile roof. Both were built by a devout Christian Scientist, Count Mankowski, an avid fisherman who loved Catalina. The count was married to an American woman named Morris; though of Polish descent the count was a British citizen who enjoyed summers on Catalina. The church next door was built at the same time and in the same Spanish style as his classic home; he kept his horses across the street in a stable that overlooked the bay. The stable has been replaced by a modern apartment building.

Continue on up to the top of the hill, from where East Whittley curves to your right and then turn left over to Marilla Ave. downhill. Follow Marilla a short distance to Hiawatha Ave. on the left and up another short street where you come to the Barlow House with its wide circular porch.

Barlow House
In the early 1900s a circus act called the Travillo Brothers came to Catalina Island on a talent hunt for a new member for their team. The search took them to Seal Rocks off the east end of the Island, where the California sea lion hauling ground was mobbed with potential ball-bouncing circus stars. While on the Island the family quickly decided that this was where they wanted to settle. This became a reality in 1906, when the Travillo family built the charming circular house. Their sea lions trained in the yard overlooking Avalon town. Mrs. Travillo had a gift shop on Crescent Ave. and sold abalone shells provided by her diver sons, Ford, Jack, and Guy. They were also among the avid coin divers who would meet the boat and shout, "Throw a coin!" These divers could hold a mouthful, and actually had a lucrative business going.

The family sold the house to an opera singer who spent her summers on the Island, and she in turn sold it to Mr. Feek, principal of the local school. In 1923, Sarah C. Smith purchased the house. It has remained in her family ever since, used as a summer home until 1973 when Sarah's daughter, Liz Barlow, retired from her teaching career and moved to Catalina. This elegant home, designated as a Historical House, will be preserved in its gracious turn-of-the-century style for future generations to appreciate. From here Hiawatha soon completes its angular half circle to meet Marilla Ave., where once again you come to Crescent Ave., your starting point.

Zane Grey Home

This walk takes you up above the Casino building for another spectacular view of Avalon and the bay. From Crescent Ave. head up Marilla Avenue. Turn right on Vieudelou and follow the curve to Chimes Tower Road. Before you arrive at the Chimes you pass the Zane Grey Hotel to your left, built in 1926 by Zane Grey, big-game fisherman and famed Western novelist. This Hopi Indian pueblo-style home fit the rough-and-ready life-style of its remarkable owner. The living and dining room, graced by a fireplace with a log mantle, has open-beam ceilings shaped from teak brought from Tahiti aboard Grey's yacht, *The Fisherman*. An oak dining table with heavy benches and a hand-hewn upright piano are some of the massive furnishings that still grace the home. Zane Grey

spent most of his later life in Avalon writing and fishing. As he said about Catalina in *What the Open Means to Me,*

> *"I used to climb the mountain trail that overlooked the Pacific and here a thousand times I shut my eyes and gave myself over to sensorial perceptions. . . . It is an environment that means enchantment to me. Sea and mountain! Breeze and roar of surf! . . . I could write here and be at peace."*

Born Pearl Zane Grey in Zanesville, Ohio, in 1872, Zane Grey wrote 89 books before his death in 1939 at age 67.

Chimes Tower

Farther up and across Zane Grey Rd. is the Chimes Tower. Manufactured by the Deagan Company in Chicago at a cost of $25,000, these chimes have been tolling the time every 15 minutes since 1925, when they were presented as a gift to the town of Avalon by Mrs. Ada Wrigley. On holidays and special occasions the electric console is played manually, the resonance blending in with the surrounding harbor-sounds

Zane Grey Home and Chimes Tower, late 1930s

WALKING TOURS
OF AVALON

© MOON PUBLICATIONS, INC.

to create a cadence unique to Catalina. From this spot, looking across the bay you'll have a good view of the Holly Hill House on the southeast tip of Avalon Bay. Its conical-shaped roof can't be missed.

Holly Hill House

In 1888, a remarkable man named Peter Gano bought what some consider to be the choicest parcel of land in Avalon from George Shatto for $500. An engineer with extensive experience in waterworks, Gano generously offered to de-

sign Avalon's first freshwater system, laying pipe from Avalon Canyon Springs to the only large building at that time, the Metropole Hotel. He shipped building supplies from the Mainland to Avalon aboard his boat, the *Osprey*. On the project, his only helper was Mercury, a former circus horse that performed the heavy labor of this monumental task. Gano designed an ingenious cable-car system to carry his equipment up the steep incline to the top of the hill. Mercury, on whistle command, walked down the hill, pulling ropes wound around pulleys to power the loaded cable car up the hill to the building site. Gano also laid water pipes directly to his home site and designed a three-cistern system to catch rainfall. He was a craftsman who took great pride in his work, building the house to last with strong, durable materials. The open-air circular cupola patio with the cone-shaped roof captures the attention of everyone who visits the Island. And living in the house must be an even greater pleasure; beautiful vistas of the sea and Avalon town from every window.

This remarkable man has a bittersweet legend associated with his name. Fable tells us that he labored on the house for the love of a lady. But when it was completed, she couldn't bring herself to give up Mainland society for life in a small seaside village—even in a fabulous house built for entertaining. She told Gano it was either her or the house. Convinced she would change her mind, he chose the house—naming it **Look Out Cottage**. The battle of wills ended when ultimately she married another, leaving Gano to live alone in his hand-built masterpiece until very old age. Old-timers who were children during Gano's time tell of signs posted around his house that stated bluntly, No Women Allowed.

The house has had four owners since it was completed in 1890. The Giddings family bought it from Gano in 1921 and renamed it Holly Hill House (for the abundant holly that grew on the hill) and for the next 40 years spent their summers in Avalon. In 1971, the Smiths (along with the Richard Land Company) bought it with the intention of developing the property below the house into condominiums. Excavation began, destabilizing the foundation of the house. To make the hill safe again extensive steel, concrete, and Gunite repairs were made, but the condos were never built. Then soon after the repairs were completed a fire destroyed the cupola roof.

In 1971, Holly Hill House was bought by Victor and Shari Kreis, frequent visitors to Catalina and longtime admirers of this Victorian house on the hill. The Kreises' first project was to rebuild the cupola; since then the family has been involved in an energetic restoration program. In an ongoing project, old photos are studied and every detail is painstakingly approached with the original Gano house in mind. Modern improvements from earlier renovations were replaced with antique or old-style carpentry and appliances. Wood was stripped and brought back to its original luster; furniture of the era was brought in—the family uses a 1907 gas stove in their 1890s kitchen. Visiting this house is a trip into the past. Contact the Catalina Museum, Box 366, Avalon, CA 90704, tel. 510-2414, for information about special group tours.

Pebbly Beach/Mt. Ada Walk

This is a good early-morning stroll. Walk toward the mole and continue on Pebbly Beach Rd. along the ocean boardwalk, where you'll meet other early risers—fishermen, walkers, and joggers. The sun rises over this part of the ocean, and it's a sparkling, invigorating walk past Lovers Cove Beach, a nice place to stop and watch the fish splashing out of the water, looking for breakfast.

At Pebbly Beach is a small airport, with a cement ramp for landing amphibious planes, and a helicopter pad. Lots of traffic flies in and out of this little airport. Freight is brought in on a special amphibian, and passenger-carrying helicopters land here throughout the day. Stop for breakfast (or lunch or dinner) at the Buffalo Nickel. If you're a plane buff, the rooftop patio offers a great vantage point from which to watch the amphibs and helicopters come and go. The restaurant also serves meals inside (you can get buffalo burgers here).

The Southern California Edison Company maintains its desalination and utility plant in Pebbly Beach, and about a dozen families live across the road. Past the houses the road turns up the hill and eventually meanders by the former home of William Wrigley Jr. In 1919, after the Wrigleys purchased the Island, they chose Mt. Ada, 350 feet above the bay, for their future home. It's said that Mrs. Wrigley (Ada) determined that from here she could see the sun rise and set with the purple hills of Avalon as a backdrop. The house was built in 1921, with only the immediate area around the structure landscaped. (At night well-positioned floodlights turn the building into a floating white mansion against the black hillside.)

In 1978, the estate was donated to the University of Southern California for use as an academic and cultural center. Managed by the university's Institute for Marine and Coastal Studies, seminars and workshops were held here year-round, hosting such groups as the U.S. Geological Survey, the U.S. Office of Naval Research, and other organizations from many parts of the world. Today, Wrigley's home is a fabulous bed and breakfast establishment called **The Inn On Mt. Ada**. For the lazies who don't hike, the Avalon Scenic Tour takes you past Mt. Ada (see "Guided Tours," below).

Mount Buena Vista

While walking, look across the street and below the entrance to Mt. Ada. There's a large white cross on the side of the hill. At one time Mt. Buena Vista was the location of a park and terminus of an old incline railway, called Island Mountain Railway. The little railroad operated two cars: one going from the amphitheater (at the end of Crescent Ave.) up to the summit at Buena Vista, and one going from the summit down to Lovers Cove. It was built in 1904 and dismantled in 1920.

For over 60 consecutive years Buena Vista has been the location of the colorful costumed Easter sunrise pageant presented by the Island community. If you happen to be in Avalon on Easter, the city provides free bus service to the hill site from downtown on Easter morning (ask the chamber of commerce for time and details). To return to Crescent Ave. from Buena Vista, continue walking down the hill and you'll end up on lower Clemente St. a half block from Crescent Avenue. The views from Buena Vista and Mt. Ada of the bay, the town, the harbor, and the purple mountains are breathtaking.

Tremont Street

From Crescent Ave. turn up Sumner Ave. and continue to the end and turn right onto Tremont Street. On your left you pass newly built rental condos and a few of the original stucco "ranchitos" built by William Wrigley Jr. for the many Mexican families that he hired to help with the development of the Island. Turn left on Metropole (another steep incline), following the hill down to Crescent Avenue.

Country Club Road Walk

From Crescent Ave. walk up Catalina Street. In the second block on the left you pass the Catalina Bible Church. This building was the home of author Gene Stratton Porter, born in 1868 in Indiana. Two of her best-sellers were *Freckles* and *Laddie*. Ms. Porter spent several summers in her home called Singing Waters before her death in 1924. At the end of Catalina St. turn right past Avalon Canyon Rd. and go left up Country Club Road. Continue on this road, which wanders past the Country Club, the exclusive Palms Restaurant, putting green, golf pro shop, tennis courts, tee-off area for the golf course, and a place to stop for a cool drink at the golf course. Farther on is the turnoff for the cemetery on the left. Country Club Rd., bordered by dozens of eucalyptus trees, takes you past the large, pleasant Catalina Canyon Hotel and Canyon Restaurant. Turn left on East Whittley (go down and veer right on Whittley), which ends at Crescent Avenue.

DAY-HIKES OUTSIDE THE CITY OF AVALON

These trails take you short distances out of town, and in some cases you must backtrack on the same trails; in others, a circular route will be given. Hike with a companion and bring water since it's not available on the trail.

Catalina Stable To Botanical Garden

From downtown, continue up Sumner Ave. and follow it to the left of Country Club Road. Pass the golf course on the left, and take the left "V" when you come to the Sand Trap Restaurant and Pitch and Putt Golf Course. Continue past the Catalina Stables, and just beyond the picnic grounds is the graded dirt road to the Botanical Garden. This easy hike takes about an hour each way.

Jail Road/Indian Trail To Stage Road
Along fire roads, most involving steep slopes. At 1,460 feet this is a spectacular vantage point. From here you can see the Island's rugged coastline and (when Mainland smog doesn't interfere) the San Gabriel Mountains across the channel. Strenuous hike.

Hermit Gulch Trail/Canyon Road/Divide Road
These steep slopes on undeveloped pathways combine for a strenuous hike, five hours for a good hiker, with little shade along the way.

Renton Mine Road/Mt. Ada Road To East Mountain
Expect moderate to steep slopes along a graded dirt road, strenuous hike; plan about three hours for the hardy hiker.

DAY-HIKES AROUND AVALON

© MOON PUBLICATIONS, INC.

KATHY ESCOVEDO-SANDERS

GUIDED TOURS

Santa Catalina Island Company's Discovery Tours offers a variety of guided tours for the visitor who wants to see as much of the Island as possible in a short amount of time. You can wander the hills and Interior on your own feet, but it's a big island—76 square miles. For most visitors these tours are the only opportunity to see the Island's interior and its distant coves. The roomy motorstage is comfortable, the boats are fun, and the guides are witty, well versed, and pleasant.

Visitor's Information Center
Ask about money-saving combinations for three of the described trips at the visitor's information center on Crescent Ave. across from the green Pleasure Pier, tel. 510-2500, Box 737, Avalon, CA 90704. Here you'll find a preview of sights available, with backlighted photos, historical exhibits, a topographic display, and videos of the Island. Visitors are invited to browse the literature racks for a wealth of information and will find enthusiastic, friendly people to answer questions and make reservations.

Avalon Scenic Tour
This 50-minute trip is especially gratifying for the one-day visitor. The bus leaves from the Sumner Ave. side of Island Plaza and passes Avalon's major points of interest. You first travel along Avalon's beaches and into the hills that surround its sparkling bay. The bus takes you by the **Inn On Mt. Ada** (today a bed and breakfast but originally the residence of Mr. and Mrs. William Wrigley Jr.), along the waterfront, through the residential section of Avalon, and to vistas that are perfect for picture taking—the views are fabulous. Fare: adult $5, senior $4.50, child $3.25.

Skyline Drive
This two-hour tour is a good way to see part of the interior if you only have a day. It takes you 10 miles inside the Santa Catalina Island Conservancy's nature preserve to the Airport-In-The-Sky. Along Catalina's skyline you see mountain scenery on one side and deep canyons and hidden coves indenting the coastline on the other. Flora here, such as the Catalina iron-

wood tree, can only be seen on Catalina. Ironwood trees, once common in the western United States, have been extinct on the Mainland for over 20,000 years. This rugged country is also the home of Catalina's wild animals: buffalo, deer, goat, boar, and fox. The tour departs from the bus terminal in the Island Plaza; reservations required. Part of the fare goes to the Santa Catalina Island Conservancy and is a tax-deductible contribution; adult $10.50, senior $9.50, child $7.

Inland Motor Tour

If you plan on spending several days in Catalina, take the four-hour Inland Tour. Though more expensive than some of the other trips, this half-day trip is well worth your time and money. The tour goes to the heart of the 66 square miles of rugged wildlands owned by the Conservancy. You travel along a high ridge, with vistas of rolling hills on one side and the vast Pacific on the other. You'll see Middle Ranch nestled in a valley with growing crops and farmhouses.

Refreshments are served at **Rancho Escondido,** where you're a guest at a demonstration where two riders (one western, one English) put the purebred Arabian horses through their paces. Wander the grounds of the ranch and visit the tack room where the Wrigley family stable gear is stored, including remarkable silver riding equipment, ornate bridles, carved saddles, and old and new photos of the family in equestrian gear. In the trophy room watch a video that shows the Arabians and tells the history of the Wrigleys, their horses, and Rancho Escondido. In another part of the ranch are old stagecoaches that at one time carried tourists along Catalina's dirt roads. Today's modern buses were designed to somewhat resemble the old stages of yesteryear. Returning to Avalon, the bus circles back by way of the Airport-In-The-Sky and along the high ridge overlooking hidden coves along the Catalina coast. The bus leaves from the Island Plaza daily at 9 a.m. and 3 p.m.; adult $19.50, senior $18, child $12.50. Reservations required.

Casino Tour

Take this 45-minute walking tour for a complete circuit of the Casino. A tram ride from the Island Plaza brings you to Casino Point, and from there the group is escorted by a guide through the landmark building. You're taken into the theater on the bottom floor to view the heroic-sized murals, intricate architecture, and see the colossal Page pipe organ (though not advertised, once in a while an organist will demonstrate its many sound effects). From here you'll walk the ramp to the mezzanine and the large ballroom. The balcony surrounding the dance floor is a perfect vantage point from which to photograph Avalon Bay—and imagine the romance of an evening, of music, and a moon lighting the sea. A tram ride back into Avalon concludes the tour; adult $5, child $4.

Coastal Cruise

The 55-minute Coastal Cruise goes to the eastern tip of Catalina—past the "working" side of the Island. Here's where boaters find the boat yard, where the Edison Company runs its desalination and electric plants, and from here the barge hauls freight back and forth to the Mainland. The cruise boat passes the small seaplane airport and helipad, and farther down is the rock quarry where millions of tons of rocks and boulders have been removed from the Island to be used in most of the seawalls and breakwaters around Los Angeles Harbor and Southern California's coast.

When the sea lions are "at home," it's a wonderful opportunity to see them in their natural habitat. Since pinnipeds (in this case California sea lions and harbor seals) are migratory animals, viewing them depends on the season. California sea lions don't pup on the Island, but the harbor seals do. So during the mating season, beginning as early as June, the males take their harems to a private cove; in July and Aug. they return to Seal Rocks in larger numbers to sun themselves, swim, and dive for fish. The tour departs from the Pleasure Pier; adult $5, senior $4.50, child $3.25.

GLASS-BOTTOM BOATS

In addition to its many other unusual "firsts," Catalina holds the distinction of being the place where a glass-bottom boat was first used. Inspired by the glass-bottomed box that fishermen used for a better view under the surface of the water when untangling lines or to spot abalone on the rocks below, Charles Feige created the first practical glass-bottom rowboat in 1896. In 1897, a glass-bottom sternwheeler was built of boiler iron by P.J. Waller; it was operated with wheels, bicycle fashion. After more study it was found that a power-driven boat didn't disturb the water and its inhabitants as originally believed.

MV *Phoenix*
Today, the MV *Phoenix*, built in Wilmington, California in 1931, is operated daily by the Santa Catalina Island Company. The *Phoenix* leisurely cruises Catalina's marine gardens in Lovers Cove. Many radiantly colored fish thrive in Lovers Cove, the most vivid resident being the golden garibaldi, a species of perch. Others you may see are the silver perch, button perch, and the toothy sheepshead. Occasionally, a transparent jellyfish will float by. Adding grandeur to the scene is the iodine kelp forest with its amber tendrils and leaves reaching up 100 feet and more to the surface, supported by air bulbs. Daylight trips depart from the Pleasure Pier frequently during the summer months. A 40-minute trip, fares are adult $5, senior $4.50, child $3.25. The new glass-bottom *Moonstone* offers night trips through the bay.

Other Discovery Tours
For the Flying Fish Tour, Sunset Buffet Cruise, or Twilight Dining at Two Harbors, see "After Dark."

Adventure Tours
Another tour company in Avalon offers a variety of tours and will give information at their office at 311 Sumner Ave., tel. 510-0409. Shuttle Bus Tours takes passengers from the heart of Avalon to the hills and beyond on air-conditioned coaches. Visit the Island's magnificent interior and enjoy peaceful coves, with breathtaking views, fascinating landmarks, and unique wildlife.

Seaview
Adventure Tours' glass-bottom boat embarks on 45-minute night trips as well as daytime cruises. The *Seaview* is equipped with a brilliant light that attracts a variety of sealife and makes it possible to view bottom dwellers not ordinarily seen by day. It departs from the Pleasure Pier daily and each evening during the summer months; ask about a combination day-and-night ticket. Fare: adult $5.50, senior $3.50, child $3.25. Other Adventure Tours: Botanical Garden Trip, City & Botanical Garden Tour, City Tour, and Inside Adventure Tour.

For more information and prices, offices are located at the Cabrillo Mole Terminal and a second at the Pleasure Pier. Call (in the L.A. area) 800-FUNSUN, in Avalon call 510-2888; P.O. Box 1314, Avalon, CA 90704.

RANCHO ESCONDIDO

Within 10 years after William Wrigley Jr. had acquired Catalina and the Santa Catalina Island Co., his son Philip began making plans for the development of the interior. After many months of traveling through the beautiful countryside, he came upon a setting called Cottonwood Canyon that he thought would make an ideal site for a horse ranch. He and the rest of his scouting group set up camp to get acquainted with the area. It was a good move; the wind howled through the canyon, and it turned out to be a cold place. As Wrigley put it, "We quickly found out from bitter experience that it was the wrong spot except during the middle of the day."

As it turned out, Cottonwood led them to the location that would prove to be just right, only a short distance away. The setting was lovely, but as they discovered, it was not easy to locate the second time. Undoubtedly that's why the ranch was ultimately called El Rancho Escondido ("The Hidden Ranch"). Even now, surrounded with tall eucalyptus, the ranch remains hidden from sight until you're just a few hundred yards away.

As the first set of buildings was begun, plans were in the making to breed a Catalina Arabian horse. Helen and Philip Wrigley were the owners of two Arabians and were much impressed by their beauty and stamina. They then had to find a horseman to take charge of this frontier location and develop it into a ranch. The choice was Jack White, a longtime cattleman. In 1931, this lanky, leathery-faced Westerner, who felt more at home on a horse than anyplace else, tackled the job. It was at about this time that the first gray stallion, called Kaaba, was transported to the Island. The horse and White did a good job; Jack didn't even mind sleeping in a tent for the first months while the ranch took shape.

The breeding program was initiated under the experienced eye of Millard

Johnson, who said he'd try it out for a "few months." Jack White eventually took over the SCI Co. cattle ranch, and Johnson ended up running the ranch—for the next 16 years. During WW II the breeding program was put on hold, but by 1949 Escondido had grown to include over 75 horses and was the largest purebred Arabian breeding ranch in Southern California.

Millard Johnson's young assistant, Joe Dawkins, took over in 1951. He knew horses and he liked people; it was at about this time that the SCI Co. began its new bus tour called the "Inland Motor Tour." Tourists were taken on a good bus tour of the interior, with a donut-and-rodeo stop at Rancho Escondido—it continues to be a favorite attraction on Catalina. Every visitor to the Island should make a point of taking the Inland Tour, not only to see Catalina's rugged interior, but to have the opportunity to see what Catalina Arabian horses are all about. Escondido's Arabians have garnered hundreds of awards over the years and have started a dynasty of Catalina Arabians. The number of Arabians on the ranch varies between 16 and 20. The Wrigley family visits the ranch several times a year, and needless to say they are all avid riders.

Since Dawkins retired in 1972, several ranchers have managed El Rancho Escondido. The newest resident manager (since October 1991) is Richard Welch, a cowboy, formerly of Scottsdale, Arizona, with a background in training hard-to-break horses. The Spanish-style ranch buildings are graceful and built mostly from Catalina materials, right up to the

showing a working horse (Inland Tour)

red tiles on the roof (from Catalina's old tile factory). Shaggy eucalyptus trees surround the buildings, giving welcome shade on hot, sunny days. The grounds are spotless and well kept. Visit the tack room, with its hundreds of ribbons, awards, interesting saddles, and pictures of the Wrigley family and their horses. A video of the Wrigleys and their horses is shown during the stopover. Also, take a look at some of the original stagecoaches that rolled along the dirt roads in the early days of Catalina's development.

The most exciting part of the visit is the show put on each day (twice daily during summer months) for visitors. Midge, Richard's wife and equine assistant, explains the history of the Arabian horse. In an arena with bleacher seats for guests, ranch-hands, in western dress as well as Arabian garb, put the horses through exercises that show what the breed is capable of doing as a working ranch animal. Don't miss this great show, even if you aren't a horse person.

KATHY ESCOVIDO-SANDERS

CATALINA'S INTERIOR

TWO HARBORS

In 1602, when Vizcaino approached the mountains of Catalina which rose out of the Pacific, the explorer was certain he had reached two islands. From a distance, the bulk of land on the east end of Catalina appears to taper to a low point. Here the sea seems to separate the east end from the small nub on the west end. Actually, there is no separation, only a low-lying neck, a half-mile-wide isthmus just 50 feet at its summit, comprising the narrowest section of Catalina Island. The ocean side of this isthmus is Catalina Harbor, the most protected harbor on the Island; the channel side is Isthmus Cove. This area is now called Two Harbors, 14 miles by ocean and 23 miles by road from Avalon.

HISTORY

For many years, Two Harbors, at one time called Union Harbor, was also referred to as the "Isthmus." It is the site of some of the most intriguing Island history. Allegedly, this is where one of the largest groups of Indians was located, along with the still-sought "temple," or *yuva'r,* observed by the Vizcaino expedition. Their description fits the worship of the religious cult of Chingichnich that was the custom of most of the Gabrielinos at the time. You can still see the sinkholes of the gold mines that flourished at the Isthmus, Cherry Valley, and Fourth of July Cove in the 1860s. The Civil War barracks, built in 1863, are still in use by the Isthmus Yacht Club. Most of the roughnecks of the gold rush were driven out after the arrival of the Union volunteers. (See "History" in the main "Introduction" for details.)

Fact Or Fiction?

The history of Catalina abounds with legends. In most cases there is a minutia of truth. But as time passes and the stories are repeated, they take on the embellishments of each storyteller. Most pirates and smugglers did not keep diaries, or, if they did, none have ever been found. Still, some stories persist; accept them for what they are, legends that may or may not be historically accurate.

Buried Treasure

The brig *Danube*, out of New York, was wrecked in 1824 on the rocks near San Pedro. Samuel Prentiss and other survivors made their way to the San Gabriel Mission. There Prentiss found an old Gabrielino Indian called Turie, alleged to be a chieftain from Catalina Island. The 70-year-old Indian, close to death, welcomed Prentiss's friendship. Before he died, Turie told Prentiss about Island Indians who had buried rich treasure beneath a tree on Catalina. He sketched a crude map, which launched the legendary treasure hunt of Sam Prentiss.

Prentiss returned to the site of the wreck in San Pedro, and ,from the salvage of the *Danube*, he built himself a small vessel and set sail for Catalina. In the middle of the channel he was caught in a severe storm. Everything he owned was washed overboard, and it was all he could do to keep himself alive in the small boat. The treasure map was buried at the bottom of the sea, but the dream was not forgotten. Prentiss

made it to the Island, remembering only that the treasure was buried at the base of a tree. He built a small cabin overlooking Emerald Bay. For the next 30 years he hunted sea otter, fished, and spent every extra moment searching for his treasure. Gripped by the dream of riches, he sold firewood from the trees he cut down and dug up in his relentless quest for the mysterious treasure.

He is purported to be the first white man to die on Catalina Island. Today, near where his cabin stood, you can see the wind-grazed tombstone erected by Joseph Banning, one of the early owners of Catalina:

In memory of
Samuel Prentiss
A native of Massachusetts
Came to California in 1824
Died on Catalina 1854—Age 72.

Apparently he never found the treasure. Keeping his secret to himself almost until the day he died, he ultimately shared it with Santos Louis Bouchette, giving rise to yet another bit of Island lore.

Catalina Harbor in the early 1900s. Today the harbor is usually filled with pleasure boats.

SANTA CATALINA ISLAND CO.

Bouchette

Santos Louis Bouchette was the son of one of the survivors of the *Danube* shipwreck. When Prentiss shared his secret with this young man, it stimulated within Bouchette's heart the same urges and desires about the treasure that had consumed Prentiss for 30 years. Bouchette also began the search, but he was luckier than Prentiss—or maybe wilier. In the midst of his treasure hunt he stumbled across rich veins of silver, lead, and gold. There are those who tell the story a little differently, saying that Bouchette "salted" the mine to encourage heavy financial backing from outsiders. Whether this is true or not, his mine was incorporated under the name of Mineral Hills Mines Company, and it became his real treasure.

Bouchette operated the mine for some years. On one of his many cross-channel trips to the pueblo of Los Angeles, after a whirlwind romance, he came back to the Island married to a French dance-hall girl. The story goes that she didn't like the rough life the miners led, so Bouchette built her an elaborate house 1 miles from Johnson's Landing, furnishing it with English mahogany furniture and a plate-glass mirror from France that cost him $1000. He kept borrowing money to keep his mining venture solvent, and continued to prospect around every tree even remotely likely to be the one that guarded the treasure of Turie, the old Indian chief.

After some time his wife was apparently still dissatisfied—or could Bouchette have finally found Samuel Prentiss's long-coveted Indian treasure? For one day in the spring of 1876 Bouchette and his wife were seen loading silver ore and a few provisions into their sailboat, and they were never seen again.

Gold

Francisco Lopez, a Mexican youth, has been credited with discovering the first gold in California, near Newhall in 1842. While digging up a wild onion he found a gold nugget entangled in its roots. However, according to Catalina legend, Captain George Yount, a friend and associate of Samuel Prentiss, discovered an outcropping of gold-bearing quartz in a canyon near Two Harbors in 1830, a full 12 years before the strike at Sutter's Mill that started the California gold rush. Yount was deeply involved in otter hunting, and the bit of quartz he chipped off and stuffed into his pocket in Cherry Valley was forgotten until the Sutter's Mill find. He returned to the Island three times over the years trying to rediscover, without success, the location of the gold quartz he had first seen.

In a fit of depression, the sea captain shared his frustrating story with gold miners on the Mainland, which began the gold stampede on Catalina Island. There are various stories concerning the amount of gold found. Some say there was a lot, but the cost of mining was prohibitive. Others say the quality of the ore was not high. In 1873, after discovering the difficulties involved in using burros to get ore out of Silver Canyon, an English syndicate forfeited its dreams and a $40,000 down payment to George Shatto.

The First Tourists

The Banning brothers, who owned the Island from 1892 to 1919, made one of the first changes to the landscape of the Isthmus. They could see its potential as a fishing paradise, so to encourage tourists a fishing bungalow was built on the hill between the two harbors in 1910. As the Bannings and then the Wrigleys developed the Island, the Isthmus, now called Two Harbors, also grew—but not in the same manner as Avalon.

As more people discoved Catalina, it remained a harbor only for those who could indulge in the luxury of yachting. This limited traffic during the 1920s and '30s to the elite. Christian's Hut, a Polynesian-style resort with a tropical-beach atmosphere, was a gathering spot for the affluent, glamorous film celebrities of that era. The Isthmus was a place where they could get away from autograph seekers and socialize with others who shared their status. The "star" status is far less important now, though some years ago everyone was thrilled when John Wayne brought his large yacht, the *Wild Goose,* to Two Harbors.

Today, Two Harbors quietly bustles with campers, boaters, and vacationers who enjoy the serenity of low rolling hills and the fresh breeze that skips across the narrow strip of land from the Pacific Ocean side of the Island.

Movies

Many films were shot at Two Harbors, especially in the days of the silents when the noise of the elements was unimportant. The shaggy palm trees and clear blue water met by a smog-free sky were the backdrop for several talkies: *Mutiny On The Bounty, Treasure Island, The Sea Witch, McHale's Navy,* and later in 1976, *MacArthur.*

For many years the *Ning Po,* a nefarious Chinese junk built in China in 1773, was an attraction at Catalina Harbor. With an unsavory history including piracy, smuggling, and destruction at sea, it was rebuilt by an enterprising businessman for use as a Chinese cafe at the Isthmus, where it was also a prop in several movies. Built of camphor and ironwood, no nails were used in its construction; each joint was carefully fitted. The *Ning Po* stood as a monument to the genius of the Chinese shipbuilding industry. It was ultimately destroyed by the sea and lies buried beneath the mud in Catalina Harbor.

Catalina Marine Science Center

Operated by the University of Southern California's Institute for Marine and Coastal Studies, courses through USC and other universities in the marine sciences both at undergraduate and graduate levels are conducted at the Marine Science Center. Located at Two Harbors' Big Fisherman Cove, the center was established in 1968 through a Santa Catalina Island Company

SANTA CATALINA ISLAND CO.

Hesperia, *the ship used in making the film version of Robert Louis Stevenson's* Treasure Island. *This classic children's adventure story, directed by Victor Fleming for MGM and starring Wallace Beery and Jackie Cooper, was filmed at the Isthmus of Catalina in 1935. For the past 63 years, Two Harbors and other Catalina coves have served as venues for such films as* MacArthur *and* The Sea Witch, *and more recently as the backdrop for TV dramas.*

gift and lease of 45 land acres and 360 acres of sea floor. The facility has been used by the National Geographic Society to film lobster moulting (lobsters shed their skins as they grow). Scientists from all over the world occasionally gather to study the sea and Catalina's undeveloped surroundings. Buildings include laboratories, dormitories for students, and a hyperbaric chamber for emergency treatment of the bends (open to anyone along the Southern California coast who needs it).

Groups of 15 or more can prearrange a guided tour of the facility, which will include an illustrated lecture about the research at Catalina Marine Science Center, a viewing of the award-winning documentary about the kelp forests of Catalina, a visit to the touch tank, and a walking tour of the laboratory and the hyperbaric chamber; takes two hours, $5 pp. The complex is a pleasant 2.2-mile hike from the center of Two Harbors, or take the shore boat which leaves from the Two Harbors dock.

The area along the waterfront of the Marine Science Center is a marinelife refuge. The public is not allowed to anchor a boat, to fish, or to take anything away, and the moorings are for Center use only. **Note:** In the event of a storm, the moorings in front of the Science Center are available to boaters in distress. For information about the program offered to marine-science students, write: Resident Director, Catalina Marine Science Center, P.O. Box 398, Two Harbors, CA 90704-5044, tel. 510-0811, (310) 743-6792. (See below.)

GETTING THERE

From The Mainland
There was a time when the only way to Two Harbors was by private boat; today it is easily accessible via several routes. Both the speedy Express boats and the fastest Super Express depart from the **San Pedro Air and Sea Terminal** and the **Express Terminal** in Long Beach (near the bow of the *Queen Mary*) on a regular schedule every day, year-round. These boats have stabilizers to smooth out the trip, individual airline-type seats, and an attendant to serve you snacks and drinks.

For reservations and schedules, call (213) 519-1212; groups of 15 or more call (310) 519-7957, elsewhere in California (800) 540-4753. Roundtrip on the **Express,** $29.20 adult, child 2-11 $21.70, child under 2 $1.50, senior $26.50. The faster **Super Express** roundtrip fares are: adult $34, child 2-11 $25, child under two $1.50, senior $31.50. Ask about the Captain's Lounge, a comfortable salon that accommodates private parties of up to eight people for $40 in addition to the regular ticket price (includes a bottle of champagne).

Catalina Island shuttle buses make several trips daily to the interior.

CATALINA
ISLAND
TRAILS

© MOON PUBLICATIONS, INC.

Catalina Cruise Line

Another large passenger boat to Two Harbors, Catalina Cruises, operates on a regular schedule throughout the year. During the summer, they make two trips daily to Two Harbors. Call for the winter schedule, tel. (310) 253-9800 or (800) 888-5939; roundtrip fares are $28 adult, child under 12 $18, under two $1.50, senior $24.

From Avalon

The *Shoreliner* cruise is a popular way to travel to Two Harbors from Avalon. The boats hug the coast from Avalon and give visitors an opportunity to leisurely view the mountains which drop to the sea and that are often alive with wild goats. Depending on the time of the year, passengers will see flying fish, porpoises, sea lions, and whales, along with pelicans and other seabirds fishing the coastal waters of Catalina. The ship passes numerous small coves, some with private schools, scout camps, and many filled with boats. These coves are favorite destinations for diving enthusiasts and Mainland boaters. Adult one-way fare (in either direction) $11.50, child 5-11 $6.50, under two $1.50. Many travelers enjoy taking the *Shoreliner* one way and the Safari Bus the other, which gives them the opportunity to see the rugged Catalina interior.

Note: Those bringing bicycles and surfboards to the Island aboard passenger boats from the Mainland pay a $3 fee each way.

Catalina Safari Bus

The Safari Bus shuttle provides daily scheduled bus transportation between Two Harbors and Avalon with stops at Little Harbor, Airport-In-The-Sky, and Black Jack Junction. The bus leaves from Avalon's Island Plaza, 213 Catalina Street. For schedules and rates (group rates available) call 510-2800; Box 5044, Two Harbors, CA 90704-5044. The drive takes passengers through the Catalina Conservancy and gives first-timers a view of the undeveloped lands of the reserve and the stunning wildlife of the Island, including herds of roaming buffalo. (See "Fauna," p. 8.)

Health And Help

There are no medical facilities at Two Harbors. However, Los Angeles County has a group of highly trained paramedics who have a fast boat, the *Bay Watch Isthmus*. It has all the high-tech equipment of an ambulance and is based year-round at Isthmus Cove. The *Bay Watch I* is based in Avalon. Between these two medical evacuation boats and the Avalon Municipal Hospital, plus an airvac helicopter between the Island and the Mainland, Catalina possesses a highly effective emergency system for both land or sea accidents. For diving accidents, a hyperbaric chamber is available at the Marine Science Center in the Two Harbors area at Big Fisherman Cove.

ACCOMMODATIONS

Banning House Lodge

The history-rich Banning House was built in 1910 by Judge Joseph Brent Banning (son of Phineas Banning). At the beginning of the century, the house served as a holiday home for the Banning family and their Mainland friends. The Bannings built a dirt road from Avalon and brought tourists on stagecoaches to the Isthmus, where they stayed in a tent village on the beach. Over the years the·Banning House has seen a variety of guests, including Hollywood stars and other celebrities who used it as a hotel while filming at the Isthmus during the early Wrigley days.

This all changed in 1941 with the beginning of WW II. At that time it was taken over by the U.S. Coast Guard and used for officers' quarters. After 1946 the Lodge was used variously as a dude ranch, girls' camp, hunting lodge, and employee housing. In 1987 Doug Bombard (life-long resident of Avalon and Two Harbors) began restoring the building into a turn-of-the-century delight.

Set on the top of a small knoll, the house enjoys views of both Isthmus Cove on the lee side and Catalina Harbor on the windward side of the Island. Today the Banning House Lodge is operated as a bed and breakfast inn with 11

Banning House

charming rooms available by reservation only. Each room has unique decor suggesting the history of the era. Continental breakfast is served in the "oak period-piece dining room" from 8-10 a.m. Guests can walk (or take the shuttle) to the beach and small village of Two Harbors. Room rates for one or two people are $100-175, each room with a view. For information and reservations write to Box 5044, Two Harbors, CA 90704-5044, tel. 510-2800.

Catalina Elderhostel Program

A popular program specifically designed for older adults, Elderhostels offer unique experiences of learning to develop new areas of interests or to expand current curiosities. Those 60 years and older (a companion can be as young as 50) enjoy inexpensive, short-term academic programs at educational institutions around the world. On Catalina Island the program is held at the Catalina Marine Science Center at Two Harbors. While at the Center, participants have the option of taking five different classes, though the requirement is only one. Offerings include a study on how Catalina's Indians utilized the underwater world, the Japanese art of *gyotaku* (fish printing), a seminar on a selected topic about conservation—and much more.

Accommodations are in the second-floor housing complex. While taking part in the program, participants will be walking several times a day to and from the waterfront research area and between buildings, with steep roads to and from. Double-occupancy rooms share bathrooms with up to four people. Registration costs, six nights' accommodations, all meals from Sunday evening through Saturday breakfast, five days of classes, and a variety of extracurricular activities are included in the tuition of $315 pp; transportation to and from the Mainland is not included. For more information contact Elderhostel, 75 Federal St., Boston, MA 02110-1941, tel. (617) 426-8056.

Camping Cabins

These basic cabins are available in the off-season only, which begins in October. Each room houses two people and comes equipped with either twin bunk beds or a double bed, and guests supply their own sleeping bags or bedding. Rooms have a refrigerator, heater, electrical outlets, and ample storage space. Separate community bathrooms for men and women offer sinks, toilets, mirrors, electrical outlets, and hot coin-operated showers. A communal cooking facility has four two-burner propane stoves, tables and chairs, two large gas barbecue grills, and cleanup areas.

Cabins are clustered in groups of seven around a large deck area. These clusters are ideal for group meetings. Plenty of fresh-water outlets around the camping cabins make it convenient to rinse off diving gear. As we go to press, the cabin rate is $42 per night. For reservations and information, call 510-2800; Box 5044, Two Harbors, CA 90704-5044.

Camping

Year-round camping is available on Catalina's west end, with campsites in the improved Two Harbors Campground; $7.50 pp per night. Tent-

CATALINA CAMPGROUNDS

© MOON PUBLICATIONS, INC.

cabins are also available (sturdy wood framed, with wood deck, canvas roof, and shaded porch. Cots and mattresses are supplied; you bring your sleeping bag. From Two Harbors to the campground is a quarter-mile-long walk on a narrow bumpy path, so carrying too much could be a problem. The rangers provide a gear-hauling service, and for $1 per item they will haul ice chests, heavy backpacks, etc. Other rental camping equipment such as propane, butane, charcoal, lanterns, tents, and campstoves is available at the campground. The campsites are located on a hillside that slopes down to the blue water. On site are barbecues, picnic tables, toilets, cold showers, sun shades, and fire rings. Fires are a real danger; please restrict all fires and smoking to the barbecue and fire ring area only. Water is provided at each site; family and group campsites are available. For reservations, call **Catalina Island Camping,** tel. 510-2800.

Parson's Landing Campground, open year-round, is about seven miles farther into the west end, and transportation is provided by the Two Harbors shore boat.

Restrictions

All groups must be accompanied by an adult (at least 18 years old) who will assume full responsibility for the group at all times. Campers must stay in assigned camping areas. Plant collecting, woodcutting, or removing any natural feature is strictly prohibited. Trash cans are provided. Motorcycles, archery equipment, fireworks, and firearms are prohibited anywhere outside the city of Avalon. No pets are allowed in the campgrounds. Keep it quiet between 10 p.m. and 7 a.m.

Bear in mind that the Coast Guard prohibits passengers onboard the cross-channel vessels from carrying propane, charcoal, gas stoves, and lanterns. All are available to rent from the campground ranger at Two Harbors. Bring a flashlight and a canteen if you plan on hiking.

(top) Santa Barbara Mission; (bottom) Catalina Yacht Club (Oz Mallan)

Gabriel Beckman tilework on Wrigley Memorial (Oz Mallan)

Eateries

Just a few feet from the beach, fine steak and seafood are served in a South Seas atmosphere at **Doug's Harbor Reef Restaurant and Saloon.** Doug's is close to the foot of the pier in the center of Two Harbors village; open for dinner. The outdoor bar/patio area has two television sets for sports viewing, and a live band or a DJ plays every weekend during the summer season. A satellite dish and cable bring in entertainment from around the world. The **Snack Bar** is open for breakfast and lunch serving great sandwiches and snacks. Doug's Harbor Reef Restaurant also offers a catering service for special events, boaters, and beach parties.

RECREATION

A day-trip from Avalon on the shuttle bus leaves you plenty of time to explore Two Harbors, take a swim in exceptionally clear water, and enjoy a leisurely lunch at the Snack Bar. Some opt to bring a lunch and picnic either at the beach or at Catalina Harbor (a short hike past the old Union Army barracks) where there are wooden tables, barbecue facilities, water, and public restrooms (coin-operated showers at Two Harbors only). The bandstand area on Isthmus Beach with tables, benches, and barbecue pits can be reserved for private groups by calling 510-0303. For those interested in tennis, two courts are available to the public for an hourly fee. A volleyball court on the main beach is open to the public—free.

Nature Hikes

At Two Harbors, several exploration trips are offered. Nature hikes are led by a naturalist who points out nature's unique exhibits, explains the colorful history, and helps you explore the plant and animal life surrounding the Two Harbors area. Hikes are conducted regularly, and walking tours can last two to three hours; wear good walking shoes and bring water. Cost is $15 and up per person, depending on the length of time. For groups, these hikes can be custom designed to fit the interest of the party, and an appropriate naturalist will be available. For information and reservations call 510-2800.

Island Safari

A van takes you into the rugged interior and you are accompanied by a naturalist. You'll have a chance to see the spectacular views of the formidable cliffs and rolling sea as well as a close-up look at Catalina wildlife, including buffalo that wander the hills. Trips are available to a wide variety of destinations in the interior of the Island and range from ancient Indian middens to a hidden waterfall to the site of an Indian village where visitors can see a soapstone quarry with half-carved Indian bowls, just as they were left hundreds of years ago. Two and a half-, three- and four-hour tours are available, starting at $15 pp. Check with Two Harbors Visitors and Information Office, tel. 510-2800.

On Your Own

For independent explorations, take the Catalina Safari bus to either the airport, Little Harbor, or Black Jack Junction. One-way fare is $14.20 per person for adults, $10.25 for children. For schedules and information call 510-2800.

WATER SPORTS

If you've come to Two Harbors for diving, you won't be disappointed; about 75% of all boat-diving off Catalina is done on the west end. Snorkeling is excellent in any of the remote coves or kelp beds at the west end of Isthmus Cove. Near the mouth of the Isthmus is Bird Rock, kept white by flocks of seagulls, cormorants, brown pelicans, and other passing seafowl that pause during their migrations. The submarine terrain in this area is well worth exploring. The shallows, which range from 15 to 40 feet, are interspersed with giant kelp fronds and patches of eelgrass which hide the small, colorful fish and strange sea creatures that feed on it. From here the bottom suddenly drops to a depth of about 100 feet, creating steep walls covered with gorgonia, sea urchins, and sea stars.

Tricky currents can be a hazard here and at some of the other popular dive spots, including Ship Rock and Eagle Reef. Blue Cavern Point offers several short underwater passageways that have been tunneled by wave action over the millennia. Probably the most attractive and treacherous dive spot on the windward side of the Island is Farnsworth Bank, three miles southwest of Ben Weston Beach. An ecological reserve, it has the only known purple coral on the Island; no souvenirs may be taken. Farnsworth has built-in hazards of strong currents and sheer sides that can plummet 35 fathoms.

Snorkeling Safari

For the snorkeler who would like to see Catalina's offshore marinelife, a two-hour snorkeling excursion is led by one of Two Harbors' leading underwater guides. Snorkelers meet at the

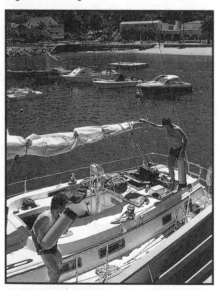

loading scuba tanks aboard for a day of diving in the clear waters around Two Harbors

dive center at the foot of the pier, where the "captain" takes them by boat to some of the richest marine habitats on the west end for shallow-water snorkeling. Explorers will investigate areas of shell-lined octopus lairs, the brilliant orange garibaldi's nesting grounds, and can often see the sea hare *(Aplysia vaccaria),* largest sea snail in the world, which can grow to the size of a basketball. Rates are $12 pp, with gear included $16 pp. All dive equipment isavailable for rent at the dive center as well as Aqua-View paddleboards. For more information call 510-0303.

Scuba Diving Safari

Scuba divers, ask about the two-hour dive trip onboard the *Garibaldi,* a boat designed for dive trips. Divers are taken to a variety of spots on the west end of the Island; advanced divers will have the opportunity of diving at more spectacular spots on the windward side of Catalina. Fee is $30 pp; bring your own regulator and your C-card; all other equipment is available for rent at the dive center.

Fishing

Many fine eating fish swarm around the Two Harbors area. Although not the easiest to capture, lobster and abalone are two big favorites (check out fishing seasons and limits.) For a good list of the fish found in Catalina waters, see "Fishing" in the Avalon chapter.

West End Cruising Club

Boaters who visit Two Harbors no longer have to pay a landing fee. The club is still active and members pay a yearly fee of $15. The money helps fund the multitude of activities sponsored by the club. There are beach parties with big bands, theme parties, and fish and steak barbecues. Planned activities include dinghy races, volleyball tournaments, and wildlife seminars. Once a year, members get together and have an underwater and shoreline cleanup in the Isthmus harbor. Doug's Harbor Reef Restaurant and Saloon is available for cocktail parties and catered events on the beach, special cruises, and a subscription to the *WestEnder* bulletin (plus a lot more).

the Two Harbors pier

The Fourth of July is a special time, with a magnificent children's summer festival and flamboyant fireworks display over the bay jointly sponsored by the West End Cruising Club, Fourth of July Cove, and others; open to the public. If you've never watched fireworks on an island, it's an experience you won't soon forget: brilliant lights reflecting off black water, the smell of explosives mixed with fresh sea air, and a cacophony of sounds from the boats as they blast horns, dingers, and bells—a thank-you for the great display. For more information about the West End Cruising Club, call 510-0303; Box 5044, Two Harbors, CA 90704-5044.

PRACTICALITIES

Two Harbors is a small village of less than 200 year-round residents. However, visitors find most everything they need, only not in such large quantities. The village moves at a slower pace than the Mainland, and that's how most Islanders want to keep it. The one-room schoolhouse is the only one left in Los Angeles County. Children from kindergarten through the fifth grade attend school in the rustic small building, which was built with a lot of help from Mainland visitors. Each day, the older children are bused into Avalon for junior and senior high school.

Catalina schools are operated under the Long Beach Unified School District.

General Store
Two Harbors General Store stocks a little of everything: most of the essential grocery items along with sundries, liquor, clothing, household supplies, marine supplies, fishing supplies and licenses. Don't forget the lending library; this is the spot to bring your "already-read" paperbacks. For large-group grocery orders call at least two weeks in advance and they'll be waiting for you when you arrive, tel. 510-0303, ext. 217.

Outboard Shop
Both inboard and outboard gas and diesel available. They offer engine repair and other boating services; dry storage available for boats 24 feet and under.

Dive Shop
At the foot of Isthmus Cove Pier, **Two Harbors Dive Station** has dive tank fills to 3,000 psi. Fins, masks, and snorkels can be rented. The selection is limited; no underwater lights or cameras, for example. Rent an Aqua-View paddleboard; they're fun for exploring the bay's underworld from the surface of the water.

KATHY ESCOVEDO-SANDERS

HIKING

Backpacking is a real adventure in the rugged hills of Catalina. Be aware of the interior's mountainous terrain and allow enough daylight to reach your destination. The network of undeveloped trails running across Catalina varies in type from goat trails and footpaths to jeep trails and fire roads. However, Los Angeles County Parks and Recreation asks that you keep to designated trails. There are no streams with potable water, so take an ample supply; there's safe drinking water at all the improved campsites. Be prepared for very few commercial contacts like stores (general store at Two Harbors), and only a few phones are found along the way (phones noted on hiking map).

Hikers should carry first-aid kits. Remember, you'll be sharing this outback with wild animals: bison, wild boar, goats, deer, and rattlesnakes. Expect to encounter poison oak. Even in winter, when the branches are bare, a brush against them will cause a reaction if you're sensitive. A hiking permit (free) is necessary before you begin your trek into the interior. These are avail-

able at the Department of Parks and Recreation in the Island Plaza, 213 Catalina St., tel. 510-0688, at Two Harbors, and at Airport-In-The-Sky.

A few tips to first-time hikers on Catalina: good hiking shoes are important, and the weather can differ between the interior and the coastal sections of the Island, varying as much as 30 degrees. Wearing layers is recommended. The days may be hot, and wearing shorts and a T-shirt is comfortable, but the evenings (even in summer) usually cool down, and long pants and a heavy sweatshirt feel good. If traveling around the Island during the rest of the year, a waterproof poncho is suggested. Don't forget to bring sun protection, e.g., a hat and sun-block lotion.

HIKING TRAILS

Route Out Of Avalon

You can start your trip in Avalon—trails and roads lead from there to within one mile of the west end of the Island. To hike out of Avalon, go toward the Casino on Crescent St., turn left on Marilla St., right on Vieudelou St., and then take a last left onto Stage Road. A paved street, it's the main road out of Avalon into the interior; expect lots of vehicular traffic. This first part of your trip is a hilly climb from the first turn on Marilla.

Silver Peak Trail To Parson's Landing
(10.1 miles—strenuous.) A backcountry trail for the experienced hiker. Use a compass. On this hike, you'll get sensational views of the mountains meeting the sea. Campsites are available at Parson's Landing, but reservations are necessary through Camp and Cove, tel. 510-0303.

Two Harbors To Parson's Landing
(6.8 miles, 0-5% grade.) This is all dirt, fairly level, a comfortable walk with beautiful views

of the ocean. The trail takes you past the Scout camps.

Little Harbor To West Summit
(4.3 miles, 5-10% grade.) This is a gradual uphill dirt trail, moderately difficult: you travel uphill for two miles.

West Summit To Two Harbors
(2.5 miles, 10%-plus grade.) This dirt trail is mostly downhill from West Summit to Two Harbors. It takes you past the turnoff to Fisherman's Cove, USC Marine Center, and Little Fisherman's Campground. While at Two Harbors notice the Isthmus Yacht Club, formerly the old Civil War barracks.

West Summit To The Airport Via Empire
(7.0 miles, 5-10%-plus grade.) This is an undeveloped dirt trail. It goes up and down. This

WEST END HIKES

SILVER PEAK TO STARLIGHT BEACH -+-+-+-+-
PARSON'S LANDING TO STARLIGHT BEACH ----------
PARSON'S LANDING TO SILVER PEAK ·················
WELLS BEACH TO SILVER PEAK -··-··-··-
TWO HARBORS TO PARSON'S LANDING -··-··-··-
TWO HARBORS TO LITTLE HARBOR CAMPGROUND -·-··-··-·-
LITTLE HARBOR TO BUFFALO SPRINGS RESERVOIR ···············

CENTRAL ISLAND HIKES

LITTLE HARBOR TO AIRPORT ··················
AIRPORT TO LITTLE HARBOR VIA BUFFALO SPRINGS RES. ··············
LITTLE HARBOR TO EAGLE'S NEST – – – – –
AIRPORT TO BLACKJACK CAMPGROUND ▬ ▬ ▬ ▬ ▬ ▬
BLACKJACK CAMPGROUND TO LITTLE HARBOR OVERLOOK —·—·—·—·—
BLACKJACK CAMPGROUND TO MT. ORIZABA •▬·•▬·•▬·•▬·
LITTLE HARBOR TO BEN WESTON BEACH – – – – – – –
OLD EAGLE'S NEST TRAIL – – – – – –
CAPE CANYON TRAIL —·▬—·▬—·▬

© MOON PUBLICATIONS, INC.

takes you past the old Empire Landing rock quarry where you can get water. It's uphill to the airport, a moderately difficult hike.

Airport To Little Harbor Overlook
(5.8 miles, 10%-plus grade.) This road is all dirt and downhill. It goes through the Wrigley family's Rancho Escondido. The trail parallels Cottonwood Canyon. If you want to make a detour through Cottonwood, make a left at the airport to hit Cottonwood Canyon. Water is available at Little Harbor. Be aware of wild pigs in the area.

Little Harbor Overlook To Little Harbor
(1.2 miles, 5-10% grade.) An all-downhill dirt

trail. Be aware of vehicle traffic through here, including tour buses.

Ben Weston Junction
To Little Harbor Overlook
(2.3 miles, 10%-plus grade.) This trail is mostly uphill—about two miles of it. You'll see the location of a WW II gunnery station at the top. From here the view of the coast and Little Harbor is breathtaking.

Old Eagles Nest Trail
(2.6 miles, 5-10% grade.) This is an undeveloped loop trail that begins at the old Eagles Nest stagecoach stop and meets the main road

into Little Harbor. Hill climbing involved, moderately difficult.

Cottonwood Trail
(5.5 miles, 5-10%-plus grade.) Moderately difficult undeveloped trail.

Black Jack Junction To Black Jack
(1.5 miles, 5-10% grade.) Dirt trail, gradual upgrade. The turnoff to the campground is marked. Black Jack is Catalina's second-highest peak at 2,010 feet. Old mine shafts dot the area. There's a telephone at the junction.

Black Jack Junction To Airport
(2.5 miles, 5-10% grade.) There are some lovely views on this hike. Runway Cafe and water available at the airport. Lots of buffalo roam the area. This is a moderately easy hike.

Middle Ranch Junction To Black Jack Junction
(2.7 miles, 0-5% grade.) Fairly level walking along Catalina's China Wall.

Middle Ranch To Black Jack Via Cape Canyon
(4.4 miles, 5-10% grade.) This dirt trail is all uphill. The last mile and a half is very steep. Cape Canyon is a pleasant hike, giving you a good look at the farming activities of Catalina. Note: the Conservancy asks that you do not cut through crops. The second bump gate is the trail marker turnoff. Difficult.

Middle Ranch To Ben Weston Junction
(2.4 Miles, 10%-plus grade.) Moderate. The dirt road passes the Camp Cactus turnoff (old Army camp). Turn at the Ben Weston Junction for the beach.

Middle Ranch Junction To Middle Ranch
(4.8 miles 0-10%-plus grade.) All dirt road and downhill. Lots of buffalo and maybe deer. Stay to the side of the road due to traffic—tour buses and other vehicles.

Bullrush Canyon Trail
(7.5 miles, 5-10% grade.) Undeveloped dirt trail, hardy trekkers call this the best hike on the Island. Lots of scrub oak and wildlife. Downhill, level.

Summit To Middle Ranch Junction
(2.0 miles, 0-5% grade.) This is a slurry road, and it's fairly level. Behind Haypress Lake are two others called Hidden Lakes, gateway to Silver Canyon—lots of poison oak. Taking a left at the third lake takes you to Silver Canyon. Moderate hike.

Hiking in Catalina's interior was only made possible since the formation of the Catalina Conservancy in 1972.

Avalon To East Summit
(3.2 miles, 10% grade.) This is all uphill. The road is slurry and lined with eucalyptus trees. You'll enjoy great views, though it gets quite steep in places. When you reach the summit, stop to admire more superior views.

Empire Landing Road From Two Harbors
(6.2 miles—moderate.) Leave Two Harbors on the surfaced main road to Avalon, and break off to an abandoned dirt road which leads to the Airport-In-The-Sky.

Hiking To Little Harbor
From Two Harbors
From Doug's Harbor Reef Restaurant and Saloon, walk to the main road toward Avalon and follow it up and over the hills past upper Buffalo Reservoir and into Little Harbor. For the highly experienced hiker in excellent physical condition there's another strenuous trail to Little Harbor by way of the old Banning House Road that cuts off about a mile from the Banning House. Follow Banning House Rd. for 3.2 miles until you run into graded, dirt Little Harbor Rd., where you turn right. Following that for another 1.9 miles brings you to Little Harbor Campground. (Beware of rattlesnakes.)

Boushey Road
(2.1 miles—strenuous.) The connecting dirt road between Silver Peak Trail and Parson's Landing. For only the hardy hiker.

Organized Nature Hikes
These treks offer you the opportunity to explore the plant and animal life surrounding the Two Harbors area. Nature hikes are conducted upon request during the summer months only. Contact the Los Angeles County or Two Harbors ranger. Slide lectures are also given at various times on the beach at Two Harbors.

CAMPING

On Catalina you'll find two types of campgrounds: primitive and improved. Primitive camps have no facilities whatsoever; improved sites include toilets, fire rings, and barbecue pits. Some have showers, most have phones, some are accessible only by boat (B), some by shuttle (S), some hike-in (H), and a few by shore boat (SB) from Isthmus Cove at Two Harbors. The five improved campgrounds are all accessible by road. Of the six primitive sites, five are accessible by boat only on a first-come first-served basis (see hiking maps). Little Fisherman's, Parson's Landing, and Emerald Bay, at the west end near Two Harbors, no longer require landing permits. For a map of the areas described, send a stamped legal size 4" by 9" self-addressed envelope and $1 cash only to the Los Angeles County Parks, Box 1133, Avalon, CA 90704. **Note**: Fires are permitted at improved campsites *only*.

Getting There

In Avalon, at 213 Catalina St. in the Island Plaza, catch the (seasonal only) shuttle bus to Hermit Gulch Campground, Airport-In-The-Sky, and to all the improved campsites in the interior. Reservations to the interior are required. For more information and seasonal schedule call 510-2078, 510-0143, or 510-0303.

IMPROVED CAMPGROUNDS

Hermit Gulch Campground

Hermit Gulch Campground is the closest camping area to Avalon and is within walking distance of all the town attractions. It can easily be reached by walking up Sumner Ave. through Avalon Canyon. Follow the sign that says "Avalon Canyon Road." From the sign it's 1 ½ miles inland on the Memorial Park Road. Operated by the SCI Co., facilities can handle 200 people. Attractively landscaped with tall shade trees, the campground offers fresh water, coin-operated inside hot showers, lighted restrooms, picnic tables, barbecue pits, vending machines, and a public phone; no electrical hookups, no pets, no wood fires. Fees: adult $7, child under 6 free; groups of 20 receive a discount. For reservations call L.A. County Office of Parks and Recreation, 510-8368; check into the ranger's office upon arrival.

Black Jack

Mount Black Jack, at 2,006 feet, is the second-highest peak on Catalina (the highest, at 2,097 feet, is Mt. Orizaba). It's the site of old Black Jack Mine (lead, zinc, and silver). Black Jack Camp, 10 miles from Avalon and 15 miles from

---

CAMPING SUPPLIES

As a camper you know what food and clothes will fit your lifestyle. The following is a checklist of other things to consider taking on your camping trip to Catalina Island:

- ✔ flashlight
- ✔ extra batteries
- ✔ sunglasses
- ✔ pen/paper/cards/book
- ✔ knife
- ✔ extra pair of broken-in shoes
- ✔ lightweight tent
- ✔ lightweight sleeping bag
- ✔ something to anchor a windbreak
- ✔ camera/film
- ✔ waterproof matches
- ✔ water supply
- ✔ canteen
- ✔ extra pair of glasses
- ✔ toilet paper
- ✔ ChapStick
- ✔ water purification tablets
- ✔ towel
- ✔ Calmitol ointment (good for burns, bites, and rashes)
- ✔ snake-bite kit

Two Harbors, is located at a 1,500-foot elevation. It is the principal inland camping area on Catalina, set in a lovely, protected pine forest. Some vantage points in the camp overlook the channel side of the Island toward the Mainland. Operated by Los Angeles County Department of Parks and Recreation, the camp offers accommodations for 75 campers. Facilities include water, toilets, fire rings, barbecue pits, public phone, and shuttle bus service to Black Jack Junction. Fees: adult $7, child six and under 50 cents. For reservations call 510-0688.

Little Harbor

The primary campground on the Pacific side of Catalina, Little Harbor is also considered by some to be Catalina's most picturesque and historic. Bring your camera for spectacular views from Indian Head Point above Little Harbor. Much of the history of the Catalina Indians has been brought to light in a deeply stratified archaeological site overlooking the twin bays of Lit-

CATALINA CAMPSITES

PRIMITIVE

Emerald Bay (H)(SB)

Ripper's Cove (SB)

Starlight Beach (SB)

Little Gibraltar Rock and Cabrillo Harbor (H)(SB)

Italian Gardens (SB)

Goat Harbor (SB)

IMPROVED

Hermits Gulch Campground (H)(V)

Black Jack (H)(V)

Little Harbor (H)(V)

Two Harbors Campground (H)

Parson's Landing (SB)

For details phone (310) 510-0303

Accessible by: SB = Shore Boat
              H = Hike
              V = Vehicle

tle Harbor (see "History"). In 1894 Dr. O.T. Fellows built an inn here as a stopover for stagecoach passengers visiting the Island. The inn has long since gone, but the old stage road, still used today, meets the sea at its twin harbors: the smaller one (Little Harbor) a placid anchorage, the larger one (Shark Harbor) a surf-pounded strand that offers exciting beachcombing possibilities (especially after a storm) and excellent bodysurfing.

Little Harbor Campground is located on the site of an ancient Indian village. A good base for day-hiking to a variety of destinations, it's seven miles from Two Harbors and six miles from Black Jack. Though on the windward side of the Island, the camp is located in a protected patch of flat land close to the road and the ocean. Operated by the Los Angeles County Department of Parks and Recreation, it can accommodate 150 campers, with toilets, cold showers, barbecue pits, fire rings, picnic tables, phone, and shuttle bus service. It offers excellent swimming, diving, and fishing. Fees: adult $7, child six and under 50 cents; call 510-0688 for reservations.

Two Harbors Campground

This privately owned campground is a half mile from Two Harbors on a bluff overlooking the rocky beach and crystal-clear waters of the cove. From here you can see right down to the bottom and watch the variegated hues of blue and green continue for some way out to sea. It's a good base from which to explore the many trails and coves of the west end. There's a general store, dive shop, restaurant, bar, and many other activities available thanks to the close proximity of the West End Cruising Club (see "Two Harbors"). Facilities accommodate 250 campers, with toilets, cold showers, fire rings, barbecues, picnic tables, phone, swimming,

fishing, and diving. Since it is illegal to carry combustible materials on public transport, be prepared to buy charcoal and lighter fluid from the park ranger. Fees: $6 pp, payable at the Camp and Cove office at the foot of the Two Harbors pier. For reservations, call 510-0303.

Parson's Landing

The easiest way to get there is to travel from Two Harbors by shore boat (seasonal schedule). The boat ride offers spectacular coastal views. By trail, Parson's Landing is seven miles west of Two Harbors. This undeveloped campground adjacent to the beach can be a quiet spot, or on a holiday weekend, very crowded. Facilities can accommodate 150 campers, with latrines, fire rings, barbecue pits, and limited water; firewood, charcoal, and lighter fluid available from the campground ranger. Fees: $6 pp, payable at the Camp and Cove office. For reservations, call 510-0303.

PRIMITIVE CAMPSITES

Camping is permitted at six different coves on the lee coast of the Island. These completely undeveloped sites are not maintained by any

Camping in Catalina's coves is a time to enjoy the sea, stars, and fauna.

agency and provide little more than a flat area to lay out your sleeping bag. Fees ($3 pp per day) are paid to Conservancy rangers who will find you. First-come, first-served.

Emerald Bay/Sandy Beach

The cove of Emerald Bay is leased to the Corsair Yacht Club, and a portion of the beach and surrounding area is leased to the Boy Scouts of America for use as a summer camp. However, public camping is available in a primitive campsite on Sandy Beach. Accessible by boat or by road from Two Harbors. Emerald Bay, too, has exceptionally clear water and its share of Catalina's colorful past. Samuel Prentiss was the first white man to build a house on Catalina, here at Emerald Bay. He is buried on the hill overlooking what almost became the mining town of "Queen City" during the gold frenzy of 1863-64. Today this out-of-the-way area continues to provide a tranquil retreat for the explorer who prefers the peace of a grassy hillside sloping down to a spacious Robinson Crusoe-style beach.

Ripper's Cove

An excellent primitive campsite, accessible only by boat. There's good anchorage on the sandy bottom, and the sloping grassland behind the beach provides vigorous safe and scenic hiking.

Starlight Beach

A small beach one mile short of Land's End, the westernmost tip of Catalina Island. Access by boat only. The diving is excellent in the transparent waters of this cove.

Little Gibraltar Rock And Cabrillo Harbor

The small leased camp at Cabrillo Harbor is operated by the Long Beach Council of Boy Scouts as a summer camp. The harbor also contains a primitive campsite for public use. Access to the interior from the beach is very difficult due to rough terrain. Boat-in only.

Italian Gardens

Named for the many Italian fishermen from San Pedro who successfully fished here some years back. This is a long beach with access by boat only for primitive camping and terrific diving. There is no hiking into the interior from the beach.

Goat Harbor

This is a rugged geological area. Access by boat to a sandy beach offers primitive camping. The cliffs are dangerous. Access to the interior from the beach is very difficult due to rough terrain.

BOATING

CRUISING CALIFORNIA'S SOUTHERN COAST

The Channel Islands are unquestionably the most popular boater's destination along the Southern California coast, with Catalina being the favorite. An island is an obvious draw for boaters, and at least one is close enough to the Santa Barbara, Ventura, Los Angeles, Orange County, and San Diego mainland to be accessible—even to smaller craft. For boaters who are looking for an active nightlife and other shore activities, Avalon is the harbor for your visit. On the other hand, if it's the quiet life you're seeking, escape to one of the other Channel islands or to one of Catalina's many small isolated coves, where the loudest thing you'll hear—aside from other boaters—is the slap of the water on your bow and maybe a squawking seagull. Most of these isolated coves show no sign of man's intrusion. Day-hikes will bring you into direct con-

tact with the natural phenomena of the islands, and diving is unparalleled along the entire California coast.

PRACTICALITIES

Weather Information

Every seaman has a big responsibility—not only for his own personal safety and that of his crew, but (as most would concede) for a large financial investment as well. Weather plays an important part in boating, and a lot of tragedies could be averted with the use of common sense. Boat owners should take advantage of all the information available to them, and in Southern California there's a lot; monitoring the weather is of prime importance.

Even though some of the islands are not long distances from the Mainland (Catalina is only 22 miles from Long Beach Harbor), the Santa Barbara/Catalina Channel is known as a formidable stretch of open sea. The crossing can be smooth or it can pitch waves that pound the hull and leap the gunwales. Fog can occur anytime, but in the winter months it's denser and hangs in there longer. Fog seldom forms when the air is at least five degrees F warmer than the water, so visibility improves with fresh southerly winds and a steady or slowly falling barometer.

During the winter months in the Catalina Channel, Santa Ana winds (also called northeasters) can shift swell-direction and render an anchorage unsafe. And although all coves and harbors in Catalina provide peaceful anchorage most of the time, safe boaters pay heed to the forecasts. When an advisory is in effect or storm warning is up, they don't go out unless

SOUTHERN CALIFORNIA COASTAL STORM WARNING DISPLAY LOCATIONS

San Diego: Ballast Point, B Street Pier, Coronado Yacht Club, Shelter Island, Mission Bay Aquatic Headquarters, Oceanside Harbor

Dana Point Harbor

Catalina Island: Avalon Pleasure Pier, Isthmus Cove

Sunset Beach

Newport Beach Harbor: Channel Entrance

Long Beach Marina: Administration Building

San Pedro: Marine Exchange Building

Redondo Beach: King Harbor on the Breakwater

Marina del Rey: Administration Building

Port Hueneme Naval Station, Oxnard: Channel Islands Harbor

Ventura Marina

Santa Barbara: Weather Signal Station

they are highly qualified sailors and have experience in the prevailing sea conditions—and it's an emergency trip! If already at sea, most make for home port—pronto!—or to the nearest harbor that offers protection from the predicted wind and sea direction. Flags and lights give warnings on the mole in Avalon and at the Two Harbors Office.

Note: One red pennant or red-over-white lights means the forecast is an 18- to 33-knot wind and/or sea, dangerous for small boats. Two red pennants or white-over-red lights means a 34- to 47-knot gale. One square red flag with black center or red-over-red lights means a 48- to 63-knot storm. For marine weather information from Los Angeles 24 hours, call 477-1463; for aircraft weather from FAA, call 776-1640 or 787-4911. By radio, 24 hours from the National Weather Service, use VHF channel Wx-1 to about 97 miles from Mt. Wilson. Or from FAA Los Angeles, use beacon band 332 kHz. Southern California harbormasters are always on call for a local weather report; Avalon's number is 510-0535.

It's wise to know where the safe harbors and coves are located in case you need to make a run in the middle of the night. The seasons generally hold true, but to eliminate any unpleasant surprises, boaters must know what's coming. One of the biggest aids in stormy conditions is to stay calm and remember everything ever learned about sailing. As in any emergency situation, panic compounds existing problems.

Radio Equipment
For about $400, boaters can buy a receiver that will pick up the weather and not take up much space or, for more money (about $1000), a ham radio rig. It's necessary to have a license to broadcast, but not to listen. Other boaters talk to each other and give good information about the weather in different areas. Anyone interested in sailing frequently and far would be wise to get a general class license (or higher) to have full capability to broadcast through the ham networks, especially helpful in emergency situations.

CALIFORNIA COASTAL
STORM-WARNING FLAGS AND LIGHTS

Daytime Signal   Night Signal

SMALL CRAFT ADVISORIES

One red pennant displayed by day or a red light over a white light at night indicates that winds as high as 33 knots (38 mph) and/or sea conditions considered dangerous to small-craft operations are forecast for the area.

Daytime Signal   Night Signal

GALE WARNING

Two red pennants displayed by day or a white light above a red light at night indicates that winds 34-47 knots (39-54 mph) are forecast for the area.

Daytime Signal   Night Signal

STORM WARNING

A single square red flag with a black center displayed during daytime or two red lights at night indicates that winds 48 knots (55 mph) and above are forecast for the area. If the winds are associated with a tropical cyclone (hurricane), the storm warning displays indicate that winds 48-63 knots (55-73 mph) are forecast.

Daytime Signal   Night Signal

HURRICANE WARNING

Displayed only in connection with a tropical cyclone (hurricane). Two square red flags with black centers displayed by day or a white light between two red lights at night indicates that winds 64 knots (74 mph) and above are forecast for the area.

DIANA LASICH HARPER

Navigation

Accurate charts are available from most marine supply stores. Valuable books that should be on board for all sailors that cruise the channel are *Pacific Boating Almanac* and *Cruising Guide To California's Channel Islands*, by Brian M. Fagan, both published by Western Marine Enterprises, Inc. The Chart Guide for Catalina is also handy to tuck away. For maximum convenience and safety ask to have your name put on a free mailing list for the "Local Notice to Mariners," which provides weekly NOAA chart editions that indicate shoreline and depth changes. For this service write to: Commander, 11th Coast Guard District, 400 Oceangate, Long Beach, CA 90822.

Towing Assistance

Members of Boat/US (which number about 215,000) now receive a reimbursement up to $50 for boat-towing service. Membership in the nonprofit organization is $17 and entitles each member to a $50 towing reimbursement per year. Broader towing coverage is available from Boat/US for an additional fee.

The association made this service available in 1984, when the Coast Guard turned all none-mergency towing over to commercial firms (except in foul weather or darkness). Other services and marine insurance are available

through Boat/US; for more information contact Boat/US, 880 S. Pickett St., Alexandria, VA 22304, tel. (703) 823-9550.

PUR Traveler

There are many gadgets manufactured for boats that make them pretty, practical, efficient, easier, or just fun. One gadget that could be a health saver is a water-filter system. There are several on the market, one of which is the PUR Traveler, tested by the University of Arizona Microbiology Dept. and the Johns Hopkins School of Hygiene and Public Health, and which meets EPA standards. The PUR is state of the art, hand held, light, compact, easy to use, and solves the safe water dilemma for travelers; there is a slight taste of iodine, especially when the cartridge is brand new. This handy travel gadget not only filters out impurities but also kills all disease-causing cysts, bacteria, and viruses instantly. Water from any source is poured into the top of the seven-inch-high cartridge and pushed through a chemical cartridge (capable of purifying 100 gallons) and within seconds one cup of pure water is available; $59.95, refill cartridge $19.95.

The PUR can be purchased at stores across the U.S. such as REI, Adventure 16, Sonora Mountaineering, Earth Store, Erewhon, and Tents and Trails, or call (800) 845-7873. Small

Don't let this happen to you.

portable desalination units are also available. For more information write PUR Traveler, 2229 Edgewood Ave. S, Minneapolis, MN 55426.

Brita Filter System
This German purifier is designed to remove chlorine and chlorine compounds, lead and copper, organic pollutants, rust, chemicals, and various other impurities—without removing valuable minerals. The basic system is a plastic pitcher and a replaceable filter cartridge. Drinking water is poured into the top section of the pitcher and filtered into the bottom for pouring or storage. Also available is a Travel Pack, which removes impurities unsafe for drinking. This includes germicidal disinfectant tablets to help destroy parasites, plus the Brita cartridge to filter out the chemical taste of the tablets. Including the Travel Pack, the price is about $50. For more information contact Brita America Marketing West, 444 Castro St., Suite 426, Mountain View, CA 94041; in Southern California tel. (800) 672-3470, ext. 825; out of state, tel. (800) 538-8157.

Underwater Repair Service
If you need an emergency underwater repair, if your line gets wrapped around the prop, or if you've dropped your only prescription glasses overboard, don't panic. In Avalon, Gary's Mooring & Diving Service, tel. 510-0779, is available for any diving jobs you need to have done. Argo Diving, tel. 510-2208, is also available for even the most creative of diving needs.

CATALINA COVES AND HARBORS

AVALON MARINAS

Mooring Information
Moorings are assigned on a first-come first-served basis. There are 400 moorings in Avalon, and on a busy weekend, rafting (two boats tied together to one mooring) increases the boat population to as much as 500. Upon arrival please stand by at the harbor entrance until a patrol boat assigns a mooring. Mooring fees are payable to the patrol boat or at the harbormaster's office. Departing without paying incurs double charges. On your day of departure, moorings must be vacated by 9 a.m. If you arrive in Avalon on a busy weekend and find all moorings occupied, you can anchor free of charge in specified areas at the discretion of the harbormaster. The Harbor Patrol maintains a 24-hour service year-round; there is no landing fee at Avalon, Descanso Bay, Hamilton Beach, or any Conservancy property. For more Avalon harbor information call 510-0535.

Note: Between Oct. 15 and two weeks before Easter, two nights' fees buy five additional consecutive nights if the moorings are available.

Services
Complete cooperation is necessary to keep the harbor and beaches clean. Harbor Department service boats pick up trash daily, free of charge, at approximately 10 a.m. and 2 p.m. Plastic trash bags can be obtained from the patrol boats or at the harbormaster's office. Leave the trash bag on the stern of your boat, making sure there's nothing around it that might be mistaken for trash and hauled away. A holding-tank pump-out station is located on float No. 5 in the southeast corner of Avalon Bay. All generators and other noisy motors must be shut off by 10 p.m.

AVALON MOORING FEES

Boats 39' and under	$12 per night
40' to 49'	$16 per night
50' to 59'	$20 per night
60' to 69'	$25 per night
70' to 79'	$30 per night
80' to 89'	$35 per night
90' to 99'	$40 per night
100' and over	$45 per night

Shore boats and fueling service are available year-round. Shore boat fees to the Pleasure Pier are $2 pp for the inner harbor and $2.50 for the outer harbor. Some summers, enterprising Island kids operate a boat-to-boat shopping service from a small outboard. You can order almost anything and it'll be delivered to your boat for a price. Please anticipate your water needs because Avalon has a water shortage. Fresh water is available at the Chevron fuel dock and at float 5.

Gas Dock

The Chevron Oil gas dock is located on Casino Pier in Avalon for all your boat fuel needs, tel. 510-0046. Diesel fuel and regular gasoline and oil are also available at Two Harbors, tel. 510-0303.

Descanso Bay

There are 47 moorings and anchorage in Descanso Bay; you are requested to keep dinghies out of the swim area, and no beach landings are permitted. For your convenience, a dinghy dock is located on the gas dock at Casino Point, another between the Tuna Club and the Yacht Club, and one at the Pleasure Pier. Dinghies up to 14 feet may be tied to any of these docks for up to 72 hours. Don't leave removable motors or anything else loose, and be aware that even an entire dinghy can be a victim of theft. Stop-ping at any dock other than the dinghy docks mentioned is permitted only long enough to transfer people.

Hamilton Beach

There are 36 moorings and uncomfortable anchorage. This cove was once the location of the prewar seaplane terminal. Today, the cove is the home of a beautiful Mediterranean village of condos that graciously climb the hillside, all with fantastic views. The architecture and design of these condos really make a lovely vista from a boat.

Lovers Cove

To encourage the growth of marinelife in this underwater preserve, there are no moorings; anchorage is prohibited. Lovers Cove is used for swimming, snorkeling, and glass-bottom boat cruising only.

OUTSIDE OF AVALON

Besides Avalon, 17 other coves have moorings, and many others provide anchorage. For more detailed information about the numerous coves on the Island, call the Camp and Cove Agency, tel. 510-0303. They can tell you where to moor, what the prices are, the hazards, and if anchorage is available.

Hamilton Cove

Note: Do not bring firearms, bow-hunting gear, or motorcycles to shore—all are prohibited. Fires are a real danger, not allowed except in designated camping and picnic areas. Make charcoal fires only (charcoal is available on the Island). Do not cut trees or shrubs or remove any artifacts you might find on shore or underwater.

MOORINGS AND ANCHORAGES AROUND THE ISLAND

Cruising around the Island gives you a glimpse into each of the coves that circle Catalina. The following information touches on each cove, the number of possible anchorages and moorings at each location, as well as other miscellaneous information.

Seal Rocks

Past Lovers Cove toward the east end is Pebbly Beach. Here the amphibian airport and ramp share the shoreline with the helicopter pad, boat yard, freight dock, Southern California Edison plant, Buffalo Nickel Restaurant, and the only gas station serving Avalon town. There are no moorings, and no anchoring is allowed.

Continuing past Pebbly you'll see one of Catalina's two rock quarries. This and the quarry at Empire Landing (in operation since before the turn of the century) have provided millions of tons of rock for Mainland seawalls and breakwaters. The Los Angeles Light Breakwater is 90% Catalina rock, Pier J next to the *Queen Mary* contains three million tons, Redondo Beach and Port Hueneme breakwaters each contain 1.5 million tons, and Playa del Rey breakwater 750,000 tons. None of this seems to make a dent in the Catalina shoreline. On past Jewfish Point is a rookery for California sea lions. Boaters: Watch for submerged rocks in this area.

To China Point

As you round the Island's east end you'll pass Church Rock before coming to the Palisades area, so named because of the steep mountains that drop to the sea. From the water you can see the web-like paths of the mountain goats that roam these hills. This is good anchorage during Santa Ana storm conditions. Going on, Silver Canyon Landing has no moorings but it does have anchorage with some westerly protection. Going ashore is risky due to the surf, but if you plan to attempt a landing you'll find the fewest breakers on the southwest corner. Continuing on past Bulldog Rock and Salta Verde Point with its "painted cliffs" will bring you to China Point. In the 1800s, this was the location of one of the camps where illegal Chinese immigrants, supposedly being returned to China by government order, were dropped off by unscrupulous sea captains before being smuggled back to the California Mainland. Between China Point and Ben Weston Point you may spot seals. There are no moorings at Ben Weston Beach, and anchorage is considered unsafe.

Little Harbor

West, beyond Indian Head Rock, you'll come to one of the most picturesque harbors on the Island, which is really two individual harbors, Little Harbor and Shark Harbor. Little Harbor has no moorings, but excellent anchorage for 10-15 boats. Shark Harbor, the larger, has no moorings; anchorage is considered unsafe. Surfing, however, is good. Little Harbor offers improved camping facilities for 150 persons. From here, you can hike to the tops of the surrounding hills for spectacular coastal vistas, see wildlife, and explore the ancient location of one of the main communities of the Catalina Indians.

Little Harbor

WEST END AND TWO HARBORS

Catalina Harbor

"Cat" Harbor has 96 moorings plus anchorage for 235; onshore facilities available for California Yacht Club. Following the coast past Pin Rock you'll sail into Catalina Harbor. This is the isthmus of the Island, its narrowest point (one-half mile wide). It is no longer necessary to pay a landing fee on any part of Catalina.

You'll find firepits, good picnic facilities and toilets, but camping is not allowed. The wreck of the nefarious Chinese pirate ship *Ning Po* is buried under the mud here. Ballast Point is said to have been formed by Yankee clippers which dropped ballast here to scrape the bottoms of their ships.

In the days before these waters were charted, this nub of land separated by Two Harbors fooled sailors into thinking that this was another island. Continuing on around Catalina Head, you come to Lobster Bay which, according to legend, was a pirate hideout. At Whale Rock, what looks like a whale's waterspout is only a "blowhole" caused by the tide hitting the rock and forcing a column of water along it and up into the air.

Ribbon Rock attracts attention with its striated layers of quartz against the high dark face of the cliff. It was here, according to Frederick Holder's story, "Adventures of Torqua" (see "Blue Cavern Point" in this section), that white settlers forever trapped a band of thieving Indians in an underground cave by sealing the exit. Iron Bound Cove has no moorings; although the anchorage is exposed, it's considered fair. From here, legend has it, Chinese immigrants left their temporary camps and hiked over to Catalina Harbor to gamble.

From Eagle Rock To Land's End

Eagle Rock is almost at Land's End, on the western tip of Catalina. Until 1952, the American bald eagle used this isolated area to breed. Today, although eagles are not seen in large numbers, an occasional bird is spotted soaring over the rocky cliffs—thanks to the ongoing Bald Eagle Reintroduction Program overseen by the Catalina Conservancy (see "Fauna"). Sizable numbers of brown pelicans cluster on the rocks. As you cruise around Land's End you'll see the West End Light; expect strong currents and swell.

Parson's Landing

Here you'll find no moorings but anchorage for 10. This is a good beach for camping, with fire rings, toilets, and barbecue pits. Call Camp and Cove, tel. 510-0303, for reservations. In all but very dry years, there's a freshwater spring up the canyon. At one time the home of miners and pioneers, the area was named for the twin brothers Nathaniel and Theoples Parsons, who lived here in the mid-1800s. Beyond Arrow Point are Johnson's Landing and Emerald Bay. Samuel Prentiss lived in a small stone house here at Johnson's Landing while he searched the Island for his elusive treasure. During the mining years of 1863-64, grandiose plans for Queen City were begun by the rough-and-tumble miners who'd set up a temporary community in the flush of the gold frenzy on Catalina. The Union Army arrived to survey the Island for a possible Indian reservation and ended the miners' dreams of riches when they were ordered to leave.

Emerald Bay
Emerald Bay, with its isolation and natural beauty, is a favorite anchorage for boaters. It has 99 moorings and anchorage for 5-10 boats. Shore land is leased to the Great Western Council of Boy Scouts through 1992; leasing changes are being discussed as we go to print, and it's possible that this will be the future location of a Cousteau ecological resort. Presently, Sandy Beach is available for day camping only.

Howland's
Just around the bend from Sandy Beach is another favorite boat harbor, Howland's Landing, with 40 moorings. High up in the canyon is the windblown stone marker of Samuel Prentiss keeping a lonely vigil as the only marked grave outside of Avalon. Land ashore is leased to Catalina Island Camps and Los Angeles Yacht Club.

Big Geiger Cove
Anchorage for 10, shore leased to the Blue Water Cruising Club. **Little Geiger Cove** has

COVES AND MOORINGS ON CATALINA

WEST END
PARSON'S LANDING
JOHNSONS LANDING
EAGLE ROCK
IRON BOUND COVE
RIBBON ROCK
WHALE ROCK
LOBSTER BAY
CATALINA HARBOR
BALLAST POINT
LITTLE HARBOR
INDIAN HEAD LOOKOUT POINT
BEN WESTON
CHINA POINT

EMERALD BAY
SANDY BEACH
BIG GEIGER COVE
LITTLE GEIGER COVE
SHIP ROCK LIGHT
HOWLAND'S LANDING   EAGLE REEF
CHERRY COVE
FOURTH OF JULY COVE
TWO HARBORS

BIRD ROCK
ISTHMUS COVE
BLUE CAVERN PT.
LITTLE FISHERMAN'S COVE
ROCK QUARRY
BIG FISHERMAN'S COVE

EMPIRE LANDING
RIPPERS COVE
LITTLE GIBRALTER COVE
GOAT HARBOR
ITALIAN GARDENS
LONG POINT
BUTTON SHELL BEACH
HEN ROCK
WHITE'S LANDING
TORQUA SPRINGS
WILLOW COVE
TOYON BAY
GALLAGHER'S COVE

TWO HARBORS ROAD
ESCONDIDO ROAD
AIRPORT ROAD
OLD STAGE ROAD
MIDDLE RANCH ROAD

HAMILTON BEACH
DESCANSO BAY
CASINO PT.
AVALON BAY
LOVERS COVE
AVALON
PEBBLY BEACH & SEA PLANE AREA
ROCK QUARRY
JEWFISH PT.
SEAL ROCKS
EAST END LIGHT
CHURCH ROCK

SALTA VERDE   PALISADES
SILVER CANYON   BINNACLE ROCK

0   2mi
0   2km

one mooring and anchorage for three, land leased to Offshore Cruising Club.

Cherry Cove

Cherry Cove has 103 moorings but no anchorage. The shore has been leased to the San Gabriel Valley Boy Scouts for many years. In late 1991 the Jacques Cousteau organization was being considered as a new lessee for an ecological resort, but Scout supporters appear to have encouraged a location change for the Cousteau organization to Emerald Bay. Cherry Cove was named for 77 Catalina cherry trees planted up the canyon. See "Flora."

Fourth Of July Cove

Here you'll find 42 moorings but no anchorage. Named for the holiday celebrations held every July by the Banning family during their era of ownership. Land is leased to Fourth of July Yacht Club.

TWO HARBORS

Home of the West End Cruising Club, membership ($15 yearly) is open to the general public; applications and cards are available at the office at the foot of the Isthmus Pier. However, it is not necessary to belong to the club in order to land at Two Harbors. There is no landing fee at Two Harbors or any other cove on Catalina Island.

Isthmus Cove

This large cove has 249 moorings available and anchorage for 100. Transient moorings are on a first-come first-served basis. Mooring fees are paid to the patrol boat or at the harbormaster's office at Isthmus Cove. Anchoring is permitted outside of established mooring areas except under special weather conditions at the discretion of the harbor patrol. They will assist you if you have any difficulty anchoring. Rafting of boats in mooring areas is not allowed unless expressly permitted by the Harbor Patrol. Speed limit within all mooring areas is five miles per hour or "wakeless" speed, whichever is slow-

TWO HARBORS MOORING FEES	
Size	**Daily**
Stringline	$9.65
10-30 feet	$10.65
31-40 feet	$13.60
41-50 feet	$17.20
51-60 feet	$20
61-70 feet	$23.40
Over 71 feet	$27.30

Day-use fee: under two hours free. Ask about weekly and holiday fee schedules. Garbage and recycling pick-up: 75¢ boatside.

est; this includes dinghies. Keep your neighbor happy—no generators or other motors before 7 a.m. or after 10 p.m. For your own safety, please carry a bright flashlight when traveling after dark in a dinghy skiff or inflatable raft which does not have navigation lights.

Bird Rock

A large white mound that can be seen by boaters from some distance at sea, this landmark was once bought by Helen Webb with Civil War scrip to build a gambling casino. However, a casino wasn't built and the tiny islet is still home to thousands of birds.

Little Fisherman's Cove

Moorings are counted as part of those of the Isthmus Cove. The southwest shore is leased to the Channel Cruising Club; the south shore has camping facilities (Two Harbors Campground, reservations necessary through Catalina Island Camping). The southeast shore is leased to King Harbor Yacht Club.

Big Fisherman's Cove

The home of USC Marine Science Center. Do not use the ramp, dock, or two moorings as they are for research use only. This entire area is now a marinelife refuge. For more information call Bill McFarland, director, tel. 510-0811. The diving-bends recompression chamber at the Science Center is open to anyone who needs it. For emergency calls only, tel. 510-1053.

TWO HARBORS SERVICES

Shore Boat
During the summer season, five shore boats run regularly between Fourth of July, Cherry, Big Fisherman's, and Isthmus coves. During the winter, they're "on call"; three blasts of a horn and a wave during the day, three blasts and a flashing light at night will summon a shore boat. All shoreboats monitor channel 9 VHF. When calling, give them your mooring number and cove name. It helps if you use a flashing light at night when you see the boat approach-

ing. Fees are: Isthmus Cove $1.25 per person, Fourth of July, Big Fisherman's, and Cherry Cove $1.50 pp.

Dinghy Dock
Floats on the Isthmus pier are for loading and unloading passengers. Dinghy docks are provided at the Isthmus Cove and Catalina Harbor for dinghies up to 13 feet. Tie them with a long bowline.

Trash
Trash cans are located at the end of the dinghy dock at Catalina Harbor and on the southwest side of the Cove Agency office at Isthmus Cove. During summer months, a trash collection boat (familiarly called the "salad boat") operates in the Two Harbors, Fourth of July, Cherry, Howland's, Emerald Bay, and White's Landing areas; it will accept your trash and recycling bags for 75 cents. In winter, harbor patrol boats will accept your the bags for 75 cents. If all else fails, take your trash with you. There is a fine of $500 and/or six months in jail for trash thrown over the side.

FROM BLUE CAVERN POINT TRAVELING SOUTH

Blue Cavern Point
With its clear deep waters, this is a favorite diving spot for taking photos. Caves and other small coves invite exploration. This is the site of one of the scenes described in Fredrick Holder's "Adventures of Torqua," a tale of Indian raiders who take valuables from the camps of the white man and make their way to Blue Cavern Point. From there an underwater opening leads into a tunnel that passes through to the opposite side of the Island. The Indians then exit at Ribbon Rock to escape with their loot. While the victims are bewildered at first, they eventually work out the puzzle. After discovering the Indians' method of escape, the disgruntled white men cement the exit at Ribbon Rock and wait for another raid. Once again the Indians creep into camp, take what they can carry and make their

NUMBER OF MOORINGS ALONG CATALINA COAST

Avalon Bay	315
Catalina Harbor	85
Parson's Landing	2
Emerald Bay	97
Howlands	39
Big Geiger Cove	1
Cherry Cove	102
Fourth of July	42
Isthmus Cove	239
Empire Landing	2
Buttonshell Beach	7
Hen Rock Cove	25
White's Landing	17
Moonstone Beach	34
Toyon	9
Hamilton Beach	36
Descanso	4

way to the point, slipping silently into the black water and the even blacker cave. The white men hide and when all the Indians are inside, seal the entrance of the cave, entombing them for eternity. Fiction?

Empire Landing
Boaters will see two moorings, but they are private; however there's anchorage for 20. Another quarry site with a dock for emergency landing only, operating intermittently over the last 30 years or more, has provided Island stone for building sites and breakwaters all along the Southern California coast. One of the largest hills of soapstone on the Island was located at Empire Landing. It was carved by the Indians into religious artifacts and everyday utensils such as ollas (for grinding acorns and other hard grains). Many fascinating artifacts were found, including remnants of half-made ollas attached by stems of stone to the outcropping, as though the carver had been interrupted and left his project unexpectedly. During the 1950s, the soapstone was blasted and removed in the course of production.

Rippers Cove
No moorings here, anchorage for 5-10. Two beaches have crystal-clear water, a fine place for swimming and diving. Look for "velvet-covered" sand dollars spinning along like miniature wheels on the sandy bottom of the bay.

Little Gibraltar
No moorings, but there's anchorage for five to seven boats. Around Little Gibraltar to Cabrillo Beach the shore is leased to the Long Beach Boy Scouts.

Goat Harbor
No moorings, but anchorage for 5-10 boats. Good camping and hiking. Supplies for Middle Ranch, a working ranch in the interior, used to be unloaded from boats here and taken inland. In 1966, Explorer Scouts were breaking camp on the beach when they discovered a half-buried chest containing gold-leaf-wrapped opium. Who knows how old it was!

Italian Gardens
No moorings, but it's a fair anchorage. A good fishing spot, it was here in this "sea-garden" that the Italian fishermen from San Pedro came regularly to take abundant catches of fish back across the channel.

Long Point
Folklore tells of a cave at Long Point that (still) whistles when the wind approaches from a certain direction, with an eerie sound which struck fear into the hearts of the Indians. Long Point Light warns boaters of the presence of this jutting finger of land.

Buttonshell Beach
Seven moorings, anchorage for 10. The land ashore, called Camp Fox, is leased to the Glendale YMCA.

Hen Rock Cove
Twenty-four moorings, anchorage for 10. Good snorkeling area. The land is leased to the Balboa Yacht Club.

White's Landing
Seventeen moorings, anchorage for 16. The land is leased to Los Angeles Girl Scouts and part of the beach to the Balboa Yacht Club. Here you'll see a well and the foundations of a smelter where a conveyor brought silver ore to the landing from Black Jack Mine high on the ridge above this beach. This mine produced more silver ore than any other mine on the Island.

Moonstone Beach
Thirty-eight moorings and anchorage for 12. This beach is leased to the Newport Harbor Yacht Club. It was named Moonstone because in years past the beach was covered with small shiny rocks.

Torqua Springs
From descriptions in old ships' logs this was probably where the Indians came to get their water. For years, this was also one of Avalon's main water sources. Today, it gets its fame from

Avalon Harbor

a 100-foot-deep artificial reef that has been established at Torqua Springs, built from old cars, pipes, machinery, and tanks, creating a good habitat for fish and an excellent dive area.

Willow Cove

No moorings, anchorage for four boats. A small quiet cove, beach camping permitted, with good swimming in clear water.

Toyon Bay

Nine moorings and anchorage for six boats. Shore area is leased to the Catalina Island Marine Institute.

Gallagher's Beach

No moorings, fair anchorage for three to five boats. Shore leased to "Campus-by-the-Sea" vacation camp.

SANTA BARBARA CONFERENCE AND VISITORS BUREAU

SOUTHERN CALIFORNIA MARINAS

SANTA BARBARA COUNTY COASTAL AREAS

The prehistory of the site of the present city of Santa Barbara includes the Chumash Indians. Here beneath the Santa Ynez Mountains was the location of some of the largest communities of Chumash Indians. In 1782 Father Junipero Serra and Captain Jose Francisco de Ortega founded a military presidio to defend against Russian explorers. In 1786, Mission Santa Barbara was built, the 10th mission under the Spanish flag. As was the case with all of the Spanish missions, the Europeans, seeking to convert the Indians to Christianity, managed instead to destroy the culture that had existed for thousands of years in the Santa Barbara area.

The peaceful Pacific coast Indians were content with a productive life of fishing in a generous sea. The first Europeans were so amazed at the quantities of sardines, tuna, and swordfish

the Indians caught so easily that they felt there was enough seafood to support a rich economy with the fishing industry alone. Santa Barbara's southern neighbor Carpinteria (in Spanish meaning "carpenter's shop"), was alive with long beaches filled with the energetic Canalino Indians industriously building their wood-plank canoes called *tomols*. In fact, two explorers (Cabrillo in 1547 and Portola in 1769) were both so impressed with the boat-building abilities of the area's Indians that even though there were more than 200 years between visits, both chose names in remembrance of the Indian canoe building. Cabrillo's name was Los Pueblos de Canoas ("Cities of Canoes"), while Portola chose to honor the carpenter with Carpinteria.

The Spanish influence in Santa Barbara lingered longer than in other parts of the West

Coast. Many historical buildings from the Spanish era can still be seen by taking a walk through "old California" on Santa Barbara's "Red Tile Tour." Begin this walk at the Courthouse at the 1100 block of Anacapa St. or anywhere along the route designated by red tiles (a brochure is available at the chamber of commerce office at 1330 State Street). The self-guided tour takes you to the Hill-Carillo Adobe built in 1826, the 1827 Casa de la Guerra, (center of Santa Barbara social life made famous in *Two Years Before The Mast),* and the Casa de Covarrubias (1817), where the last Mexican Assembly met in July of 1846.

Since the early 1920s Santa Barbara has attracted the celebrity class. There are many lovely homes and horse ranches close by—especially in the rolling hills behind town (former President Ronald Reagan's included). Along the often rough Santa Barbara coast, a 2,364-foot breakwater was constructed in the 1920s. It covers 84 acres, creating a safe harbor for fishing boats and pleasure craft alike. Santa Barbara's Stearns Wharf, established 1872, is touted as the oldest operating wharf on the West Coast. In the early days the wharf was used for steamers going up and down the coast; a trip by ship was the quickest way to get to San Francisco or San Diego. Today it's fun to walk on the restored wharf, eat at one of the restaurants, buy fresh seafood at the fish market, take pictures of the town and coastline, or just watch the gulls screech and dive when a fishing boat docks alongside.

MARINA INFORMATION

Santa Barbara Harbor
The marina and fishing boat anchorage are located in Santa Barbara Harbor. For information and reservations contact City of Santa Barbara, 132 A. Harbor Way, Santa Barbara, CA 93109, tel. (805) 564-5520. There are 100 transient slips available; altogether 1,000 slips accommodate both pleasure craft and fishing boats. Slip fees are 40 cents per foot per day, 14 day limit, issued on a first-come, first-serve basis.

Fresh water is available at each slip. A convenience food store is located on the premises, open 8 a.m.-7 p.m. The closest supermarket is a two-block walk. Marine supplies are available 8 a.m.-6 p.m. Marine services also available. Fuel dock hours are 7 a.m.-6 p.m. No laundry facilities at the marina.

Santa Barbara Yacht Club
Visiting members of reciprocal yacht clubs are always welcome to use the facilities of the Santa Barbara Yacht Club. You'll find showers, bar, good food, and active racing programs; 130 Harbor Way, Santa Barbara, CA 93109, tel. (805) 965-8112. **Harbormaster**: Located on the breakwater at the west end of Cabrillo Blvd. at 132 A Harbor Way, Santa Barbara, CA 93109, tel. (805) 963-1737 or 963-1738. The office is open 24 hours a day; a patrol boat operates 24 hours a day. There's a 24-hour radio watch on VHF channel 16. Julia Hazard is the harbormaster.

MARINE SERVICES

Union Marine Station, On-The-Breakwater, Santa Barbara 93109, tel. (805) 962-7186, has a fuel dock open daily 7 a.m.-6 p.m. The **Coast Chandlery**, On-The-Breakwater, Santa Barbara, CA 93109, tel. (805) 965-4538, offers a variety of marine supplies, clothing, marine repair, and boat sales; open 8 to 6. **Sailors Emporium,** Marine Center, 117 B Harbor Way, Santa Barbara, CA 93109, tel. (805) 962-5155, open daily offering canvaswear, nautical gifts, sewing repairs, new sails; "everything for the fair weather sailor in you." A marine outfitter that will dress up you or your boat. **Pacific Marine Electrical & Refrigeration,** 31 Breakwater, Santa Barbara, CA 93109, tel. (805) 963-8000 is open 8 a.m.-5 p.m., and offers electrical and corrosion control consulting. **The Boat Yard,** On-The-Breakwater, Santa Barbara, CA 93109, tel. (805) 965-0887, has a travelift with a capacity of 30 tons, plus a shipyard with do-it-yourself facilities.

Fishing Information

There's a four-lane, concrete **launching ramp** operated by the City of Santa Barbara. Enter through the main harbor entrance. **Carter's Sportfishing Center,** On-The-Breakwater, Santa Barbara, CA 93109, tel. (805) 962-4720, has everything for the fisherman, including bait, rods, tackle, and repairs. Open 7 days. **Santa Barbara Boat Rentals,** 827 Margo, Santa Bar-

bara, CA 93109, tel. (805) 962-2826, is next to the launching ramp; also sail and power rentals.

SANTA BARBARA ATTRACTIONS

Spend some time poking around Santa Barbara, a modern city that carefully preserves its early Spanish beginnings. A stop at the Santa Barbara Visitors Bureau at 1330 State St., tel. (805) 965-3021, will get you good information and maps of the town. If you plan on visiting the Santa Barbara area in August, do stay for the Old Spanish Days Fiesta. This is a citywide good time of five days celebrating the city's Spanish heritage and offers parades, dancing, flamenco and concert music, an arts and crafts show, rodeo, barbecues, theatrical performances; everyone dresses in the Spanish costumes of early California. It's colorful and has been ongoing for more than 20 years. Boaters, make reservations early; the harbor is packed during this time. Other busy times are during Semana Nautica Regatta (great sailing races)

Santa Barbara Harbor

SANTA BARBARA CONFERENCE AND VISITORS BUREAU

One of Southern California's busiest marinas is in Santa Barbara.

and the Santa Barbara to King Harbor Race, one of the most popular sailing races of Southern California. Take the opportunity to see a polo match in July and attend free concerts in the park from June 1 to mid-Sept. (Alameda Park Band Stand).

Museums

The **Museum of Natural History** is on Puesta del Sol Rd. (two blocks north of the mission), tel. (805) 682-4711. Along with exhibits featuring mammals, birds, fish, reptiles, plantlife, and geology of the Channel Islands, there's a planetarium. Also of interest is a diorama of prehistoric Indian life and a 72-foot blue whale skeleton in front of the museum; guided tours, admission adults $3, teens and seniors $2, children $1.

The **Historical Museum** is at 136 E. de la Guerra St., tel. (805) 966-1601. Here you'll see treasures from Santa Barbara's colorful past: documents, paintings, costumes, and many rare mementos from three eras, Indian, Mexican, and American. Admission free, call for hours.

Fernald House and Trussell-Winchester Adobe, 414 W. Montecito St., P.O. Box 578 Santa Barbara, CA 93102-0578, tel. (805) 966-1601. Admission is free, but donations are greatly appreciated. Tours Sun. 2-4 p.m. Fernald House is a two-story Queen Anne Victorian home, partially restored to circa-1900 period furnishings, fine arts, and decorative arts. Originally the home of Judge Charles Fernald and

his family, the Trussell-Winchester Adobe is a 19th-century adobe with authentic furnishings. Timbers from the shipwreck of the *Winfield Scott* were used in construction.

Museum of Art, 1130 State St., tel. (805) 963-4364, is one of the nation's outstanding regional museums, with important holdings of American art, featuring examples by O'Keeffe, Eakins, Sargent, and Hopper; 19th-century French art including impressionist works by Monet, Pissarro, and Chagall; Asian art, classical antiquities, photography, 20th-century art, modern European art, and prints and drawings. Special exhibitions throughout the year explore a variety of themes; some are originated by the museum and others are drawn from national and international traveling exhibitions. Admission $3 adults, $1.50 children 6-16, under 6 free; free Thursdays and first Sunday of the month. Hours: Tues.-Sat. 11 a.m.-5 p.m., Thurs. to 9 p.m., Sun. 12-5 p.m., closed Mondays, Thanksgiving, Christmas, and New Year's Day.

Santa Barbara Mission, located at the upper end of Laguna St., tel. (805) 682-4713, is called the "Queen of the Missions" because of its graceful beauty. It is still in use as a parish church. Take a self-guided tour of the museum, garden, chapel, cemetery, and the remnants of the original water system on the hill north of the mission. Open daily 9-5; admission $1; children under 16 free.

NATURE TREKS

The **Botanic Garden** is at 1212 Mission Canyon Rd., tel. (805) 682-4726 (1½ miles north of the mission). Wander through 65 acres of native trees, shrubs, wildflowers, and cacti in natural settings, or explore the five miles of easy-to-walk nature trails. Visit the historic dam built in 1806 by Indians under the supervision of the mission padres. Open daily 8 a.m. until sunset. Guided tours daily at 2 p.m. and on Thurs. and Sat. at 10:30 a.m., specialty tours Mon. at noon.; admission is $3 for adults, $2 for seniors and teens, $1 children 5-12, free to Garden members and on Tues. and Wednesday.

The **Santa Barbara Zoological Gardens** are at 500 Ninos Dr. off Cabrillo Blvd., tel. (805) 962-6310. In a garden setting the zoo has a delightful variety of elephants, monkeys, lions, sea lions, exotic birds, and other animals. Great for children of all ages with a miniature train ride, playground, farmyard petting area, and botanical gardens. Snack bar and spacious picnic facilities. Open Mid-June to Labor Day, 9 a.m.-6 p.m., 10 a.m.-5 p.m. the rest of the year; admission $4 adult and junior, $2 senior and children under 12. Train ride $1 adults, 50 cents children.

Santa Barbara is home to the **Moreton Bay Fig Tree** on Chapala St. and Highway 101. The tree, native to Australia, is the largest of its kind in the States. It was planted in 1877 by a pioneer family and it is said that more than 10,000 people could stand in its shade at noon—the branch spread is over 160 feet. If you are suffering from cabin fever, take a stroll along the paved walkway on top of the breakwater. This is a half-mile walk around the harbor with great views of the city and mountains. Anyone interested in tidepools should go to Carpinteria Beach during the once-a-day low-low tide. Visitors can view the constant battle for survival by nature's feisty organisms. Where shore and sea are tangent, the tidal ebb and flood probably sustains more life per square foot than any other natural ecosystem. Remember, California's aquatic life, plants, and animals are protected by law; especially prohibited is the taking of specimens. Tidepooling is a recreation of looking and learning.

NEARBY RESTAURANTS

Breakwater Restaurant, On-The-Breakwater, tel. (805) 965-1557. **Char West**, 221 Stearns Wharf, tel. (805) 962- 5631. **Azteca Restaurante**, 623 State St., tel. (805) 965-9059. **John Dory**, On-The-Breakwater, tel. (805) 966-4418. **Moby Dick**, 220 Stearns Wharf, tel. (805) 965-0549. Lobster House, 15 E. Cabrillo Blvd., tel. (805) 965-1174. **Suishin Sukiyaki**, 511 State St., tel. (805) 962-1495.

sea otter

VENTURA COUNTY COASTAL AREAS

History

The Chumash Indians were much the same all along the Pacific coast; their life-style was closely associated with the sea. It was only after the arrival of the Spaniards that the "sameness" began to change. Mission San Buenaventura was founded in 1782 and many of the Indians were enlisted to do the menial work of the padres. As time went by Indian country became white man's country. The few remaining Indians became ranch hands and were gradually assimilated into the population. In the mid-1800s settlers from the East and Midwest began to discover the fertile valleys of Ventura County, and farming became the number one economic activity.

Close behind, another activity began. From as early as 1896, oil has been removed from offshore wells. (Even earlier, the Indians made use of the asphaltum that oozed from the earth in isolated places along the shore to seal their *tomol* canoes and to waterproof their basketry.) The oil business continued to grow and though the economic rewards of the industry along the California coast are great, ecologists are greatly concerned over the damage that the occasional spill causes the wildlife of the Pacific.

VENTURA COUNTY MARINAS

The harbormaster for Ventura County is located at 1603 Anchors Way Dr., Ventura, CA 93001, tel. (805) 642-8618.

Ventura West Marina

Phase one of the marina is located on the northeast portion of Ventura Harbor; Phase two is on the harbor's west side. Mailing address for both is 1198 Navigator Dr., Ventura, CA 93001. Transient slips available, number varies. Slip fees are 30 cents per foot per night. There's a deli and small food store on the premises, open 8:30 a.m.-5:30 p.m. daily. Fresh water is available at all slips and there's a pump-out station. Marine supplies available 8:30 a.m.-5:30 p.m. On premises, 18 washers and dryers open 24 hours daily.

Harbortown Marina Resort Hotel

At 1050 Schooner Dr., Ventura, CA 93001, tel. (805) 658-1212, CA only (800) 622-1212; rooms from $58-105. Guest slips and transient accommodations available.

Ventura Isle Marina

Located at the south end of Ventura Harbor, 1363 Spinnaker Dr., Ventura, CA 93001. Slip fees are $12 a day up to 35 feet, $15 a day over 35 feet; average per foot for permanent slip is $8.50. Small food stores are available in the harbor within walking distance. There's a water hookup at each slip, also showers, ice, electricity, and a pump-out station. No marine service or supplies available. Laundry services available 24 hours with a guest card.

Vintage Marina

Located near Channel Islands Blvd. next to the Harbor Landing, with restaurants, shops; parking lot faces Harborwalk condos. Office directly across from the Pacific Corinthian Marina. Mailing address is 2950 S. Harbor Blvd., Oxnard, CA 93055. The number of transient slips available varies. Slip fees are $6.50 per foot for under 36 feet; $6.75 per foot for over 36 feet: $7.25 per foot for catamarans and trimarans or boats measuring over 70 feet (N-ties). Nearest food store is less than five miles, located in the Harbor Landing area; open Tues.-Sun. 9 a.m.-5 p.m. Fresh water is located at the dock boxes. No marine services or supplies available. Laundry facilities are available for guests.

Channel Islands Marina

Located on the west side of Channel Islands Harbor, the mailing address is 3850 Harbor Blvd., Oxnard, CA 93030. Number of transient slips varies according to season. Slip fees from $5.85 per foot monthly up to a 25-foot slip to $7 per foot monthly up to a 48-foot slip. Closest food store is about one-quarter mile away, open 7 a.m.-11 p.m. Water is available on the docks. Marine supplies available 8:30 a.m.-9 p.m., and the fuel dock is open 8 a.m.-5 p.m., tel. (805) 985-7558.

Anacapa Isle Marina

Located at 3001 Peninsula Rd., Oxnard, CA 93035, tel. (805) 985-6035. Call for transient slip information and fees. Regular slip fees begin at $225 monthly for 25 feet to $518 monthly for

50 feet. Food stores are within walking distance, berths for boats of all sizes, clean restrooms, concrete docks, fresh water, electrical hookups, 24-hour security and laundromats, telephone, lockable dock boxes. Also available are apartments, three pools, jacuzzi, gym, saunas, locker rooms, clubhouse, tennis courts, laundry, and ice. Guest dock, hotel, and restaurants adjoin the marina. When you join Almar Marina, you enjoy free guest privileges at five marinas (Dolphin Isle Marina at Fort Bragg, Ballena Isle Marina at Alameda, Ventura Isle Marina at Ventura, Anacapa Isle Marina at Oxnard, Cabrillo Isle Marina at San Diego).

ATTRACTIONS IN VENTURA COUNTY

One of the most important facilities in the area is the **Channel Islands National Park Building**, located across from the ocean at 1901 Spinnaker Dr., Ventura, CA 93001, tel. (805) 644-8262; visitor center open year-round, summer 8 a.m.-5:30 p.m., fall/winter 8 a.m.-5 p.m. The visitor center offers a well-stocked bookstore with a good collection of books concerning the area, the Channel Islands, the history, and the sea. Exhibits introduce the visitor to the Channel Islands National Marine Sanctuary—what it does and what its goals are for the future of the Channel Islands.

Also available to the public are excellent films about the Channel Islands and tidepool exhibits where children (and adults) experience a hands-on introduction to the small creatures of the sea. These precious resources have been misused in the past but now the federal government is ensuring the islands will be preserved for future generations. They show us what California must have been like when the first white man arrived. The Channel Islands National Park Center is the best source of information for travelers interested in visiting the Channel Islands; that goes for campers, who must obtain a permit.

Island Packers (authorized concessionaire to Channel Islands National Park) next door offers transportation to and from the Channel Islands on a variety of boats from motor launch to sailing vessels for day-trips and/or to drop off campers. They offer swim and snorkel days, tidepool exploring, whalewatching, camping trips, and special group trips. See individual island chapters below for more information; reservations are necessary, tel. (805) 642-1393; information tel. (805) 642-7688.

Island Flights
Channel Islands Aviation makes charter flights to Santa Rosa and San Miguel islands from Camarillo Airport. The trip takes a half-hour each way. Permits must be obtained from the Channel Islands National Park Headquarters. From the same airport the company makes day-trips to Santa Rosa Island. Passengers are encouraged to bring picnics and to wear good walking shoes. An itinerary (five hours) will be arranged when reservations are made and can include a trip with the island ranger to the scenic points, Indian middens, wildlife and botany vistas, or just a quiet spot for a picnic. Adults, $75 RT, children $50. For reservations and information call (805) 987-1678.

Area Museums
The **Albinger Archaeological Museum** is located at 113 E. Main St., downtown, tel. (805) 648-5823. The **Olivas Adobe Historic Park** at 4200 Olivas Park Dr., tel. (805) 644-4346, a historic early California adobe built in 1847, offers a glimpse into the early days of California living. The grounds are open daily, house open Tues.-Sun., free weekend tours at 11 a.m., 1 and 2 p.m. A 12-minute video on the ranchos of California is offered free on weekends. The **Ortega Adobe Historic Residence** at 215 W. Main St., downtown, tel. (805) 648-5823, is an 1857 middle-class structure. **Ventura County Museum of History and Art**, 100 E. Main St., downtown, tel. (805) 653-0323, 653-5469 is open Tues.-Sun. 10 a.m. 5 p.m., closed New Year's, Thanksgiving, Christmas. Nonprofit, private museum, founded in 1913. Members free; adults, $2, ages 6-12, $.50; no admission charge on Tuesday. Visitors will find a permanent collection of Ventura County historical items as well as changing art exhibits and George Stuart Historical Figures relating to the famous and infamous of the world. Look for an extensive collection of horse-drawn farm implements. The library/archives contain historical records and more than 20,000 historic photographs; newspapers and Sanborn fire insurance maps on microfilm.

Nature Treks
For those interested in nature, a visit to the **Santa Clara Estuary Natural Reserve** is well worth the time. It's accessible from Peninsula Beach to the north or McGrath State Beach to the south. This marshland wildlife preserve is

located at the mouth of the Santa Clara River. North of the river along Spinnaker Dr. the wastewater lagoons are fenced off, making an outstanding habitat for migratory waterfowl. This is a must for serious birdwatchers.

A larger spot (1,800 acres) is the **Mugu Lagoon**, the largest between Morro Bay and San Diego County. The lagoon is located entirely within the grounds of the Navy's Pacific Missile Test Center. In order to see the lagoon, it's necessary to make reservations at least 30 days in advance with a minimum of 15 persons. Public access is limited to weekend interpretive tours. For more information call the Public Affairs Office, tel. (805) 982-8094.

Seaside Wilderness Park is a small park of palm trees and Monterey pines where the bird-watching is good. The only way to get there is by three-quarter-mile walk from **Emma Wood State Beach** in the north. Continue along the beach and sand dunes west of the railroad tracks.

MARINE SERVICES

Dave's Marine Fuel, 1404 Anchors Way Dr., Ventura, CA 93001, tel. (805) 644-6776. Open Mon.-Fri. 8 a.m.-5 p.m., Sat.-Sun. 6 a.m.-6 p.m., off-hours fuel by appointment. Commercial and volume fuel prices at Unocal fuel dock; bait, ice, tackle. **Ventura Harbor Village**, at 1559 Spinnaker Dr., Ventura, CA 93001, tel. (805) 644-0169. You'll find specialty shops, restaurants, as well as a full-service shipyard, a self-service boatyard, marine fuel dock, and a commercial fish unloading, processing, and distribution center. Take a stroll along the mile-long bayside walkway; here visitors see yacht activity as well as busy commercial fishing traffic.

Ventura Harbor Boatyard, Inc., 1415 Spinnaker Dr., Ventura 93001. For the full-service yard call (805) 654-1433, for the self-service yard call (805) 654-8265, fax (805) 654-8066. **Cruise Marine Refrigeration** is at 1660 Callens Rd., Ventura 93001, tel. (805) 644-COLD.

Marine Books
Trade Winds Nautique, in Beacon Marine Center, 1198 Navigator Rd., Ventura, CA 93003, tel. (805) 644-6545, is open daily 9 a.m.-6 p.m. and carries marine books and cruising guides.

NEARBY RESTAURANTS

Alexander's, 1080 Navigator Dr., tel. (805) 658-1212. **Andrea's Seafood**, 1449 Spinnaker Dr., tel. (805) 654-0546. **Bedford's**, 1583 Spinnaker Dr., tel. (805) 644-3333. **Bramsway Deli/Restaurant**, 1559 Spinnaker Dr., tel. (805) 642-3116. **Colony Kitchen**, 2401 E. Harbor Blvd., tel. (805) 642-0261. **Denny's**, 2148 E. Harbor Blvd., tel. (805) 643-9192. **Waterfront Deli** (at Ventura West Marina), 1198 Navigator Dr., tel. (805) 644-3354. **First Mate Deli** (next to National Park Visitor Center), 1869 Spinnaker Dr., tel. (805) 654-1300.

Hornblower's, 1559 Spinnaker Dr., tel. (805) 658-2345. **Hungry Hunter**, 2046 E. Harbor Blvd., tel. (805) 648-5146. **Love's**, 2070 E. Harbor Blvd., tel. (805) 648-3021. **Pierpont Inn**, 550 Sanjon Road, tel. (805) 643-6144. **Ramon's**, 2401 E. Harbor Blvd., tel. (805) 642-0261. **Scotch & Sirloin**, 1510 Anchors Way Dr., tel. (805) 644-2229. **Seaview-On-The-Pier**, Fishing Pier, tel. (805) 643-7030. **Village Inn**, 1591 Spinnaker Dr., tel. (805) 658-0844.

LOS ANGELES COUNTY COASTAL AREAS

In 1860, Los Angeles had a population of 4,355. By 1870 it had only grown to 5,728. Then in 1876 the transcontinental railroad was completed, and things started to move a *little* faster. By 1890 the population had grown to more than 51,000. It's been growing rapidly ever since. Today the population of Los Angeles County is over 10 million and many of those people are boat owners. In 1986, small pleasure boats registered in Southern California alone increased by 14,457—across the state the increase was 23,102. According to an unofficial report from the Department of Motor Vehicles, pleasure boat registration count in the state is 666,089, making it second in the nation, behind only Michigan. These totals do not include the really big vessels registered directly with the Coast Guard; minimum size for Coast Guard registration is five tons.

Los Angeles Harbor is one of the largest manmade harbors in the world. It engulfs 7,000 acres of land and water and boasts 28 miles of waterfront. The largest commercial fishing fleet in the U.S. calls Los Angeles Harbor home. Fish canneries thrive and cargo ships from all over the world include Los Angeles Harbor as a port of call. The pleasure boater has all that he could want—except isolation. Marinas with thousands of slips, plus boat yards, hoists, cranes, equipment centers, fishing supplies, boat landings, and terminals for luxury cruise lines can all be found pretty close together. The waterfront has been spruced up in recent years; many of the old ports like San Pedro and Long Beach have undergone complete face-lifts. Modern hotels, convention centers, and restaurants have been built next to new state-of-the-art marinas with quaint fishing village-like complexes and shopping centers to attract out-of-town visitors—as well as local boaters.

Part of the greater Los Angeles Harbor, Marina del Rey is the largest artificial small-craft harbor in the world. Built in 1960, it accommodates more than 6,000 pleasure boats and there's a waiting list! This is a busy harbor with every kind of marine service available, including dry storage. Guest berths are located at Basin H; check with the harbormaster. Advance reservations are suggested.

MARINA DEL REY HARBOR

Marina del Rey is the largest manmade small craft harbor in the world. Built in 1960, it accommodates more than 6,000 recreational boats in 23 anchorages and yacht clubs. This is a busy harbor with every kind of marine service available, including dry storage. Guest Boat Docks are located along the main channel and Basin H, adjacent to Burton Chace Park. Dock office is in the Community Building in the center of the park, which is located at the western end of Mindanao Way. Park and dock office telephone is (310) 305-9595, open daily 6 a.m.-10 p.m. Mail: Los Angeles County Department of Beaches and Harbors, 13837 Fiji Way, Marina del Rey, CA 90292. There are 1,900 feet of dock space, including ten 57-foot slips. Rates are 50 cents per foot per day and include water and power hookups, trash collection, hot showers, and picnic facilities. One-week maximum stay. Many restaurants are within walking distance. Nearest food store is Marina Market in the shopping center one block east of the docks, open 24 hours daily. Laundromat within one mile and marine services nearby. Special events include Christmas Boat Parade, California Cup, free summer concerts in the park, July 4 fireworks, and annual In-The-Water Boat Show.

Call or write for information and reservations to Burton Chace Park Transient Docks, 13837 Fiji Way, Marina del Rey, CA 90292, tel. (310) 305-9545. **Harbormaster**, tel. (310) 823-7762. The **Marina Visitor's Information Center** is located at 4701 Admiralty Way, Marina del Rey,

CA 90292, tel. (310) 822-0119. Open daily from 9 a.m.-5 p.m. There are 36 transient slips available.

Deauville Marina
Located in Basins B and C, Marina del Rey. Mailing address is 13900 Marquesas Way, Marina del Rey, CA 90292, tel. (310) 823-4655. No transient slips available. Slip fees range from $8.34-$15 per foot for slips 30-55 feet. Fresh water is available at each slip and the nearest food store is four blocks away, open 9 a.m.-6 p.m. Captain's Wharf Restaurant is located on premises.

Special Attractions
Fisherman's Village is a commercial area with trendy shops, art galleries, and good restaurants along with shops that cater to the boater; fishing licenses are available here also. Visit the **Burton Chace Park** for a nice change of pace. You'll find an eight-acre park with a great view of the main channel, plus transient docks,

fishing dock, picnic area, and watchtower. Free parking on weekdays.

Marine Services
Basin G Boatyard, 4643 Admiralty Way, Marina del Rey, CA 90292, tel. (310) 827-2870. Hoist capacity to 30 feet. Hull and bottom painting, open daily 8 a.m.-5 p.m. **Mare Co. Sails,** 4080 Lincoln Blvd., Marina del Rey, CA 90292, tel. (310) 822-9344. A full-service sail loft including sail repairs, custom sewing, wire rope splices, multihull nets and trampolines, and marine hardware. Open Mon.-Fri. 8:30 a.m.-5:30 p.m.

An all-year fuel dock, **Marine Fuels and Service, Inc.,** is located on the west side of the main channel; 13800 Bora Bora Way, Marina del Rey, CA 90292, tel. (310) 823-2444. Boaters will find fishing supplies, frozen bait, and tackle as well as ice, marine accessories, and pumpout station. Open summer 7 a.m.-6 p.m, winter 8 a.m.-5 p.m. **Maritime Communications, Inc.,** 766 Washington Blvd., Marina del Rey, CA

MARINA DEL REY

COURSES FROM MARINA DEL REY

To:	Magnetic Course	Reverse Course	Distance in Nautical Miles
Pt. Conception	271	91	100
Anacapa Light	260	80	44
Santa Cruz Light	254	74	67
Santa Rosa Light	252	72	82
Begg Rock	225	45	70.5
San Nicholas Island, West End	219	39	68.5
Pt. Vincente	155	335	13.5
Santa Barbara Island	209	29	39
Osborn Bank	203	23	45.5
Tanner Bank	189	9	82
Bishop Rock	184	4	96.5
Catalina Island, West End	179	359	29
Catalina Island Isthmus	166	346	30

90291, tel. (310) 821-4958. There's a good selection of clocks, watches, sextants, and navigational instruments along with compass adjusting, sales, and repair. Marine electronics sales, service, installation. Open year-round Mon.-Fri. 8:30-5, Sat. 8:30-noon, closed Sunday.

Nearby Accommodations

Dolphin Marina, Basins C and D, 13900 Panay Way, Marina del Rey, CA 90292, tel. (310) 823-4875. Apartments with slips available. **Jamaica Bay Inn**, Basin E, 4175 Admiralty Way, Marina del Rey, CA 90292, tel. (310) 823-5333; small-boat launching ramp. **Doubletree Hotel Marina del Rey**, Basin E, 4100 Admiralty Way, Marina del Rey, CA 90292, tel. (310) 301-3000, (800) 528-0444. $165-275, special weekend rates available. **Marina del Rey Hotel**, 13534 Bali Way, Marina del Rey, CA 90292, tel. (310) 301-1000; slips available. Rooms $120-205, suites $350-400. **Marina International Hotel**, 4200 Admiralty Way, Marina del Rey, CA 90292, tel. (310) 301-2000, (800) 8-MARINA.

The Marina International Hotel and Bungalows is a full-service European-style hotel situated in the heart of the world's largest man-made yacht harbor—Marina del Rey. Five miles north and 10 minutes away from L.A. International Airport, offering complimentary shuttle service. One hundred and thirty-five guest rooms (25 are charming bungalows), featuring private balcony or patio. A true hideaway, yet convenient to all the glitz and glamor Los Angeles has to offer!

Restaurants

Akbar, 590 Washington St., tel. (310) 822-4116. **Benihana of Tokyo**, 14160 Panay Way, tel. (310) 821-0888. **Casa Escobar**, 14160 Palawan Way, tel. (310) 822-2199. **Casola's Fish House**, 4211 Admiralty Way, tel. (310) 823-5339. **Charley Brown's**, 4445 Admiralty Way, tel. (310) 823-4534. **Cheesecake Factory**, 4142 Via Marina, tel. (310) 306-3344. **Cyrano's**, 13535 Mindanao Way, tel. (310) 823-5305. **Don the Beachcomber**, 13530 Bali Way, tel. (310) 823-5435. **El Torito** (Fisherman's Village),

13715 Fiji Way, tel. (310) 823-8941. **Fish Market** (Fisherman's Village), 13723 Fiji Way, tel. (310) 823-8444. **Jamaica Bay Inn**, 4175 Admiralty Way, tel. (310) 823-5333. **Red Onion**, 4215 Admiralty Way, tel. (310) 821-2291. **Shanghai Red's**, 13813 Fiji Way, tel. (310) 823-4522.

Church Services

Second Community Baptist Church, 1041 Washington Blvd., Venice, tel. (310) 392-5632. **St. Mark's Catholic Church**, 940 Coeur d'Alene Ave., Venice, tel. (310) 821-5058. **20th Church of L.A.**, 132 Brooks Ave., Venice, tel. (310) 396-1390. **Marina del Rey Episcopal Chapel**, 4201 Via Marina, Marina del Rey, tel. (310) 823-8643 or 670-4777. **Beth Shalom Jewish Temple Reformed**, 1827 California Ave., Santa Monica, tel. (310) 453-3361. **First Lutheran Church of Venice**, 815 Venice Blvd., Venice, tel. (310) 821-2740. Nondenominational **Church of the Marina** meets every Sunday morning at 9 in the Burton Chace Park Community Building. For information call (310) 823-9598.

Emergency Services

Sheriff's harbor patrol offices are located adjacent to the Department of Beaches and Harbors Administration Offices at 13837 Fiji Way. Harbor patrol offices are staffed 24 hours, every day of the year, and can be reached by calling (310) 823-7762, or 911 (emergency) to report a fire or to request the paramedics.

REDONDO BEACH AND KING HARBOR

Redondo Beach's King Harbor continues to grow more popular and more crowded each year. The harbor can handle more than 1,500 pleasure boats. Between boaters and visitors to the Redondo Municipal Pier, the International Boardwalk, and Monstad Pier, King Harbor attracts thousands of people, especially in the summer. There are four marinas in King Harbor. None maintain transient docks; however, arrangements can be made if slips are available.

COURSES FROM REDONDO BEACH

To:	Magnetic Course	Reverse Course	Distance in Nautical Miles
Palos Verdes Point	191	11	4.5
Catalina Island, West End	191	11	24
Santa Barbara Light	221	41	38
San Nicolas Island, East End	218	38	62
Tanner Bank	193	13	77.5
Begg Rock	231	51	70.5
Santa Rosa Island, South Point	257	77	85
Anacapa Light	267	87	49
Point Dume	279	99	27

King Harbor Marina
Located in Basins One and Two, mailing address is 212 Yacht Club Way, Redondo Beach, CA 90277, tel. (310) 376-6926. Laundry, restaurant, and cocktails close by.

Port Royal Marina
Located in Basin Two, mailing address is 555 North Harbor Dr., Redondo Beach, CA 90277, tel. (310) 376-0431.

Portofino Inn and Marina
Located in Basin Two, mailing address is 255 Portofino Way, Redondo Beach, CA 90277, tel. (310) 379-8481, ext. 432, (800) 468-4292, fax (310) 372-7329. The office is open Wed.-Sun. 9 a.m.-5 p.m. The newly remodeled Portofino Inn is on the premises, offering upscale rooms with sports facilities, jacuzzis, luxury amenities, and lovely views of the harbor; room rates from $110. Try the Marina Cafe and Grill and watch the parade of boats while enjoying the excellent food and bar.

Redondo Beach Marina
Located at 189 North Harbor Dr., Redondo Beach, CA 90277, tel. (310) 374-3481. Restaurant on premises, close to fish market. Redondo Sport Fishing at 233 N. Harbor Drive, Redondo Beach, CA 90277, tel. (310) 372-2111, offers deep-sea sportfishing on a variety of vessels, including the *Isle of Redondo* barge. Pole rentals, tackle sales, and whalewatching in season round out their offerings. Open 24 hours.

Marina Services
All four of these marinas offer dockside water and electricity. The average overnight fee is $10, higher for larger boats. **Laundry** facilities are offered to guests of King Harbor, Redondo Beach, and Portofino marinas. There are no food stores located within King Harbor, though there are delis and liquor stores within a few blocks. A large supermarket is one quarter mile away.

Note: The city of Redondo Beach offers free anchorage to transient boats. A bow and stern anchor are required. Transients must provide their own shore transportation. A permit is required from the harbormaster and is limited to a 72-hour stay.

Restaurants
King Harbor is encircled with fine restaurants. The pier located at the south end of the harbor offers a plethora of good dining and entertainment.

Marine Services

King Harbor Marina Inc. is located in Basin One, next to King Harbor Marina, at 212 Yacht Club Way, Redondo Beach, CA 90277, tel. (310) 374-8923, fax (310) 374-6067. The boatyard is open daily from 9 a.m.-6 p.m. The marine store is open seven days a week; 24-hour emergency service is available. The Portofino Oasis Petroleum fuel dock is located at the entrance to Basin Two, 310 Portofino Way, Redondo Beach, CA 90277, tel. (310) 374-9858; open daily 6-6, with marine supplies, ice, cold drinks, and snacks.

LOS ANGELES HARBOR ATTRACTIONS

Catalina Boat Terminal

Boats to Catalina Island leave from Catalina Landing in downtown Long Beach and from San Pedro at the Catalina Air and Sea Terminal under the Vincent Thomas Bridge, daily, year-round. For complete information see "Getting There."

Cabrillo Marine Museum

The original **Cabrillo Marine Museum** at 3720 Stephen M. White Dr. was begun in 1920. Rather a casual affair instigated by a local lifeguard, John Olguin, who collected sea specimens in mayonnaise jars and exhibited them in an old bathhouse. For years children and their parents were intrigued with John's collection. Eventually, the museum grew up and John's energetic enterprise hired a curator with a degree. John is still around as curator emeritus and the new large facility includes an auditorium, classrooms, laboratories, an exhibition hall with interpretive displays, touch tanks, and aquariums containing marine flora and fauna.

LOS ANGELES HARBOR

© MOON PUBLICATIONS, INC.

COURSES FROM POINT VINCENTE

To:	Magnetic Course	Reverse Course	Distance in Nautical Miles
14-Mile Bank	120	300	29
60-Mile Bank	146	326	68.5
Catalina Island, East End	153	333	26
Gallagher Cove, Catalina Island	157	337	22.8
White's Cove, Catalina Island	158	338	21
Lone Pt., Catalina Island	158	338	20
Isthmus Cove, Catalina Island	178	358	18.6
Emerald Cove, Catalina Island	183	3	17.6
San Nicholas Island, East End	222	42	60
Santa Barbara Island, North End	228	48	35
Anacapa Island	275	95	50
Pt. Hueneme	285	105	46
Pt. Dume	292	112	24.5
Avalon, Catalina Island	152	332	24
Coronado Island	128	308	99
San Diego, Entrance Buoy	123	303	90
Del Mar	107	287	60.5
20-Mile Bank	118	298	30
Newport Entrance Buoy	93	273	29.5

The **Gift and Book Shop** is open 12:30-3:30 p.m. The museum is open Tues.-Fri. noon-5 p.m., Sat. and Sun. 10 a.m.-5 p.m. Call (310) 548-7562 for information (a recorded message) regarding guided tidepool tours at the Point Fermin Marine Life Refuge. The museum also sponsors whalewatching tours, trips to the Channel Islands, grunion run programs, and Cabrillo Day celebrations. **Note:** The city parking lot charges $5.50 because of beach access.

Ports O' Call Village And Whalers Wharf
A favorite for out-of-towners is to stroll through the "re-created" atmosphere of Ports O' Call, an old California seaport, and then into Whalers Wharf, a 19th-century New England seaside community. Both offer shops, restaurants, harbor excursions, and a view of the main harbor channel. Open 11 a.m.-9 p.m. all year.

At **Abalone Cove Ecological Reserve**, investigate the tidepools. **Point Fermin Lighthouse**, closer to the harbor, was built in 1874. Visitors are not allowed into the lighthouse, but the park and grounds surrounding it are a perfect spot from which to watch the whales during their yearly migration. Along with picnic facilities, playground, and small amphitheater, you'll find the **Cetacean and Community Building**. The whale station offers a free 20-minute whale movie; open Sat. and Sun. 9 a.m.-4 p.m.

COURSES FROM SAN PEDRO

To:	Magnetic Course	Reverse Course	Distance in Nautical Miles
Newport Bay Bell Buoy	96	276	20
San Diego Entrance Lighted Whistle Buoy	126	306	82
14-Mile Bank	131	311	22
Horseshoe Kelp	145	325	3.2
60-Mile Bank	153	333	65
Catalina Island, East End	172	352	24
Avalon, Catalina Island	174	354	21.7
Gallagher Cove, Catalina Island	178	358	21
White's Landing, Catalina Island	183	3	19.8
Lone Pt., Catalina Island	183	3	18.6
Isthmus Cove, Catalina Island	202	22	19.8
Emerald Cove, Catalina Island	208	28	19.8
Catalina Island, West End	219	39	22.6
San Nicolas Island, West End	229	48	65
Santa Barbara Island, North End	236	56	40.5

LONG BEACH AREA

Though the Long Beach Marine Stadium was used for the 1932 Olympics, it was built in the 1920s. A mile long and a mile wide, this connection to Alamitos Bay is perfect for a multitude of water sports.

Cerritos Bahia Marina
Located at 6289 East Pacific Coast Hwy., Long Beach, CA 90803, tel. (310) 431-6575. No transient slips are available. There is a food store on the premises that's open 24 hours. Water is located at every dock. Marine supplies available 7 a.m.-6 p.m. Fuel dock available 6 a.m.-6 p.m.

Restaurants
Chart House, 221 Marina Dr., tel. (310) 598-9411. **Edgewater Inn**, 6400 E. Pacific Coast Hwy., tel. (310) 434-8451. **Golden Sails**, 6285 Pacific Coast Hwy., tel. (310) 430-0585. **Hof's Hut**, 6257 E. 2nd St., tel. (310) 498-2110. **Jolly Roger**, 168 Marina Dr., tel. (310) 598-9431. **Rusty Pelican**, 6550 Marine Dr., tel. (310) 594-6551. **Schooner or Later**, 241 Marina Dr., tel. (310) 498-3185. **Todd's**, 190 Marina Dr., tel. (310) 597-7771. **Windrose**, 110 Marina Dr., tel. (310) 597-3607. **Adolph's Restaurant**, 700 Queensway Dr., tel. (310) 435-7676.

Alamitos Bay Marina
Located at the Pacific Ocean and the San Gabriel River. Mailing address is Long Beach Marine Bureau, 205 Marina Dr., Long Beach 90803, tel. (310) 594-0951. There are 80 transient end ties available. Slip fees are 50 cents per foot per night. The nearest food store is **Lucky Market**, one-half mile away, open 8 a.m.-9 p.m. Fresh water at each end tie; bring a hose.

COURSES FROM LONG BEACH HARBOR

Long Beach Breakwater To:	Magnetic Course	Reverse Course	Distance in Nautical Miles
Avalon, Catalina Island	183	3	23.5
Isthmus, Catalina Island	208	28	22.5
Horseshoe Kelp	194	14	4.5
14-Mile Bank	140	320	21.5
San Clemente Island, East End	174	345	54.5
Newport Bell Buoy	105	285	17.5
San Diego Entrance Buoy.	130	310	81
Catalina Island, West End	220	40	26
Santa Barbara Island	236	56	44.5
San Nicolas Island, East End	229	49	68
Point Fermin	236	56	5.5
Long Beach Marina East Breakwater Light To:			
Oceanside	116	296	48
San Diego, Entrance B	131	311	80
N. Coronado Island	136	316	87
45 Fathom Bank	157	337	64
14-Mile Bank	145	325	21
209 Fathom Bank	145	325	40
San Clemente Island, East End	176	356	55
Catalina Island, East End	183	3	26
Avalon, Catalina Island	187	7	24.5
Isthmus, Ship Rock C.I.	213	33	24
Catalina Island, West End	223	43	28
Santa Barbara Island	238	58	47
San Nicolas Island, East End	229	49	70
Osborn Bank	229	49	50

Dock carts are provided. Marine supplies are available at **West Marine Products Store** from 9 to 6. Marine services are available at **Marina Shipyard** from 8 to 5. Fuel at the **76 Dock**, open 8 to 8. No laundry facilities; restaurant located on premises.

***Queen Mary* Complex**
Anyone visiting Long Beach for the first time should by all means take an afternoon and visit the *Queen Mary* and *Spruce Goose*. The *Queen* was originally engaged in crossing the Atlantic between Europe and the U.S. She's a grand

example of luxury liners of the past. Close by, the *Spruce Goose* was the brainstorm of the eccentric though brilliant Howard Hughes. The *Goose* is the largest plane ever to get aloft, and that's about as much as it did. In the Geodome that houses the giant plane, exhibits and films give the public the history and events that brought about the construction and follow-up of Hughes's brainchild.

Downtown Shoreline Marina
Located at the Pacific Ocean and Los Angeles River (near *Queen Mary)*. Mailing address is 450 E. Shoreline Dr., Long Beach, CA 90802, tel. (310) 437-0375. There are 64 transient end ties available; 50 cents per foot per night. Water available at end ties; bring a hose. Nearest food store is **Safeway**, one mile away, open 8 a.m.- 8 p.m. Marine supplies are available from 9 a.m.-6 p.m. Fuel dock is open 8 a.m.-6 p.m. Restaurant located on premises. Special attractions: Shoreline Village, *Queen Mary,* and the *Spruce Goose.*

Queensway Bay Marina
Located near the *Queen Mary* and *Spruce Goose,* behind the Viscount Hotel. Mailing address is 900 Queensway Dr., Long Beach, CA 90801, tel. (310) 436-0411. There are 40 transient Catalina-style moorings available; mooring fees range from $12 to $20 per day. Nearest food store is one mile away, fresh water available. Marine supply store open from 10 a.m.-6 p.m. Fuel dock available across the river, open 6 a.m.-5 p.m. No laundry facilities. Water taxi service to the *Queen Mary,* Shoreline Village, and town; full use of Viscount Hotel swimming pool and tennis courts.

LONG BEACH ACCOMMODATIONS

Families traveling to the island from out of town often enjoy sightseeing in Long Beach either before or after a trip to Catalina Island. The Hyatt Regency in Long Beach is a convenient stopover. The hotel is modern (built in 1989), close to the major sights along the waterfront including the *Queen Mary* and Howard Hughes's *Spruce Goose.* Located across the street from **Shoreline Village** and its trendy shops and restaurants, it's only minutes away from a choice of boats and helicopters that make daily trips to and from Catalina Island. Transportation is available from the hotel to Disneyland, Knott's Berry Farm, and many other Southern California attractions. Room rates are $130 s, $150 d; 200 S. Pine Ave., Long Beach, CA 90802, tel. (213) 491-1234.

Travelodge Hotel Resort And Marina
On Queensway Bay, at 700 Queensway Dr., Long Beach, CA 90802, tel. (310) 435-7676 (for reservations from U.S. and Canada call 800-255-3050), Travelodge is a modern, world-class hotel. The hotel is a five-minute walk from the *Catalina Express* boat along with many other attractions. The hotel offers a swimming pool and tennis courts, as well as Adolph's Restaurant, which serves scrumptious fresh seafood.

LONG BEACH HARBOR

COLORADO LAGOON

LONG BEACH

MARINE STADIUM

PACIFIC COAST HWY

LIVINGSTON DR.

BELMONT SHORE

2nd ST

MARINE PARK

OCEAN BLVD

BELMONT PIER

NAPLES

PUBLIC WALKWAY

LONG BEACH MARINA

BAYSHORE WALK

ALAMITOS BAY

ALAMITOS PENINSULA

MARINA DR.

1

SEAL BEACH

0   1 mi
0   1 km

© MOON PUBLICATIONS, INC.

ORANGE COUNTY COASTAL AREAS

HISTORY

Indians

California Chumash Indians of the Gabriolino and Jauneno groups lived along the coast of what is now Orange County for hundreds of years before the coming of the Spaniards. San Juan Capistrano, several miles inland from the ocean at San Clemente, was the seventh mission (circa 1776) along the California coast. This mission and its priests, along with all the other missions established up and down the coast, drastically changed the lifestyle of the Indians. Because of this change and the exposure to unknown diseases brought by the outsiders, most of the Indian population didn't survive very long after the coming of the Europeans. Surprisingly, an exception to this is a small group of Juaneno Indians still living in Orange County. Not too many years ago, a few archaeological artifacts dating back to the first Juanenos were found at the site of the new Crystal Cove State Park.

Settlers

The first Americans settled in Orange County around 1859 in the Anaheim area. Inland farmers, away from the swampy coastal regions, were successful raising orange trees, peanuts, barley, corn, pigs, and sheep. From there the colonists spread out and it wasn't long before there was a small dusty village called Newport next to the sea. It was tough going for the adventurous settlers during those early years. The landscape provided few natural materials to help them establish a town. (The Indians had solved the housing problem by building their oval-shaped huts from branches and tule grasses found along the rolling hills that bordered the Pacific.) The settlers brought everything overland in crude, wooden wagons.

Shipping

In Newport, McFadden's Wharf—the first along this part of California's southern coast—was built at about the time the first orange groves were planted inland. The wharf helped to initiate the shipping and trade industry early on, a boon to farmers shipping their products. Wool alone was big freight—about 80,000 merino sheep grazed the fields close by.

It wasn't long before the American entrepreneurial spirit rose to the occasion—why bring an empty ship from the north to the southern part of the state when picking up wool and other agricultural products? And so in 1873, a forward thinker gambled on a load of redwood aboard a southbound ship, just what was needed to fence off areas of farmland south of Santa Ana in order to keep the wild horses out. (Historical accounts mention hundreds of them in the area.) Timber was a hot seller and in great demand—the shipping industry in Southern California was growing up. By 1889 steamships were doing a booming business carrying freight and passengers between San Diego and San Francisco with a stop in Newport.

But the trains would change all that very shortly. The same forward-thinking men who developed the shipping business in Orange County also introduced the railroad for both passengers and freight. The premier line was an 11-mile run between Santa Ana and Newport. It cost 50 cents per person and took 30 minutes going north, 40 minutes going south. The difference was a 10-minute stopover at artesian wells to pick up water. (Until 1905, Newport had to import all of its drinking water.) New railroad lines were built connecting all the cities of California, and the southern state grew by leaps and bounds!

Newport

With the advent of the railroad, the quiet little village of Newport began a transition that would ultimately make it a popular resort destination. A moderate year-round climate attracted people from all over California to its long white beaches, craggy cliffs, and beautiful clear ocean. For years outlying acreage in Orange County remained untouched. In the mid-1950s another American with great foresight gambled millions of dollars to build an amusement park in Anaheim, many miles away from Southern California's established business centers. The man was Walt Disney and he called his unique park Disneyland. Since that time, Orange County has developed into a thriving metropolis. Hundreds of thousands of people and many big corporations left busy inner cities to go to the sunny countryside. The close-by coastal areas were also affected—new ports and marinas are added each year, with Newport the oldest and perhaps the queen of the Orange County coast.

ORANGE COUNTY ATTRACTIONS

Marine Events And Attractions

If visiting an Orange County port for the first time, you may wish to leave the boat docked at the marina for a day or two and visit one of the

Newport Harbor

NEWPORT VISITORS BUREAU

many fine attractions scattered about. Close by is the **Orange County Marine Institute** where, through classes and talks, visitors get an opportunity to view and understand the natural marinelife of this coastal area. Young people spend a day and night aboard the brig *Pilgrim* learning history and basic shipboard tasks, and standing watch.

The ship is a replica of the brig which carried Richard Henry Dana to these waters in 1834. Dana's experiences are recounted in his classic, *Two Years Before the Mast*. Another program is held onboard the tall ship *Californian*, a replica of a 19th-century revenue cutter.

The **Nautical Heritage Society Museum** offers seamanship training for young people aged 16 to 25, focusing on California maritime history. If you happen to be visiting during whale-watching season, the **Festival of the Whales** begins mid-February and continues for a month. Daily whalewatching cruises offshore, lectures, movies, displays, and demonstrations are open to the public.

Amphitheaters

Fine year-round entertainment is presented at many open-air amphitheaters. Check the schedules for **Festival of Arts of Laguna Beach**, 650 Laguna Canyon Rd., Laguna Beach, mailing address P.O. Box 37, Laguna Beach, CA 92652, tel. (714) 494-1145.

This is the home of the summer presentation, **Pageant of the Masters**. Grounds admission $2, $1 seniors, children and preteenagers admitted free. Pageant ticket prices are $9-38. The **Pacific Amphitheatre**, corner of Fair Dr. and Fairview in Costa Mesa (next to the Orange County Fairgrounds), tel. (714) 546-4875, seats 19,000; it's the largest outdoor amphitheater in California and presents concerts and name entertainment.

Fine Arts

Call for events at the **Idylwild School of Music and Arts**, P.O. Box 38, Idylwild, CA 92349, tel. (714) 659-2171. **Segerstrom Hall**, Costa Mesa, CA 92626, tel. (714) 556-2121, is a 3,600-seat multipurpose theater.

Theaters

Spend an evening at one of the many fine theaters in the area, such as **Cabrillo Playhouse/San Clemente Community Theatre**, 202 Avenida Cabrillo, San Clemente, CA 92672, tel. (714) 492-0465. **Costa Mesa Civic Playhouse**, 661 Hamilton St., Costa Mesa, CA 92627, tel. (714) 650-5269, is now entering its 27th year, and offers shows Sept. to June, with one children's production in January. The program includes such gems as *Come Back to the Five and Dime Jimmy Dean, Jimmy Dean, The Deadly Game, The 1940s Radio Hour,* and *Everybody Loves Opal.* There is also an Annual Yuletide Pageant and a Youth Theatre Production. Prices are $8.50 Thurs. and Sun., $9.50 Fri.-Sat., musicals $13.50 and $15.50. Senior rates offered on Thurs. and Sunday.

Irvine Community Theater, 12 Fuchsia, Irvine, CA 92658, tel. (714) 857-5496. **Laguna Playhouse**, 606 Laguna Canyon Rd., Laguna Beach, CA 92651, tel. (714) 494-8021. Tickets $11-22 Mainstage, $4-8 Youth Theater. **Newport Theatre Arts Center**, 2501 Cliff Drive, Newport Beach, CA 92660, tel. (714) 631-0288. Tickets $15 musicals, $13 plays; shows year-round. **South Coast Repertory Theatre**, 655 Town Center Dr., Costa Mesa, CA 92626, tel. (714) 957-4033 (tickets/info), tickets $15-32. Offers live theater Sept.-June.

Dinner Theaters

For a complete evening of entertainment including a good dinner, visit: **Elizabeth Howard's Curtain Call Theatre**, 690 El Camino Real, Tustin, CA 92645, tel. (714) 838-1540. **Southampton's Dinner Theatre**, 140 Avenida Pico, San Clemente, CA 92672, tel. (714) 498-7576.

Special Attractions

Don't forget the old favorites, **Disneyland**, 1313 South Harbor Blvd., Anaheim, CA 92835, tel. (714) 999-4565, and **Knott's Berry Farm**, 8039 Beach Blvd., Buena Park, CA 90679, tel. (714) 220-5200. **Balboa Island** is a picturesque community on a small island with trendy shops and specialty restaurants reminiscent of the New

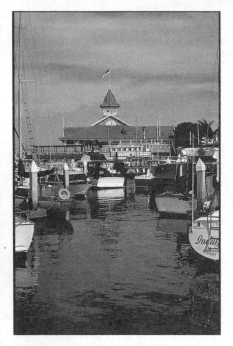

historic Balboa Pavilion

England coast. And the favored way to get there is onboard the **Balboa Island Ferry**. This is a small ferry for a short trip, holding only three cars, passengers, and bikers traveling between Balboa and the "fun zone" of the Balboa Peninsula.

Step into the past with a visit to **Mission San Juan Capistrano.** If it happens to be March 19, you'll witness the annual return of the swallows; the Mission is only 10 minutes east of Dana Point.

Nature Treks
Explore the **Corona del Mar tidepools** at Big Corona State Beach and Little Corona Beach. One of the few places in Orange County to observe firsthand the intriguing organisms of the sea. Or visit the **Orange County Marine Institute** (24200 Dana Point Harbor Dr., Dana Point, CA 92629) at the far end of Dana Point Har-

bor. This is an educational facility for exploring the ocean environment. Birdwatchers, check out the **Bolsa Chica Ecological Preserve** and **Upper Newport Bay Ecological Reserve** (see map). The Bolsa Chica Ecological Preserve consists of 1,200 acres of marshland. From two parking lot viewing areas you may see three birds on the endangered species list: **the clapper rail, California least tern,** and the **savanna sparrow**. Take the loop trail across from the beach entrance; interpretive signs are posted along the way. **Note**: Most of the marsh is private land, so stay within the viewing areas; one is at Pacific Coast Hwy. across from the main Bolsa Chica Beach entrance, and the other is at Pacific Coast Hwy. and Warner Avenue.

The Upper Newport Bay Ecological Reserve is an estuary. Contact **Friends of Upper Newport Bay,** which offers interpretive bird tours Saturday during the winter: P.O. Box 2001, Newport Beach, CA 92663. Are you docked at Dana Harbor and getting cabin fever? Take a walk to the northern end of the harbor to the jetty and offshore **Dana Point Marine Life Refuge**.

Events Along The Orange County Coast
Some events are held annually in the communities of Orange County. At the **Robert Moore Theatre** on the Orange Coast College Campus, workshops, seminars, classes, performing arts, tours, swap meets, and other special events are held daily, so ask for current brochure information; 2701 Fairview Rd. or P.O. Box 5005, Costa Mesa, CA 92628-5005, tel. (714) 432-5880. Open year-round Mon.-Thurs. 9 a.m.-6 p.m., Fri. 9 a.m.-5 p.m., Sat. 8 a.m.-12 noon. Ticket prices range from $8 to $12.

Each April, sailboats from both local and distant ports arrive to take part in the **Newport Ensenada Race** from Newport Harbor to the waters of Ensenada, Mexico, tel. (714) 640-1351. **Around the Bay in May** celebrates the coming of summer with 10-mile jogging/running races around the Newport Beach area, tel. (714) 644-8211.

The **Baroque Music Festival** celebrates the musical heritage in Corona del Mar each June.

The **Newport Beach Bike Tour** in June is a six-mile ride around the back bay, returning to East Bluff Park (and a picnic), tel. (714) 650-1000. It's fun to play in the sand in October's **Sandcastle Contest** at Big Corona Beach in Corona del Mar. Here you'll see some fabulous sand sculptures done both by individuals and groups. Each December brightly decorated boats follow an eight-mile parade route through Newport Harbor nightly for two weeks in the middle of the month; the event is called the **Festival of Lights Parade**. For details about getting your boat into the fun, call (714) 644-8211.

ORANGE COUNTY MARINAS

Sunset Aquatic Marina
Located at the end of Edinger Ave. in Huntington Beach, P.O. Box 538, Sunset Beach, CA 90742. For reservations or information, call (310) 592-2833 or (714) 846-0179. Eight transient slips are available, plus a guest dock. Slip fees are $6.80-10.20 per night. No food store on the premises; the nearest is 2 miles away. Hours are 9 a.m.-5 p.m. daily. Water hookups located at all slips and guest dock.

    Harbormaster: tel. (310) 592-2869 or (714) 846-2873/839-3800. A rescue boat is based here and may be contacted on channel 16. If no contact is made, call KDG Newport on 156.8 MHz.

NEWPORT HARBOR MARINAS

Balboa Marina
Located at 201 East Coast Hwy., Newport Beach, CA 92660, there are 132 slips available; live-aboards are not allowed. Fees according to size are 20-55 feet, $9-9.50 per foot monthly. Also available: water, electricity, dock box, phones, showers, restrooms, pump-out, parking. There's a waiting list; contact Daryl Landrum, tel. (714) 644-9730.

Balboa Yacht Basin
Located at 829 Harbor Island Dr., Newport Beach, CA 92660, tel. (714) 673-1761, there are 171 slips available, live-aboards not allowed. Slip fees according to size are 31-75 feet, $9.50 per foot. Facilities include water, electricity, dock box, phones, showers, restrooms, pump-out, parking, garage walk-in, and hardware store. Absolutely no dry storage. There's a waiting list; contact Don Jones.

Bay Shore Marina
Located at 2572 Bay Shores Dr., Newport Beach, CA 92660, tel. (714) 644-9730, there are 134 slips available, live-aboards not allowed. Slip fees according to size are 18-82 feet, $8.50-9.50 per foot monthly. Facilities include water, electricity, dock box, phones, showers, restrooms, pump-out, parking. There's a waiting list according to length. Contact Daryl Landrum.

Bayside Marina
Located at 1137 and 1353 Bayside Dr., Corona

NEWPORT BEACH

SANTA ANA RIVER

HUNTINGTON BEACH

PACIFIC

55

SUPERIOR AVE

IRVINE AVE

UPPER NEWPORT BAY ECOLOGICAL RESERVE

COSTA MESA

COAST HWY

DOVER DR

NEWPORT BEACH

BALBOA BLVD

NEWPORT DUNES AQUATIC PARK

MARINA PARK
PIER
NEWPORT BEACH

NEWPORT HARBOR

BALBOA ISLAND

BALBOA PAVILION

BALBOA BEACH

0   1 mi
0   1 km

© MOON PUBLICATIONS, INC.

A sunny day brings out small and large vessels in Newport Harbor.

DENISE BICKNELL

del Mar, CA 92625, tel. (714) 644-9730, there are 250 slips available, live-aboards not allowed. Slip fees according to size are 18-75 feet, $9.50 per foot monthly; facilities include water, electricity, dock box, phones, showers, restrooms, pump-out, parking. There's a waiting list according to length. Contact Daryl Landrum.

De Anza Bayside Marina
Located at 300 East Coast Hwy., Newport Beach, CA 92660, tel. (714) 673-1331, there are 265 slips available; live-aboards are not allowed. Slip fees according to size are 14-50 feet, $7.75 per foot monthly; 21-30 feet, $9.50 per foot monthly; 31 feet and up, $9.75 per foot monthly. Facilities include water, electricity, dock box, phones, laundry, message service, dry storage, showers, restrooms, paging service, parking. No waiting for some, a year's wait for others; contact Shirlene Burrill.

Little Inn On The Bay
Located at 617 Lido Park Dr., Newport Beach, CA 92663, tel. (714) 673-8800, there are 14 slips available, live-aboards not allowed. Slip fees range $10-11 per foot per month; facilities include water, electricity, dock box, phones, mail/message service, showers, restrooms, restaurants, security. There's a waiting list of six months; contact Mike Saber.

Newport Dunes Marina
Located at 101 North Bayside Dr., Newport Beach, CA 92660, tel. (714) 729-1100, there are 430 slips available, 18 are live-aboard, plus 17 guest slips. Slip fees are 20-46 feet, $11.50-14.75 per foot by boat length or slip length, whichever is longest. Facilities include water, electricity, TV and phone hookups at each slip; parking, restrooms with showers, clubhouse, fitness center, pool and spa, lockers, ice and vending machines, laundry, security, and

HUNTINGTON HARBOR

PACIFIC COAST HWY

SEAL BEACH

NAT'L. WILDLIFE REFUGE

ANAHEIM BAY

HUNTINGTON BEACH

SUNSET AQUATIC REGIONAL PARK

SURFSIDE

TRINIDAD ISLAND

SUNSET BEACH

HUNTINGTON HARBOR

WARNER AVE. BOAT LAUNCH

WARNER AVE.

BOLSA CHICA ECOLOGICAL RESERVE

0   2 mi
0   2 km

© MOON PUBLICATIONS, INC.

NEWPORT YACHT CLUBS

Bahia Corinthian Yacht Club
1601 Bayside Dr.,
Corona del Mar, CA 92625
tel. (714) 644-9530

Balboa Island Yacht Club (and Ferry)
410 S. Bay Front,
Newport Beach, CA 92662
tel. (714) 673-1070

Balboa Yacht Club
1801 Bayside Dr.,
Corona del Mar, CA 92625
tel. (714) 673-3515

Lido Isle Yacht Club
701 Via Lido Sound,
Lido Isle, CA 92663
tel. (714) 673-6170

Newport Harbor Yacht Club
720 W. Bay Ave.,
Balboa, CA 92660
tel. (714) 673-7730

Shark Island Yacht Club
1099 Bayside Drive,
Newport Beach, CA 92662
tel. (714) 760-0221

South Shore Yacht Club
2527 W. Coast Highway,
Newport Beach, CA 92660
tel. (714) 631-9969 (Port)
tel. (714) 646-3102 (in house)

mail/message service (for live-aboards only). Also on property is a marine repair, cafe, grocery store, quiet saltwater lagoon and beach, as well as a premier RV resort. There's a waiting list; contact Tom Ginger, open year-round, seven days a week.

Newport Arches Marina
Located at 3333 West Coast Hwy., Newport Beach, CA 92663, tel. (714) 642-4644, there are 76 slips available, five are live-aboard. Slip fees are 25-66 feet, $12-15 per foot monthly. Facilities include water, electricity, dock box, phones, mail/message service. Fuel dock available with mini-mart, showers, restrooms, restaurant, parking, security, brokerage. Availability varies; contact Judy Owens.

Twenty-eighth Street Marina
Located at 2800 Lafayette Ave., Newport Beach, CA 92663, tel. (714) 675-2486, there are 25 slips available. Fees are $11-14 per foot monthly. Facilities include water, electricity, dock box, phones, showers, restrooms, parking, security. No waiting list, contact Mike Singer.

Other Area Marinas
California Recreation Co., 1137 Bayside Dr., Corona del Mar, CA 92625, tel. (714) 644-9730. **Lido Yacht Anchorage**, 717 Lido Park Dr., Newport Beach, CA 92663, tel. (714) 673-9330.

Area Restaurants
Ruby's Diner, 1 Balboa Pier, Newport Beach, tel. (714) 675-7029. **The Cannery**, 3010 Lafayette Ave., Newport Beach, tel. (714) 675-5777. **Amelia's On Balboa Island**, 311 Marina Ave., Balboa Island, tel. (714) 673-6580.

DANA POINT

Once a major port for square-rigged ships, the new harbor was named for Richard Henry Dana, author of *Two Years Before the Mast*. The classic novel is an account of the adventures of a young man from the U.S. East Coast working onboard a merchant ship that plied the waters of the West Coast in the mid-1830s. The flavor of early California is depicted in a very real manner. Richard Henry Dana would be amazed and proud to have this harbor named in his honor. It isn't only a gathering spot for modern pleasure boats, but is a popular dock for whalewatching excursions and research vessels. Here at Dana Point in 1986, significant fact-finding was accomplished on the subject of whales' voices and underwater communication. One of the largest and most popular waterfront festivals in

Orange County, the **Tallships Competition**, is held here each year; what a beautiful sight!

Dana West Marina
Located at 24500 Dana Point Harbor Dr., Dana Point, CA 92629; 1,462 slips available. Fees 23-63 feet are $4.56-7.05 monthly. Water, electricity, dock box, phones, laundry, pump-out, parking, showers, restrooms, security. If you wish to add your name to the waiting list call (714) 496-6137.

Dana Point Marina Company
Located on the east side of Dana Point Harbor, it is 60 miles equidistant from Los Angeles and San Diego. Mailing address is 24705 Dana Dr., Dana Point, CA 92629, tel. (714) 496-6137. Call the harbormaster for guest berth assignment. Anchorage is available for visitors but vessel must be attended at all times. Transient slips available. Slip fees: $5.50-9 per foot per month. A number of restaurants and small shops are located in the harbor.

Marina office hours are Tues.-Sat. 8 a.m.-12 p.m. and 1-5 p.m. Fresh water available at each slip. Fuel dock hours 8 a.m.-5 p.m. weekdays, 6 a.m.-5 p.m. weekends. Laundry facilities available 24 hours daily.

Restaurants
The Brig, 25010 del Prado (Mariner's Village), tel. (714) 496-9046. **Casa Maria**, 25052 del

COURSES FROM NEWPORT BAY

To:	Magnetic Course	Reverse Course	Distance in Nautical Miles
Dana Point	121	301	11
San Diego Bell Buoy	136	316	66.2
60-Mile Bank	170	350	56.3
14-Mile Bank	192	12	13
San Clemente Island, East End	192	12	52.5
San Clemente Island, West End	213	33	50
Tanner Bank	214	34	83.2
Catalina Island, East End	216	36	27
Avalon, Catalina Island	222	42	26.4
Gallagher Cove, Catalina Island	225	45	26.9
White's Landing, Catalina Island	229	49	27
Lone Pt., Catalina Island	230	51	26.4
Isthmus Cove, Catalina Island	239	59	31.5
Emerald Cove, Catalina Island	242	62	33.5
Catalina Island, West End	244	64	36.6
Santa Barbara Island, North End	249	69	58.2
Pt. Fermin Buoy	272	92	21.5
San Pedro Breakwater	276	96	20

Prado, tel. (714) 496-6311. **Harpoon Henry's**, 25200 del Prado, tel. (714) 493-2933. **Jolly Roger's**, 25100 del Prado, tel. (714) 496-0855. **Quiet Cannon**, 34344 Street of the Green Lantern, tel. (714) 496-6146. **Skippers Galley**, 25116 del Prado, tel. (714) 496-0424. **Wind & Sea**, 25152 del Prado (Dana Wharf), tel. (714) 496-5959. **Beach Cities Pizza**, 34473 Golden Lantern, tel. (714) 496-2670.

Marine Facilities
Dana Point Fuel Dock, 34461 Puerto Place, Dana Point, CA 92629, tel. (714) 496-6113. Summer hours, weekdays 6 a.m.-6 p.m., weekends 6 a.m.-5 p.m. Off-season hours 8 a.m.-5 p.m. **Kettenburg Marine**, 34467 Golden Lantern, Dana Point, CA 92629, tel. (714) 496-3640 or (714) 499-3950 for marine hardware, charts, electronic sales and service; open 8:30 a.m.-5 p.m. year-round. **Dana Book and Navigation**, 24402 del Prado, Suite B, Dana Point, CA 92629, tel. (714) 661-3926. Open daily 10 a.m.-5:30 p.m. for nautical magazines, books, charts, instruments.

    Dana Point Shipyard (north of the fuel dock), 34671 Puerto Place, Dana Point, CA 92629, tel. (714) 661-1313; travelift capacity 50 tons, crane capacity seven tons. For boat and engine maintenance, repairs, parts, prop and shaft repairs; open Mon.-Sat. 8 a.m.-5 p.m. **Black Bart's Aquatics**, 34145 Pacific Coast Hwy., Dana Point, CA 92629, tel. (714) 496-5891, for diving supplies, sales, rentals, fishing licenses, air refills, charter dive boat, and marine hardware.

IMPORTANT INFORMATION

Harbormaster: 25005 Dana Dr., Dana Point, CA 92629, tel. (714) 496-2242/834-3800, emergency tel. (714) 496-1121; the harbormaster assigns guest berths.

    Speed limit: Five mph in Dana Point Harbor.

    Dockmaster's: 24705 Dana Dr. in the southeast part of east basin.

    Dana Point Harbor Patrol: Equipped with rescue and fire-fighting equipment and stationed in the harbor, they maintain a 24-hour radio watch on VHF-FM channels 12 (156.60 mHz) and 16 (156.80 mHz). During late hours contact the Newport Harbor Patrol via VHF channel 16, or use emergency phone at foot of the Harbor Patrol stairs (most southeasterly building once through the breakwater).

SAN DIEGO CONVENTION AND VISITORS BUREAU

SAN DIEGO COUNTY COASTAL AREAS

History

San Diego is sometimes referred to as the Cradle of California Civilization. Juan Cabrillo's discovery of San Diego in 1542 was the beginning of the Spanish influence that has always been part of California's modern life-style. Mission San Diego de Alcala, built in 1769, was the first in a chain built by Father Junipero Serra, the beginning of the Camino Real ("Royal Highway"). Ultimately 21 missions were built, each a day's walk from the next going from San Diego toward Northern California. San Diego was organized as a town in 1834, and by 1850 was incorporated as a city.

San Diego Harbor is considered one of the finest natural harbors in the world. For years the biggest fleet was that of the U.S. Navy. Today, the biggest fleet is the pleasure boats that fill the many marinas in San Diego. Vessels vary from simple and small to luxurious and large. The temperate climate is perfect for the sailors to whom San Diego is either home base or just a favorite port of call.

OCEANSIDE

The second California mission was Mission San Luis Rey, constructed in 1798 in Oceanside. A large group of Native Americans called this area home. The missions were generally built near large Indian villages since the object was to convert them to Christianity.

More boaters are discovering the $10 million marina and small craft harbor. Equidistant from San Diego and Newport Beach, Oceanside has its advantages for boaters, whether for permanent docking or for a good transient "halfway house." The boat harbor accommodates 900 permanent boats with slips reserved for transient boatmen. Other facilities include good restaurants, shopping, marine supplies, launching ramps, fuel docks, boat repairs, good fishing supplies, and a quarter-mile-long fishing pier. All slips are handled through the Harbor District.

Oceanside Harbor Marina
Located at Oceanside Harbor in the city of Oceanside, mailing address is 1540 Harbor Dr. North, Oceanside, CA 92054, tel. (619) 966-4580. Boaters will find 51 transient slips. Slip fees vary according to season: from May 1 to Sept. 30, 60 cents per foot; Oct. 1 to April 30, 45 cents per foot. Water hookups are at each slip. A marine supply store is open 8-6. Marine services are available 8-5. Fuel dock is open from sunrise to sunset; laundromat open 24 hours. A mini-mart on the premises is open 8-6. **Note**: Boaters wishing an overnight slip or docking, please check at the Headquarters Building, 1540 Harbor Dr. North.

Marine Services
Oceanside Marine Centre, Inc., 1550 Harbor Dr. North, Oceanside, CA 92054, tel. (619) 722-1833, is open year-round, weekdays 8-5, Sat. 9-4:30, Sun. 10-3. Fifteen-ton travelift available plus hardware, engine repair, maintenance, sales, and brokerage. **Oceanside Sailboats** is at 1400 C Harbor Dr. North, Oceanside, CA 92054, tel. (619) 722-3509, fax (619) 722-0036. Open 9-5 p.m. year-round, closed Monday. Chandlery and brokerage, new and used available. **Oceanside Fuel Dock** is at 1380 North Pacific St., Oceanside, CA 92054, tel. (619) 722-5853. Open all year except Christmas, New Year's Day, and Thanksgiving afternoon. Hours May through Oct. are 7:30-5, Nov. through April, 8-4:30.

Area Accommodations
Villa Marina Resort is at 2008 Harbor Dr. North, Oceanside, CA 92054, tel. (619) 722-1561.

Nearby Restaurants
The **Chart House**, 314 Harbor Dr. South, tel. (619) 722-1345. **Cape Cod House**, 258 Harbor Dr. South, tel. (619) 722-5556. **Harbor Deli**, 272 Harbor Dr. South, tel. (619) 722-7228. **Harbor Fish & Chips**, 282 Harbor Dr. South, tel. (619) 722-4977. **Harbor Light**, 264 Harbor Dr. South, tel. (619) 722-4855. **Jolly Roger Restaurant**, 1900 Harbor Dr. North, tel. (619) 722-1831. **Monterey Bay Canners Seafood**, tel.

(619) 722-3474. **Pappy's**, 270 Harbor Dr. South, tel. (619) 439-9648.

Water Sports
San Diego offers a multitude of aquatic activities, from the obvious—sailing and power boating—to water-skiing, windsurfing, swimming, wet-biking, and deep-sea fishing. Sportfishermen know they have a good chance (in season) to catch albacore, barracuda, bluefin tuna, marlin, yellowtail, swordfish, mackerel, and white sea bass. Without going too far out to sea (three to 14 miles), bottom fishing is another favorite pastime with fishermen, bringing in kelp bass, rock bass, ling cod, rock cod, grouper, halibut, black sea bass, sheepshead, and sole. And don't overlook fishing from your skiff in Mission Bay, where you'll have access to croaker, smelt, bass, halibut, flounder, perch, and sea trout.

SAN DIEGO AREA ATTRACTIONS

Balboa Park
It would be possible to stay in San Diego for a month and take in a different outstanding attraction every day (if you didn't run out of money first!). Balboa Park, in the heart of the city, is the location of 1,074 acres of museums, art galleries, theaters, sports facilities, and one of the world's largest zoos. What's left over is green grass and tall trees. The park's museum and gallery complex is amazing. Within walking distance you find the **Reuben H. Fleet Space Theatre and Science Center**, the **Hall of Champions, Museum of Man, Natural History Museum, San Diego Museum of Art**, and the **Timken Art Gallery**. Most of the Spanish/Moorish buildings in the park were originally part of the Panama-California Exposition of 1915-16 and the California-Pacific International Exposition of 1935-36. Every day the 100-bell carillon chimes each quarter hour from the lovely **California Tower**, another city landmark and example of Spanish/Moorish architecture.

Cabrillo National Monument
The Cabrillo National Monument overlooks what Juan Cabrillo called San Miguel Bay and what today is called San Diego Bay. The monument was established to remember the first man to visit the entire California coast, beginning in 1542. Stop by the visitor center for an exhibit which tells of Cabrillo's explorations and discoveries. Programs about the monument are presented daily.

Sea World
A desolate marshland several miles north of downtown San Diego has been brilliantly transformed into a 4,600-acre aquatic playground called **Mission Bay Park**. In the heart of this complex, Sea World offers visitors one of the finest marinelife facilities in the world. Along

Sea World is one of the fun places to visit while in the San Diego Area.

SAN DIEGO TOURISM OFFICE

with a high-flying killer whale named Shamu, there's the Penguin Encounter in a 5,000-square-foot re-created Antarctic neighborhood behind a 100-foot viewing window, a 28° F home for more than 400 penguins. In the California Tidepool exhibit, visitors may pick up and examine starfish or sea urchins, or wander around to see dolphins, sea lions, otters, and even a walrus. Plenty to see and do for the whole family.

Gaslamp Quarter

Step back in time to the 1890s and one of San Diego's historic districts. You'll get the sights, sounds, and feeling of a bustling California waterfront before the turn of the century with restored Victorian homes. One of the best ways to learn about the Quarter is via walking tours offered every Sat. from 10 a.m.-noon and 1 p.m.-3 p.m. Custom tours can be arranged by calling (619) 233-4694.

Animals

For the animal lover a trip to **San Diego Wild Animal Park** at 15500 San Pasqual Valley Rd., Escondido, CA 92027, tel. (619) 480-0105, is well worth the time. You'll find 2,200 acres of simulated natural habitats for more than 3,000 animals roaming free as they would in their birth-

places. The park, 30 miles from downtown San Diego, includes an African village as well as a five-mile (50-minute) monorail trip (with narrator-guide) that glides silently through expansive Asian and African enclosures. Don't miss the Nairobi Center with its lowland gorilla colony. Along with its Animal Care Center, the park has achieved national acclaim with its condor program. Of the 52 condors in the U.S., 25 were hatched at the Wild Animal Park. This is one of the few preserves in the world where the animals run free and the people are contained! The park is open every day of the year; $16.50 adult, $9.50 child (3-15).

Closely related in operations is the **San Diego Zoo** at Balboa Park in downtown San Diego. One of the highlights is the Children's Zoo. Double-decker buses with narrator-guides take visitors on a 40-minute trip through three miles of safari land, including sprawling canyons and mesas. Open daily.

More Attractions

Old Town is the site of the first European settlement in California. In 1967, the state provided 2 million dollars to buy six blocks in the heart of Old Town. It has been restored and the State Park Old Town Historical Society offers walking tours led by park rangers at 2 p.m. daily

lions and tigers and bears—at the renowned San Diego Zoo

SAN DIEGO TOURISM OFFICE

The sunny shores of San Diego attract boaters, windsurfers, and picnickers.

SAN DIEGO CONVENTION AND VISITORS BUREAU

from the **Machado y Silvas Adobe** across from the plaza. For more information, call Old Town State Park, (619) 237-6770.

The **Maritime Museum** is a trio of ships, each telling its story of the past. The most familiar, the *Star of India,* is the oldest merchant sailing vessel afloat. The steam-powered ferryboat *Berkeley* was the first successful propeller-driven ferry on the West Coast and was responsible for carrying thousands to safety during the 1906 San Francisco earthquake. The 1904 steam yacht *Medea,* built for a wealthy Scot and later owned by members of Parliament, served in both world wars. Moored on the Embarcadero, the "fleet" is open daily from 9 to 8, admission $4, tel. (619) 234-9153.

The Mexican border at **Tijuana** is a 25-minute trip on the trolley from downtown ($1.50 RT). From the border it's another 20-minute walk to Avenida Revolucion in downtown Tijuana, where there are dozens of shops. No passport or visa is required of U.S. citizens for a stay of less than 72 hours, within 75 miles of the border. You may bring $400 in retail value of duty-free goods back into the States. A good destination for visitors to Tijuana is the **Cultural Complex**, where, in the Omnimax Theater, you relive Mexican history. On the grounds also visit the **Anthropological Museum** and the **Performing Arts Center**. For the sports fan there's **horse racing, jai alai,** and **bullfighting** in season.

For nonboaters interested in a small ocean cruise, take a trip to Catalina Island on *Seajet.* The computer-stabilized vessel makes the trip between San Diego and Avalon from Seajet Harbor Village. Call for schedule. Fare of $69 includes continental breakfast and a complimentary tour of your choice on Catalina Island. For more information and reservations, call (800) 622-CJET.

MISSION BAY AREA

Mission Bay Marina
Located on the northwest corner of Quivira Basin next to the harbor patrol and hospitality point. Mailing address is 1500 Quivira Way, San Diego, CA 92109, tel. (619) 222-6488. The number of transient slips available varies. Slip fees range from transient, 50 cents per foot, to permanent slips at $6.25-$8 per foot per month. Fresh water is available. Clean restrooms and showers, as well as free hookup to master TV antenna, dock boxes, and telephone service available to guests. Marine supplies are available Mon.-Sat. 8-5, Sun. 10-3. A full-service boatyard, **Knight Carver Yacht Center,** is open weekdays 7:30-5; fuel dock is nearby. No laundry facilities available, although a deli, liquor store, several restaurants, and a seafood market are nearby. The closest food store is about 1½

miles away, open weekdays 8-5, weekends 8:30-4:30. (May close on Sunday in the winter.)

Seaforth Marina

Located on Quivira Basin in Mission Bay. Mailing address is 1677 Quivira Rd., San Diego, CA 92109, tel. (619) 224-6807, open daily 9-5. Slip fees are $7.25 per foot per month. There's a freshwater hookup at each slip, and a marine supply store is open 9-5. Marine services and repairs are available 9-5. A fuel dock is located one block away. The nearest food store is also one block away; no laundromat. A restaurant is located on the premises.

Sea World Marina

Located at Perez Cove in Mission Bay, next door to Sea World. Mailing address is 1660 S. Shores Rd., San Diego, CA 92109, tel. (619) 226-3915. **Harbormaster**: 2581 Quivira Court, San Diego, CA 92109, tel. (619) 221-8899, open 24 hours a day. The number of transient slips available varies; slips will accommodate boats from 24 to 50 feet. Slip fee is $15 per night. At each slip guests find electricity, phone hookup, dock boxes, and fresh water. A food store on the premises is open from 7 a.m. to 7 p.m. in the summer and 8-5 in the winter.

Marine services include washdown, wax, and hull-painting service. Fuel dock available, 7 a.m.-

MISSION BAY AREA

7 p.m. summer, 8-5 winter. No laundry facilities. Sea World Marina is within easy walking distance of Sea World. There is no fee to tie up for the day and visit Sea World. Special 20% Sea World admission discounts are provided to marina tenants. The marina is 10 minutes away by car from San Diego International Airport, downtown San Diego, and most major resort hotels and restaurants. Special events: hydroplane racing, bathtub races, the Christmas Parade of Lights.

Area Accommodations

Catamaran Hotel, 3999 Mission Blvd., San Diego, CA 92109, tel. (619) 488-1081, (800) 288-0770. **Bahia Resort Hotel,** 998 W. Mission Dr., San Diego, CA 92109, tel. (619) 488-0551, (800) 288-0770. **Dana Inn and Marina,** 1710 West Mission Bay Dr., San Diego, CA 92109, tel. (619) 222-6440, (800) 445-3339; guest docks. Located on scenic Mission Bay Park, a 4,600-acre aquatic playground offering skiing, sailing, fishing, a jogging path, and plenty of warm sunshine. Easily accessible to Interstate 5 and San Diego International Airport, the Dana Inn and Marina places you just minutes from major attractions such as Sea World and the world-famous zoo. This excellent location offers bay-view rooms and pathways from the hotel that lead you along San Diego's longest beachfront boardwalk. **San Diego Hilton Beach and Tennis Resort,** 1775 East Mission Bay Dr., San Diego 92109, tel. (619) 276-4010; guest slips.

Campland on the Bay Campground and Marina, 2211 Pacific Beach Dr., San Diego 92109, tel. (619) 274-0601, (800) 4-BAYFUN, (619) 581-4224, has RV and tent campsites, boat slips, storage, and launch ramp. This is a 43-acre landscaped park with sandy beach on Mission Bay. Pools, whirlpool spa, Frisbee golf, restaurant, market, laundromat, planned activities, boat and RV storage, video game room, "howling contests," and marina. Close to all San Diego attractions, open 365 days a year.

Nearby Restaurants

Atlantis, 2595 Ingraham St., tel. (619) 224-2434; guest dock at Sea World Marina. **Bahia Hotel,** 998 W. Mission Dr., tel. (619) 488-0551. **Catamaran Hotel,** 3999 Mission Blvd., tel. (619) 488-1081. **The Red Hen Country Kitchen,** 1710 W. Mission Bay Dr., tel. (619) 226-6440; guest dock. **Islandia Hyatt House,** 1441 Quivira Rd., tel. (619) 224-3541; guest dock. **Trade Winds (Hilton Hotel),** 1775 E. Mission Bay Dr., Mission Bay, tel. (619) 276-4010; guest dock. Vacation Village Hotel, 1404 Vacation Rd., tel. (619) 274-4630.

SAN DIEGO'S SHELTER ISLAND AREA

Bay Club Marina/Half Moon Anchorage

These two marinas next door to each other are located at Shelter Island. Mailing address is 2131 Shelter Island Dr., San Diego, CA 92106, tel. (619) 222-0314/224-3401. Boaters will find three to five transient slips available. Slip fees are $12 per foot under 30 feet; $15 30-40 feet; $18 40 feet and up per month. Freshwater faucets and electricity on docks (sometimes a pigtail is needed). The nearest food store is a 10-minute walk; hours are 8-5:30. Laundry facilities are at Bay Club Marina. The Bay Club Hotel and Kanaka's Restaurant on premises.

Kona Marina Inn

Located on Shelter Island. Mailing address is 1901 Shelter Island Dr., San Diego, CA 92106, tel. (619) 222-1191. Open daily 9-5 year-round. Transient slips available when there are vacancies in the marina. Slip fees are $8.25 per foot per month. Freshwater hookups are near the boat slips. Nearest food store is two miles away. Restaurant is on the premises. Hours are daily 9-5.

Shelter Island Marina Inn

Located at Point Loma, Shelter Island. Mailing address is 2051 Shelter Island Dr., San Diego, CA 92106, tel. (619) 222-0561, ext. 307. Number of transient slips varies. Slip fees range from $10-30. Live-aboards are allowed. There's a freshwater hookup at each slip. Nearest food

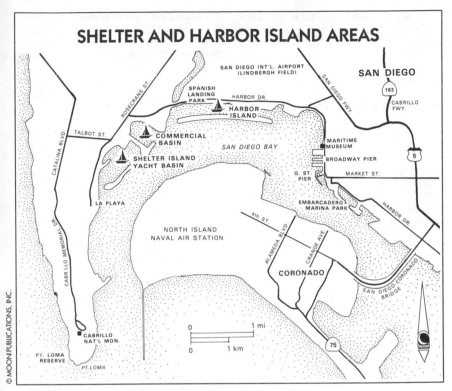

SHELTER AND HARBOR ISLAND AREAS

store is one mile away, open 9-5. Laundromat is open 24 hours a day. There's a restaurant on the premises. Special services include meeting and banquet facilities to accommodate groups from 20 to 500 people.

Sun Harbor Marina

Located near Point Loma. Mailing address is 5104 N. Harbor Dr., San Diego, CA 92106, tel. (619) 222-1167. No transient slips available; slip fees are $7 per foot per month. The nearest food store is three blocks away, open 9-4:30. You'll find a freshwater hookup every three slips. There's a restaurant on the premises. Special attractions include sportfishing.

Nearby Accommodations

Humphrey's Half Moon Inn, 2303 Shelter Island

Dr., tel. (619) 224-3411. **Kona Inn**, 1901 Shelter Island Dr., tel. (619) 222-0421. **Kona Kal Club**, 1551 Shelter Island Dr., tel. (619) 222-1191. **Posada Inn**, 5005 N. Harbor Dr., tel. (619) 224-3254. **Travelodge Point Loma**, 5102 N. Harbor Dr., tel. (619) 223-8171.

Nearby Restaurants

Bali Ha'i, 2230 Shelter Island Dr., tel. (619) 222-1181. The **Brigantine Seafood Restaurant**, 2725 Shelter Island Dr., tel. (619) 224-2871. The **Chart House**, 2760 Shelter Island Dr., tel. (619) 222-2216. **Coconuts on Shelter Island**, 1901 Shelter Island Dr., tel. (619) 286-6887. **Dock Masters**, 2051 Shelter Island Dr., tel. (619) 223-2572. **Point Loma Seafoods**, 2805 Emerson St., tel. (619) 223-1109. **La Terraza Restaurant**, 2830 Canon St., tel. (619) 224-

2777. **Miguel's Mexican Restaurant**, 2912 Shelter Island Dr., tel. (619) 224-2401. **Red Sails Inn**, 2614 Shelter Island Dr., tel. (619) 223-3030.

Sportfishing/Yacht Charters
H & M Landing, 2803 Emerson St., tel. (619) 222-1144. **Set Sail Yacht Charters**, 2131 Shelter Island Dr., tel. (619) 224-3791, (800) 553-7245, fax (619) 224-8736, has beautifully maintained yachts, 29-53 feet. The location at the Bay Club Hotel and Marina places the fleet in sight of both the San Diego Yacht Club front dock and the Humphrey's outdoor concert stage. Also, the Italian and America's Cup syndicate headquarters are located within easy walking distance. Rates from $130-540.

Marine Supplies And Services
Custom Marine Electronics, Inc., 2525 Shelter Island Dr., tel. (619) 224-3646, open Mon.-Fri. 8:30-5, Sat. 9-12, sales and service. **Capt. Franke Marine Surveyors, Inc.**, 1310 Rosecrans St., tel. (619) 224-2944. **Hall and Mal-**

one Marine Insurance Brokers, 2812 Canon St., tel. (619) 226-8661. **Kettenburg Marine**, 2810 Carleton St., tel. (619) 221-7400. **Pacific Marine Supply**, 2804 Canon St., tel. (619) 222-7084. **Pearson's Marine Fuels**, 2435 Shelter Island Dr., tel. (619) 222-7084; gas, diesel, oil change service and diesel tank cleaning.

San Diego Marine Exchange, Inc., 2636 Shelter Island Dr., tel. (619) 223-7159, (800) 540-SDMX. **Driscoll Custom Boats**, 2438 Shelter Island Dr., tel. (619) 224-3575. **Marine Management**, 1050 Anchorage Lane, tel. (619) 222-0328, boat repair and maintenance; open all year, Mon.-Fri. 8-5, on-call after hours. **Nielsen Beaumont Marine**, 2420 Shelter Island Dr., tel. (619) 222-4255; power boats to 70 tons, open year-round, 7:30 a.m.-4 p.m. Mon.-Friday. **Shelter Island Boatyard**, 2330 Shelter Island Dr., Suite 1, tel. (619) 222-0481; open Mon.-Fri. 8 a.m.-5 p.m., year-round.

SAN DIEGO'S HARBOR ISLAND AREA

Harbor Island West Marina
Located on San Diego Bay. Mailing address is 2040 Harbor Island Dr., San Diego, CA 92101, tel. (619) 291-6440. Number of transient slips varies; slip fees range from $10.50-19.25 per night. Fresh water available at each slip except side ties; dock carts are provided and on docks. Marine supplies for sale from 9 a.m.-6 p.m. Fuel dock open 7 a.m.-10 p.m. Laundromat open 8 a.m.-10 p.m.

Cabrillo Isle Marina
Located at Harbor Island, mailing address is 1450 Harbor Island Dr., San Diego, CA 92101, tel. (619) 297-6222. Transient slips are available; the number varies. Guest slip fees $16-33 per day, 30-56 feet. Special charges for liveaboards. Fresh water available at each slip along with lockable dock boxes, telephone, concrete docks, clean restrooms. Marine supplies available within one mile from marina. Marine services and repairs available; fuel dock one-quarter mile away. Laundry facilities available.

SAN DIEGO FUEL DOCKS

Chevron Oil Company
High Seas Fuel Dock
2510 Shelter Island Drive
tel. (619) 224-5522

Chevron Oil Company
Pearson Marine Fuels, Inc.
2435 Shelter Island Drive
tel. (619) 222-7084

Cortez Fuel Dock
1880 Harbor Island Drive
tel. (619) 296-2331

Pelican Marine Sales
2040 Harbor Island Drive
tel. (619) 297-3735

Tonga Marine Fuel Dock
2385 Shelter Island Drive
tel. (619) 224-3090

COURSES FROM SAN DIEGO

From San Diego Whistle Buoy To:	Magnetic Course	Reverse Course	Distance in Nautical Miles
Oceanside	332	152	35
Dana Point	320	140	56
Newport	316	136	66
Los Angeles Light	306	126	82
Avalon, Catalina Island	293	113	70
Pyramid Cove, San Clemente	266	86	58
Cortez Bank	248	68	95
60-Mile Bank	222	42	60
North Coronado	181	1	12

Deli and restaurant on premises, open from 7 a.m. to 7 p.m.; supermarket is one mile away.

Marina Cortez
Located on San Diego Bay; mailing address is 1880 Harbor Island Dr., San Diego, CA 92106, tel. (619) 291-5985. Number of transient slips available varies. Slip fees are $25 per night. Fresh water available at docks. Marine supply store open 9-5. Fuel dock open 7:30-6. Laundromat, restaurant, and food store located on premises. Hours 8-7 during the summer.

Area Restaurants
Anthony's Fish Grotto, 1360 N. Harbor Dr., tel. (619) 232-7408. **Barnacle Bill's**, 1880 Harbor Island Dr., tel. (619) 297-1673. **Boat House** (Harbor Island Marina), 2040 Harbor Island Dr., tel. (619) 291-6440; guest dock. **Boll Weevil**, 2743 Shelter Island Dr., tel. (619) 224-2871. **Chart House**, East Harbor Dr., tel. (619) 223-7391; guest dock. **Chart House** (Glorietta Bay), 1701 Grand Way, Coronado, tel. (619) 435-0155; dinghy dock.
   Tom Ham's Light House, 2150 Harbor Island Dr., tel. (619) 291-9110; guest dock. **Humphrey's**, 2241 Shelter Island Dr., tel. (619) 224-3411; guest dock. **Intercontinental Hotel**, 385 West Harbor Dr., tel. (619) 234-1500/231-0972. **Reuben E. Lee River Boat**, 880 Harbor Island Dr., tel. (619) 291-1974. **Sheppard's** (at Sheraton Harbor Island Hotel), 1380 Harbor Island Dr., tel. (619) 291-2900. **Tarantino's**, 5150 Harbor Dr., tel. (619) 224-3555.

BOATING SAFETY

Boating accidents can be avoided with simple education. Boaters in California are urged to look into the many safety classes offered by several statewide organizations. The largest of these are provided by the U.S. Coast Guard Auxiliary and the U.S. Power Squadrons. These classes last six to 16 weeks and include information on aids to navigation, rules of the road, charts and compasses, boating regulations, marlinspike seamanship, marine engines, and boat trailering practices. Call the Coast Guard Auxiliary at (213) 590-2217. A list of boating safety classes in your area is available by writing to: Department of Boating and Waterways, 1629 S Street, Sacramento, CA 95814, tel. (916) 445-2616.

DOWNTOWN AREAS

Chula Vista Marina

Located south of downtown San Diego, just off
I-5 on the J St. turnoff. Mailing address is 550
Tidelands Ave., Chula Vista, CA 92010, tel.
(619) 691-1860. Ten to 20 transient slips are
available. Slip fees range from $6.50-7.50. Food
store located on premises and open 8-7. Fresh
water is available at each slip. Marine supplies
available 9-7. Laundry and restaurant located on
premises. Special attractions very close by are
boat rental, RV resort, launching ramp, swimming beach, deli, and a fishing pier.

Intercontinental Marina

Located one mile north of the Coronado Bridge in downtown San Diego. Mailing address is 385 West Harbor Dr., San Diego, CA 92101, tel. (619) 230-8955. Number of transient slips avail-able varies. Slip fees are $1 per foot. Nearest food store is one-quarter mile. Hours: weekdays 8-5, weekends and holidays 9-5. Fresh water is available at each slip. Laundry facilities and restaurant located on premises. Special attractions close by are theaters, shops, luxury hotels, swimming pool, spa, sauna, tennis.

MORE MARINAS AND LAUNCHING RAMPS

Glorietta Bay Marina, 1715 Strand Way, Coronado 92118, tel. (619)435-5203, open daily 9 a.m.-5 p.m. year-round. Fees from $8.30-9.25. Dock master is Jack Swartz. **Coronado Cays Yacht Club**, Grand Carible Isle, Coronado 92118. **Dana Inn Docks**, 1710 West Mission Bay Dr., San Diego 92109. **Hilton Inn Docks**, 1775 East Mission Bay Dr., San Diego 92109.

SAN DIEGO CONVENTION AND VISITORS BUREAU

San Diego's boating population grows each year.

KATHY ESCOVIDO-SANDERS

THE CHANNEL ISLANDS

THE LAND

There are eight islands in the Channel Islands group, which extends off the California coast in a chain from Santa Barbara south to the Oceanside area. All share similar geologic origins, but each has evolved over the millennia into its own special environment with its own unique history. Geologists disagree over what once was believed to be fact: that from 70 million years ago to less than 20,000 years ago, the four northern Channel Islands were one colossal "super-island" connected to the Mainland by a land bridge. The theory was that the Anacapa end of this supposed island was joined to the Mainland at Point Mugu and was part of the Santa Monica Mountains. Earlier scientists believed that a land bridge might have existed because of the presence of land animals; the bridge gave them a logical reason for how the fauna traveled to the islands. Many other theories are now being studied that would be plausible explanations for the presence of wildlife on the islands without a land bridge.

Other geologists believe that the islands were formed 14 million years ago when volcanic activity along the Southern California coast was at its maximum. Islands, peaks, and ridges rose out of the sea, only to settle down again as the volcanic activity subsided. Ultimately, this left what we now call the Channel Islands. With the coming of the Ice Age over a million years ago, freezing water and subsequent melting eroded the offshore peaks. Geologic stresses from all the changes caused buckling, folding, fractures, and tears in the earth. Cliffs were formed, ridges slid into the sea, and islands appeared and disappeared into the ocean.

Geology buffs, while traveling around the Channel Islands, study the cliffs, bluffs, terrain, and underwater floor. In most cases it's rugged and craggy with horizontal and vertical strata and flat terraces above and below the sea. To a scientist this tells the story of many changes in ocean levels over the centuries. A relatively shallow submarine shelf at an average depth of 300 feet extends three to six miles around each of the islands. Here, the mingling of the cold current of the north with the warmer countercurrent of the south, along with the unique topography of the ocean bottom, contribute to making this one of the richest marine environments in the United States.

FLORA

Coreopsis
All eight Channel Islands have many natural similarities. On each of the islands many of the same plant communities thrive. One of the most common, coreopsis, also called sea dahlia and sunflower tree, has been variously described as a dwarf or miniature tree. The grotesque, odd plants average two feet in height but can grow as tall as 10 feet. In the fall, the clustered plants, bare of blossom or leaf, look like a dwarfed, misshapen, mysterious forest, all black and brown with knobby branches. But with winter rains, a change spreads over the hills; delicate fern-like fronds begin to appear. By spring, the plant blooms profusely (depending on the amount of winter rainfall) though just for a short time, bearing brilliant yellow/orange flowers; this splash of color is seen clear to the Mainland.

Coreopsis is found on all of the islands but San Clemente, spreading a bright carpet along the gentle hills of Santa Barbara Island, poking up even from craggy pockets and crevices of Anacapa and San Miguel. Rabbits destroyed most of the coreopsis on Santa Barbara, eating

DIANA LASICH HARPER

coreopsis

all the greenery they could reach, and then even girdling the trunks, ultimately destroying the trees and their bright flowers.

Cactus

The **prickly pear**, an *Opuntia* species, is a common Channel Island cactus, seen over much of the southern part of California and on into Mexico. The oval, disk-like pads are edible, as is the fruit—the pear. The plant bears beautiful satiny-yellow blossoms that wither and drop as the fruit begins to develop. The fruit becomes sweet and juicy if allowed to ripen on the plant, and is commonly eaten not only on the Channel Islands but in Mexico, Central America, and parts of Africa as well. An account given in *The Diary of a Ship Captain's Wife,* by Margaret Holden Eaton, who lived on Santa Cruz Island with her husband and baby girl from 1909, tells of making syrup for pancakes from the prickly pear. The trick is to peel the spines very carefully, then it's ready to enjoy. Oddly enough, sheep were known to eat the pear, prickly spines and all. The land was severely overgrazed—that's real hunger!

Another relative of the species growing on the islands is the **cholla cactus**. It's shaped differently from the prickly pear but is just as deadly with its curled barb-like spines. It too produces a flower, a delicate blossom sprouting at the joints. Long trails of **snake cactus** hang from rocky walls and canyons on the islands.

Wildflowers

The purple **blue-eyed grass flowers** have six graceful petals with yellow star-like centers. The **western thistle** blooms a bright pink on top of its feathery tassel. After a rainy winter, spring bursts forth on the islands, and even the sand dunes come alive with blue **lupine** and golden **California poppies. Dudleya**, grayish green and similar to common ice plant, grows side by side with the orange-blossomed **mimulus**, or monkey flower, on the steep walls of rocky southern-exposed cliffs. White **morning glories** steadfastly climb over and around **sea cucumbers** and **island sage. Ferns** and **mosses** grow at the bottom of steep canyons.

Trees

Island cherry, island oak, and **ironwood trees** grow on California's offshore islands. One of the most unusual of nature's quirks is a stand of **Torrey pines** on Santa Rosa Island. This is the only example of these pines outside Torrey Pines State Park, north of San Diego. These, along with the **Santa Cruz Island pine**, are remnants of an archaic Pleistocene forest that have survived a multitude of climatic changes over thousands of years.

FAUNA

Island Fox

The unique island fox, a relative of the Mainland gray fox, is an inhabitant of the six larger Channel Islands (not Anacapa or Santa Barbara). The animal differs from his Mainland relative in several ways. It's small—about the size of a house cat; in fact it has many feline characteristics, a scampering movement, and a yowl resembling a domestic cat's. It lives on a diet of mice, fish, birds and their eggs, crabs, fruit, insects, berries, and yes, even prickly pears. The fox has little fear of humans and a great curiosity (another catlike characteristic); it will stop and give you a good look if you meet on a mountain path.

There's no certainty about how it arrived on the islands. One possibility is that it rafted on a tree trunk washed out to sea from the Mainland during a heavy rainstorm; another is that it could have been brought to the islands by Indians traveling from the Mainland. The fox also suffers from the introduction of "exotic" grasses. Wild oat seeds (the kind that stick on your shoelaces when you hike the hills) get into the foxes' eyes and blind them. The island fox is just a little different on each of the Channel Islands; a bit bigger or smaller with slight color variations.

Rodents

The **white-footed mouse**, also known as the deer mouse, is endemic to the particular island it inhabits and is an important part of the food chain. Its chief predator is the fox. The rodent has white undersides, oversized feet, a hairy tail, and wide ears. It eats a varied diet—seeds, bark, twigs, fruit—and if it can get into a camper's tucker, it recognizes gourmet heaven. The mouse reproduces readily and survives nicely in the nooks and crannies of the rocky coastline, meadows, or sandy shore. It can be found on all eight of the Channel Islands. As with the fox, each island has developed a subspecies with subtle differences. Those on Santa Rosa and Santa Barbara have even developed their own variety of ticks and fleas.

Other small rodent relatives found on the islands are the **meadow mouse** and the **harvest mouse**. It is said there is an **island shrew**, but it must be extremely shy, since it has only been spotted a couple of times in over a hundred years. The **ground squirrel** is also part of the island family and lives in underground burrows in the meadow areas.

Wild Goats

This feral animal was introduced to the islands sometime during the Spanish arrival. It's believed that domestic goats were dropped off so the ship's crew would have fresh meat the next time they passed through. It doesn't take many generations for the goat to revert to its wild stage, and they reproduce quickly; the female generally delivers two kids a year.

island fox

DIANA LASICH-HARPER

On Catalina and San Clemente the goats increased freely for many years, building up large free-running herds. They are destructive animals with voracious appetites. Since ecologists have begun to see the need to preserve these islands in their natural states, many of the goats have been hunted or removed. On Catalina the occasional hunt keeps the herds down to a reasonable number. On San Clemente, the Navy Wildlife Biology staff has been trying to rid the island of the animals through hunts and bodily removal to Mainland sites. The staff has had not only the spritely goats to contend with (they can scamper up the tiniest trail and walk sideways where few humans dare to tread), but also animal lovers who feel that goats have a right to life on San Clemente. So while the environmentalists and the animal lovers argue, the goats keep right on reproducing and devastating the landscape with their natural eating habits.

BIRDS

An enormous variety of birds nest on the rocky cliffs and shores of the Channel Islands. Here it is easy to see that the **brown pelican**, only a few years ago in danger of being destroyed, is now flourishing. These large birds fly in a wedge formation, gracefully flapping their wings close to the wave tops. Spotting a fishy morsel they dive into the sea and, forgetting all grace, scoop up as many fish as their large beaks will hold, ending up a crumpled heap on the water's surface.

Not too long ago, pelican reproduction slowed down to a point of concern. Eggshells were so

DIANA LASICH HARPER

thin they could not support the weight of the brooding mother, cutting down dramatically on the number of chicks hatching each year. It was discovered that the problem was caused by DDT found in small fish ingested by the pelican. The pesticide accumulated in the tissues of the bird, eventually reaching such high levels that it affected, among other things, the shells of the eggs. Since DDT has been banned, the pelican has made a remarkable comeback and can be seen in large healthy numbers on Channel Island rookeries.

Pelicans have a few bad habits that get them into other troubles. One is trying to steal fish from fishermen—often right off the hook. If a pelican should get caught on your hook *do not* just cut the line at your end. If you do, you're condemning the bird to death; the line almost always ends up wrapped around the bird's body, including his wings, leaving him helpless, unable to fly, and doomed to starvation. Don't be afraid to reel the pelican in.

Other Birds

Along with a flourishing brown pelican rookery on Anacapa Island, thousands of other birds have found that the Channel Islands are nirvana. With little outside influence to disturb them, the relatively shallow near-shore waters around the islands supply 11 species of breeding seabirds with a rich food source of fish and invertebrates. On Santa Barbara, bird enthusiasts will find the largest colony of **Xantus' murrelet** and **black storm petrels** in the U.S. These timid seabirds are usually noticed only on or above the open ocean; they return to shore but once a year to breed and nest. Migratory fowl and other birds such as **loons, grebes, herons, plovers, ducks**, and **geese** are also seen on the islands. Some stop just to rest on their long journeys while others take time out for nesting and breeding before continuing.

Other feathered inhabitants of the islands include the **Brandt's cormorant**, a powerful web-footed diver that swims underwater after its pelagic prey. The **western gull**, a noisy old friend seen all over the West Coast, vigorously

UNTANGLING A PELICAN FROM YOUR LINE

1. Keep reeling! Although it'll struggle and flap its wings, remember you know what's best. As large as the bird appears, it only weighs about six pounds and is quite harmless if handled correctly.

2. When you've got the bird close enough, grab the closed bill and hold it securely with one hand. The inside edges of the bill are sharp, but unless you rub your hand up and down the edge, a pelican bite will not hurt you.

3. Fold up the wings into their normal closed position and hold them there. This quiets down the bird and it should stop struggling.

4. Turn the bird's head around so it lies along the middle of it's back (that's how pelicans sleep) and the bird is easier to handle. Tuck the pelican under your armpit, or between your legs while removing the fishing line and hook. But remember, keep a firm grip on the bird's bill. Certainly it would be easier for two people instead of one, but one person can do it.

5. The most important thing you can do for the bird is cut off every bit of fishing line. Do not throw scrap pieces of line into the water to ensnare another bird or wrap around a boat prop shaft.

6. If the hook is embedded in the pelican's flesh, try to cut off the barb and back the hook out. Or cut off the loop end of the hook and push the rest of the hook through. If you lack wire cutters, remove the line from the hook and push it forward. Do not rip the hook out; if it's impossible to remove the hook, leave it in. Pelicans do not seem to get infections and the bird's skin will heal around the hook.

7. If the hook has been swallowed and the line is very long and hanging out of it's bill, you will need the help of another person to hold the pelican's bill open (wear gloves) while you cut the line off as short as possible. If you're alone, just cut the line at the edge of the bill.

8. Set the bird down, step back a few feet and release it. You just did a very good deed for one of mother nature's favorites.

DIANA LASICH HARPER

A FOOD CHAIN IN THE OCEAN

Phytoplankton   Zooplankton   Small Fish   Larger Fish

1st Order   2nd Order   3rd Order

PRIMARY   CONSUMERS
PRODUCERS

nests on the Channel Islands high above the sea. **Sandpipers** are seen not only on the sandy shore, but also on the rocks and cliffs above, where nature has provided ample food and few predators.

MARINE CREATURES

An action of the sea called **upwelling** occurs along the California coast. Actually it happens all over the world, near the equator as well as in the Antarctic. In simple terms, coastal upwelling occurs when water from deeper levels of the ocean is brought to the surface to replace the surface waters when they are moved offshore by heavy winds. The upwelled water is colder and contains richer nutrients such as nitrates, phosphates, and silicates. These nutrients act as fertilizer for marine plants and ultimately help the fishing industry. Sometimes large areas of the sea become red, green, or brown from the rapid reproduction of microscopic plant and animal organisms called plankton. During this "plankton bloom," these tiny organisms are grazed upon by small animals. The smaller animals are fed upon by larger animals, including fish, which are in turn food for the larger fish. And when the whales graze in these colorful "pastures," they consume up to a ton of plankton per mouthful.

Tidepools

It's hard to describe the myriad marine crea-

tures of the Channel Islands without first mentioning the tidepools that thrive along their rocky shores. A tidepool is a pocket of the sea trapped regularly after the tide has gone out. The miniworlds that exist in each of these tiny pools are replicas of sealife in the larger picture. The fight for existence against such mighty forces as the pounding surf in high tide, drying sun and smothering heat during low tide, ultraviolet radiation from the sun, rain that dilutes the salinity, and constant predators presents ongoing adversity for these sturdy survivors.

One major predator is man. The creatures of the sea have not yet evolved a defense system to fight such calamities as oil spills or chemical pollution. It's up to us to do everything in our power to protect these fascinating creatures. When exploring or studying tidepools, each person has a responsibility to leave it as found. Apparently, it does no harm to the tiny creatures to pick them up (carefully), or turn them over, or scoop them up in a jar to watch them swim freely, as long as everything is returned *exactly* the same.

Note: Wear sturdy rubber-soled shoes that you don't mind getting wet, as most of the rocks around the intertidal zone are slick. Be sure to check the tide table in the local paper or marine store, and keep track when you're meandering at low tide; it could be difficult to return when the tide is barreling back in, especially in a rocky area.

Intertidal Zone

The intertidal zone is the area between the highest high tide and the lowest low tide. It's created by the coming and going of the ocean current each day. The currents also change with the time of the month, the year, and the quarter of the moon. This creates a continuum of habitats, from high rocks that regularly get the splashing surf at the highest tides to the deepest level of pools that are only exposed during the lowest tides at certain times of the year. All of the species in the zone have learned to live with the ocean and its capricious nature. Those with the least tolerance to atmospheric pressure are found at the lowest part of the zone or closest to the sea. Tolerant ones live toward the tops of rocks or reefs. The poor little creatures that would get washed into the sea (and probably eaten) every time a large wave crashes into their rocky homes occupy the protected pockets and crevices on the lee side of the rocks. Nature thinks of everything.

The following intertidal organisms are found along the entire Pacific coast from the top of Alaska to the southern edge of Mexico. For an excellent pocket guide that identifies and explains Pacific tidepool life, get a copy of *Pacific Intertidal Life,* by Ron Russo and Pam Olhausen, Nature Study Guild, Box 972, Berkeley, CA 94701.

Sand Creatures

The smooth sand constantly brushed by the incoming and outgoing sea hides a multitude of organisms. Everyone has seen the tiny **sand crab** burrowing its way into the wet sand of the backwash of each wave, straining for tidbits of food. Other small creatures (all different) come in many sizes and shapes: some have antennae, some hop sideways, some are gray, white, or the color of the sand. At night swarms of tiny **sandhoppers** leap onto kelp fronds in search of food. These, too, are part of the food chain with their own set of predators.

Marine Flora

Some brown algae (seaweed), called kelps, form large tangled forests consisting of **giant kelp, feather boa kelp, bull whip kelp**, and **elk kelp**. All of these brown algae depend on gas-filled bulbs, called pneumatocysts, to buoy their long, swaying stems, and blades that transfer energy from the sun into the dim depths of the bottom regions of the "holdfasts," which anchor the kelp to the sea floor. These kelp forests are habitats for a great variety of marinelife that depend on them for food and shelter. The fish that live within the forests are colorful and varied.

Among the most flamboyant algae is giant kelp, growing as much as 100 feet from the sea floor to the surface. They grow amazingly fast, as much as three feet a day, fed by the rich nutrients of the colder water brought in by upwelling, and plenty of sunshine. A new plant usually doubles its size every three weeks. The long stems are buoyed up by brown, tear-shaped pneumatocysts. From the surface, the

---

TIDEPOOL ORGANISMS

shield limpet	sun star
ribbed limpet	brittle star
owl limpet	green urchin
plate limpet	giant red urchin
horned slipper shell	isopod
black abalone	barnacle
chiton	crab
mussel	shrimp
black turban snail	eel
leafy hornmouth	bristleworm
checkered periwin-	ribbonworm
kle	flatworm
dog winkle	green alga
octopus	brown alga
sea slug	red alga
anemone	sponge
sea star	hydroid

kelp resembles a jumbled mass of brown rubberlike stems and vines and tobacco-like leaves, a place you want to stay away from. In reality this is just the canopy; the remainder of what continues to grow just gets longer and lies on the surface of the water.

From the diver's point of view, the stems grow a good distance apart from each other on the sea floor and indeed resemble a forest of tall trees. The holdfast is not a root in the sense of a land plant, gathering nutrients from the surrounding soil. It is simply an anchorage. The alga takes nourishment directly from the seawater through all exposed surfaces.

Reproduction is through microscopic cells known as spores, produced by a female plant and fertilized by a male; free-floating spores then germinate and begin to form separate new plants. Some seaweeds produce mini-plants which eventually separate and become new plants. Eventually giant kelp becomes so top-heavy that the holdfast lets go and the entire plant ends up floating on the surface of the sea

until caught by a current and thrown in a heap on a beach or rocky shoreline. However, it continues to nurture, harboring a variety of crabs, worms, clams, starfish, and other invertebrates.

Just as tidepool life exists because it can sustain itself despite drying, temperature change, salt level, and tide level, so it is with kelp. One of the more hardy, able to resist and persist, is a green alga called **sea lettuce**, which can lose up to 75% of its tissue water and recoup to fine fetter once in the water again. A brown alga, common **branched rockweed**, can withstand up to 48 hours of exposure without drying out. On the other hand, most red algae are extremely sensitive to heat and light and exist in the low intertidal zone because they cannot survive more than two or three hours of exposure.

Algae Aquaculture
Aquaculture is the farming of aquatic plants and animals and is practiced in many countries in the world. In Japan and other Oriental countries it has been a flourishing business for years; in

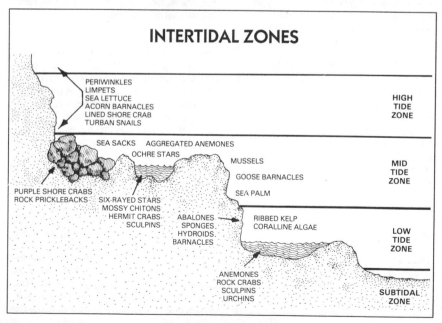

INTERTIDAL ZONES

PERIWINKLES
LIMPETS
SEA LETTUCE
ACORN BARNACLES
LINED SHORE CRAB
TURBAN SNAILS

HIGH TIDE ZONE

SEA SACKS   AGGREGATED ANEMONES
OCHRE STARS
MUSSELS
GOOSE BARNACLES
SEA PALM

PURPLE SHORE CRABS
ROCK PRICKLEBACKS   SIX-RAYED STARS
MOSSY CHITONS
HERMIT CRABS   ABALONES
SCULPINS   SPONGES
HYDROIDS
BARNACLES

MID TIDE ZONE

RIBBED KELP
CORALLINE ALGAE

LOW TIDE ZONE

ANEMONES
ROCK CRABS
SCULPINS
URCHINS

SUBTIDAL ZONE

the U.S. it's still in the developing stages. A multimillion-dollar business in algae harvesting is one area of aquaculture that has been very successful here. Algin, a derivative of kelp, is found in many products that you see in the supermarket every time you buy ice cream, chocolate milk, pudding, salad dressing, cheese, or fruit juice, take a close look at the ingredients. Algae derivatives furnish a gel used to emulsify and stabilize foods. It's used in diverse ways, in dental molds, beer, fertilizer, animal feed, paint, and cosmetics; approximately 15% of the world's iodine comes from Japan, where it is manufactured from kelp.

The kelp beds off California are leased out by the state, which accepts bids from companies that do the actual harvesting in specially designed ships that often harvest 400 tons of kelp a day. San Diego is a very popular area for kelp harvesting because of good year-round weather conditions. Under the auspices of the Department of Fish and Game, kelp can be cut up to a maximum of four feet below the surface of the water. Opening up the surface directs more sunshine beneath the sea and onto the plants, encouraging new growth. Harvesting is a healthy process.

AVOIDING SHARKS

Boaters, swimmers, surfers, and divers by the millions safely enjoy California's beaches and coastal waters. However, once in a great while a shark attack is reported. Be aware of the facts without stressing out while you're in the water of the Pacific. One of the easiest precautions to take is to avoid areas where seals and sea lions congregate. Another place *not* to go is the location of a previous shark attack. Since 1926, there have been 65 shark attacks recorded off the California coast, 44 attributed to great whites. Two of the attacks were at San Miguel Island, and three were off Point Conception. Most of the other confrontations occurred north of Point Conception, which should help put Southern Californians at ease. Sharks seem to avoid kelp beds, which should make skin divers exploring the beds around the Channel Islands feel a little more relaxed. A few statistics: most attacks on humans occur at the surface (not because the person looks like a seal as some believe, but for territorial reasons); and in Northern California, most attacks took place in clear water under 60 degrees rather than in warm or murky waters.

Seaweed Dishes

Some countries (Japan, China, and the Philippines, plus the state of Hawaii) have recognized the value of eating seaweed for centuries. These algae are nutritious and rich in vitamins A and E. The red, green, and brown algae are also very high in niacin and vitamins C, B-12, and B-1. They contain digestible proteins—highest in the red and green varieties. Three ounces of red algae supplies one-half the adult daily protein requirements. Common sea lettuce is high in iron, protein, iodine, magnesium, vitamins A, B-1, and C, and sodium. Pluck or cut the blades from rocks at low tide, wash well, dry at room temperature, and then use as a soup base.

Be aware that *except* in state parks and reserves, gathering algae for noncommercial use does *not* require a California fishing license or permit. In a state park or reserve, you must obtain a permit from the state Dept. of Parks and Recreation. In the course of collecting algae in intertidal areas, you will find many invertebrates, including clams, crabs, worms, and snails, living among the seaweeds. These animals can be taken only in legal seasons and with a fishing license. Outside of bureaucratic permission, all you need is a sharp knife, a bucket, some plastic bags, and don't forget your rubber-soled shoes. A good guidebook is handy to have along.

The best time to collect is at low tide—in California tides reach high and low levels twice a day. Tidal charts are found in many beach community newspapers, or check at your local sporting goods store or bait and tackle shop. Rocky shorelines are your best bet for collecting algae; the sides of the rocks are richer in plant life than the top. To get the freshest seaweed, take it directly from the place of attachment. Don't get lazy and grab a bunch that's been washed ashore —it's seldom fresh and will be full of debris. Take only what you need.

MARINE MAMMALS

Marine Mammal Protection Act

More than 25 species of marine mammals inhabit the Channel Islands Sanctuary. After being nearly demolished by the extensive hunting in the 18th and early 19th centuries, seals, sea lions, and a variety of fur seals have made a remarkable comeback. The Marine Mammal Protection Act of 1972 was passed with the intention of protecting the mammals, and management was transferred from the coastal states to the federal government. Many feel this law was enacted primarily to protect whales, but it was written to include all marine mammals—to the dismay of many.

There's much controversy among fishermen who feel the sea lion and sea otter are interfering with their business. According to divers, the sea otter eats a tremendous amount of abalone each year. Commercial fishermen complain that the growing sea lion popula-tion is taking a larger share of fish often right from their

SEAWEED RECIPES

Some seaweed is good raw, others cooked. Some make good additions to salads combined with cucumber and radish. All ingredients, including the seaweed, should be finely chopped.

NEREOCYSTIS KELP CAKE

3 eggs
2 cups sugar
1½ tsp cooking oil
1 tsp baking soda
1 tsp baking powder
1 tsp cinnamon
½ tsp powdered ginger
1½ cup grated kelp
1 cup crushed pineapple, drained

Use portion of "head" or float of nereocystis, the brown alga (kelp) found on beaches in California. A float about four inches in diameter will not be too old or tough. Cut into pieces, peel with vegetable peeler, and grate or chop finely. Wash (to remove excess salt that is released in grating) and drain well in colander.

Beat eggs until thick and lemon colored, gradually adding sugar. When combined, add cooking oil and stir briefly. Stir together flour, baking soda, baking powder, cinnamon, and powdered ginger. Add to egg mixture, then fold in the finely grated kelp and crushed pineapple. Bake at 350° F for 45 minutes in a greased and flour-dusted 10- by 10- or 9- by 12-inch pan.

This recipe makes a moist spice cake which may be frosted with butter-lemon frosting or left unfrosted with powdered sugar sifted over the top, according to taste. (From I.A. Abbott.)

KIM CHEE

Based on the Korean method of preparing their famous pickled cabbages, using a red alga, gracilaria.

2 lbs. gracilaria   chopped into two- to three-inch pieces
handful of coarse salt
2 cloves garlic   chopped per quart of wilted seaweed or to taste

1-2 chopped bulb onion or ½ cup chopped green onions
chili pepper,   chopped, or tsp cayenne (to taste— should be hot)

½ tsp paprika

Wash and clean the seaweed. Salt and wilt by letting it stand overnight. Drain off liquid; add garlic, onions, chili pepper, and paprika. Pack tightly in jars, seal, and refrigerate. Let stand a few days before using. (From Abbott and Williamson.)

northern Alaskan fur seal

The pinniped family includes two basic groups, the eared seals: **fur seals** and **sea lions,** and the hair seals, so-called true seals: harbor seals, **ribbon seals,** and **elephant seals**. Eared seals have small external flaps for ears. They move rapidly on land since they can turn their hind flippers forward, almost like feet, and they use their large forward flippers to swim quickly in the water. These mammals return year after year to special breeding areas called rookeries, commonly on offshore islands. Breeding season is a noisy, hectic time at the rookery. Males fight for territories and to the victors go groups of 25 or more females, accurately called "harems." Males go more than two months without feeding during breeding time.

Hair seals have no external ears. They have small front flippers, and use their hind flippers for swimming. They cannot turn their hind flippers forward, making them very clumsy on land. Five species of pinnipeds gather to breed, pup, and nurse their young in the Channel Islands: the harbor seal, **Steller sea lion, California sea lion,** northern fur seal, and elephant seal.

northern elephant seal

nets, not only creating a decrease in income, but fouling up expensive gear, creating "down time," and worst of all (according to the fishermen), they cannot destroy an animal that persists without first obtaining a special permit from National Marine Fisheries Service.

Ecologists argue that nature provides its own means of thinning the herds: many newborn pups are trampled to death each season in the rookeries as the herd multiplies. But fishermen are still demanding the right to destroy a seal that is making a nuisance of itself in the nets. Right now, there are no clear-cut answers. The law says it is illegal to harass a marine mammal. Harassment is interpreted as human activity which changes the behavior of the animals. You cannot harm, capture, kill, interfere with or enter a rookery, or closely pursue a whale with a boat.

Pinnipeds

Pinniped means "featherfeet" and refers to the modification of the front and hind feet to form flippers. Many of the seals, such as the **harbor seal,** spend six to eight months at sea. Others, such as the **northern fur seal,** spend considerable time on land. These creatures have thick hides with heavy layers of fat underneath and in some cases fur to protect them from the cold.

Sea Otters

After being around for at least three million years, the sea otter was almost totally annihilated in the middle 1800s. It was quite a thrill when, in 1938, a large herd of 100 sea otters was discovered about 15 miles south of Monterey. This marine mammal, part of the weasel family, can grow to about 4 feet long and reach a weight of 60-87 pounds. Their hind feet are large and webbed, with the fifth digit (comparable to man's little toe) the longest. The tail is used to help guide the animal while swimming, which it can do very efficiently. Its most impres-

DIANA LASICH HARPER

sea otter

sive feature, however, is its beautiful soft fur, which in the past made many coats and nearly caused its extinction.

The otters' front paws are stubby with retractable claws. However, the animals are quite adept with them, using them much like a human uses fingers. Anyone who has ever tried to remove an abalone attached to a rock knows that it is impossible to do without a metal bar. The otter, however, is quite an accomplished underwater hunter, easily capturing abalone and other shellfish. It is commonly seen floating on its back with a rock in one paw, holding a shellfish in the other, pounding away at the shell 'til it frees the flesh, ready to be nibbled.

The otter has no blubber as do seals and sea lions; its fur is not efficient enough to maintain its body temperature at 100° F, so it has a high metabolic rate and must consume large quantities of food each day. It forages (very efficiently) day and night. As the herds grow, the prognosis is that certain fishing industries will be greatly affected: Pismo clam, abalone, sea urchin, shallow-water red and rock crab, Dungeness crab, lobster, razor clam, and all open mariculture (marine farming) projects. The otter lives about 20 years and produces one pup approximately every two years. Its only enemy (besides man) is the white shark.

The first record of sea otters was made in 1741 after Vitus Bering (the explorer for whom the Bering Sea was named) spotted them in the Commander Islands and eastward in the Aleutians. The famous explorer was accompanied

by a German naturalist, George Wilhelm Steller. The group obtained about 800 pelts from Indians, who hunted them for the pelt and food in reasonable numbers. These were taken home to Europe—the first time Europeans were exposed to otter pelts. After that, in 1778, English explorer James Cook returned from extensive travels along the north Pacific coast and revealed to the world the potential profit awaiting the hunter. Thus, the sea otter fur trade began, which would attract people in ships from many parts of the world, weakening and ultimately loosening the hold of the Spanish flag on California.

Whales

When whales are mentioned, most West Coast dwellers think of the **gray whale**, which is enthusiastically observed as it migrates along the Pacific Coast from the Bering Sea to Baja and back each year. Others remember fondly the fun and games created by "Humphrey the humpback," which led the Coast Guard and many boaters on a romp up the Sacramento River Delta in 1986. But many more species of this usually gentle, giant mammal (part of the cetacean family) live in and around the coast near the Channel Islands. Although we think of all whales as being gigantic, the **pygmy sperm** grows to only 13 feet maximum, and some of the **beaked whales** only grow to 15-17 feet. The **false killer** isn't a true whale, but belongs to the dolphin (Delphinidae) family and gets huge, to 18 feet. The **killer** grows to 31 feet, and the **pilot**, to 22 feet.

Various sources say there are 78-91 species of cetaceans in the world. The cetaceans store thick layers of blubber under their skins. This provides insulation against cold, and some scientists believe it enables them to go for long periods without food. It's becoming more evident that the gray whale feeds heavily during the four months spent in the Bering Sea and feeds lightly during the eight months of migration to and from Baja. Rather amazing, considering the energy it must take to swim thousands of miles, and on the return, nurse a baby as well (if it's a blue whale, the baby could be 25 feet long and weigh up to two tons at birth!).

Some whales feed on plankton, minute organisms floating in the sea, straining them through baleen plates, the fine net-like apparatus in their mouths. Although the mammoth mammals have been known to snack on a passing school of anchovies or other small fish, they are mainly plankton eaters. So the largest animal on earth feeds on the smallest organisms lowest on the food chain, where the supply is more abundant. When in captivity, the animals are fed a variety of soft-boned fish, like mackerel, and squid.

The killer whale is the only known enemy of the great whales—along with man. But attacks are not as common as some would think. Pods of killer whales have been known in isolated instances to attack a lone whale; but its reputation as a killer whale rises mostly from tales related by whalers who have had their slaughtered whales (under tow) attacked by killer whales. The killer is ordinarily a fish eater.

Great whales appear to be unusually healthy

finback whale

California gray whale

Baird's beaked whale

CALIFORNIA WHALES

northern right
fin or rorqual
minke
sei
blue or sulphurbottom
finback
humpback
gray
sperm
pygmy sperm
dwarf sperm
beaked or bottlenose
Baird's beaked
Hubb's beaked
Cuvier's beaked
orca or killer

animals; the slow movers attract acorn barnacles, which are really just "hitchhikers" and do no physical harm. Parasites on the other hand can be a disabling menace, maybe even causing the aberrant behavior of "beaching." Scientists have found large quantities of parasites on these beached mammals.

Whaling

For centuries the whale has been a source of food and oil (and for a while, whalebone), especially for the polar region natives. Seven thousand years ago, Eskimos on Canada's east coast were using toggle harpoon heads. In the mid-19th century they were "invented" again by the Yankee whaling fleet. Whaling was begun off the coast of California by Yankee whalers in the early 1800s. By the late 1800s, the gray whale was thought to be extinct. Shore whaling (referred to as "whaling by hand") is part of California's history, and the first whaling station was built in Monterey in 1854. Others were built up and down the California coast and down to Baja but were short lived. In 1874, Charles Melville Scammon (the whaler who discovered and exploited Scammon's Lagoon in Baja) wrote: "This particular branch of whaling is rapidly dying out, owing to the scarcity of the animals which now visit the coast."

During this time, the Americans dominated the whaling industry. Their chief target was the **right whale**, so called because it was the "right" whale to catch: it was slow moving, didn't sink when killed, contained valuable baleen used for women's corset stays (big business in those days), and of course was a great source of valuable oil used for lamps and smokeless candles. (Petroleum was discovered in 1859 and Edison came through with the incandescent bulb in 1879; otherwise we may never have had the privilege of seeing a whale.) When overhunting pretty well wiped out the right whale, the new target was the **sperm whale**; these were taken for oil and ambergris (used in perfume).

The industry was really making inroads into the whale populations with the development of the explosive harpoon gun in 1868, fast steam-powered catcher boats, and later with the use of floating factory-ships. The whaling industry methodically went about their business, destroying one species of whale after the other. After 1880, whaling was just about finished. However, interest was revived again in the States between 1940 and 1965. Whales were slaughtered and used mostly for pet food until it was no longer economically feasible to hunt them.

Only two nations—Japan and Russia—continue to hunt, and they aim primarily at the sperm whale for its oil. Whale meat is eaten in Japan but accounts for only two percent of the fishing industry and is steadily declining. Russia takes a small number each year for the subsistence of Siberian natives. Except for Eskimos, it is illegal for Americans to hunt whales under both the Marine Mammal Protection Act and the Rare and Endangered Species Act. The Fisheries Conservation Act of 1976 prohibited whaling within a 200-mile ocean zone off the U.S. coast. The last "killer" ship registered in the U.S. was the *Sioux City*, now used for marine research.

Dolphins And Porpoises

If there were a popularity contest for sea animals, hands-down winners would be porpois-

rough-toothed dolphin

Risso's dolphin

es and dolphins. They always appear to have smiles on their faces, their squeaky "talk" is a happy sound, they impart a playful attitude, and certainly their friendly rapport with human beings in marine parks around the U.S. has endeared them to millions of people. Also of the cetacean family, many of their habits are similar to those of their big brother, the whale. The terms "dolphin" and "porpoise" are continually confused. Strictly speaking, the dolphin is the long-beaked variety. The porpoise is the snubby-nosed form. Porpoises and dolphins have intrigued man for centuries.

They have been written about, sung about, drawn, and fought over. Aristotle compared them to man: ". . . dolphins are born of a womb, take milk from nipples, breathe with lungs, make a variety of sounds, copulate rather than spawn, and care for their young, often with the help of an 'auntie.'" When you see "dolphin" on menus, it is not a cetacean, but is actually a fish called mahimahi or dolphinfish. Around the Channel

PACIFIC DOLPHINS AND PORPOISES

common or white-belly
Pacific pilot
Risso's
Pacific white-sided
harbor
Dall
false killer
striped
rough toothed
Pacific bottlenose

Islands, it isn't unusual to see hundreds of **white-sided dolphins** cavorting in the wake of a fast-moving boat. The largest herds are seen from Aug. to Jan.—or individual performers can be seen at San Diego's Sea World.

HISTORY

INDIANS

Canalinos

Humans have been touching these islands for centuries. Remnants of prehistoric man place him here 11,000 years ago. Today, the only people we can learn about are the Chumash Indians, inhabitants of the Channel Islands at the time of the arrival of the Spaniards. The Indians are referred to by several names. Even though their language, based on the original Shoshonean, evolved into many dialects, all Channel Island Indians are known as Canalinos.

These particular Indians are considered to have possessed higher than average technical abilities. They are credited with many contributions to the culture of the time, but the most outstanding was their wood-plank canoe called a *tomol.* Before this boat was developed, there is evidence that a primitive craft made from large bundles of tule grass was used. It had obvious disadvantages: it only lasted one or two times in the sea and long distances could not be undertaken. On the other hand, the *tomol,* a fine wooden craft, was sturdy and fast, had two prows, and sometimes had wing boards as well.

The canoe was constructed of planks split from driftwood logs with wedges made of whalebone or antler (they had no metal tools). Holes were drilled and reamed with stone drills. Strong cord made of fiber was strung through to hold them together. They were then buried in wet sand with fires built over them to steam the boards so that they could be bent to the desired shape. The seams were caulked with asphaltum (thick black oil that oozes at certain rocky areas along the Southern California coast, such as Carpinteria), and even then, the craft took on water. However, these 12- to 16-foot vessels were more than adequate for taking 12-20 mariners long distances, to the Mainland and from island to island—even though they had to include a youth or two to bail water.

The Canalinos were hunters and fishermen. They hunted sea lions, otters, and seabirds. They fished from their wood-plank boats and used shiny hooks carved from abalone shells that fooled the big fish into thinking the hook was a little fish—the first man-made lure? It apparently worked well, as indicated in the many kitchen middens found all over the Channel Islands; obviously seafood was an important part of the Canalino diet.

The Indians were talented in other areas also. They wove sturdy, handsome baskets from plant fibers, varnishing those they wished to make waterproof. They painstakingly made tiny beads from the marine snail (purple olivella), among other shells. These were strung and valued for trade with Mainland Indians. Besides beads, islanders traded otter skins, seal pelts, shellfish, and carved stone figures (often depictions of whales or seals) used as charmstones. The island Indians had quantities of stone to work with, as on Catalina where there's an abundant supply of soapstone, steatite, and obsidian. These island objects were traded for Mainland goods scarce or not available on the islands such as acorns, rabbits, deer, and a hard rock called chert.

Canalino Indians built huts from branches and tule grass.

Indian Cult

All the villages of the Channel Islands were independent of each other, each with a *wot* (chief) and a shaman. The life of the Indian villager was controlled by these two men. There were rules and ceremonies and the chief depended on the mysterious prowess possessed by the shaman to help him through difficult times, such as drought or eclipse. A few important ceremonies consistently held in the village dealt with birth, death, and puberty for both boys and girls. Puberty ceremonies were so universally celebrated among the hunting and gathering Indians that historians believe them to have been brought from Asia itself.

The boys went through a rigorous ceremony, the *toalache* cult, which involved the ingestion of a narcotic, called *toalache* (see p. 7). The girls' rite was more in the nature of a debut, a presentation to society of a marriageable young woman. It was a time of moral lectures and a test of virtue. First, virtue was tested with the girl swallowing a ball of tobacco. If she could retain it without regurgitating, she was indeed a virtuous Indian maiden; if she regurgitated, she was considered a fallen woman and held in contempt. Sad for the girl with a queasy stomach! During the three-day rite, some of the old taboos remained, such as not eating meat, and using a stick to scratch her head instead of her fingers. But mostly it was a preparation for life as a wife, mother, and efficient member of the community —and for her future health.

These qualities were enhanced by practically baking her in a pit for three days and nights, protected from hot stones only by a mattress of branches from such plants as the California mugwort and the western ragweed. During this time she was the center of attention, and although she did fast from all food, she could drink, was bathed with warm water, and was the central figure in hours of dancing and singing and the distribution of gifts.

After three days, her face was painted by the wife of the visiting official (guests from a neighboring village) in charge of the ceremony. Anklets and bracelets of (highly valued) human hair and shell necklaces were placed on her. A sand painting was made on the ground and she was given moral lectures, instructing her on how to act in order to be socially acceptable. She should be industrious and not a gadabout, bathe each day, be hospitable, have a straightforward manner with no malice in her heart. At the end of the ceremony, she was given a ball of sage meal and salt that she then spit into a hole in the center of the sand painting and she watched as the entire "painting" was brushed into the hole and the earth packed in on top of it—her future was sealed.

The Indians of the Channel Islands were all part of the cult called Chingichnich that originated on Catalina Island. The medicine men exercised incredible exploitations of the people. The shaman was considered a wizard, a powerful man deserving of the people's respect. He induced spells, producing items from his mouth that he said were sent to him from the heavens. He would take credit for magically causing the death of an enemy in another village.

The medicine man also explained the signs of nature to the people; a rainbow was a sign of good fortune, while an eclipse was a certain omen of calamity. During an eclipse the people were reduced to shouting and weeping, pounding with sticks on the ground, all to scare away the monster trying to steal the moon or sun. The shaman must have been right, since in each instance they eventually managed to scare away this evil monster that was eating their celestial body. Falling stars were children of the moon; the morning and evening stars were the Big Stars, and Polaris was the "star that does not move."

The Advent Of The White Man

It appears that life went on among these Indians for centuries with very little outside intrusion. This was claimed to change shortly after the Spaniards declared the west coast of the continent for the king of Spain in the mid-1700s. It was shortly after this time that the Russians and Americans discovered that the coast was home to a precious little sea creature, the otter, that was desired for its velvet-like fur by a ready market in Asia and Europe. The otter hunts that would change the destiny of a country (Spain) and a culture (the Indians') began. For a while the Russians and Americans were competitors, each trying to outhunt the other. After realizing what was happening, the Spaniards, too, began hunting the otter, at the same time placing strict embargos on all foreign ships, ordering them to leave the territory. These orders didn't stop either the Russians or the Americans, nor for that matter ships from other countries that were beginning to enviously eye the beautiful California coast.

The Spanish didn't have the manpower to police the entire Pacific coast—outsiders had their way. The beginning of the end for the Spanish regime was on the horizon; the hunts continued. The otter was slaughtered on a grand scale and soon it was all but wiped out. But neither the Americans nor the Russians considered that, and in fact they ultimately joined forces, employing experienced hunters, the Aleut Indians with their sleek *bidarkas*—kayaks made from seal skins stretched over whalebones. The Aleuts made temporary camps on the islands while they massacred the sea otter for its fur.

The hunters found there was also a market for certain species of pinnipeds and then virtually destroyed the Guadalupe fur seal, northern fur seal, and northern elephant seal, which was prized for the superior lubricating qualities of its oil. One large bull might produce more than 200 gallons of this oil, while his whiskers fetched a handsome return in China as opium-pipe cleaners.

In the midst of all this turmoil, the Channel Island Indians were caught up in the outsiders' frantic search for money. The peaceful Canalino Indians were no match for the aggressive Aleuts. Their women were raped, the men murdered, and entire families commandeered by the invaders from the north while they stayed on the islands. White man's diseases were rampant; syphilis and measles were responsible for the deaths of most of the Indians who weren't murdered. The few that remained agreed to go to Mainland missions. By 1857, there were no Indians left on the Channel Islands. The end of an era—the white man's entrance to the California coast was totally destructive.

Pioneers

In a different spirit, even the pioneers wreaked havoc to nature's balance. In the latter half of the 19th century, settlers began to arrive with their sheep. What better place? No fences were needed, there were no other farmers to disturb, just massive grazing areas. These voracious animals were allowed to roam and reproduce freely. Overgrazing destroyed native plants; the introduction of oats and other "exotic" crops further damaged the natural vegetation of the islands. People have tried to tame these bits of land, but in most cases the greatest equalizers of all, nature's elements, have maintained the upper hand. Today, bowing to this natural power, man has wisely chosen to preserve most of these islands as they are and were in prehistoric times.

Chinese

The Chinese were heavily discriminated against during and after the gold rush. They were often smuggled into the country by dishonest sea captains to sell (yes, like slaves) for cheap labor. It was sometimes necessary for these ships from the Orient to lay over or hide the Chinese on the Channel Islands in order for the captain to complete his nefarious dealings and sneak by wary customs agents.

While spending time on the islands, the Chinese were made aware of the profusion of abalone along the islands' shores. After the sea otter slaughter (sea otters eat thousands of abalone each year) and the destruction of the Indian (who also harvested his share of the shellfish) the abalone was ignored and allowed to replenish for many years. At the first opportunity, the Chinese returned and harvested cove after cove of the delicately flavored abalone meat that had been prized by Orientals for centuries. This quietly administered industry (California's first organized fishing industry, if you don't count the Indians') flourished in all of the Channel islands and by 1879 more than four million pounds a year of dried abalone meat were being exported.

The hard-working Orientals were eventually driven away by other immigrants: Italians, Portuguese, slavs, and Japanese. By 1890 Chinese fishing villages were nonexistent. Commercial divers over the past 30-40 years have made their dent in the population as well. Abalone has become more scarce each year; now the meat is sold at local fish markets for around $48 a pound!

The First Oil Boom
Southern California's first oil boom took place in the late 1800s. Much like the gold rush, it brought economic rewards to the state, and everyone wanted to get into the oil business. The industry was a baby. It wasn't until much later, in the 1890s, with technical improvements in drilling, storing, and refining, that it became a viable business. As the years passed, Southern California continued to upgrade the industry until it was producing 25% of the world's oil. Offshore leases of the outer continental shelf

were first obtained in the 1950s. Today, San Pedro and Long Beach Harbor still bustle with the comings and goings of large oil tankers from all over the world; the pro-ecology groups keep their fingers crossed that each year will be "spill-free."

Channel Islands National Park
San Miguel, Santa Rosa, Santa Cruz, Anacapa, and Santa Barbara, the five northernmost of the eight Channel islands, make up Channel Islands National Park, established on March 5, 1980, when President Carter signed a bill into law creating the National Park and Marine Sanctuary to preserve the area's delicate ecology. The entire Channel Islands National Park is a reserve included in the Man and the Biosphere Program, an international effort to define and solve worldwide environmental problems and issues. National marine sanctuaries are under the administration of the National Marine Sanctuary Office, National Oceanic and Atmospheric Administration (NOAA), and the U.S. Department of Commerce, and are managed by the National Park Service and the California Department of Fish and Game under an agreement with NOAA. The sanctuary includes the land areas of Anacapa, Santa Barbara, San Miguel, and most recently acquired (1987) Santa Rosa, plus a band of sea extending six miles around each of the five northernmost Channel islands.

PRACTICALITIES

Camping

Camping is permitted on Anacapa, San Miguel, and Santa Barbara with a free permit from Park Headquarters at 1901 Spinnaker Dr., Ventura, CA 93001, tel. (805) 644-8262. Visitors planning to take their own boats should study U.S. Coast and Geodetic Survey Charts 18720, 18729, and 18756. Anchoring at either Anacapa or Santa Barbara islands can be hazardous due to sea conditions. A maximum of 30 people per day are allowed to camp at each island and only in designated areas. Everything for your stay must be hauled in, including water and fuel. When you leave you must take all trash with you.

The facilities at the campgrounds include pit toilets and tables. No open fires are allowed. If you plan to cook you must bring a small stove. There are restrictions on using the stoves, all meant to control the possibility of a wildfire on the arid islands, which would destroy the years of effort by the National Park Service to restore the land to its original condition. A fire department is nonexistent. Also, discharge of firearms and fireworks is not allowed in the park or within the one-nautical-mile seaward boundary of ocean within the state ecological reserves.

Activities

When you get right down to it, there's not a whole lot to do on the Channel Islands. In fact there are probably many people who wouldn't be interested in this kind of a trip at all. Let's find out how you rate. Do you need electronic entertainment, a regular bed, or a close-by fast-foodery to make your getaway worthwhile? If you answered yes to any or all of these questions, cancel your trip to the Channel Islands—*right now*. On the other hand, does the shock of a black velvet sky sparkling with brilliant stars always bring a lump to your throat? Can you gaze fascinated for hours at a time into a small rocky pool filled with the colorful minutiae of marinelife? Do you somehow mistake the sound of the sea crashing onto a rocky shore for a lullaby? If you answered yes to any or all of *these* questions, you will have the time of your life on the Channel Islands.

All visitors to the islands should know that most of what you get from a visit is a glimpse of life before the advent of modern man. Because of the importation of domestic animals allowed to overgraze the land and the intrusion of "exotic" plants, including fast growing grain types such as oats, barley, and sea grasses, the native vegetation was choked out almost entirely. These introduced seeds were broadcast in open plowed fields by well-intentioned farmers, further crowding out the native grasses. This combination of events all but destroyed the original landscape. Today, with a lot of TLC, the native plants are returning. With this in mind, hiking on the islands (where permitted) is restricted to formal paths.

Getting There

The ocean around the northern Channel Islands can change from placid to rough and choppy very quickly, especially in the afternoon. It's wise to study local conditions and be prepared. **Island Packers Boat Company** provides regular transportation to Anacapa, Santa Barbara, Santa Rosa, and San Miguel islands; reservations should be made at least one to two weeks in advance; check seasonal schedules. Located next door to the Channel Islands National Park Headquarters at 1867 Spinnaker Dr., Ventura, CA 93001, call for reservations, (805) 642-1393, for information (805) 642-7688. Several commercial boat companies operate open-party and charter trips the rest of the year, especially during the whalewatch season, Jan. through March. For more detailed information call Park Headquarters, tel. (805) 644-8262.

San Miguel, Santa Rosa, And Santa Cruz

A permit to visit San Miguel is free through Park Headquarters in Ventura. Access is by excursion boat only. For permission to land on Santa Rosa Island contact Park Headquarters. To visit Santa

Cruz, contact the Nature Conservancy, Santa Cruz Island Preserve, 213 Stearns Wharf, Santa Barbara, CA 93101, tel. (805) 962-9111. For further information write to: Channel Islands National Park Visitor Center, 1901 Spinnaker Dr., Ventura, CA 93001, tel. (805) 644-8262. Boat transportation and package tours are provided by Island Packers, 1867 Spinnaker Dr., Ventura, CA 93001, tel. (805) 642-1393.

Romance And Adventure

Sailing charter trips are available from **Navigators Channel Island Cruise.** Luncheon trips start at $40; overnight island cruises for two are $450 and up. These trips are available April through November; 1621 Fernald Point Lane, Santa Barbara, CA 93108, tel. (805) 969-2393. Twilight and sunset cocktail harbor cruises offered at Captain Jack's Landing, 4151 S. Victoria Ave., Oxnard, CA 93030, tel. (805) 985-8511 and (213) 457-9221.

ANACAPA ISLAND

Anacapa lies 11 miles southwest of Oxnard, 14 miles south of Ventura, and 26 miles southeast of Santa Barbara. Isolated and remote, it stretches five miles across the sea but has a total area of only one square mile. Anacapa is actually three separate islands separated by narrow channels, inaccessible from each other except by boat. West Anacapa, largest of the islands, is punctuated with sea-etched caves and craggy peaks. On Middle Anacapa, surrounded by high cliffs, meadows of green grass display giant coreopsis with their distinctive yellow flowers that, when in bloom (on a clear day), can be seen from the Mainland and far out to sea.

GEOLOGY

A volcanic rock, Anacapa is riddled with labyrinthine caverns in the submarine lava flow eas-

Escorted groups to the Channel Islands are often accompanied by knowledgeable guides.

VENTURA VISITORS BUREAU

ily observed at the island's base. Anacapa Island is made up almost entirely of dense deposits of Miocene volcanic rock, lava ash, and breccia (rock consisting of sharp fragments embedded in compacted sand, clay, or lava ash). As time, wind, and sea continue to erode the cliffs, gravel and pebbles of different minerals are exposed. Near Frenchy's Cove, look for a large vein of almost-white chalcedony (a translucent quartz commonly pale gray or blue with a wax-like luster) and on the south shore of West Anacapa near Cat Rock the geology buff can spot San Onofre blue-green breccia. While browsing Cat Rock, notice the surge channel and the adjacent blowhole that makes a beautiful photo subject with a little patience.

The famous Arch Rock, a natural "bridge" formed by constant sea erosion, is at the easternmost extension of the island. This is Anacapa's trademark and the sight most people remember after visiting the Channel Islands. It was first brought to the attention of the public when sketched by James Whistler during his time in the Coast Guard. Arch Rock is 80 feet high and the archway is 50 feet high—product and victim of the pounding sea. Along the island's coast, the erosion from the perpetually crashing waves has created blowholes, surge channels, caves, benches; the black sand seen

on a few beaches during low tide is actually tiny flakes of the black lava of which the island is made. Earthquake faulting, folding, lifting, and the ancient volcanic eruptions (from a still unknown source) created steep-sided cliffs that fall precipitously into a deep sea. Viewing the rugged splendor of Anacapa is one of those lifetime events not soon to be forgotten.

FLORA AND FAUNA

There are practically no trees on Anacapa. The landscape is reminiscent of California's high desert, with only low-growing scrubby shrubs that include **cholla, dudleya,** and **coreopsis.** The most readily noticed animals are the birds. You'll see **cormorants, scoter ducks, black oystercatchers, western gulls,** and **brown pelicans** gliding low over the sea and high along the rugged cliffs. The once nearly extinct brown pelican uses the slopes and cliffs of West Anacapa as its only large nesting site on the west coast of the United States. Because West Anacapa has been designated a research nature area for the pelican rookery, no landings are permitted without written permission from the superintendent.

Brown kelp hugs the shoreline, providing a

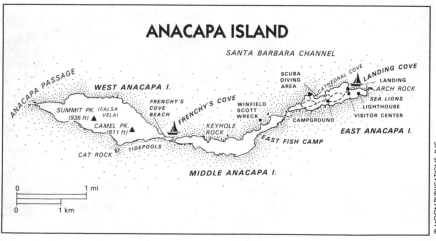

ANACAPA ISLAND

SANTA BARBARA CHANNEL

haven for a myriad collection of fish, invertebrates, and other curious sea creatures. This is a favorite place for divers to photograph, explore, and to see **abalone, lobster**, and **scallops**. Fishermen (with a valid fishing license) will find **sheepshead, rockfish, perch**, and **sand dabs. Sea lions** and **seals** frolic in the surrounding waters, and the top of the cliff on Middle Anacapa is an ideal viewing location during the Jan.-March migration of the **gray whales** that passes close to the island.

HISTORY

Indians
Because there is no water source, most historians believe that the Canalino Indians didn't live on the island permanently. Instead they used Anacapa as a hunting ground for shellfish, sea lions, and seals. They also used the ready supply of sturdy minerals to make arrowheads. Many kitchen middens have been found, and other remnants of the past can still be seen on Anacapa; remember, everything on the islands is protected by federal law, so don't take any souvenirs—whether Indian, animal, plant, or mineral.

Europeans
The first outsiders to see Anacapa were the crew of Cabrillo's ship that anchored near the small island in Oct. 1542. It wasn't mentioned again until 1769 when Portola made notes in his log, calling it Las Mesitas ("Little Tables"). But it was Juan Perez, supply-ship captain of the Portola expedition, who named it Falsa Vela ("False Sail"). This name is still in use today for the tallest point on Anacapa. On a clear day seamen have a remarkable view of the 936-foot peak. The island was renamed Anacapa by Captain George Vancouver, sailing under the British flag on his journey down the California coast in 1793.

The closest islands to the Mainland, the Anacapa group was probably the easiest for smugglers to reach in the mid-1800s, as well as ruthless sea captains who deposited their deported Chinese slaves here 'til buyers could be found. As a result, the industrious Chinese gathered abalone, a money-making bonanza that abounded in West Anacapa's tidepools.

Navigational Aids
It is believed that the Indians traveled between islands in their *tomols* (wooden canoes) at night after the westerly winds calmed down. Open fires on island promontories were tended by the Indians as navigational aids. By the early 1800s, the Indians were gone from the Channel Islands, and Europeans began settling the California coast. As traffic increased, maritime disasters became commonplace. Now, as then, fog appears when least expected and a calm sea becomes a churning chaos—often too quickly for a ship to escape its torment. Though the Channel Islands were on the course traveled between New Spain (Mexico) and the Philippines, Spanish galleons soon learned to give these formidable rocky bits of land a wide berth. For years ships went aground around the islands and it was evident that a lighthouse was needed.

The East End Lighthouse
Only after a disastrous accident (December 2, 1853) brought attention to the channel's need for a lighthouse was it seriously considered. A 225-foot sidewheel steamer called the *Winfield Scott* went aground in a thick fog on Middle Anacapa's rocky coast. Two hundred and fifty passengers (and $800,000 in gold bullion) waited eight days on the barren island with virtually no food, water, or shelter before they were rescued. In 1854, a United States Coast Survey team agreed that Anacapa was the ideal spot for a lighthouse, but after careful exploration concluded that it was impossible to build on the steep-cliffed island. Many years passed before something more than talk took place. In 1912, an unattended automatic acetylene beacon was built; in 1932, the present lighthouse was erected by the United States Lighthouse Service (later to become the U.S. Coast Guard).

When first built, the lighthouse was attended by a group of Coast Guardsmen accompanied by their families. In 1969, the light was automated, and at an elevation of 277 feet it's one of the most powerful on the California coast. The catadioptric light has 1.2 million candlepower and can be seen 23 miles in all directions. Housed in a traditional white cylindrical structure, a foghorn sounds every 15 seconds in foggy weather. A radio beacon close by transmits with a full range of 10 miles. The Anacapa light on East Anacapa continues to serve as a beacon for the many ships that pass, endangered by the fog that often shrouds these rocky islands. Today the lighthouse is attended by personnel stationed in Port Hueneme on the Mainland coast. A park ranger lives year-round in one of the former Coast Guard houses on East Anacapa, still white with a red-tiled roof. Another house has been transformed into a museum for visitors to the island.

ISLANDERS

The Websters

Anacapa's history includes very few permanent residents. And like all the other Channel islands, it was sheep that brought the first settlers to Anacapa. In 1907, Heaman Bayfield ("Bay") Webster (son of the Ventura postmaster of the era), his wife Martha, and their two young sons Morris and Harvey bought the lease to Anacapa from the Department of the Interior for $75. They set up housekeeping and lived on the island for the following 10 summers. They raised sheep and opened a tourist resort, calling it the Webster Sheep Ranch and Fishing Camp. It was primitive—with sand-flushed toilets. (A trapdoor on the windward side of the outhouse received gusts of wind-blown sand—flush courtesy of Mother Nature.) Water was brought from the Mainland in five-gallon jugs. With no fresh water on Anacapa, it's curious how the sheep survived; one bit of lore claims that each morning after heavy night fog had soaked their wool, the animals licked the moisture from one another's coats. A good part of their diet was the dudleya

plant, a low-growing succulent that provided some liquid.

Webster instigated one of the first package tourist trips on the California coast. For a budget sum, he brought families to the island in one of his boats, offered them fishing, swimming, hunting, hiking, and Indian artifact hunts; a smokehouse was available for fishermen. Who wouldn't jump at the chance for that vacation on the Channel Islands today! Entrepreneur Bay Webster was way ahead of his time.

Frenchy The Hermit

Born Raymond Ledreaux in Brittany, his colorful past is said to have included a bitter experience of aborted studies for the Catholic priesthood followed by a seaman's life that took him around the world and, finally, from China to America. Contentment was cut short by the death of his young wife during the 1918 influenza epidemic. Perhaps it was these tragedies that first turned Frenchy to his reclusive life on tiny Anacapa Island in 1928. The Frenchman survived alone over the years through fishing and by using his ever-ready supply of seafood to trade for other necessities with local fishermen and occasional campers. All who knew Frenchy enjoyed a visit to the rocky island, and never arrived without a jug of wine to loosen his tongue. Their evening might include a dinner of cioppino and lobster (he was a good cook), and tall tales of the sea, or perhaps discussions of classic literature and fine music.

Frenchy was a diamond in the rough, and though he lived a life far from the madding crowds (with his crowd of cats), he didn't fit the stereotype of "hermit"; he was always happy to have the company of visitors to the island. In 1954, Frenchy turned 68 and the Park Service employees decided he should be moved ashore after 26 years on Anacapa Island. A lovely cove on West Anacapa's north shore bears his name.

GETTING THERE

Being the closest to the Mainland, East Anacapa is the island most frequently seen by visi-

Special excursions take visitors on occasional overnight cruises stopping at several of the Channel Islands.

tors. Camping, hiking, and picnicking in small groups are encouraged by Channel Islands National Park Service.

Island Packers, a commercial carrier, provides transportation between Ventura and East Anacapa, with seasonal schedules available. The boating company offers a variety of trips to other parts of Anacapa as well as the rest of the Channel islands. Some are day-trips; some are multiday island adventures. A popular trip takes passengers to Frenchy's Cove Landing on special low-tide days to explore the tidepools for several hours. Island Packers also delivers campers to East Anacapa and makes arrangements to pick them up on a designated day. You can't change your mind—remember, there's no phone on the island! However, the Park Service has a radio for emergencies—only.

For further information, prices, and schedules, contact Island Packers, 1867 Spinnaker Dr., Ventura, CA 93001, tel. (805) 642-1393. For information about other commercial carriers, contact Channel Islands National Park Headquarters, 1901 Spinnaker Dr., Ventura, CA 93001, tel. (805) 644-8464. Sportfishing and

scuba-diving boats frequent the island, and all boaters are invited to anchor offshore.

ACTIVITIES

Hiking On East Anacapa
The first thing you must do when arriving on East Anacapa Island is climb a steep stairway of 154 steps up the side of the mountain; after that you've really arrived. The park ranger is very helpful, and with advance planning through the Park Service, you may arrange for tours, walks, and other programs. A self-guiding trail acquaints you with the magic of nature on Anacapa. The walk is short (1¹² miles), and the park requests that you stay on the trails in the interest of protecting fragile island resources and for your own safety. If you happen to visit on a foggy day and the foghorn is operating, *do not* visit the lighthouse. Severe hearing damage may result. Picnicking is allowed, but you must carry all trash off the island. Latrines are available, but there is no fresh water, so bring along whatever water you think you'll need.

hiking the dry hills of
the Channel Islands

CHANNEL ISLANDS NATIONAL PARK

CAMPING

Anyone wishing to camp on the Anacapa group is restricted to the campground on East Anacapa. Facilities are free on a first-come, first-served basis and limited to 30 persons or six groups; therefore reservations and permits are a must. The permit gives you 14 days on the island; reservations may not be made more than 90 days in advance. Bring everything you need; there is nothing on Anacapa Island except the artistry of Mother Nature. But travel light; remember, you haul everything up the side of the cliff (shelter, food, fuel, water, etc.) and then walk another quarter mile to the campgrounds. You'll find picnic tables, so bring a portable stove if you plan to cook. Be prepared in the event that a strong wind comes up (one frequently does), and bring a tent that can be well anchored.

Note: There's no room to run free, throw a football, or even a Frisbee. Expect time on Anacapa to be spent tuning in to nature and enjoying the solitude, a subtle interaction with what life must have been like hundreds of years ago. This is unique, life on a desert island with its many changing moods and faces. Pets are not allowed.

Weather
The weather is something to be considered when planning a camping trip on the Channel Islands because in most cases you can't just pack up and go home. The wind often blows for several days at a time—even in summer—at speeds up to 20-30 miles per hour. Your only protection will be the shelter you bring along; tube tents are not recommended; a small mountain tent is best. Wet, thick fog can also set in for several days. Spring and winter rains turn the trails into thick quagmires of mud; and when the sun shines there are no shade trees to provide relief. If all of these possibilities don't discourage you, you'll have the time of your life.

What To Bring
Bring an extra day's supply of food in case the weather turns bad and you cannot leave when planned. Plan on a gallon of water per person for each day. Take an extra change of clothes in case you take an unplanned swim. Bring at least one heavy jacket, a rain poncho (the boat ride can be wet), and a woolly cap is nice. Bring also: a ground cloth, a windbreak, and a medium-weight sleeping bag. A backpacker's stove is necessary. Gathering live or dead plants on the island is prohibited. Use biodegradable soap *only*. Do not pour waste in the ocean or on plants; dispose of it in gravel areas. You'll be

glad you brought a brimmed hat, sunscreen, first-aid kit, binoculars, and camera. Bring the usuals: matches, flashlights, etc.

Swimming, Fishing, And Diving

Beaches on East Anacapa are inaccessible, but on hot, still summer days, swimming is great in the landing cove. This means you'll enter the water from the landing dock several feet above the water. Snorkelers will find kelp beds not too far from the dock. A favorite scuba spot, the water is crystal clear, though many areas are thick with seaweed. Here marinelife flourishes with the usual and the unusual darting in and out of the brown leaves and bulbs of the tall kelp forest. **Note:** The waters for one nautical mile around each of the park's islands are part of the California State Reserve. State fish and game laws apply. Some areas in these reserves are available for sportfishing only. Check with your local Fish and Game officer or the park ranger, and remember to come with a valid California fishing license. Spear guns are not allowed.

FOR BOATERS

As your boat approaches East Anacapa and you begin to look for the park entry, watch for a cluster of white buildings on the bluff. A white-painted wall marks a small dent in a cliff used as a landing for traffic in and out of East Anacapa. Though there's room for a good-sized vessel, there's usually a surge. Put on your muscles; a dinghy can and should be hoisted the 11 feet to the platform because the surge and movement from the blowhole will surely bounce the dinghy against the dock. This is the loading area for supplies for the National Park Service personnel. Everything is hauled up the cliff with the help of a crane. Boaters will see two buoys off the dock, but overnight mooring is definitely discouraged.

Cathedral Cove

This cove is considered a marginal fair-weather anchorage but is one of the loveliest coves on the island. Some boatmen leave their boats anchored here when going ashore to the ranger station, a half mile east. Be prepared for thick kelp along the coast. Underwater nature trails are in the planning stages for Cathedral Cove. For adventurers, Cathedral Cave is a multi-chambered sea cave and can be explored by skiff in calm weather; beware of surge.

Frenchy's Cove

Frenchy's Cove is a great beach, a good picnic spot, and an outstanding snorkeling area. And for nature lovers, this is the place to explore the extensive tidepools at low tide. Most sailors agree that Frenchy's is the most sheltered anchorage on Anacapa—in calm conditions. When the sea rises, there isn't a good anchorage on the island. Frenchy's is popular, not only for its tidepools but also for the caves in the cliffs northwest of the cove. In calm water you can land a dinghy on the beach; there are no facilities. If the sea is surging, landing can be touchy. The vaulted interior of the nearby caves (Frenchy's and Indian Water Cave) can be explored by skiff.

The *Winfield Scott*

Close by, divers will find the *Winfield Scott*, a steamer that grounded and sank here in 1853. Clear water in the area makes ideal conditions for good underwater photos. Just take pictures, no souvenirs please!

Cat Rock Anchorages

On the south side of West Anacapa, three-quarters of a mile west of the West Passage, is Cat Rock. Head at least 200 yards west of that for a safe anchorage. Expect some kelp. East anchorage is under the lee of the land east of Cat Rock. Pick your way through the kelp and you'll find deep water close to the shoreline.

East Fish Camp

East Fish Camp is a popular anchorage with fishing boats. Here you'll find protection from west to north winds—but expect an occasional surge in the anchorage. In a calm sea this is an adequate overnight refuge. East Fish Camp shore is usually thick with kelp.

SANTA BARBARA ISLAND

Of the eight Channel Islands, Santa Barbara is the smallest, roughly one by one-half mile, containing a total of 640 acres. The island is 38 miles west of San Pedro and 25 miles west of Catalina Island.

THE LAND

The tiny triangle-shaped rock is a remnant of an ancient Miocene volcano and geologically associated with the Guadalupe Islands of Mexico. It's a marine terrace on top of steep, jagged cliffs, some as high as 500 feet. From the cliffs, two peaks gently swell from the center of the island: the highest, called Signal Peak, rises to 635 feet. The second highest, at 562 feet, is North Peak. The island shares the rough-hewn look of the other Channel Islands with caves, coves, blowholes, rocky ledges, and dramatic drops to the sea.

Climate
Santa Barbara Island is mild, with daytime temperatures varying from 50°-80° F. Frost is almost unheard of, but fog is another matter. The island is often shrouded in fog early in the morning and in the evening. As on the Mainland close by, rainfall averages 10-12 inches yearly, falling mostly in the winter months. The winds can be devastating, rising quickly and blowing hard across the desolate landscape of Santa Barbara Island.

FLORA

Because of the lack of water and the frequent mighty winds, the island has no trees and only low-growing scrub vegetation. The closest thing to a tree is the **coreopsis** plant, which often grows to 10 feet on the island, showing bright yellow, daisy-like flowers across the landscape in the spring. Even the coreopsis growth has been reduced over the years to just a few stands scattered around the island. Other native plants are the **prickly pear cactus** and **sea blite**.

Nonnative plants imported over the years include the devastating **crystalline iceplant** (native to South Africa). No one is certain how it arrived, but since before the turn of the century it's been steadily taking over the terrain. Perhaps a lone seed carried by a migrating bird was the first culprit. Because of its ability to thrive while absorbing salt-laden sea air, it gradually encroached upon the native plants. And when it withers and dies it deposits its salt-loaded tissues into the soil, further destroying the possibility of survival for the native plants.

On the eastern terraces are fields of grasses including **rye, barley**, and **oats** introduced in

DIANA LASICH HARPER

Santa Barbara Lighthouse on Arch Point

the days when farmers tried to tame the wild elements of the island by raising farm animals. Due to the lack of rain and frequent high winds it was not a successful venture. With the protection and care of the National Park Service, native plants are making a slow recovery.

FAUNA

Only two vertebrates make their home on Santa Barbara, the **night lizard** and the **white-footed mouse**. In the early 1900s a large number of

feral rabbits and cats roamed the island. The rabbits furthered the destruction of plants and the cats decimated the bird population. The rabbits proved almost worse than the voracious sheep on other Channel islands. When the rabbits could no longer reach the leaves, they began nibbling the trunk of the coreopsis, girdling it, which caused the plant to die, leaving toppled trunks in their wake. However, the rabbits are gone, and the cats were rounded up and the last of them shipped off the island in 1978; the result is now a birdwatcher's paradise. The

Audubon Society frequently brings groups to the island for a week of observing **barn owls, meadowlarks, burrowing owls, American kestrels, hummingbirds, orange-crowned warblers, island horned larks**, and **finches**. The skies are thick with coastal birds, including a variety of **gulls, cormorants, pelicans**, and the **black oystercatcher.**

Sea Creatures

The rugged shoreline is surrounded with rich kelp beds that make an ideal habitat for a wide variety of sea creatures, including abalone, lobster, sea urchins, crabs, and myriad varieties of fish. Webster Point cove is a haul-out area for **sea lions** and **sea elephants**. Watching them frolic in the coastal waters is a good pastime; bring binoculars and a long lens for your camera. If you spend much time here you'll get used to the raspy bark of these sea mammals and even begin to distinguish when it's just a call from mom for the pups to come for dinner, or the harsh, commanding call of the courting male.

In early summer you might see pups being taught to swim and fish. They depend on their mothers for food for the first couple of months, but at six or seven months they join groups of the same age and are ready to try their flippers and venture out to sea. Remember, it's against the law to interfere in any way with marine mammals.

HISTORY

The Indians living on nearby islands were known to have visited Santa Barbara Island and used it as a campsite while hunting seals and other sealife. Evidence of this is found in several middens scattered around the island. But because of the lack of water there was never a permanent settlement. Explorer Sebastian Vizcaino arrived on the island December 4, 1602, which is the special day of remembering Saint Barbara—and so this little bit of rock was named Santa Barbara Island. As with all of the islands, it was peaceful and undisturbed by the white man until the mid-1800s, when shipping and otter hunting became common along the Pacific coast.

In the early 1920s, a group of farming families led by Alvin Hyder tried their hands at farming on the island. They are responsible for clearing large stands of coreopsis to plant barley and hay used to feed about 200 sheep. They also began raising Belgian hares (all of which were gone by 1940). By the mid-1920s the farming venture failed and the settlers left the inhospitable island.

A story has circulated for years about a barefooted wanderer who found shelter on Santa Barbara during the Depression. He cared for the wild cats that had been left behind by settlers long gone. It is said that he eked out an existence by trading fish with passing boats. After his departure the island was left to nature's capricious whims until World War II. The U.S. Navy used the island as an early-warning outpost; in the 1950s it was used as a missile-tracking station. Santa Barbara Island became part of the National Park system in 1938 and was designated part of the Channel Islands National Marine Sanctuary in 1980.

ACTIVITIES

Camping

Camping is permitted on Santa Barbara Island, but it is a trek for the hardy. The camping area is located next to the ranger's headquarters; the ranger is on the island most of the year. You are off-loaded onto a landing dock and then you must carry all equipment up a steep quarter-mile trail to the campground. A maximum of 30 people are permitted at five campsites. And be forewarned, your camp will probably be only a few feet from your neighbor; in other words, there's no privacy. Once at the campsite things get a little easier.

Remember to bring everything you need: drinking water, campstove, charcoal, food, garbage bags (yes, you must haul out all your trash), and clothes for wide variations in weather. There are toilet facilities, picnic tables, and one fire ring and four charcoal grills where charcoal cooking is permitted only when open fires are allowed. In times of heavy winds, and May

sea elephant

to October, open fires are prohibited. (See "Anacapa—Camping," p. 212.) Yes, this is camping on the proverbial desert island. Permits (free) are required and obtained from Channel Islands National Park Headquarters in Ventura, tel. (805) 644-8262. (See "Camping," p. 206.) Pets, slingshots, firearms, and fireworks are prohibited.

Hiking

Hiking is permitted only on six miles of established trails. Ask the ranger about the **Canyon View Self-guided Trail** and the booklet that interprets much of what you see. Two trails begin at the campsite. One (to the left) wanders the gentle terrain to a gorge where one of the few stands of coreopsis can be seen. This is good birdwatching country; don't forget the binoculars and bird identification book. The second trail eventually leads to Signal Peak, the highest peak on the island. Expect a steady ascent over several hills until finally you reach the summit, with a dramatic view of the sheer drop into the rocks and swirling sea below. From here you can see across the narrow channel to Sutil Island, a huge, barren rock. Hikers: Do not wear Vibram-soled hiking boots, please, as they tear up the fragile landscape.

Water Sports

Access to the sea is at the Landing Cove only. Climbing down the trail from the campsite, you have a choice of a variety of water activities on Santa Barbara Island, such as **swimming** and **snorkeling** off the rocky shore, or from the landing dock. The water is crystal clear and makes for fantastic **underwater photography. Fishing** is permitted off the landing platform; don't forget to bring your fishing gear and license, and note seasonal regulations.

Nature Watching

The best thing to do on Santa Barbara Island is to observe nature. Even if you've never been intrigued with winged creatures before, get out your binoculars, perch on a craggy cliff to view the coastal birds, or hike into the canyon near the coreopsis, and you'll be entertained and educated by the antics of these sky creatures. The best time to watch the birds is early in the morning or at dusk when they're all looking for food. You can spend hours watching the agile sea lions jumping the waves, diving, and playing much like small children at the shore. At certain times of the year the sea elephants join in. When a seal moves on land it is called "hauling." The two main hauling areas are on the southeast and northwest shores of Santa Barbara Island.

Tidepools

At low tide you can explore the tidepools. This is a mesmerizing activity. No doubt you'll see purple sea urchins, limpets, starfish, and minute organisms. Please take care not to interfere with their life cycles; these delicate life forms are a California treasure that must be guarded for future generations to enjoy. Wear sturdy rubber-soled shoes (no sandals); the rocks you'll be climbing around on are very slick. Be aware of when the tide comes back or be prepared to swim to shore.

Getting There

Public transportation is available next to Park Headquarters in Ventura aboard one of several Island Packers sail or power boats. Boats leave

Park rangers give visitors an orientation onboard excursion boats headed for Anacapa, Santa Barbara, and San Miguel Islands.

CHANNEL ISLANDS NATIONAL PARK

for Santa Barbara daily during the summer months. Day-trips and roundtrip transportation for campers are available. Winter weather gets rather nasty around this outer island, and few trips are scheduled. Write for yearly schedule: Island Packers, 1867 Spinnaker Dr., Ventura, CA 93001, tel. (805) 642-1393. Private boats travel to the island, but visitors must have a camping permit and reservations before arrival if planning to spend the night.

For Boaters
Boaters planning the trip to Santa Barbara Island should first study U.S. Coast and Geodetic Survey Charts 18720, 18729, and 18756. The trip from Santa Barbara Channel will take you across the Pacific Missile Range, which is often in use. For information about firing times call

(805) 982-8841. A Coast Guard lighthouse is located on Arch Point. Anchorage is usually limited to the Landing Cove area, and the dock is not acceptable for boats. Those wishing to go ashore must do so in a skiff or small boat. Be prepared for sudden rising sea and wind, especially in the afternoon and during the fall and winter months. If a strong northeast wind develops, get out immediately.

A safe daytime anchorage in calm weather is off the north coast in about 35 feet of water with a sandy bottom. From here you can explore the coastline by skiff and no doubt you'll meet the friendly sea lions that live along the shore. They like to watch you almost as much as you enjoy watching them. A calm day anchored offshore Santa Barbara Island can be a soothing interlude between you and Mother Nature's creatures.

SAN MIGUEL ISLAND

THE LAND

The most remote island off the California coast, San Miguel is harassed by northwesterly gales that blast it continuously. Eight miles long and four miles wide, San Miguel Island encompasses an area of 14 square miles and is 26 miles from Santa Barbara, the closest point on the Mainland. Two peaks just over 800 feet tall in the center of the island are San Miguel's highest points. Surrounded by treacherous reefs and shoals, San Miguel exhibits a shoreline of gentle sandy beaches as well as rugged rocky cliffs.

Prince Island, a tiny islet close offshore Cuyler Habor as you approach San Miguel, has steep-walled canyons that drop straight to the sea, adding to the stark landscape as you approach.

In many places the 10,000-acre island is smothered by sand that all but strangles the struggling plantlife. To complete this moonscape facade is a caliche "ghost forest" where macabre remnants of broken trees line up like white tombstones on the desolate sand-covered surface. The scientific explanation is quite fundamental: caliche is a calcium carbonate sand composed mainly of the shattered lime skeletons of innumerable sea creatures that blows inland from the beaches, engulfing the existing vegetation. Organic acids in the plants reacting chemically with the sand cement the fine grains together. After the inner plant decays, perfect castings remain. Some of these strange forms have been standing for thousands of years while others are new—the process continues. These startling caliche forms can also be seen on Santa Rosa and San Nicolas but are quite rare in other areas of the world.

Climate

This isolated, windswept bit of land lies vulnerable to the capricious whims of nature's violent northwesterly storms, unguarded by the landmass of the Mainland. San Miguel is the westernmost island of the Channel group. Yearly rainfall is about 11 inches, and as on the other islands in this unfriendly channel, fog can descend quickly and unexpectedly. Dress for the wind, whether it be hot or cool.

© MOON PUBLICATIONS, INC.

FAUNA AND FLORA

San Miguel is the California coast's largest breeding ground for six species of pinnipeds (fin-footed mammals), the seals and sea lions. The **California sea lion, Steller sea lion, northern elephant seal, harbor seal, Guadalupe fur seal**, and **northern fur seal** return to San Miguel's Point Bennett to "haul out," sometimes traveling great distances from throughout the northeastern Pacific. In late spring and early summer the cows come ashore at this sandy peninsula to bear their young and then breed again almost immediately. After a gentle summer of mother's nursing and care, the pups learn to fish amidst a rich supply of food. By autumn most are ready to begin their nomadic lives in the sea. Because of the rugged, isolated cliffs, three major sea bird colonies live here undisturbed. **Auklets, gulls, guillemots, cormorants, snowy plovers**, and many others breed on San Miguel and Prince Island. The few vertebrates on the island include the **island fox** and the **white-footed mouse. Barn owls, peregrine falcons**, and **red-tailed hawks** are among the birds of prey often seen.

A few rare plant species are found on San Miguel: the **live-forever, wild buckwheat**, and **rose mallow**. The bright orange bloom of the coreopsis can be seen each spring climbing the hill from Cuyler Harbor. In a wet year San Miguel produces a blazing crop of California poppies.

HISTORY

San Miguel is said to have supported a large community of Canalino Indians. Many middens are known to be on the island, and with relatively little activity over the years it is hoped that some are still undisturbed by pot diggers. Though the wind has been known to unbury Indian graves, hopefully some day these pristine sites will reveal more about the long-gone Canalino Indians.

Most historians agree that "Isla de Posesion" was the name that Cabrillo gave to San Miguel on his voyage of discovery in 1542. How tragic that he was never able to boast of his wondrous discoveries—Cabrillo died in January 1543. It's believed that he died in Cuyler Harbor on San Miguel Island. His fellow voyagers changed the island's name to La Isla de Juan Rodriguez in his honor. Though Cabrillo is reportedly buried on San Miguel, his grave has never been found.

Charts from the later Vizcaino expedition identified San Miguel as La Isla de San Lucas. The final change came in 1770 when cartographer Miguel Costanso changed the name to honor himself. In 1793, British Captain George Vancouver traveled south along the California coast and fixed the names of the islands on nautical charts.

The Fascinating People

George Nidever of San Nicolas fame was the first to try ranching on San Miguel Island, in the mid-1800s, grazing cattle, horses, and hogs as well as sheep. After Nidever, a parade of hermits, boatmen, and would-be ranchers came and went, unobtrusively struggling with the land and the tempests. Time was spent building and patching from what they could scavenge from nature's collection of flotsam and jetsam violently thrown on San Miguel's shores.

Captain Waters, a salty character who ranched the island during the late 1800s, declared it a separate sovereignty. Obviously that didn't take hold. San Miguel has been owned by the federal government since the signing of the Hidalgo Treaty in 1848 and leased to various ranchers over the years. In 1906, rancher John Russel built a V-shaped fenced compound, outbuildings, and a ranch house from planks, timber, and scraps, much of which was combed from the beach. The shape of the building was to urge the winds to rush by the house and out to sea without damage, similar to the windshields seen today on large trucks. The man was ahead of his time! By 1930 he was gone.

Probably the name that lingers with the desolate little island more than any of the others is the "king" of San Miguel, Herbert Lester, and his family. Lester and his wife Elise, both New Yorkers, arrived on the island as honeymooners.

From the stories that filter down from the past, Herbie and Elise learned to love the island and led a blissful life for a long time. Herbie was thrilled when asked to manage the sheep ranch. The couple happily filled their days with the not-so-easy chores of day-to day living on the little island: gathering firewood, dealing with the water situation, trying to keep the constant wind-blown sand out of the house (Would you believe a revolving door?), the struggle to make ends meet when there was little money, and very little to make do with. But the Lesters were happy and ingenious and loved the freedom to explore and enjoy their "island paradise."

Two daughters were born while the Lesters called San Miguel home. Elise taught the girls, Marriane Miguel and Betsy, in their own small schoolhouse with the help of the 500-volume library she brought with her to the island. It was a life that today many folks would envy. Mostly through the efforts of the Lester family, a small monument was placed on the island to honor the memory of the first visitor to San Miguel—Juan Rodriguez Cabrillo.

The Lesters welcomed many visitors from the Mainland—by sailboat, airplane, fishing boat, and official Coast Guard vessel; Elise kept a guest book and in 12 years recorded several thousand entries. Unfortunately, the story does not have a happy ending. When WW II hit the country, the government began to make plans to take over the "Lesters' island." Eventually two sailors were put on the island as "guards." Apparently the intruders and the thought of leaving his island was more than Herbert Lester could handle; he ended his life with a gun. His wife and daughters moved to the Mainland and have never returned to San Miguel.

The Navy did take over. The sheep were removed and the Navy used the island as an aerial bombing range during WW II and the Korean War. After that it was a missile target area. The bombing of San Miguel was finally stopped in May of 1960 after protests by ecologists. The National Park Service signed an agreement with the Navy to preserve and manage the island. The breeding colony of pinnipeds at Point Bennett has increased and multiplied since that time.

PRACTICALITIES

San Miguel Island is managed by the National Park Service and has a resident ranger for most of the year. The island is open to the public on a limited-access basis; camping is allowed by permit. This protects the large seal and sea lion rookeries that are thriving at Point Bennett. For years the island was used as an aerial bombing target, and though all precautions are taken, every once in a while an old bomb shows up. A free permit is required to visit the island and you *cannot* obtain permits at the island. Get your permit from the Channel Islands National Park office in Ventura, 1901 Spinnaker Dr., tel. (805) 644-8262. Public transportation is available aboard Island Packers boats, tel. (805) 642-7688. San Miguel is well worth a visit, especially to see the rookeries and the unusual caliche. A knowledgeable park ranger will guide you around the island; hiking is restricted to the designated trails. No fishing is allowed from shore.

For Boaters

Anchoring overnight is permitted only at Tyler Bight and Cuyler Harbor. Inexperienced boaters are warned of the dangers of the unpredictable wind and sea conditions. Cuyler Harbor was named after its original government surveyor and was a favorite anchorage for the explorers of the past. The shore is covered by sand dunes on the south side of the anchorage. Cuyler Harbor can be a comfortable and uncrowded anchorage, but it's not unusual for a cranky surge to suddenly appear and for sweeping winds to rage over the cliffs.

San Miguel is an island of great extremes; you can anchor in calm conditions at Cuyler one moment and be taken on a roller coaster ride the next. Take all precautions possible and be alert to the changeable weather.

There's a government-designated "danger area" over the eastern half of San Miguel Island. Look into the regulations in chapter two of the *U.S. Coast Pilot*. The coastline at Tyler Bight is covered with large areas of sand dunes. Adams Cove is at the east end of the sandy beach extending east from the point with an indented cove of sloping rocks and sand. San

Miguel is a dangerous destination and should be attempted only by the most experienced boaters.

SANTA ROSA ISLAND

THE LAND

Santa Rosa is the second largest of the Channel Islands, about 15 miles long from east to west and nine miles across at its widest point. Its 55,000 acres offer the same rugged landscape as its brother islands but with the soothing touch of gentle slopes covered with grass sprawling to the edge of the sea, some ending in sand, some ending abruptly in rocky ledges and rugged cliffs. Some say that Santa Rosa resembles the Azores in the mid-Atlantic. Fortunately, Santa Rosa has fresh water year-round, which gives it

a rosier future than its neighbors. Two high mountains, Soledad Peak (1,574 feet) and Black Mountain (1,298 feet), rise above the deep canyons and high coastal cliffs that dominate portions of the island.

Climate
Santa Rosa doesn't have as much protection from the Point Conception headland as the islands to the east and south, therefore winds can be ruthless: 20-knot winds are common, and winter gales have been clocked at 90 knots. By some meteorological quirk, Santa Rosa receives only half the rainfall of the adjacent coast-

SANTA ROSA ISLAND

SANTA BARBARA CHANNEL

CARRINGTON PT.

TALCOTT SHOAL

BROCKWAY PT.

NORTHEAST ANCHORAGE

BECHER'S BAY

SANDY PT.

BLACK MTN.
(1298 ft)

SOUTHEAST ANCHORAGE

TORREY PINES

SKUNK PT.

SAN MIGUEL PASSAGE

SOLEDAD PK.
(1574 ft)

EAST PT.

EAGLE ROCK

ABANDONED MILITARY BASE

FORD POINT

S.S. CHICKASAW

JOHNSON'S LEE

SOUTH PT.

0   5 km

0   5 mi

© MOON PUBLICATIONS, INC.

line. But the consistent fog shrouds the island with moisture, which helps to keep the grasses green, in some areas year-round. In a really wet year, the island spring is alive with the color of California poppies and lupine. When planning a visit to the island, be prepared to dress in layers. It can be cold or it can be hot—it really depends on the wind.

FLORA

As with all the other islands, the introduction of alien animals and plants has been hard on Santa Rosa's own natural environment. Spanish and Russian sailors left pigs on Santa Rosa for future food sources. Santa Rosa has one of only two stands of **Torrey pines** in existence. (The other stand of Torreys is located in the pine groves around La Jolla, a community called Torrey Pines.) Fortunately, the pines have survived the animals' rooting habits. The pigs did just fine thank you, and their rooting instinct which destroys all seedlings has made it impossible for native plants to survive. Why and how the pines made it are questions that so far have not been answered. The trees survived monumental climatic changes over the years

thistle

in *only* these two isolated spots. Even the Torrey pines have mutated somewhat to adjust to island living. Growing in deep-cut canyons and ravines, the tops of the trees are whipped constantly by the wind; maybe that's why they grow to only about 35 feet. **Coastal, scrub**, and **island oak, willow**, and **Catalina cherry** also survive on Santa Rosa Island.

FAUNA

The island has the usual introduced animals and the only native mammals left are the **island fox, white-footed mouse**, the **island spotted skunk**, and the **California myotis**, the smallest bat found on the Channel Islands. Other natives include a species of **salamander**, a species of **frog**, and two types of **lizards**. The **harbor seal** and the **California sea lion** make yearly stops on Santa Rosa.

HISTORY

Prehistoric Remains

The remains of a dwarf mammoth (only six feet tall) were found on Santa Rosa in a depression which has been called a "fire pit"; in other words the little-big beast was barbecued. Radiocarbon tests indicate that this feast was held 29,700 years ago! This electrifying discovery has opened a door on the past. Some scientists conjecture that this prehistoric cousin to the elephant may have arrived from the Mainland after having been washed out to sea by a torrential storm and by swimming or just keeping afloat (after all, an elephant does come equipped with a built-in snorkel), or perhaps rafting, it survived until it reached a friendly shore. Another theory is the familiar old "land-bridge" idea. At some point, sections of this bridge to the Mainland along the coastline sank, creating Santa Rosa Island and stranding the elephant-like behemoth (known to have roamed the west coast of the Mainland during the prehistoric era). Being stranded on a small island with limited food sources and interbreeding may have caused

*Santa Rosa Island's
Carrington Point*

CHANNEL ISLANDS NATIONAL PARK

stunting. All of this is conjecture; will we ever *really* figure out what happened so many years ago?

The Spanish Explorers
It is believed that the Vizcaino expedition named the island San Ambrosio and more than likely Juan Perez, who explored the area in the early 1770s, named the island Santa Rosa.

The Earthquake Of 1812
The missionaries had little luck luring the island Indians to the Mainland missions because of the Indians' isolated location. It was not easy for the priests to get to the islands, and the Indians were happy with their life-style, at least until the invasion of outsiders hunting the otters. Then in 1812 a destructive earthquake hit the adjacent Mainland and the Channel Islands. Its epicenter was along Santa Rosa's canyon called Canada Lobo. A tear in the earth 1,000 feet long, 100 feet wide, and 50 feet deep still remains as proof of nature's devastating force on that day. The rumbling earth, crumbling boulders, and mammoth waves crashing onto the coast are said by historians to be the factors that finally led the Indians to the Mainland missions and Christianity.

Settlers
After the Indian era, the island was part of a land grant from the Spanish Crown presented to Don Carlos and Don Jose Carrillo. Don Carlos gave half the island to his two daughters as their dowries when they were married. For many years the families raised sheep on the island and Santa Rosa was known far and wide for the great fiestas at shearing time. Before the turn of the century, most of the sheep were removed by the island's then-new owners, A.P. and W.H. More, and replaced with cattle and racehorse stock. In 1902 Walter Vail and J.V. Vickers bought the island and strengthened the cattle herds, grazing some of the finest cattle in California. Santa Rosa Island does not show the severe abuse that some of the other islands suffered, proving that with balanced grazing, the ecology can be preserved.

In December of 1986 the island was sold (for $29.58 million) and it is now part of the Channel Islands Marine Sanctuary. Over time most of the cattle will be removed, but the park's representative advises that they are planning to keep a small herd in operation so that visitors will understand the importance of the cattle ranch and its effect on the island for so many years. There are high hopes that the island will soon be open to the public for camping, backpacking, and specialized nature treks. The former owners of Santa Rosa, the heirs of Vail and Vickers, have retained the ranch house near Becher's Bay for their private use for the next 25 years.

ACTIVITIES

Hiking

A landing permit (free) is required to go ashore on Santa Rosa Island. You cannot get a permit on the island; it must be obtained at the Channel Islands National Park Headquarters, 1901 Spinnaker Dr., in Ventura; tel. (805) 644-8262. Visitors are met by the knowledgeable National Park ranger and guided on a three- to five-mile trek with a good historical and geographical lesson. He also points out the interesting facts of the island's flora and fauna. You are not given free run of the island; hikers are restricted to designated paths (which at this time are existing dirt roads left over from the former owners) and taken on a sample hike around the lovely, lonely island.

Fishing And Diving

The thick kelp beds and offshore reefs provide a rich haven for scallops, gamefish, abalone, and lobster. The comparatively small number of divers who do brave the poor anchorage find a fish paradise. (Don't forget your license, and note the seasons.) On a calm day the water is clear and underwater photography in the kelp forest can be spectacular. These same reefs have proven deadly for a number of vessels that failed to recognize the danger in these waters, where gale-force winds can rise unexpectedly.

BOATING ANCHORAGES

Santa Rosa is without a good natural harbor. Its westernmost extremity is **Sandy Point**, aptly named for the 400-foot white sand dunes that extend from that point inland. **Becher's Bay** is a long open bay 4 miles across backed by low sandstone cliffs. Though it can be a comfortable daytime anchorage, it's described by some sailors as a wild and interesting spot for an overnight stay. A pier at Becher's is used by the cattle ranch; landing there is by permit only. **Eagle Rock Anchorage** is considered a tem-

porary anchorage under the cliffs with good shelter. **Ford Point Anchorage** is another temporary anchorage in the lee of a small point. It offers little shelter for anything but a short stay. Note the inviting sandy beach nearby.

Johnson's Lee is immediately northeast of the southernmost point of the island (there's a light at this end). Experienced sailors call it the best anchorage on Santa Rosa; however, spring and winter can be uncomfortable. On the cliffs above the anchorage notice the old abandoned military barracks. Beware of the dilapidated Navy pier. The shore is lined with thick kelp beds here. The anchorage is fairly comfortable as long as the weather is good. As most boaters already know, there isn't a good safe anchorage at Santa Rosa in bad weather.

PRACTICALITIES

Day-trips are now offered and visitors have begun going to the island on Island Packers boats (next to the park office in Ventura). For schedules and reservations call (805) 642-1393; adult $60 RT, child $50. Right now, part of the adventure is just getting on the island. A dock has yet to be built, so visitors are landed six at a time from a small motorized skiff launched from the larger boat. Becher's Bay can show a strong, turbulent surf, so it's a given that passengers are going to get a little wet (more than likely *very* soaked). With the proper spirit it's all part of the fun, and visitors are advised to bring an extra set of clothing and to keep cameras in plastic bags until safely ashore. Be sure to bring food, water, film, towels, or anything else with you. The only facility so far is the portable latrine. Landing permits (free) must be obtained from the Channel Islands National Park Headquarters, 1901 Spinnaker Dr., Ventura; tel. (805) 644-8262.

Channel Islands Aviation

Day-trips allowing five hours on Santa Rosa Island are made via small plane leaving Camarillo Airport. For more details call (805) 987-1678.

SANTA CRUZ ISLAND

THE LAND

Santa Cruz Island is a verdant surprise compared with the drier islands of the channel. The usually abundant supply of water has given the island the look of a magnificent green paradise. The beauty of this, the largest island, has attracted boaters for generations. Within its boundaries are rolling meadowlands, rugged slopes, rivers, waterfalls, sandy beaches, thick stands of pine trees, babbling brooks, picturesque old wooden bridges, craggy bluffs, deep wooded canyons, and giant caves—a natural wonderland surrounded by the beautiful Pacific.

Santa Cruz is composed primarily of igneous rock from earlier volcanic eruptions; sedimentary sandstones and shales fringe the island's shores. It boasts gigantic sea caves and its tallest peak is 2,450 feet. A few geologists contend that the northern and southern parts of the island were originally on two different small plates of the earth's crust, the southern part having originated near the San Diego area. The island encompasses 62,000 acres, is approximately 25 miles long and two to seven miles wide. It lies 23 miles southwest of Santa Barbara.

FLORA

Ferns add rich beauty to the **closed-cone pine** forests in the northern and western parts of the island. **Eucalyptus** trees were brought to the island years ago. With controlled grazing, Santa Cruz seems to have suffered less than some of the other islands. Endemic plants are still found, even though wild boar and at one time over 40,000 feral sheep ran free on certain parts of the island. A native plant, the **dudieya**, adds a touch of gray-green against the stark cliffs. A rainbow of colorful wildflowers covers the rolling meadows in spring, including the **California poppy, blue lupine, thistles,** and many more.

Over 600 species of plants are found on the island in 10 different plant communities; 40 species are restricted to the Channel Islands, and eight occur only on Santa Cruz. Some of the more notable examples are **Santa Cruz Island ironwood** and the **island oak**.

FAUNA

Santa Cruz Island fauna is more varied than on many of the other Channel islands except Catalina. Along with 10 species of terrestrial mammals, including the **white-footed mouse** and the **big-eared harvest mouse**, four kinds of bats, plus hundreds of **Channel Island foxes**, and the **island spotted skunk**, you'll find two species of **salamanders**, one type of **frog**, three kinds of **lizards**, and a small group of **snakes**. More then 140 species of land birds have been identified, including **quail, pheasant, ravens, meadowlarks, doves,** plus an occasional **eagle**. An example of island endemism is the **island blue jay**, which is larger and bluer than its Mainland cousin.

The 77 miles of shoreline, cliffs, beaches, offshore rocks, and tidepools provide an important breeding habitat for colonies of nesting **seabirds**. Hundreds of **California sea lions** and **harbor seals** make the island's isolated coves home. In fact, at Painted Cave you will often find a bull sea lion and his harem on the rocks in the last chamber. Scorpion Rock near the east end of the island has become a popular rookery for the **pelicans** that are coming back strong after a few years' setback during the DDT scare. At one time elk and boar were introduced to the island for hunts; now they are gone.

SANTA CRUZ ISLAND

SANTA BARBARA CHANNEL

ANACAPA PASSAGE

SCORPION ANCHORAGE

LITTLE SCORPION ANCHORAGE

SAN PEDRO PT.

HUNGRYMANS ANCHORAGE

SMUGGLER'S COVE

YELLOWBANKS ANCHORAGE

MIDDLE ANCHORAGE

SANDSTONE PT.

POTATO HARBOR

COCHE PT.

CHINESE HARBOR

PRISONER'S HARBOR

PELICAN BAY

TWIN HARBORS

PLATTS HARBOR

FRYS HARBOR

DIABLO ANCHORAGE

BABY'S HARBOR

LADY'S HARBOR

CUEVA VALDEZ ANCHORAGE

HAZARD'S ANCHORAGE

PROFILE PT.

PAINTED CAVE

DEVILS PEAK
(2450 ft)

CENTRAL VALLEY

VALLEY ANCHORAGE

BLUE BANKS ANCHORAGE

ALBERT'S ANCHORAGE

COCHES PRIETOS ANCHORAGE

WILLOWS ANCHORAGE

BOWEN PT.

SIERRA BLANCA
(1528 ft)

LAGUNA HARBOR

PUNTA ARENA

GULL ISLAND

MORSE PT.

KINTON PT.

BLACK PT.

FORNEY'S COVE

WEST POINT

POZO ANCHORAGE

SANTA CRUZ CHANNEL

5 mi

5 km

0

0

© MOON PUBLICATIONS, INC.

HISTORY

Prehistoric Indians

A survey of the Indian sites on Santa Cruz suggests there are as many as 3,000 undisturbed Indian sites. It seems natural that this would be the location of one of the largest Indian communities because of its size and extraordinary natural resources. (Water, a problem for so many of the other islands, appears to have been abundant on Santa Cruz.) It wasn't unusual for early settlers to run into an interesting piece of Indian stoneware lying on the surface of the ground. Fortunately, the "pot hunters" who destroyed so much archaeological information in the early 1900s did not manage to dig on this island. Today's scientists know the value of approaching the middens slowly and with great care even if it means postponement. Technology just keeps improving and one day more light will be shed on Santa Cruz's prehistoric Indians. Many pieces have already been carefully preserved in museums and private collections in Southern California.

The First Spanish Visitors

In 1769, a supply ship traveling north along the Pacific coast from Mexico accompanying the Gaspar de Portola and Father Junipero Serra expedition (of mission fame) got lost and sailed right past San Diego, its scheduled port of call. Ultimately the *San Antonio*, with Spanish Captain Juan Perez at the helm, sailed into the bay of an island occupied by many Indians (scientists estimate the population at the time was between 2,000 and 3,000). As it turned out, these Indians were friendly and curious. Visits were exchanged; the crew went to shore and the Indians came aboard the *Antonio*. The crew gave the islanders small gifts, and the Stone-Age Indians were in awe of everything made of iron: weapons, equipment, chains, and gadgets.

When the time came for the ship to depart, the ship's priest, Fray Juan Vizcaino, realized that he had left his staff (topped with an iron cross) on shore. He presumed he would never see it again

and preparations were made to hoist anchor. To the priest's great surprise, he saw a canoe approaching the ship. It was the Indians returning the lost staff. In honor of the kindness, friendly nature, and honesty of its people, the island was named then and there La Isla de Santa Cruz, Island of the Holy Cross.

Prisoner's Harbor

In 1839, 25 years after the last of the Chumash Indians had left the Island, Santa Cruz was granted to Andres Castillero by the governor of California. In 1857, the island was sold to William E. Barron, who in turn sold it to Justinian Caire and associates. The island is the center of many fascinating stories. A legendary or historical anecdote about Prisoner's Harbor has persisted through the years.

In the early 1800s, the Mexican government was in need of colonists to settle California towns. Other countries had already begun sending ships and casting a covetous eye on this desirable new country. One method of colonization was to release prisoners who would agree to settle in one of the distant communities. In the spring of 1830 a boatload of prisoners was taken to the lovely (but small) town of Santa Barbara and dropped off.

This was not to the townspeople's liking, and after much plotting and planning they suggested to the prisoners that they could begin a cattle ranch on the lovely verdant island of Santa Cruz. Santa Barbarans supplied the convicts with cattle, supplies, seeds, equipment, and transportation to Santa Cruz. The new islanders were dropped off at the cove named in their honor, Prisoner's Harbor.

In the fall, a fire destroyed the colony and all of their hard work. As goes the story, the convicts built rafts from the hides of freshly slaughtered cattle and headed for the Mainland. Now this is where history falters. One version says that the green cow hides attracted sharks, and the prisoners never made it to the Mainland. A more romantic ending has it that they all made it to shore, were eventually assimilated in the community, and lived happily ever after.

BROWN AND RED ALGAE
OF THE CHANNEL ISLANDS

wing kelp

rock weed

rock film alga

rock weed

sea tongue alga

feather boa kelp

coralline alga

ribbed kelp

coralline alga

sea sacks

sea palm

DIANA LASICH HARPER

DIANA IASICH HARPER

Justinian Caire

Justinian Caire, an immigrant from France, was the original developer of Santa Cruz Island. Living in San Francisco around the time of the gold rush, Caire and nine associates purchased Santa Cruz Island in 1869. Legend tells us that that was the beginning of a love affair between Justinian Caire and the island. Caire bought his other partners out one by one until, in 1887, the island was all his.

Originally attracted to the island because the climate and territory were similar to the islands off the French Mediterranean coast, Caire began to build a small European colony on Santa Cruz. He brought craftsmen from Italy and France and began creating a typical Old World estate in the island's lovely central valley. By the end of the century, there were close to 100 people living on the island, mostly French and Italian immigrants. Vineyards had been planted and bricks fired from island clay were used to build a huge winery. It's said that the winery produced some of the finest wine in the state.

The community boasted two-story French-colonial brick buildings with delicate wrought-iron balconies (made on the island); a tiny brick chapel was complete with stained-glass windows, altar, candles, tower, and bell, and it was always ready for a visiting priest to say mass. There was a bakery, laundry, blacksmith shop, wagon shop, stables, and well-built living quarters. Caire grazed cattle and merino sheep. Olive groves and fruit orchards, including apple, peach, and pear, were established, and rolling hills of barley and oats were raised for livestock. The Caire children and grandchildren enjoyed idyllic summer visits on their beautiful island.

Justinian died in 1897, and his wife in 1911.

Prohibition forced the winery to shut down; it operated only a few years after that era. Changes in the ranch operation began after Caire's death, and the colony suffered setbacks during the Depression. In 1936 the family made overtures to the government, offering to sell the island explicitly for creation of a national park. The price was $750,000. It was a sensational idea and the public went for it in a big way. As often happens in bureaucratic affairs, a lot of time passed without a decision. When no offers were forthcoming to form a national park, Los Angeles businessman Edwin L. Stanton bought all but 8,000 of Santa Cruz's 62,500 acres from the Caire estate for one million dollars. An article appeared in the *L.A. Times* on April 24, 1937, lamenting the loss of a possible national park on Santa Cruz Island. The price was *so* right! In 1986, when Santa Rosa Island (similar in size) was purchased by the federal government for the express purpose of creating a national park, the price was $26.58 million.

Edwin Stanton's son, Dr. Carey Stanton, moved to the island in 1957 to run the Santa Cruz Island Company. In 1975, Dr. Stanton approached **The Nature Conservancy** about a possible joint conservation effort to ensure the preservation of Santa Cruz. With the generous arrangement with Dr. Stanton and tremendous public support, The Nature Conservancy was able to acquire a limited interest in the island by 1978, which was to mature to ownership of approximately 90% of the island not later than 2008. Dr. Stanton passed away in December of 1987, the end of an era of family ownership. At this time, The Nature Conservancy assumed full responsibility for ownership and management of the western 90% of Santa Cruz.

The island has been touched by a fascinating parade of people over the years, from Charley the Hermit, who lived in an old shack at China Harbor, to the Navy personnel who kept track of the missiles, to Otis Barton, who in 1949 climbed into a strange-looking giant steel sphere he called a benthoscope and sank to 4,500 feet below the ocean's surface. His only connection with the world was a telephone and a cable. Through a small window he saw little in the pitch blackness except occasional streaks of phosphorescence and a few fish he called miter and lantern. After seven minutes in the depths, with 2,000 pounds of pressure per inch closing around the ball, the crew of the barge and tug assisting him in the experiment brought him slowly to the surface. All told he was submerged for two hours and 19 minutes.

ACTIVITIES

Diving

Diving is good around the island. Although there's less kelp than around some of the others, there's still rich marinelife to observe and photograph. At Santa Cruz many coves and bays are within easy access of the beach, but remember your permit restricts where you may go ashore. Lobster and abalone are very popular game on the island; don't forget your fishing license.

BOATING

Painted Cave

The immense sea caves in various places around the island are fascinating to visit. Painted Cave just west of Profile Point is best entered in a small dinghy or skiff. (You might want to bring a flashlight or two.) The water is usually placid unless there's a swell. It's an easy boat ride for those anchoring in Cueva Valdez. Painted Cave's walls are approximately 80 feet high at the entrance, and the ceiling rises to over 130 feet inside and then slopes to about 20 feet at the back end. It's easy to see how it got its name: beautiful reds, yellows, and greens glow in the low light as you enter the cave. The first section is more than 600 feet into the base of the island; row all the way in and when you reach the back turn hard to starboard, which will bring you into a side chamber, 150 feet into darkness. But here you'll find a beach and rock ledges with seals and sea lions. If you choose to use a flashlight the pinniped tenants will quickly slide into the water and disappear. Three more caves 1.1 miles west of Painted Cave are also great to explore. They all have large entrances.

Cueva Valdez

Cueva Valdez is a popular anchorage for beach-loving families. There's a great sandy beach for the kids, and swimming is good, with a few patches of kelp here and there. Three-quarters of a mile west of Cueva Valdez anchorage you'll find a sandy beach with limited anchorage at Hazard's Anchorage.

Lady's Harbor

This is really two harbors; one is a small cove, and the larger one is great anchorage for just a few boats. This harbor tends to be crowded on fine summer days. Little Lady's is considered only a fair-weather anchorage and is much smaller. Boats over 35 feet may have trouble turning around once inside the harbor. Landing (with permits) is allowed in both coves. This is lovely terrain with a stream and pools running into the sea.

Diablo Anchorage

Immediately west of Diablo Point is Diablo Anchorage and a half mile east is Fry's Harbor. Diablo is rarely crowded and is a good stopover when the weather is quiet.

Fry's Harbor

This is one of the most popular anchorages at Santa Cruz Island and can be crowded. But if you're lucky—maybe in the middle of the week—and it's deserted, you'll find it a beautiful place to be lazy for a few days. The rocky cliff immediately southeast of the beach provided the rock for the Santa Barbara breakwater in 1929. You'll notice remnants of the operation. If you have a choice, the best spots to anchor are tucked in under the west cliff. Take a picnic and make a dinghy trip to the small cove immediately east of Fry's, or explore the cave 600 feet west.

Prisoner's Harbor
Traveling the four miles between Fry's and Prisoner's harbors is spectacular. More than likely you'll pass a few commercial diving and fishing boats. Along the way you'll see ragged cliffs and sloping hills that become low-lying cliffs, dotted with small coves all the way. Kelp is common for a quarter mile offshore. One of the coves, Orizaba Cove, is a lovely spot in good weather and usually entertains a few harbor seals in the bay. Another pretty place is Twin Harbors; either makes a good lunch stop. For the naturalist, notice the ironwood trees in the wooded canyon of the west anchorage. Along with the rugged cliffs, Prisoner's Harbor has a pier, tall eucalyptus trees, and a few small buildings. This is the main landing for the Santa Cruz Island Company; freight boats arrive on a regular basis. Please note the signs that say "Landing closed to permit holders." Your landing will be on the beach; wade ashore.

Pelican Bay
Pelican Bay is a large anchorage and will accommodate a good number of boats on a calm, sunny day. In spring the scenery is beautiful with myriad wildflowers in bloom. This is where Ira and Margaret Eaton lived with their little girl and later operated a hotel. This was also a favorite spot for filming movies in the early days of Hollywood. Some boaters prefer Pelican to any other harbor on the island. (Others say it can be bumpy and prefer Fry's.) In calm weather take a dinghy to Tinker's Harbor or Little Pelican (pull your dinghy out of the grasp of the waves and rising tides.) This is a great place to explore the nearby woods and canyons or take a dinghy and investigate the many coves and dents along the coast.

Chinese Harbor
This open bay provides little protection for more

than a brief stop. If you see smoke rising from the northeast cliff of the anchorage several hundred feet above the beach, don't be concerned; it's a fumarole, the only one on the offshore islands.

Potato Bay
Formerly known as Tyler's, this is a beguiling bay, though narrow and between steep cliffs. Not recommended for an overnight anchorage unless in very calm weather.

Scorpion And Little Scorpion Anchorages
Scorpion is the main landing area for the Gherini Ranch. Little Scorpion is the favored of the two for anchoring with a little better protection. A good trip is exploring along the coast in a dinghy in the early hours of the morning, where you'll see spectacular scenery, including caves, alluring little coves, and ragged cliffs.

SANTA CRUZ SOUTH

In Brian Fagan's excellent boating guide, *Cruising Guide to California's Channel Islands,* a warning states that all south coast anchorages of Santa Cruz are subject to heavy surge from tropical storms off the Mexican coast which can come in without warning, especially in summer.

Smuggler's Cove
Smuggler's Cove is a large open roadstead where a large number of small craft anchor in calm weather. This is a small bight with Caire's old olive groves and tall eucalyptus trees overlooking the cove. Landing is not allowed due to a hazardous beach break.

Yellowbanks
This is one alternative to Smuggler's Cove either in calm or heavy weather. Yellowbanks is usually not as crowded as Smuggler's.

Albert's Anchorage
This anchorage is a fairly comfortable one in calm weather, with good shelter from west through north. Some boaters complain that the

steep cliff to the west shadows the cove in the late afternoon and it can be dark and coolish. The view of the island's southeast coast is lovely and you can even see (in the distance) Anacapa Island from Albert's Cove. There's a small beach at the head of the anchorage. Albert's can be bumpy when there's a surge. Landing is on the beach and there's limited access inshore.

Sandstone Point Anchorage
This is not recommended for an overnight stop.

Coches Prietos
Another picturesque cove (Coches Prietos means "black Pigs"), considered by some the best anchorage on the south side of Santa Cruz Island. There's a great sandy beach and good shelter, but it can be crowded with visitors, especially in the summer. This beautiful, semicircular beach extends into an inland valley. Landing is on the beach.

Willow's Anchorage
This is another popular anchorage. It's very pretty but recommended only in good weather. Landing is on the beach.

Pozo Anchorage
Pozo Anchorage has lovely scenery but cannot be recommended for more than a brief stay.

Forney's Cove
Forney's is another of the most popular anchorages on Santa Cruz Island. It's isolated, with breathtaking scenery, great skin diving, and excellent fishing nearby. Landing can be tricky on the beach because of the shallow and irregular surf. Take off your shoes because you'll probably get soaked. Forney's is a boater's paradise, and in the spring the rioting color of wildflowers is intoxicating. They have to be seen to be appreciated; bring your camera!

Potato Patch
An extra warning should be given about the rough area called Potato Patch, which extends two miles west of West Point. This rough water is caused by the meeting of opposing currents in

---

20,000-YEAR-OLD TUSK
A six-foot, nine-inches-long tusk from an imperial mammoth that roamed the continent 20,000 years ago was found in 1984 on Santa Cruz Island. The tusk, found by a young boy, was imbedded in rock. The immense mammoth stood some 14 feet tall at the shoulder and thrived during the late Pleistocene Epoch. It died out as a species at the end of the most recent ice age, about 10,000 years ago. The tusk can be seen at the Santa Barbara Museum of Natural History.

---

the Santa Cruz Channel and the main channel. Even in the calmest weather you'll have ripples and mild turbulence.

PRACTICALITIES

Obtaining Permits
Ninety percent of Santa Cruz is privately owned by The Nature Conservancy and visiting is allowed on a limited basis only. Permits for boats to land on the western 90% of the island must be obtained in advance from The Nature Conservancy. In Santa Barbara call (805) 964-7839. An application must be completed and island rules must be adhered to. Boaters, for example, must have complete sleeping and cooking facilities on board. Landing permits are for day use only. Permit fees are $15 for 30 consecutive days or $50 for a calendar year. The Nature Conservancy conducts a limited number of day-trips to the island each year for a fee. For information contact The Nature Conservancy, Santa Cruz Island Preserve, 213 Stearns Wharf, Santa Barbara, CA 93101, tel. (805) 962-9111.

Note: Anyone interested in contributing to The Nature Conservancy's Santa Cruz Island Preserve can forward checks to the address above. Your contribution is tax deductible and entitles you to all regular benefits of The Nature Conservancy, including a periodic newsletter on the Santa Cruz Island Project.

SAN NICOLAS ISLAND

If nothing else, San Nicolas Island's claim to fame is a fascinating story about 1,000 Indians who lived here at one time—and about one Indian woman especially, Juana Maria. Today much of the island appears lonely and desolate, with only a few hardy government people enjoying life on this high-tech, windy bit of land.

THE LAND

San Nicolas Island covers 22 square miles, and is 53 miles (almost due west of Catalina Island) from the California coast. The island topography is not very spectacular, made up of plateaus, terraces, and a few peaks (its highest is 907 feet above sea level). San Nicolas forms the outer corner of a quadrangle with the other southern Channel Islands, Santa Barbara, Catalina, and San Clemente. Its easternmost point is an ever-changing sandspit. Over the last century the continuous attack of the wind and the sea has considerably altered this part of the island.

Climate

The climate is temperate, with a mean temperature of 60.4° F, lows and highs averaging within four degrees. Fog keeps the humidity up to about 76%. The winds can rage, with the prevailing northwest winds averaging between 35 and 50 miles per hour almost every day of the year. Sandstorms can happen anytime; the island is often described as a mountain of shifting sand.

FLORA AND FAUNA

Sea Creatures

The rugged coastline of San Nicolas provides stone ledges and platforms where the **harbor seal**, the **California sea lion**, and the **northern elephant seal** bathe in sun and sea. Elephant seals, almost extinct during the 1800s, are found in a large rookery on San Nicolas. In 1950, 168 were counted and they've continued to increase their numbers.

Sea Otters

In 1938, when the southern sea otters were presumed to be extinct, a herd of 100 were discovered along the central California coast. Ports at Moss Landing in the north and Port San Luis in the south bracket the otter's 180-mile range. In 1977, the U.S. Federal Wildlife Service estimated that the count had grown to 1,800, and the herd continues to grow. The federal government, under the authority of the Marine Mammal Protection Act, has moved a small population of sea otters from the central California coast to San Nicolas. The motivation is the fear that an oil spill would wipe out the growing herd, since oil-tanker traffic is heavy along the California coast.

Unlike many marine mammals, the otter does not have a layer of blubber beneath its skin to keep warm in the chilly waters of the Pacific. Instead, it relies on a blanket of air pockets within its fur. When covered with oil, the fur mats down, destroying the air bubbles and losing its insulating quality. Within 24 hours, the "oiled" otter will die. At present the otter is included in the *threatened* species list, and certain environmentalist groups (Friends of the Otter is one) would like its status to be upgraded to *endangered*.

Commercial fishermen are lobbying for the otters to be relocated north of Point Conception since they believe the otters will spread to other islands nearby, destroying sealife. The otter has a voracious appetite, eating one-quarter of its weight each day. The teddy bear lookalike dines mostly on the lobster, scallops, and abalone which thrive in the Channel Islands' offshore kelp beds—delicacies of man and a big part of the commercial fishermen's income.

sticky monkey flower

Other Sea Organisms
The western perimeter of the island, called Land's End, is a mass of tidepools alive with **barnacles, snails, sea urchins, limpets**, and multicolored **sea anemones**. Rocky pockets and crevices are a gathering spot for **purple sea grass, sea lettuce, brown sea moss**, and **black sea snails**.

Land Creatures
Despite the construction of a Navy complex on the island, the sturdy animals seen on all of the Channel islands continue to persist on San Nicolas. The few endemic animals include the small **island fox**, the **white-footed mouse**, the **rock hen**, a species of small **lizard**, and a type of **beetle**. For some reason the fox grows slightly

longer than related foxes on the other islands, and its coloring is somewhat different. The San Nicolas fox has a black back. The skies and cliffs are rampant with **ravens, seagulls, cormorants**, and **horned larks**.

Over the years, the last of the sheep have been removed from the island and the land is beginning to recover. With the help of high humidity from intense fog that prevails much of the time, spring flowers once again cover the landscape. The blue coastal **sage** blossoms and the yellow **coreopsis** brighten the otherwise dismal panorama. Native plants are regaining the land with the absence of the constantly foraging sheep. Firmly established plants also lessen the erosion and blowing sand.

HISTORY

Indians
It's not certain whether San Nicolas Island was sighted by the Cabrillo party in 1542 or not. In 1602, Spaniard Sebastian Vizcaino followed Cabrillo's path and claimed San Nicolas on December 6. (This is a presumption by historians but seems plausible since the 6th is the feast day of St. Nicolas.) Early sea logs report that the island supported a large Indian population.

DIANA LASICH HARPER/2

The arriving padres named these Indians Nicolenos. Some scientists theorize that the Nicolenos were more peaceful than the other Channel Island Indians because so few arrowheads were found.

Many middens and burial sites have been found, however. Another fascinating remnant left behind on the south coast of San Nicolas was a sample of the Nicolenos' artistic talent; petroglyphs—large inscriptions of the sea and whales (some as long as six feet)—were discovered in a cave nicknamed by early ranchers the "Cave of the Whales." There are so many questions—and so few answers. Was there some religious significance to these large whale drawings? Why weren't others found? We'll probably never know. Part of the wall fell in 1961 and was given to the Southwest Museum in Los Angeles by the United States Navy.

The Nicolenos led peaceful lives and seldom saw visitors. (It's questionable whether the Spanish actually got off their ships and *explored* the island, since there's very little good anchorage for vessels.) The island's extensive kelp beds, rich with sealife, were overrun with otters. Then the otter hunts began, and almost the entire population of Nicoleno Indians was ravaged and murdered—the plight of all the Channel Island Indians—by hunters for the Russian and American traders. In 1835 the few remaining Indians were taken to Mainland missions.

The Abandoned Woman Of San Nicolas

In 1835, the priests discovered the population was down from more than 1,000 to 17-20 people. A vessel, *Peor Es Nada,* was commissioned by Franciscan padres to relocate the remaining Nicolenos. When Captain Charles Hubbard arrived at San Nicolas to remove them, without warning a gale riled the sea. The small schooner bobbed on its anchor as the crew, in haste and confusion, rounded up the remnant group of Indians (mostly women and children) and their modest belongings. The rising sea forced the captain to leave as soon as possible. As the ship was about to set sail with all Indians aboard, a young woman noticed that her child was not among them. In a state of hysteria she leaped into the agitated sea and swam to shore to search for the child. The captain, fearful for the safety of his crew, passengers, and ship, scurried for the Mainland—without the Indian woman or her baby.

Captain Hubbard told his story to the padres at San Gabriel Mission and expressed his intention to return for the woman after he completed a voyage to San Francisco. As it turned out, the trip to San Francisco was the last for the *Peor Es Nada.* Less than a month after the trip to San Nicolas the schooner sank, and Captain Hubbard with it. More than a few Mainland people had heard the story of the woman left on San Nicolas, but no one ever tried to do anything about it. Years passed, and the occasional hunter or fisherman mentioned signs of someone living on the island. No one was ever seen so no one investigated, convinced the woman couldn't possibly have survived alone all that time.

In 1850, George Nidever and Thomas Jeffries sailed with a crew of Mainland Indians to San Nicolas to hunt otter and, if possible, find the remains of the Indian woman and her child and return them to the Mainland mission. They remained on the island for six weeks, hunting and preparing the otter and seal hides. One night, an Indian working with Nidever hiked around the island and was convinced he saw a running figure some distance away. He tried to catch up with this surprise visitor, but was unsuccessful. His report put Nidever on the alert, and each time he visited the island he searched for the phantom.

Three years later, he and his hunting companions, including Carl Detman, stumbled on a basket filled with a feather dress. Nidever was determined to find the woman this time, and he and his companions conducted a thorough search, cave by cave, beach by beach, every inch of the island. Finally, several days later, Detman followed fresh footprints to one of the high peaks and a grass shelter.

Found at last—it was almost unbelievable. The woman appeared to be about 50, healthy and active. She was in a beautiful dress of shiny green cormorant feathers matching the one the men had stumbled upon earlier. Through sign language it was learned that her child had not survived, in fact had been found dead the day she swam ashore. She had managed quite well over the years, surviving on birds, fish, abalone, seal blubber, and roots. After her early experiences with the vicious hunters who had wiped out most of her people, it was no surprise that she was fearful of the otter hunters she observed on the island occasionally, and did her best to remain hidden.

After gathering her few possessions (including bone needles and feather dresses that so impressed her discoverers) into a basket, she joined the men and journeyed to the Mainland. She was welcomed into the home of Captain Nidever. The shy woman appeared quite pleased with her new world and enjoyed the many wondrous things that she was introduced to. The rest of her people had been taken 18 years earlier either to Los Angeles or San Gabriel missions, yet it was almost impossible to find anyone left who could speak her language. Finally, after much searching, an old Indian at Santa Ynez was brought to meet Juana Maria (a name not given to her 'til she was baptised on her deathbed).

After 18 years of desolation, loneliness, and a struggle for survival, Juana Maria was being cared for. The story goes that she liked the variety of foods that were new to her, including hardtack bread, fresh fruit, and (especially) sugar. Some blame the foods for her death; but again, who will ever know. She was treated very kindly, but despite everything, was dead within seven weeks of her rescue, marking the end of five civilizations on San Nicolas Island. She was buried in the graveyard at Santa Barbara Mission; a plaque erected in her memory in 1928 reads:

Juana Maria
Indian Woman Abandoned on
San Nicolas Island eighteen years
Found and brought to
Santa Barbara
by
Captain George Nidever
in 1853
Santa Barbara Chapter
Daughters of the American Revolution 1928

It was said that her feather dress and possessions were sent to Rome by the local priest, but no one knows where any of these things are today. In 1957, archaeologist Arthur R. Sanger of Los Angeles, who searched the Channel Islands for 30 years collecting Indian artifacts for the Museum of the American Indian in New York and the Los Angeles County Museum, was certain he had the skeleton of Juana Maria's child. He related at the time that this particular infant skeleton was found buried much deeper than the others, and that beads buried with the child were imported in the 19th century. Anything is possible. An exceptionally fine children's book called *Island Of The Blue Dolphins,* by Scott O'Dell, gives a fictionalized account of Juana Maria's years alone on the island.

Ranching

In 1857, only four years after Juana Maria's removal from San Nicolas, the first rancher, Captain Martin Kimberly, brought in sheep, whose descendants defoliated the island for the next 84 years. San Nicolas didn't go through the line of private ownership as did most of the other Channel Islands. However, it was leased to a variety of ranchers—Howland and Vail, L.P. Elliot, Roy Agee, and Martin Kimberly, running thousands of sheep and continuously planting grasses that would survive in the salty, windy environment.

Over the years overgrazing was a way of life. In 1840 the island boasted trees, brush, and moss, but by 1900 San Nicolas was devastated. At one time, the smallest fully accredited school in the county with a full-time teacher (Miss Alma R. McLain) was conducted on San Nicolas Island. The entire student body of San Nicolas Elementary School consisted of two students, Frances Agee and John Scrimiger.

Navy

In 1933 President Hoover gave jurisdiction of San Nicolas to the Navy. After temporary administration by the Army from 1942 to 1947, Point Mugu regained administrative control of the island for use by the Navy. Since then it has been closed to the public and used for various training programs. Now part of the Pacific Missile Test Center's Sea Test Range, San Nicolas maintains a far different landscape from that of the other Channel islands. The multimillion-dollar government complex includes a 10,000-foot runway with ground-controlled approach facilities that accommodates supersonic target aircraft and planes from the Mainland during operations. The entire program, including sophisticated missile-tracking instrumentation, is closely coordinated with those on the Mainland at Point Mugu. White telescope domes dot the plateau, and approximately 180 military and civilian technicians live on the windswept island.

The marine environment is essential to the testing of airborne weapons from the Pacific Missile Test Center. San Nicolas offers an un-

obstructed area over which the Navy can test its new weapon systems. This activity is conducted over a rectangular plot of ocean 200 miles long and 80 miles wide, between San Nicolas Island and Point Mugu. All of the information is then fed into complex computer systems and studied by scientists and engineers.

Management

A joint agreement between the Department of the Navy, Department of the Interior, and California Department of Fish and Game provides for the care, management, and protection of the flora and fauna, and recovery of the land on San Nicolas. Indian artifacts are protected by the Antiquities Act, which governs historic and prehistoric remains. Excavation and collection is controlled and must be approved by the Department of the Interior. Proposed scientific research is reviewed by a Project Review Board to determine scientific merit, justification, and impact on the environment. The uncontrolled "pot hunters" of the last century inflicted much damage and destroyed archaeological treasures that could have helped in determining more historic data about the original inhabitants of San Nicolas. These government bodies are making certain that history does not repeat itself.

PRACTICALITIES

San Nicolas and San Clemente islands are off-limits to the general public, as they are military reservations. If you want to visit either, you must adhere strictly to government regulations regarding each island, which can be obtained by writing Naval Air Station, Point Mugu, CA 93042, or call (805) 982-7567.

Boating

Boaters interested in San Nicolas should check out Chart 18755. The restricted naval area extends three miles around the island. An aerolight is 981 feet above the east end. Marine lights are shown from white pyramid-like structures on the south, east, and north sides of the is-

---

In the mid-1950s, an old sheepherder's shack was torn down and two Navy men found a fascinating piece of parchment with the following message:

At Christmas time when gifts are sent
They're from the saint, a kind old gent.
On an isle which bears his name
Is treasure, hid for you to claim
In an iron chest so strong
Buried where the land is long.
If you walk where the tides do meet
You will find it at your feet
Coins so rare, coins so old
Coins of silver and of gold.
If he who finds it is my friend,
All my fortune he may spend.
If he who finds it is my foe,
Curses, misery and woe.

This fascinating ditty should whet the appetites of treasure hunters; or is this just a practical joke perpetrated by a bored sheepherder spending a lonely night on windblown San Nicolas?

land. A lighted buoy is 1.3 miles southeast of the east sandspit. Another landmark to beware of is **Begg Rock**, 15 feet high and eight miles northwest of the west point of San Nicolas Island. A reef extends north and south of the rock more than 100 yards in each direction. The rock rises abruptly from depths of 50 fathoms and can disappear into a foggy day. A lighted whistle buoy is 500 yards north of the rock. Anchorage around San Nicolas is usually uncomfortable, and in many cases restricted.

SAN CLEMENTE ISLAND

THE LAND

The grass-covered promontories and ragged cliffs of volcanic rock give San Clemente an arid look most of the year. Only in early spring is there a fresh green coverlet on the island. Even that lasts only a short time. Twenty miles long and two to four miles wide, San Clemente is the fourth largest of the Channel Islands, covering an area of 56 square miles. Its highest peak is 1,965 feet. The island is a labyrinth of caves; at least one of them reaches up two stories. The shoreline shows masses of bubbled rock formed from ancient volcanic eruptions of sizzling lava hardened by the cooling sea into strange forms. Not far from the shore, dozens of steep sand dunes (300 to 1,000 feet high) are located at West Cove.

FLORA AND FAUNA

Flora

There are 10 endemic plants on San Clemente, more than on any of the other islands. It is believed that **stipa**, an endemic bunchgrass, was probably the island's main ground cover in the past. Bits of it can still be seen on the weathered side of the island in deeply cut canyons. In spring, the island boasts myriad wildflowers, including mountains of succulents called **dudleya**, the orange flowers of **mimulus, prickly pear cactus, wild cucumber, coastal sage, poppies, San Clemente larkspur, San Clemente Indian paintbrush, San Clemente island bush mallow, San Clemente broom, thistles, lupine, white morning glories**, and **cholla cactus; ferns** and moss are found at the bottoms of sheer-walled canyons hung with long trails of **snake cactus**. But the colorful flowers last but a brief time. The Navy's Natural Resources Program Office has started an effort to restore the previous balance with a native plant nursery that includes about 50 species.

Fauna

The most abundant animals are the feral **goats** that have all but taken over the island. They run free into deep canyons and along ribbon-sized paths, easily outwitting the intermittent hunters that the government allows and would like to see succeed. A program of trapping the goats and releasing them in Mainland areas is one effort tried, but the goats multiply and replace the departing animals faster than the trappers can keep up with them. Certain groups of animal lovers have complained loudly about any massive hunts that would thin out the goats, even though they are destroying the flora on San Clemente.

The **island fox**, two species of **island mice**, and four types of **bats** still make their home on the island. An occasional **osprey** can be seen flying high over the mountains, along with **mourning doves, hummingbirds, San Clemente Island sage sparrows, finches, meadowlarks**, and **ravens**. The seabirds include **pelicans, gulls**, and the **black-footed albatross** plus many more varieties. **Seals, sea lions**, and **elephant seals** don't seem to mind the Navy bombardments, since their numbers are growing. As many as 300 elephant seals use San Clemente as their hauling ground.

HISTORY

It's presumed that what Cabrillo's party first called La Victoria on Oct. 7, 1542, was indeed San Clemente. Vizcaino, during his travels along the west coast in 1602, also sighted the island and renamed it San Clemente.

Indians

Although archaeologists have not conducted as many investigations on San Clemente as on some of the other Channel Islands, archaeology classes from local Mainland colleges have uncovered over 1,000 midden sites. The Indians used the huge caves scattered around the island as living quarters. San Clemente Indians traded widely with the other islands and Mainlanders; many artifacts from neighboring Catalina Island have been found on San Clemente along with other proof that these Indian mariners traveled the channel extensively. San Clemente Indians suffered the same indignities at the hands of the Aleut otter hunters as did the rest of the Channel Islanders. Only after the populace had been almost totally destroyed did they move to the Mainland in the 1820s to San Gabriel Mission.

Island People

The island was largely uninhabited over the years, but a variety of people have touched it in some way. Documents indicate that a Spanish land grant was awarded to Pio Pico. However, the grant was never claimed. Several ranchers with interests on the other Channel Islands also used San Clemente to raise sheep, but the island's single owner has been the U.S. Government since the Hidalgo Treaty in 1848. The Chinese collected abalone from San Clemente, dried them, and shipped them from about 1890 to 1910.

After the Indians were gone it was used at various times as a hiding place for pirates and then by bootleggers who hid their illegal liquor in the many caves along the shore. Later a number of hermits found the island soothing for short periods of time, but those who stayed the longest were the sheep ranchers.

Navy

In 1934, the U.S. government assumed management of San Clemente Island. During WW II the island, under Navy jurisdiction, was used as a fleet training base and artillery target.

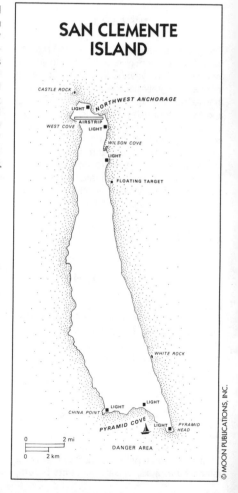

SAN CLEMENTE ISLAND

CASTLE ROCK
LIGHT   NORTHWEST ANCHORAGE
AIRSTRIP
WEST COVE   LIGHT
WILSON COVE
LIGHT
FLOATING TARGET
WHITE ROCK
CHINA POINT   LIGHT   LIGHT
PYRAMID COVE   LIGHT   PYRAMID HEAD
0   2 mi
0   2 km
DANGER AREA

© MOON PUBLICATIONS, INC.

PRACTICALITIES

Boating

There is anchorage at Pyramid Cove, but as it's part of the Navy target area, it's off-limits to boaters during periods of bombardment which usually take place every Tues., Wed., and Thursday. For detailed information contact the Commander, Amphibious Force, the Pacific Fleet, Naval Amphibious Base, Coronado, tel. (619) 437-2231, or the 11th U.S. Coast Guard District, 400 Oceangate, Long Beach, CA 90822.

Fishing

Thick kelp beds grow directly off the lee side of the island, where steep cliffs drop to the sea. The ocean bottom deepens quickly here. Sport-fishermen and divers as well as the commercial fishing fleet come together at these rich fishing grounds. The Navy allows fishing and diving except in target areas but prohibits landing on any part of the island. Undersea caves hide abundant sealife, including swarms of gamefish and elusive lobsters that have managed to stay away from the ever-present lobster traps of Mainland fishermen.

DIANA LASICH HARPER

BOOKLIST

Dana, Richard Henry. *Two Years Before The Mast.* New York: Airmont, 1965

Davis, Charlie. *Hook Up.* California: Charles Davis, 1977.

Eaton, Margaret Holden. *Diary Of A Sea Captain's Wife.* Santa Barbara: McNally & Loftin, 1980.

Fagan, Brian M. *Cruising Guide To California's Channel Islands.* California: Western Marine Enterprises, Inc., 1983.

Hillinger, Charles. *The California Islands.* California: Academy, 1958.

Holder, Charles F. *The Channel Islands of California.* McClurg, 1910.

Johnston, Bernice Eastman. *California's Gabrielino Indians.* California: Southwest Museum, 1962.

Kallman, Robert and Eugene Wheeler. *Shipwrecks, Smugglers, and Maritime Mysteries of the Santa Barbara Channel Islands.* Santa Barbara: McNally & Loftin, 1984.

Kroeber, A.L. *Handbook of the Indians of California.* Dover Publications, 1976.

Landberg, Leif C.W. *The Chumash Indians of Southern California.* California: Southwest Museum, 1965.

Moore, Patricia Anne. *The Casino.* California: Catalina Island Museum Society, 1979.

Overholt, Alma. *The Catalina Story.* California: Catalina Island Museum Society, 1962. Edited and updated by Jack Sargent, 1971.

Udvardy, Miklos D.F. *The Audubon Society Field Guide to North American Birds, Western Region.* New York: Knopf, 1977.

Windle, Ernest. *Windle's History of Santa Catalina Island.* California: Catalina Islander, 1940.

DIANA LASICH HARPER

INDEX

Page numbers in **boldface** indicate the primary reference.
Italicized page numbers indicate information in callouts, charts, illustrations, or maps.

THE METRIC SYSTEM

1 inch = 2.54 centimeters (cm)
1 foot = .304 meters (m)
1 mile = 1.6093 kilometers (km)
1 km = .6214 miles
1 fathom = 1.8288 m
1 chain = 20.1168 m
1 furlong = 201.168
1 acre = .4047 hectares (ha)
1 sq km = 100 ha
1 sq mile = 59 sq km
1 ounce = 28.35 grams
1 pound = .4536 kilograms (kg)
1 short ton = .90718 metric ton
1 short ton = 2000 pounds
1 long ton = 1.016 metric tons
1 long ton = 2240 pounds
1 metric ton = 1000 kg
1 quart = .94635 liters
1 US gallon = 3.7854 liters
1 Imperial gallon = 4.5459 liters
1 nautical mile = 1.852 km

To compute centigrade temperatures, subtract 32 from Fahrenheit and divide by 1.8. To go the other way, multiply centigrade by 1.8 and add 32.

ABOUT THE AUTHOR

Chicki Mallan never forgets that she is one of the "lucky people" who grew up on Catalina Island. Growing up on a small island is an experience that has colored her entire life. Traveling since childhood, Chicki has logged thousands of miles around the world, first with her parents, then with her own large family. Chicki and children have lived in the Orient and Europe, but she still counts Catalina as the number-one island in the world. When not traveling, lecturing, or giving slide presentations, Chicki, husband Oz, and teenage twins Patty and Bryant live in Paradise, a small community in the foothills of the California Sierra Nevada. She does what she enjoys most, writing newspaper articles in between researching travel books. In June of 1987, Chicki was awarded the *Pluma de Plata* ("Silver Pen") writing award from the Mexican government for articles she had written about Mexico. She has been associated with Moon Publications since 1983, when the first edition of *Guide to Catalina* was published. Presently Chicki is working on the fourth edition of her *Yucatan Handbook*.

Oz and Chicki Mallan

ABOUT THE PHOTOGRAPHER

Oz Mallan has been a professional photographer for the past 36 years. Much of that time was spent as chief cameraman for the *Chico Enterprise-Record*. Oz graduated from Brooks Institute of Santa Barbara in 1950. His work has often appeared in newspapers across the country via UPI and AP. He travels the world with wife, Chicki, handling the photo end of their literary projects, which include travel books, newspaper and magazine articles, as well as lectures and slide presentations. The photos in *Catalina Island Handbook* were taken on the many trips to Catalina as well as the Southern California coast.

Moon Handbooks—The Ideal Traveling Companions

Open a Moon Handbook and you're opening your eyes and heart to the world. Thoughtful, sensitive, and provocative, Moon Handbooks encourage an intimate understanding of a region, from its culture and history to essential practicalities. Fun to read and packed with valuable information on accommodations, dining, recreation, plus indispensable travel tips, detailed maps, charts, illustrations, photos, glossaries, and indexes, Moon Handbooks are ideal traveling companions: informative, entertaining, and highly practical.

To locate the bookstore nearest you that carries Moon Travel Handbooks or to order directly from Moon Publications, call: (800) 345-5473, Monday-Friday, 9 a.m.-5 p.m. PST

The Pacific/Asia Series

BALI HANDBOOK by Bill Dalton
Detailed travel information on the most famous island in the world. 12 color pages, 29 b/w photos, 68 illustrations, 42 maps, 7 charts, glossary, booklist, index. 428 pages. **$12.95**

INDONESIA HANDBOOK by Bill Dalton
This one-volume encyclopedia explores island by island the many facets of this sprawling, kaleidoscopic island nation. 30 b/w photos, 143 illustrations, 250 maps, 17 charts, booklist, extensive Indonesian vocabulary, index. 1,000 pages. **$19.95**

SOUTH KOREA HANDBOOK by Robert Nilsen
Whether you're visiting on business or searching for adventure, *South Korea Handbook* is an invaluable companion. 8 color pages, 78 b/w photos, 93 illustrations, 109 maps, 10 charts, Korean glossary with useful notes on speaking and reading the language, booklist, index. 548 pages. **$14.95**

SOUTHEAST ASIA HANDBOOK   by Carl Parkes
Helps the enlightened traveler discover the real Southeast Asia. 16 color pages, 75 b/w photos, 11 illustrations, 169 maps, 140 charts, vocabulary and suggested reading, index. 873 pages. **$16.95**

BANGKOK HANDBOOK   by Michael Buckley
Your tour guide through this exotic and dynamic city reveals the affordable and accessible possibilities. Thai phrasebook, color and b/w photos, maps, illustrations, charts, booklist, index. 214 pages.   **$10.95**

PHILIPPINES HANDBOOK   by Peter Harper and Evelyn Peplow
Crammed with detailed information, *Philippines Handbook* equips the escapist, hedonist, or business traveler with thorough coverage of the Philippines's colorful history, landscapes, and culture. Color and b/w photos, illustrations, maps, charts, index. 587 pages.   **$12.95**

HAWAII HANDBOOK   by J.D. Bisignani
Winner of the 1989 Hawaii Visitors Bureau's Best Guide Book Award and the Grand Award for Excellence in Travel Journalism, this guide takes you beyond the glitz and high-priced hype and leads you to a genuine Hawaiian experience. 12 color pages, 86 b/w photos, 132 illustrations, 86 maps, 44 graphs and charts, Hawaiian and pidgin glossaries, appendix, booklist, index. 879 pages.   **$15.95**

KAUAI HANDBOOK   by J.D. Bisignani
Kauai Handbook is the perfect antidote to the workaday world. 8 color pages, 36 b/w photos, 48 illustrations, 19 maps, 10 tables and charts, Hawaiian and pidgin glossaries, booklist, index. 236 pages.   **$9.95**

MAUI HANDBOOK: Including Molokai and Lanai   by J.D. Bisignani
"No fool-'round" advice on accommodations, eateries, and recreation, plus a comprehensive introduction to island ways, geography, and history. 8 color pages, 60 b/w photos, 72 illustrations, 34 maps, 19 charts, booklist, glossary, index. 350 pages.   **$11.95**

OAHU HANDBOOK   by J.D. Bisignani
A handy guide to Honolulu, renowned surfing beaches, and Oahu's countless other diversions. Color and b/w photos, illustrations, 18 maps, charts, booklist, glossary, index. 354 pages. **$11.95**

BIG ISLAND OF HAWAII HANDBOOK   by J.D. Bisignani
An entertaining yet informative text packed with insider tips on accommodations, dining, sports and outdoor activities, natural attractions, and must-see sights. Color and b/w photos, illustrations, 20 maps, charts, booklist, glossary, index. 347 pages.   **$11.95**

SOUTH PACIFIC HANDBOOK   by David Stanley
The original comprehensive guide to the 16 territories in the South Pacific. 20 color pages, 195 b/w photos, 121 illustrations, 35 charts, 138 maps, booklist, glossary, index. 740 pages. **$15.95**

MICRONESIA HANDBOOK:
Guide to the Caroline, Gilbert, Mariana, and Marshall Islands by David Stanley
Micronesia Handbook guides you on a real Pacific adventure all your own. 8 color pages, 77 b/w photos, 68 illustrations, 69 maps, 18 tables and charts, index. 287 pages. **$9.95**

FIJI ISLANDS HANDBOOK by David Stanley
The first and still the best source of information on travel around this 322-island archipelago. 8 color pages, 35 b/w photos, 78 illustrations, 26 maps, 3 charts, Fijian glossary, booklist, index. 198 pages. **$8.95**

TAHITI-POLYNESIA HANDBOOK by David Stanley
All five French-Polynesian archipelagoes are covered in this comprehensive guide by Oceania's best-known travel writer. 12 color pages, 45 b/w photos, 64 illustrations, 33 maps, 7 charts, booklist, glossary, index. 225 pages. **$9.95**

NEW ZEALAND HANDBOOK by Jane King
Introduces you to the people, places, history, and culture of this extraordinary land. 8 color pages, 99 b/w photos, 146 illustrations, 82 maps, booklist, index. 546 pages. **$14.95**

OUTBACK AUSTRALIA HANDBOOK by Marael Johnson
Australia is an endlessly fascinating, vast land, and *Outback Australia Handbook* explores the cities and towns, sheep stations and wilderness areas of the Northern Territory, Western, and South Australia. Full of travel tips and cultural information for adventuring, relaxing, or just getting away from it all. Color and b/w photos, illustrations, maps, charts, booklist, index. 355 pages. **$15.95**

BLUEPRINT FOR PARADISE: How to Live on a Tropic Island by Ross Norgrove
This one-of-a-kind guide has everything you need to know about moving to and living comfortably on a tropical island. 8 color pages, 40 b/w photos, 3 maps, 14 charts, appendices, index. 212 pages. **$14.95**

The Americas Series

NORTHERN CALIFORNIA HANDBOOK by Kim Weir
An outstanding companion for imaginative travel in the territory north of the Tehachapis. 12 color pages, b/w photos, 69 maps, illustrations, booklist, index. 759 pages. **$16.95**

NEVADA HANDBOOK by Deke Castleman
Nevada Handbook puts the Silver State into perspective and makes it manageable and affordable. 34 b/w photos, 43 illustrations, 37 maps, 17 charts, booklist, index. 400 pages. **$12.95**

NEW MEXICO HANDBOOK by Stephen Metzger
A close-up and complete look at every aspect of this wondrous state. 8 color pages, 85 b/w photos, 63 illustrations, 50 maps, 10 charts, booklist, index. 375 pages. **$13.95**

TEXAS HANDBOOK by Joe Cummings
Seasoned travel writer Joe Cummings brings an insider's perspective to his home state. 12 color pages, b/w photos, maps, illustrations, charts, booklist, index. 483 pages. **$11.95**

ARIZONA TRAVELER'S HANDBOOK by Bill Weir
This meticulously researched guide contains everything necessary to make Arizona accessible and enjoyable. 8 color pages, 194 b/w photos, 74 illustrations, 53 maps, 6 charts, booklist, index. 505 pages. **$13.95**

UTAH HANDBOOK by Bill Weir
Weir gives you all the carefully researched facts and background to make your visit a success. 8 color pages, 102 b/w photos, 61 illustrations, 30 maps, 9 charts, booklist, index. 452 pages. **$12.95**

ALASKA-YUKON HANDBOOK by Deke Castleman and Don Pitcher
Get the inside story, with plenty of well-seasoned advice to help you cover more miles on less money. 8 color pages, 26 b/w photos, 95 illustrations, 92 maps, 10 charts, booklist, glossary, index. 384 pages. **$13.95**

WASHINGTON HANDBOOK by Dianne J. Boulerice Lyons and Archie Satterfield
Covers sights, shopping, services, transportation, and outdoor recreation, with complete listings for restaurants and accommodations. 8 color pages, 92 b/w photos, 24 illustrations, 81 maps, 8 charts, booklist, index. 400 pages. **$13.95**

OREGON HANDBOOK by Stuart Warren and Ted Long Ishikawa
Brimming with travel practicalities and insider views on Oregon's history, culture, arts, and activities. Color and b/w photos, illustrations, 28 maps, charts, booklist, index. 422 pages. **$12.95**

IDAHO HANDBOOK by Bill Loftus
A year-round guide to everything in this outdoor wonderland, from whitewater adventures to rural hideaways. Color and b/w photos, illustrations, maps, charts, booklist, index. 275 pages. **$12.95**

WYOMING HANDBOOK by Don Pitcher
All you need to know to open the doors to this wide and wild state. Color and b/w photos, illustrations, over 60 maps, charts, booklist, index. 427 pages. **$12.95**

MONTANA HANDBOOK by W.C. McRae and Judy Jewell
The wild West is yours with this extensive guide to the Treasure State, complete with travel practicalities, history, and lively essays on Montana life. Color and b/w photos, illustrations, maps, charts, booklist, index. 393 pages. **$13.95**

COLORADO HANDBOOK by Stephen Metzger
Essential details to the all-season possibilities in Colorado fill this guide. Practical travel tips combine with recreation—skiing, nightlife, and wilderness exploration—plus entertaining essays. Color and b/w photos, illustrations, maps, charts, booklist, index. 422 pages. **$15.95**

BRITISH COLUMBIA HANDBOOK by Jane King
With an emphasis on outdoor adventures, this guide covers mainland British Columbia, Vancouver Island, the Queen Charlotte Islands, and the Canadian Rockies. 8 color pages, 56 b/w photos, 45 illustrations, 66 maps, 4 charts, booklist, index. 381 pages. **$11.95**

CATALINA ISLAND HANDBOOK: A Guide to California's Channel Islands
by Chicki Mallan
A complete guide to these remarkable islands, from the windy solitude of the Channel Islands National Marine Sanctuary to bustling Avalon. 8 color pages, 105 b/w photos, 65 illustrations, 40 maps, 32 charts, booklist, index. 245 pages. **$10.95**

BAJA HANDBOOK by Joe Cummings
A comprehensive guide with all the travel information and background on the land, history, and culture of this untamed thousand-mile-long peninsula. Color and b/w photos, illustrations, maps, charts, booklist, index. 356 pages. **$13.95**

YUCATAN HANDBOOK by Chicki Mallan
All the information you'll need to guide you into every corner of this exotic land. 8 color pages, 154 b/w photos, 55 illustrations, 57 maps, 70 charts, appendix, booklist, Mayan and Spanish glossaries, index. 391 pages. **$12.95**

CANCUN HANDBOOK and Mexico's Caribbean Coast by Chicki Mallan
Covers the city's luxury scene as well as more modest attractions, plus many side trips to unspoiled beaches and Mayan ruins. Color and b/w photos, illustrations, over 30 maps, Spanish glossary, booklist, index. 257 pages. **$10.95**

BELIZE HANDBOOK by Chicki Mallan
Complete with detailed maps, practical information, and an overview of the area's flamboyant history, culture, and geographical features, *Belize Handbook* is the only comprehensive guide of its kind to this spectacular region. Color and b/w photos, illustrations, maps, booklist, index. 212 pages. **$11.95**

JAMAICA HANDBOOK by Karl Luntta
From the sun and surf of Montego Bay and Ocho Rios to the cool slopes of the Blue Mountains, author Karl Luntta offers island-seekers a perceptive, personal view of Jamaica. Color and b/w photos, illustrations, maps, charts, index. 213 pages. **$12.95**

The International Series

EGYPT HANDBOOK by Kathy Hansen
An invaluable resource for intelligent travel in Egypt. 8 color pages, 20 b/w photos, 150 illustrations, 80 detailed maps and plans to museums and archaeological sites, Arabic glossary, booklist, index. 510 pages. **$14.95**

PAKISTAN HANDBOOK by Isobel Shaw
For armchair travelers and trekkers alike, the most detailed and authoritative guide to Pakistan ever published. 28 color pages, 86 maps, appendices, Urdu glossary, booklist, index. 478 pages. **$15.95**

MOSCOW-LENINGRAD HANDBOOK by Masha Nordbye
Provides the visitor with an extensive introduction to the history, culture, and people of these two great cities, as well as practical information on where to stay, eat, and shop. 8 color pages, 36 b/w photos, 20 illustrations, 16 maps, 9 charts, booklist, index. 205 pages. **$12.95**

NEPAL HANDBOOK by Kerry Moran
Whether you're planning a week in Kathmandu or months out on the trail, *Nepal Handbook* will take you into the heart of this Himalayan jewel. Color and b/w pages, illustrations, 50 maps, 6 charts, glossary, index. 378 pages.   **$12.95**

NEPALI AAMA by Broughton Coburn
A delightful photo-journey into the life of a Gurung tribeswoman of Central Nepal. Having lived with Aama (translated, "mother") for two years, first as an outsider and later as an adopted member of the family, Coburn presents an intimate glimpse into a culture alive with humor, folklore, religion, and ancient rituals. B/w photos. 165 pages.   **$13.95**

Moonbelts

Made of heavy-duty Cordura nylon, the Moonbelt offers maximum protection for your money and important papers. This all-weather pouch slips under your shirt or waistband, rendering it virtually undetectable and inaccessible to pickpockets. One-inch-wide nylon webbing, heavy-duty zipper, one-inch quick release buckle. Accommodates traveler's checks, passport, cash, photos. Size 5 x 9 inches. Black.   **$8.95**

**New travel handbooks may be available that are not on this list.
To find out more about current or upcoming titles,
call us toll-free at (800) 345-5473.**

IMPORTANT ORDERING INFORMATION

FOR FASTER SERVICE: Call to locate the bookstore nearest you that carries Moon Travel Handbooks or order directly from Moon Publications:

  (800) 345-5473 · **Monday-Friday** · **9 a.m.-5 p.m. PST** · **fax (916) 345-6751**

PRICES: All prices are subject to change. We always ship the most current edition. We will let you know if there is a price increase on the book you ordered.

SHIPPING & HANDLING OPTIONS:

  1) Domestic UPS or USPS first class (allow 10 working days for delivery):
    $3.50 for the first item, 50 cents for each additional item.

Exceptions:

  · **Moonbelt** shipping is $1.50 for one, 50 cents for each additional belt.
  · Add $2.00 for same-day handling.
  2) UPS 2nd Day Air or Printed Airmail requires a special quote.
  3) International Surface Bookrate (8-12 weeks delivery):
    $3.00 for the first item, $1.00 for each additional item. Note: Moon Publications cannot guarantee international surface bookrate shipping.

FOREIGN ORDERS: All orders which originate outside the U.S.A. must be paid for with either an International Money Order or a check in U.S. currency drawn on a major U.S. bank based in the U.S.A.

TELEPHONE ORDERS: We accept Visa or MasterCard payments. Minimum order is US $15.00. Call in your order: 1 (800) 345-5473. 9 a.m.-5 p.m. Pacific Standard Time.

WHERE TO BUY THIS BOOK

Bookstores and Libraries:
Moon Publications Handbooks are sold worldwide. Please write our sales manager for a list of wholesalers and distributors in your area that stock our travel handbooks.

Travelers:
We would like to have Moon Publications Handbooks available throughout the world. Please ask your bookstore to write or call us for ordering information. If your bookstore will not order our guides for you, please write or call for a free catalog.

MOON PUBLICATIONS INC.
722 WALL STREET
CHICO, CA 95928 U.S.A.
tel: (800) 345-5473
fax: (916) 345-6751

ORDER FORM

Be sure to call (800) 345-5473 for current prices and editions or for the name of the bookstore nearest you that carries Moon Travel Handbooks · 9 a.m.-5 p.m. PST
(See important ordering information on preceding page)

Name:_____Date:_____

Street:_____

City:_____Daytime Phone:_____

State or Country:_____Zip Code:_____

Quantity	Title	Price

Taxable Total	
Sales Tax (7.25%) for California Residents	
Shipping & Handling	
TOTAL	

Ship: ☐ 1st class   ☐ UPS (no P.O. Boxes)   ☐ International Surface

Ship to: ☐ address above   ☐ other_____

_____

_____

Make checks payable to:
Moon Publications Inc., 722 Wall Street, Chico, California 95928 U.S.A.
We Accept Visa and MasterCard
To Order: Call in your Visa or MasterCard number, or send a written order with your Visa or MasterCard number and expiration date clearly written.

Card Number: ☐ **Visa** ☐ **MasterCard**

☐☐☐☐ ☐☐☐☐ ☐☐☐☐ ☐☐☐☐

Exact Name on Card: ☐ same as above   expiration date:_____

☐ other_____

signature_____

When in Catalina- stop here first

❏ All sightseeing tickets
❏ Reservations for Pavilion Lodge and Hotel Atwater
❏ Displays and videos highlighting Catalina's activities
❏ Free map of Avalon ❏ Restaurant information
❏ Group and Senior rates

Visitor's Information Center

Look for theVisitor's Information Center in the center of town across from the green Pleasure Pier. For more information call (toll free in CA) 1-800-4-AVALON or (outside CA) 1-310-510-2000 from 8 a.m. – 5 p.m.

**Look for the "Saludos" girl ~
Your assurance of satisfaction.**
Santa Catalina Island Company